AF361440

FROM LAWMEN TO PLOWMEN:
ANGLO-SAXON LEGAL TRADITION
AND THE SCHOOL OF LANGLAND

From Lawmen to Plowmen: Anglo-Saxon Legal Tradition and the School of Langland

STEPHEN M. YEAGER

UNIVERSITY OF TORONTO PRESS
Toronto Buffalo London

Library and Archives Canada Cataloguing in Publication
Yeager, Stephen M., 1979–, author
From lawmen to plowmen : Anglo-Saxon legal tradition and the School of Langland/
Stephen M. Yeager.

(Toronto Anglo-Saxon Series; 17)
Includes bibliographical references and index.
ISBN 978-1-4426-4347-5 (bound)

1. English poetry – Middle English, 1100-1500 – History and criticism   2. English
language – Middle English, 1100-1500 – Versification.   3. Law and literature – England –
History – To 1500.   4. Religion and literature – England – History – To 1500.
Alliteration.   I. Title.   II. Series: Toronto Anglo-Saxon series; 17

PR317.A55Y42 2014   821'.1093554   C2014-902502-5

This book has been published with the help of a grant from the Canadian Federation
for the Humanities and Social Sciences, through the Awards to Scholarly Publications
Program, using funds provided by the Social Sciences and Humanities Research Council
of Canada.

University of Toronto Press acknowledges the financial assistance to its publishing program
of the Canada Council for the Arts and the Ontario Arts Council, an agency of the
Government of Ontario.

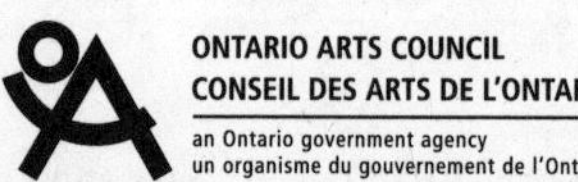

University of Toronto Press acknowledges the financial support of the Government of
Canada through the Canada Book Fund for its publishing activities.

Contents

Acknowledgments

Of the many colleagues and friends who have helped to shape this project, I am particularly grateful to Andrew Galloway, Manish Sharma, Jonathan Newman, Magda Hayton, Michael Van Dussen, Fiona Somerset, and Nicholas Watson, for taking the time to read and discuss variously sized portions of this book in the course of its gestation. Thanks also to my many colleagues and friends from University of Toronto, whose mentorship and advice continues to bear fruit these many years after my departure. Thanks in particular to Andy Orchard, Will Robins, David Townsend, Toni Healey, David Klausner, Suzanne Akbari, Lawrin Armstrong, and Alexandra Gillespie for their feedback and mentorship. Thanks also to Suzanne Rancourt, Charles Stuart, Stephen Shapiro, and everyone at University of Toronto Press, for applying their professionalism and skill to the production of this volume, and the many other beautiful books in their catalogue. Last and far from least, the two readers assigned by the press gave this book exactly the kind of thoughtful attention that one hopes for. All of these individuals and many others were immeasurably helpful in shaping this project; any infelicities or errors that remain are entirely my own.

Though I have made an effort to cite electronic sources when they have been consulted, a smattering of footnotes is poor recognition for the importance of several resources that were absolutely essential for this project. In particular I made constant use of the corpus searches in the Dictionary of Old English (DOE) and also the Middle English Dictionary (MED), and frequently consulted the British Academy Royal Society's Anglo-Saxon Charters homepage, whose resources have evolved considerably since I began this project in 2006. In particular I relied heavily on Dr Sean Miller's searchable database of Anglo-Saxon charters before it was modified for inclusion in the *Electronic Sawyer* website (http://www.esawyer.org.uk/). The *Electronic Sawyer* and the *Early English Laws* site (http://www.early englishlaws.ac.uk/) are excellent resources, which invite only the criticism that they did not come into existence fast enough to play the central role in this study that they otherwise would have. I have attempted to integrate them as much as possible, to facilitate the work of future scholars who will no doubt rely upon them heavily.

Portions of this book were presented as invited lectures and conference papers at McGill University, Columbia University, the Canada Chaucer Seminar, and the annual medieval congress at the University of Western Michigan. Thanks to all of those who attended these presentations for their questions and insights. Work done on this book was also supported financially by Wayne State University and Concordia University. Thanks to the many wonderful colleagues in both places for their advice and personal support, including especially Ellen Barton, Robert Aguirre, Arthur Marotti, Ken Jackson, Simone Chess, and Liz Reich at Wayne State and Jason Camlot, Jill Didur, Marcie Frank, and Kevin Pask at Concordia.

Portions of this book are also forthcoming or in print, in journal articles and as book chapters. My article "The New Plow and the Old: Law, Orality, and the Figure of the Plowman in Passus B 19," forthcoming in the volume *Truth and Tales: Medieval Popular Culture and the Written Word*, contains an earlier version of an argument from the first half of chapter 5; my article "Lollardy in *Mum and the Sothsegger*: A Reconsideration" in the *Yearbook of Langland Studies* overlaps with several of the arguments in chapter 6; and the relationship between diplomatic and literary textual criticism worked out in chapter 1 informs my edition of the *South English Legendary* "Life of St. Egwine" and my chapter in the volume *Rethinking the South English Legendary* edited by Heather Blurton and Jocelyn Wogan-Browne (Manchester University Press). Most recently, an article on the manuscripts of Laȝamon's *Brut* overlapping with some of the claims in chapter 4 has been accepted at *Arthuriana*. Thanks to the editors and peer reviewers of those pieces for their feedback and suggestions.

Finally, I would like to thank my family and friends, especially my parents Scott and Susan, my brother David and sister Christine, my parents-in-law Donald and Bea Quarrie, and my children Sam and Clara. I have appreciated that they only occasionally asked very vague questions about this book, even when I interrupted our time together to work on it. Last and far from least, thanks to my wife and colleague Cynthia Quarrie, for giving me purpose, fixing my grammatical errors, and otherwise keeping me honest.

Abbreviations

ASPR	*The Anglo-Saxon Poetic Records: A Collective Edition.* Ed. Elliott Van Kirk Dobbie, and George Philip Krapp. 6 vols. New York: Columbia University Press, 1931, 1932, 1936, 1942, 1953.
Bethurum	Wulfstan, Archbishop I of York / II of Worcester. *The Homilies of Wulfstan.* Ed. Dorothy Bethurum. Oxford: Clarendon Press, 1957.
BL	British Library
DOE	Antonette diPaolo Healey, ed. *Dictionary of Old English A to G online.* http://www.doe.utoronto.ca/.
EETS	Early English Text Society
ES	"The Electronic Sawyer: Online Catalogue of Anglo-Saxon Charters." Ed. Susan Kelly and Sean Miller. http://www.esawyer.org.uk/about/index.html.
Gesetze	*Die Gesetze der Angelsachsen.* Ed. Felix Liebermann. 3 vols. Halle: Niemeyer, 1903.
I–II Cn	"I–II Cnut ." *Gesetze*, 1:279–371.
LHP	*Leges Henrici Primi.* Ed. L.J. Downer. Oxford: Clarendon Press, 1972.
MED	Frances McSparran, ed. "The Electronic Middle English Dictionary." Last Updated 18 December 2001. http://quod.lib.umich.edu/m/med/.
MoEL	Patrick Wormald. *The Making of English Law: King Alfred to the Twelfth Century.* Oxford: Blackwell Publishers, 1999.
OE Corpus	Antonette diPaolo Healey et al., eds. "Dictionary of Old English Old English Corpus in Electronic Form, TEI-P3

conformant and TEI-P4 conformant version, 2004 Release." Toronto: DOE Project, 2004. http://www.doe .utoronto.ca/pages/pub/web-corpus.html.

PPTrad   *The Piers Plowman Tradition*. Ed. Helen Barr. London: Everyman, 1993.

FROM LAWMEN TO PLOWMEN:
ANGLO-SAXON LEGAL TRADITION
AND THE SCHOOL OF LANGLAND

Introduction

Though examples of persistent alliterative sound-patterning appear in poetry and prose from every century of the medieval period, there are many reasons to be cautious about positing the existence of a continuous tradition of alliterative writing with its origins in the Anglo-Saxon era.[1] The alliterative poems dated to the fourteenth and fifteenth centuries, once grouped together as the works of "the alliterative revival," have proven particularly difficult to explain in relation to the *longue durée*.[2] Scholars have been rightly sceptical for some time that the poets who wrote these texts could have known classic Old English poems like *Beowulf* or the Exeter elegies, much less that they might have written in self-conscious imitation of Old English metre. Though recent scholarship has shown that Old English had a much larger influence after the Norman Conquest than scholars have traditionally recognized, Old English literary traditions seem to peter out at around the turn of the thirteenth century.[3] Presently, the consensus hovers around the idea that, if anything, the evidence reflects an undocumented oral tradition of vernacular alliterative poetry and stressed prose that must have stretched from the Anglo-Saxon period to the Lancastrian era.[4] If such a "tradition" existed – and indeed, if we may

---

1 I use the term "sound-patterning" to refer to a sustained use of alliteration that is not necessarily prosodic, though it can be; I choose this looser definition of alliteration both because of the active debate surrounding the distinctions between Old English "stressed prose" and verse, and because the alliterative poems studied are arguably linked as much by the informality of their metre as they are by any particular metrical characteristics.
2 For discussion of this corpus's "unity" of purpose and theme, see Lawton, "Unity."
3 On the afterlife of Old English, see particularly the work of Elaine Treharne, most recently and fully her book *Living Through Conquest*.

even refer to it in the singular – it intermingled in a variety of local contexts with the traditions of Latin, Anglo-Norman, and non-alliterative English that appear alongside alliterative texts in their manuscripts, and whose influence on both the form and content of late-medieval alliterative poetry has been demonstrated time and time again.[5]

The present book aims to initiate a re-examination of the continuities between the various generations of alliterative English writing, by turning away from the metrical and linguistic analyses that have traditionally dominated the question. Instead, this book will examine the ideological conditions of literate formalism in representative examples of early medieval English writing, not only poetic but also homiletic and legal.[6] The alliterative long line is not simply a different verse form from rhyme royal or heroic couplets; it constructs a notion of "verse" itself, as opposed to "prose," which is entirely distinct from the English "verse" based on Latinate and Continental models. I will approach the relatively broad implications of this claim by constructing a genealogy of the formal strategies discernible in the "*Piers Plowman* tradition," which begins with what I shall call "Anglo-Saxon legal-homiletic discourse."

I define Anglo-Saxon legal-homiletic discourse as a set of formal authenticating strategies originating in the Anglo-Saxon era and continuing in the record-keeping practices of post-Conquest ecclesiastical institutions. Anglo-Saxon writing in both Latin and Old English cannot be easily divided into homiletic literature and legal records; in most instances, the

---

4 This thesis is first articulated by Oakden, *Alliterative Poetry*, 242–4. See also the conversation between Geoffrey Russom and Robert Fulk in Curzan and Emmons, eds, *Unfolding Conversations*, 279–314. Arguments for a continuity based on alliterative English stressed prose include McIntosh, "Wulfstan's Prose"; Blake, "Rhythmical Alliteration"; Salter, "Alliterative Revival" and "Alliterative Modes"; Cable, *English Alliterative Tradition*; Bredehoft, *Early English Metre*.

5 On the debts of alliterative Middle English poetry to non-alliterative, non-poetic, and / or non-English writing, see for example Hanna, "Alliterative"; Lawton, "Gaytryge's Sermon," "Unrhymed," "Unity," "Alliterative Style"; Salter, "Alliterative Revival," "Alliterative Modes"; Pearsall, "Origins"; Matonis, "Alliterative Poetry"; Morgann, "A Talking," "A Treatise."

6 I will use the term "homiletic" to mean "in the style of religious oratory," both because this is the preferred term of legal scholars, and because the particular kinds of oratory associated with legal texts and documents are by nature expository of other authoritative texts. For challenges to the applicability of distinctions between "homily" and "sermon" to Anglo-Saxon literature, applied by scholars like T. Hall ("Early Medieval Sermon," esp. 205), see Orchard, "Wulfstan as Reader," 319; Conti, "Preaching Scripture," 10.

two categories of texts appear to occupy the same discursive field.[7] Heavy alliteration is only one of several features of this discourse that mark it as "sententious," which is to say that it authorizes its claims via recourse to its own construction of traditional oral wisdom. This sententious formalism of Anglo-Saxon legal records places them in marked contrast to their later medieval counterparts, which typically employ the heavily regulated forms that were developed by the professional bureaucracies of crown and papacy after the eleventh century.

Hence even though the scattered survivals of fourteenth-century alliterative writing do not constitute a coherent "revivalist" movement, the alliterative metre of these texts may still share a common origin, in the institutional uses of English writing after the Norman Conquest. These legal documents may not have provided alliterative poets with their precise form, but they certainly provided alliterative metre with its authoritative air of antiquity. Unlike the Old English poetic canon, Anglo-Saxon charters and the law codes of Anglo-Saxon kings were continuously copied and studied throughout the Middle Ages.[8] These texts rarely achieved the level of formal consistency that would allow us to classify them as metrical. However, they frequently use alliterative sound-patterning, most immediately recognizable in the use of doublets like *sake and soke* to refer to the right of a tenurial landlord to hold a court, or *have and hold* to refer to the rights of possession. The appearance of these doublets in legal records alongside embedded Old English legal terms and boundary clauses perform an "orality" of origin and purpose, which would persist in the highly traditionalist legal conventions of England throughout the medieval period and beyond.[9]

---

7 I will refer to the *Piers Plowman* tradition collectively, in the loosest possible sense of the manuscripts that witness writing considered by scholars to be "Langlandian," including the versions of *Piers Plowman* (which I will define as "A-version" etc. when I refer to them individually). "Langlandian," meanwhile, denotes the inherited scholarly construct of formal attributes cited in arguments for the inclusion of various texts in the *Piers Plowman* tradition. Thus both terms are used only for the sake of clarifying the relationship between the current terminology of "Langland studies" and my own construct of Anglo-Saxon legal-homiletic discourse, and not to make claims for the authorship of any particular *Piers Plowman* tradition text.

8 See Richards, "Manuscript Contexts" and "Anglo-Saxonism"; *MoEL* 162–260.

9 On the orality of Old English law see Oliver, *Beginnings of English Law*, 34–41; Richards, "Manuscript Contexts"; Danet and Bogoch, "Orality, Literacy, and Performativity"; Harmer, *Anglo-Saxon Writs*, 85–92; Bethurum, "Stylistic Features." On orality in later medieval law, see Alvares, "Oral Features."

This book claims that the apparent traditionalism of alliterative verse had the potential to evoke this legal traditionalism, and that the *Piers Plowman* tradition particularly exploited this potential. The formal debt of *Piers Plowman* to preaching handbooks has long been acknowledged, including in particular those devotional texts that are alliterative and quasi-metrical, such as the *Lay Folk's Catechism*[10] and the works of Richard Rolle.[11] As a result the main stream of *Piers Plowman* scholarship has focused on the poem's sophisticated engagement with theological issues, for example, the spiritual implications of poverty and the efficacy of penance.[12] Even still, the poem has a long history of being read as a kind of historical document, and many critics have read the text for its representations of law, legal documents, and contemporary political events.[13] In one study that attempts to bridge the gap between these two critical conversations, Emily Steiner observes that "to read *Piers Plowman* as a penitent is also ... to do the work of a notary scribe, chancery clerk, or monastic chronicler: to witness, transcribe, and justify a number of disordered legal instruments."[14] As this study will demonstrate, Steiner's insightful observation about the quasi-documentary form of the *Piers Plowman* tradition points towards the origins of Langlandian discourse in Anglo-Saxon legal-homiletic discourse. The contributors to the *Piers Plowman* tradition and the "lawmen" who wrote and recorded Anglo-Saxon documents both treated their homiletic themes and legal authorizing modes as aspects of the same writing practice, and the analogy between penitent and clerk implicit in Steiner's formulation finds ample precedent in English writing all the way back to the age of Bede.

To describe the formal conventions of Anglo-Saxon poetry, homily, and law for the purposes of this argument, I will rely on studies that examine the formal conventions of proverbial wisdom, referred to above

---

10 Salter, "Alliterative Modes"; Lawton, "Gaytryge's Sermon."

11 Watson, "Middle English Mystics," 551; Godden, "Plowmen and Hermits"; Hanna, "Will's Work," 41–3, 46; Lawton, "Unity," 82.

12 On *Piers Plowman* and sermon literature, see Siegfried Wenzel, "Medieval Sermon" and *Summa Virtutum*; Owst, *Preaching* and *Pulpit*; Salter, *Introduction*, 47–8. On *Piers Plowman* and poverty, see for example Aers, *Sanctifying Signs*; Scott, *Poor*. On *Piers Plowman* and penance, see for example Watson, "Pastoral."

13 For example, Galloway, "Making History Legal"; Steiner, *Documentary*; Middleton, "Acts"; Green, *Crisis*; Birnes, "Advocate"; Alford, "Literature and Law" and *Glossary*; Baldwin, *Theme of Government*; Stokes, *Justice and Mercy*.

14 Steiner, *Documentary*, 93.

and throughout this study as "sententious formalism." Proverbs, commonplaces, and maxims draw their authority not only from their familiarity and their self-evidently true content, but from their patterned regularity and structural parallelisms. Susan Deskis has observed that alliteration is a particularly prominent convention in Middle English proverbs, much more so than rhyme.[15] It is telling that French court records in the wake of the Norman Conquest tended to copy English proverbs appearing in testimony untranslated, as if the native form of these statements were somehow more procedurally relevant than their meaning.[16] Alliteration is only among the most obviously English of the sententious forms employed in the *Piers Plowman* tradition to claim the cultural authority of traditional wisdom, as the poems sought a defensible ground from which to resist the ongoing centralization of English bureaucratic practices around the royal court and papal curia. Though theoretically traditional wisdom is verified by a community's collective memory of oral prehistory, such memory was surely coloured by the surviving quasi-legal texts of the Anglo-Saxon period, which then (as now) were the only sources from which an oral prehistory of English cultural and legal precedent could possibly be reconstructed. Hence whether or not Anglo-Saxon laws and documents can help us to chart the particular evolution of Langland's alliterative metre (as future studies very well may show), examining these traditions of textual transmission in juxtaposition with the *Piers Plowman* tradition and its antecedents can tell us a great deal about the possible reasons why an apparently archaic and / or regional poetic form was adopted by cosmopolitan and highly literate social critics in the fourteenth and fifteenth centuries.[17]

As the most resolutely presentist and cosmopolitan of late-medieval alliterative poems, *Piers Plowman* may seem at first to be an idiosyncratic end point for this study of Anglo-Saxon legal-homiletic discourse in post-Conquest England. But as I will demonstrate, Langland and his followers are in fact the writers who engage most directly with the themes and concerns manifest in the Anglo-Saxon texts that were most widely circulated in the later medieval period. Though alliterative texts like *Sir Gawain and the Green Knight* and *William of Palerne* certainly have their place in the

---

15 Deskis, "Echoes," 312. On alliteration in modern English proverbs relative to other languages, see F. Williams, "Alliteration."

16 Brand, "Languages," 67.

17 The fullest study of Langland's style remains Schmidt, *Clerkly Maker*.

narrative constructed here, that place is not nearly as central to the surviving evidence as that occupied by *Piers Plowman* and its continuators and imitators, and so these affiliated texts will not be considered in this book until its conclusion. I will, however, discuss the early alliterative poems *The First Worcester Fragment*, *The Proverbs of Alfred*, and Laʒamon's *Brut*. These texts have been grouped together for their similar prosodic properties,[18] and their manuscripts are all affiliated with the Worcester region, whose Malvern Hills feature in the opening lines of *Piers Plowman*, and so they provide a basis for tracing the evolution of alliterative formalism in the historical gap between the procedural obsolescence of Old English law at the turn of the thirteenth century and the first versions of *Piers Plowman* in the middle of the fourteenth.

For reasons that will become apparent, this analysis will also necessarily resist the traditional distinctions that hold variation among witnesses to be a different kind of "form" than alliteration, as metre occurs "inside" the text while variants and revisions seem to either distort that text or create new texts. Looking simultaneously at both literary and documentary formal aspects of the *Piers Plowman* tradition will shed new light on two of its more unusual features. The first of these features is its eccentric and sometimes prose-like alliterative poetic idiom, markedly different from comparable major alliterative poems like the ones listed above.[19] The second concerns the evolution of *Piers Plowman*, which over the course of its transmission history is famously complex, certainly more so than any other Middle English alliterative text. The A, B, C, and Z versions of *Piers Plowman* appear in close to fifty witnesses, while the next-most-popular *Siege of Jerusalem* appears in nine.[20] Even the coherence of individual *Piers Plowman* "versions" into unified texts has been debated, with earlier critics favouring a division of the B and C versions of the poem each into two separate texts, a *visio* and a *vita*, while later ones prefer to read the two as sections of one continuous work. The many efforts to divide and subdivide the versions of the poem into narrative units, undertaken not only by critics but also by the text's medieval scribes, further drives home the basic

---

18 Heningham, "Precursors"; Brehe, "*First Worcester Fragment*"; Frankis, "Regional Context."

19 Turville-Petre, *Alliterative Revival*, 59–60; Cable, *Alliterative Tradition*, 86; Lawton, "Alliterative Style." See also recently Smith, "Alliterative Line(s)," on Langland's complex inter-lineal alliteration.

20 Chism, *Alliterative Revivals*, 16.

problem posed by the text to critics: it is too open-ended to cohere as a poem, and yet it is too clearly poetic to be classified as anything else.[21]

Indeed, one might expect modern critics to be even more puzzled by the freedom taken with the text by its medieval scribes and readers, given the *Piers Plowman* tradition's keen thematic interest in protecting authoritative texts from distortion by literate professionals. And yet on the contrary, the openness to non-authorial revision that characterizes the manuscripts of the *Piers Plowman* tradition is widely accepted as being somehow central to that tradition's "public" function, constitutive of both its structure and content.[22] Because this study focuses more on the formal impact of this "public" function on the survival of *Piers Plowman* than it addresses the authorial intentions of Langland himself, this study will account for these features of *Piers Plowman* by looking not at the "authorial" versions of that text, but at the works of its later readers and imitators. More than Langland's own works ever could, fragments like *Richard the Redeless* and *Mum and the Sothsegger* reveal the quasi-documentary nature of the Langlandian, "public" mode. These fragments situate themselves in relation to *Piers Plowman* not as imitations of a literary antecedent, but as new documents based on an exemplum of sententious formal conventions. It is the very informal and poetic open-endedness of those conventions that makes them suitable for criticizing the excessively formalistic and hypocritical legal conventions of fourteenth-century literate professionals.

This strategy is able to work because the "informal" form employed by the *Piers Plowman* tradition had the appearance of great antiquity. Sententious formalism is clearly less able to establish authorship or authenticity than later and more rigid bureaucratic formalisms; the only reasonable argument in its favour is that it came first. And indeed, the informality and open-endedness of Langlandian discourse finds ample precedent in the generic "leakage"[23] that characterizes early English law and literature. It is a truism of Anglo-Saxon Studies that distinctions

---

21 The tripartite "Dowel," "Dobet," "Dobest" scheme, derived from what appear to be unauthorial scribal glosses, is thought to model either the modes of spiritual life (Wells, "Construction"; Dunning, "Structure") or the ascent of the soul (Meroney, "Life"; Hussey, "Langland, Hilton"). See also Robertson and Huppé, *Scriptural*; Spearing, *Verbal Repetition*; Carruthers, *Search*, 6–9; Alford, "Design," 30; Middleton, "Critical Heritage," 14; Kerby-Fulton, "*Piers*," 514.
22 Middleton, "Audience" and "Public Poetry."
23 Foley, "How Genres Leak."

between poetry and prose are blurry at best, not least because Old English "poetry" is not lineated as such on the manuscript page. Nor does subject matter or theme provide much help: for example, it cannot be assumed that Old English prose was considered a preferable mode to Old English poetry for transparently representing historical events, given that so many poems document important events in the *Anglo-Saxon Chronicle*.

The generic fluidity of Old English poetic manuscripts is addressed by Katherine O'Brien O'Keeffe in her groundbreaking study *Visible Song*, where she posits that the scribal "performance" of the text in Anglo-Saxon manuscripts is such that the manuscript is merely preparatory to an unwritten "text," and not fully representative of it.[24] As a result, the text is open to scribal reinterpretation, as demonstrated in the differences between the manuscripts of the Old English wisdom poem *Solomon and Saturn*.[25] Building on this work, Alger Doane, Carol Pasternack, and Elizabeth Tyler have each suggested different ways of modelling Anglo-Saxon scribal performance;[26] and most recently Thomas Bredehoft has pointed out that the so-called oral formulaic aspects of Anglo-Saxon poetic practice might in fact be better called "literate formulaic," which is to say that these poets have in some cases clearly reworked written sources, in much the same way that it appears a *Piers Plowman* tradition poem like *Mum and the Sothsegger* is a reworked expansion of *Piers Plowman*.[27] More similar to Anglo-Saxon literature than the mere fact of alliteration in the *Piers Plowman* tradition, then, are the particular types of resistance offered by that tradition to modern critical presumptions about the nature of poetry and its purposes. In the case of the *Piers Plowman* tradition, it appears that this resistance was deliberately cultivated, to lend authority to its satire of the literate institutions of its day.

As I will argue, then, the primary difference between the *Piers Plowman* tradition and its Anglo-Saxon antecedents is that the scribal performances in the former are self-consciously modelled in opposition to the more professional and rigid scribal practices of the fourteenth century. In *Richard the Redeless* and *Mum and the Sothsegger*, it is clear that the very practices whereby fourteenth-century professional readers ensured that their texts were stable and accurate were also the practices that enabled those

---

24 O'Brien O'Keefe, *Visible Song*.
25 O'Brien O'Keefe, *Visible Song*, 47.
26 Doane, "Ethnography"; Pasternack, *Textuality*; Tyler, *Old English Poetics*, 6.
27 Bredehoft, *Authors, Audiences*, 199. For the fullest enumeration of the specific parallels between *Mum and the Sothsegger* and *Piers Plowman*, see Blamires, "Langlandian Idiom."

professionals to distort the text for their own purposes. The poet(s) responsible for these texts therefore rewrote *Piers Plowman* the way Anglo-Saxon scribes rewrote *Solomon and Saturn*, because this older and more "oral" interpretive practice enabled them to avoid the distortions of the text created by the more recent literate practices of lawyers, clerks, doctors and friars.

As I have said, the continuators of *Piers Plowman* are far more likely to have learned about Anglo-Saxon scribal performance in their legal documents, law codes, and other historical materials, which were consulted by late-medieval institutions with far greater frequency than were the manuscripts of Old English laws and homilies. One example of the remarkable continuity of Old English law is provided by the law code of King Æthelberht (titled *Æthelberht* according to the conventions of Anglo-Saxon legal scholars). This rhythmic and sometimes alliterative text was apparently transcribed in the sixth century from laws that had been orally transmitted for generations, and yet it is uniquely witnessed in the *Textus Roffensis*, a manuscript precisely dated to between 1122 and 1124.[28] Bede refers explicitly to these laws in the *Historia ecclesiastica gentis Anglorum*, in the sole surviving reference to an Anglo-Saxon law code outside of the codes themselves from the entire Anglo-Saxon period.[29] The fact that he finds them worthy of comment might well indicate that even in the time of Bede, the code was a remarkably early example of written English. And yet because of the late date of the *Textus Roffensis* manuscript, *Æthelberht* is also part of the twelfth-century tradition of Old English literature that is the crucial link in the chain connecting Old English verse to the alliterative revival.[30]

As Patrick Wormald has observed, *Textus Roffensis* "would have made an impressive weapon for a churchman seeking to defend the position of his English foundation against prowling Norman predators."[31] The ecclesiastical institutions like Rochester that preserved Old English laws and literature did so not as revivalists, but as the heirs to a long-established practice of studying Old English alongside Latin as an educational foundation for their bureaucratic practices of literate estate management.[32] This

---

28 The code is edited in Oliver, *Beginnings of English Law*.

29 *MoEL* 29. On this code, see also Blair, *World of Bede*, 88; Jurasinski, "Continental Origins"; Lendinara, "Kentish Laws."

30 On Old English in the twelfth century, see Treharne, *Living Through Conquest*, 129–36.

31 *MoEL* 252.

32 Chapman, "*Uterque Lingua*"; Treharne, "Categorization, Periodization," and "Bishops and their Texts"; Richards, "Manuscript Contexts," 186.

practical purpose for post-Conquest Old English literacy is important, because it helps to account for the politicization of the vernacular that accompanied its resurgence in fourteenth-century writing. When a twelfth-century scribe copied the vernacular sermons and biblical translations of an Anglo-Saxon author like Ælfric, he may have earned the scorn of someone like William of Malmesbury, but his actions would have had none of the outsider charge that the literature of the Lollard "English Heresy" would have in the fourteenth century.[33] And yet it is a shorter leap than one may think from the Old English and Anglo-Latin records of monastic endowments to the texts of the *Piers Plowman* tradition, even though the latter is most famous now for its readership of reformers and revolutionaries who did so much to challenge the legitimacy of precisely those monastic endowments in the centuries leading to the Reformation.[34]

A crucial aspect of Anglo-Saxon legal-homiletic discourse in this regard is its openness to revision and even forgery as a critical practice. As Fred Robinson observes, the first original imitations of Old English to be written by speakers of later English dialects were not literary texts at all, but legal documents created "with intent to defraud," or at the very least to document previously undocumented legal claims.[35] The same monasteries and ecclesiastical institutions that benefited from these documents were often centres for the study of Old English homilies.[36] The concentration of creative energies in this arena suggests that the need to access and, if necessary, invent Old English law provides a specific practical motive for the conservation, preservation, and study of Old English literature in the centuries after the Norman Conquest. These acts of inventive scribal performance originated in the practices of the Anglo-Saxon era, and did not fully cease until the dissolution of the monasteries.

This context for the survival of Anglo-Saxon scribal practices explains their political, satirical thrust in the late-medieval period. Again, the *Textus Roffensis* provides a helpful point of reference. By its very existence, the

---

33 On the subversiveness of English in the twelfth century, see Treharne, *Living Through Conquest*, 149–50. On "the English heresy," see for example Hudson, "Lollardy: The English Heresy?"; Irvine, "Compilation and Use."

34 On Langland's own views of disendowment, see for example Kerby-Fulton, *Reformist*, 33, and "*Piers*," 510; Baldwin, "Historical Context," 73–6; Galloway, "Making History Legal," 21–3. On disendowment in fourteenth-century political discourse, see also Scase, *New Anticlericalism*; Aston, *Faith and Fire*, 95–131.

35 Robinson, "Afterlife of Old English," 277.

36 Frankis, "Regional Context," 62. On the favourability of Old English legal texts to the church of this period, see Hudson, "Administration," 95.

manuscript demonstrated that the legal and procedural innovations of the twelfth and thirteenth centuries were in fact innovative, and as such intrinsically suspect. And yet the manuscript's very methods for compiling English law mark it as a symptom of those same innovations. This is perhaps most succinctly signalled in the manuscript's copy of the *Instituta Cnuti*. The *Instituta Cnuti* is mostly faithful in its Latin translation of the Old English law code *I–II Cnut*, but one of its few changes to the original is the addition of counterfeiters to a list of criminals who should be tried by ordeal.[37] The irony of this editorial intervention, which invents a legal record precisely to advocate punishment for the unlicensed invention of legal records, anticipates the contrast between the "public" and open form of the *Piers Plowman* tradition and the obsession of its writers with the evils of rewriting authoritative texts. Paradoxically, the very openness of Anglo-Saxon documentary culture to revision and reinterpretation was the aspect of that culture that made it function so well in later eras as a basis for performances of legal traditionalism, even when those performances were aimed at undermining the very institutions that had preserved Anglo-Saxon documentary culture in the first place. By extension, it was the very destabilizing nature of legal-homiletic "traditionalism" that made its forms so rhetorically appropriate for the satire of the *Piers Plowman* tradition.

As Anglo-Saxon legal-homiletic discourse began to circulate outside of its institutional origins, it also began to manifest most clearly in formal alliterative poetry, often in texts that attributed themselves to legislating authors, like the *Brut* of "Law Man" and *The Proverbs of Alfred*.[38] The composition of these texts in the late-twelfth and early-thirteenth centuries is roughly contemporary to the rise of the English legal profession, a transition symbolized by the importance of the dates 1143 and 1189; the former marks the arrival of Vacarius, England's first professional canon law teacher, and the latter came to mark the conclusion of English common law's "time out of mind."[39] The rise of new Continental and Angevin legal forms deprived Old English law of its procedural relevance. But because Anglo-Saxon legal style still impressed audiences who were used to regarding that style as authoritative, formalized imitations of that style began to manifest in Middle English literature. In *The Proverbs of Alfred*,

---

37 O'Brien, "*Instituta Cnuti*," 195.
38 Tatlock argues that "Law man" may have been itself an archaic term that was particularly associated with the Danelaw: Tatlock, *Legendary History*, 512–14.
39 Brundage, "Professional Canonists," 12.

the *Brut*, and also *The First Worcester Fragment*, we see the forms of Anglo-Saxon law and history employed to advocate not for specific legal claims, but more generally for notions of legal propriety that were in the process of being forgotten. *Piers Plowman* the dream vision is only one step further along this trajectory, abandoning history itself to make legal arguments about English government from an allegorical and apocalyptic perspective.[40]

As this introduction has already indicated, then, alliterative style and metre in the *Piers Plowman* tradition are merely among the more obvious indicators that it participates in the post-Conquest continuation of Anglo-Saxon legal-homiletic discourse. Langland's simultaneous employment of literary and legal formalisms, manifest for example in his tendency to address specific political issues with vague sententiousness and Christian allegory, is a late manifestation of the kinds of strategies used in Anglo-Saxon law codes and legal documents since before the age of Bede. Even as Anglo-Saxon legal-homiletic forms outlived the licit legal practices that produced them, the discourse surrounding them persisted and even gained rhetorical authority, as a satirical voice particularly useful for criticizing social problems related to literacy itself.

Summary of the Chapters

In the first chapter, I will define the concepts of "orality," "literacy," "literature," and "law" that inform the subsequent study. I will define orality and literacy as strategies for mitigating anxieties about the veracity of statements – which is to say, "authorizing" them – that are particularly appropriate to their respective spoken and written technologies of communication. The oppositional strategies of literary criticism and "diplomatic" documentary criticism, employed by literary critics and historians to assess and describe the authority of written texts, are designed to engage specifically with the anxieties about authority that arise in written texts, and hence they apply imperfectly to texts that reflect the anxieties of relatively "oral" cultures. To resolve the problem, I will borrow from paremiology the terminology for describing what I call "sententious formalism," which is to say the strategies of formalizing claims to make them sound proverbial and therefore self-evident. Such strategies are constitutive of

---

40 On apocalypticism in *Piers Plowman*, see Kerby-Fulton, *Reformist Apocalypticism*; Bloomfield, *Apocalypse*.

the Anglo-Saxon legal-homiletic discourse that is the subject of this study; indeed, one can even characterize the Anglo-Saxon law code as a subset of the "maxim collection" genre exemplified also by Old English poems like *Maxims I* and *II* and *Precepts*.

When I have established this vocabulary I will then turn to an examination of the transmission of a single Anglo-Saxon charter, S 1166. This forged charter is copied by William of Malmesbury in the twelfth century; it is identifiable as a forgery because it includes a tenth-century documentary formula, though it is attributed to the seventh-century saint Aldhelm. My reading of this document will ground my terminology in the narrative of literacy's emergence in England, to provide the backdrop for this text's genealogy of the *Piers Plowman* tradition's alliterative, sententious, and quasi-legal idiom.

Chapter 2 begins with Wulfstan Archbishop II of York / Bishop I of Worcester, sometimes called "Wulfstan the homilist." Wulfstan is the legislator of the Anglo-Saxon period to have exercised the widest-ranging influence on the laws of England after the Norman Conquest. This chapter begins by describing the particular admixture of legal and homiletic discourse witnessed in his texts. The analogy that connects the authority of Wulfstan the homilist to that of Wulfstan the legislator is based in Wulfstan's literacy: the same technical competence in reading that provides Wulfstan with the moral authority to preach on biblical topics also proves his ability to read and quote from the laws of Cnut's predecessors for the purposes of reiterating those laws. I then apply my characterization of Wulfstan's form to read two important works by Wulfstan, the *Sermo Lupi ad Anglos* and *I–II Cnut*, before concluding the chapter with an examination of Anglo-Saxon legal-homiletic discourse in one of Wulfstan's most important Latin translators, who wrote the legal treatises now titled *Quadripartitus* and *Leges Henrici Primi*. Traces of Wulfstan's influence are discernible in the *Leges Henrici Primi*, indicating that the translator aimed to preserve not only the content of Wulfstan's laws but also the form that encapsulated them.

The third chapter will look at the early vernacular traditions from the Worcester region and in particular *The First Worcester Fragment* and *The Proverbs of Alfred*. Both of these poems arose from a tradition of vernacular literacy conditioned by the needs of ecclesiastical institutions, whose foundational legal texts were written in the Anglo-Saxon period; hence both of them perform a nostalgia for an Englishness that is completely circumscribed by the institutions of the church. In *The First Worcester Fragment*, a lament for the decline of English literacy in the present encodes also a lament for the loss of English traditional law. Because such laments are commonplace in Old English literature, the poem's very complaint about the decline of English literacy is itself indicative of the poet's own knowledge of Old English literature, and hence of the continuity between his poem and the tradition from which it originated. In *The Proverbs of Alfred*, meanwhile, traditional English law is presented as wisdom in a broader sense, as Alfred repeats the procedures that initiate legislative sessions in Anglo-Saxon law codes to disseminate proverbs and maxims instead. Though these texts retreat from the legal specificity of Old English documents and laws, they reinvent Anglo-Saxon legal-homiletic discourse as an authoritative mode for articulating the shared values that more contemporary ways of teaching and writing generally obscured. At the same time, these texts reflect the impact of their contemporary bureaucracies on literate practice, as the combined legal and literary force of Anglo-Saxon legal-homiletic discourse becomes simply "literary" in the poems by default.

The fourth chapter will build on this analysis to study Laȝamon's *Brut*, a much longer text nonetheless representative of the same textual community as *The First Worcester Fragment* and *The Proverbs of Alfred*. In both its historical narrative and in its unusual, "archaic" poetic mode, the *Brut* asserts that the true law of England was inherited from the relatively oral customs witnessed in Old English legal texts and documents. My reading will offer a new interpretation of the Saxon invaders led by Hengest and Horsa, whose invasion is one of the most expanded portions of the poem's translation of Wace's *Roman de Brut*. Laȝamon's treatment of the Saxons signals not an "ambivalence" about the author's ethnic forebears, as readers of the *Brut* have typically argued, but rather uses the pagan conquerors as negative examples of secular advisors. The text therefore echoes similar criticisms of the aristocracy discernible in Wulfstan's writing, and also anticipates the criticisms of hypocritical formalism in the fragments of the *Piers Plowman* tradition.

The final two chapters will apply both the critical methodology and the historical narrative of the preceding chapters to a reading of key texts from the *Piers Plowman* tradition. Chapter 5 begins with a brief survey of Anglo-Saxon legal-homiletic discourse in some of the most immediate antecedents to the *Piers Plowman* tradition, to show how that discourse may have made its way into Langland's original work. Despite the exclusion of "time out of mind" from official legal precedent, memorials of Anglo-Saxon legal customs nonetheless persisted in the fourteenth century, in a construction of "oral" prehistory exploited by the various interests in late-medieval England who wished to frame their innovations as returns to ancient precedent. The idiom of the *Piers Plowman* tradition derives its power from this construction of legal tradition. The chapter culminates in a reading of *Richard the Redeless*. This continuation of *Piers Plowman* constructs its source tradition as an alternative educational program, particularly appropriate for would-be royal advisors.

Chapter 6 concludes the study with a reading of *Mum and the Sothsegger*, a fragment connected to *Richard the Redeless* that is particularly concerned with describing and authorizing the poetic mode of the *Piers Plowman* tradition in terms of its relationship to documentary culture. The fragment examines "literacy" itself in ambivalent terms, as constructed through an original use of the division between "text" and "gloss." The problem of the text is that the "text" of true wisdom is far too vague to be applied in specific contexts without a "gloss," and yet "gloss" is by its very nature deceitful. In *Mum and the Sothsegger*, Langland's dream-vision poetic idiom is itself evoked as a mode of documentation that transcends the text/gloss dichotomy. The fragment's recourse to the authorizing formulae of *Piers Plowman* prevents this solution from being fully satisfying, however, as the poem's dream vision ultimately proves to be just another document, subject to the same anxieties as those documents found in the "bag of books" surveyed in the poem's final section. In *Mum and the Sothsegger*, as in all of the texts examined in this study, complaints about the corruption of English literacy serve the paradoxical end of authorizing English literacy, as the text's very nostalgia for an indefinite and idealized point of origin drives the poet to participate in one of the most original and innovative poetic traditions of the late-medieval period.

1 From Written Record to Memory: A Brief History of Anglo-Saxon Legal-Homiletic Discourse

In his introduction to his edition of *Piers Plowman*, W.W. Skeat provides a description of the narrator Will's voice, which could just as easily be applied to the homiletic voice of the Anglo-Saxon author Wulfstan: "He does not write to please, but to express earnest and deep convictions, and from a love of contemplating the great problems of life; and there is much that may teach a reader to be earnest, pure, loving, and simple-minded, much that may profit all such as care to be instructed in such things."[1] For Skeat, Langland writes with the "earnest" intention of defining the ideal reciprocal relationships between king and subjects, teaching his readers for their own benefit. Skeat is also responsible for the foundational statement of what C. David Benson has (rather forcefully) called "the Langland myth": this is the presumption that a poet named William Langland wrote an original version of the poem *Piers Plowman* and revised it twice.[2] In the subsequent studies that have enshrined this "myth" and rejected theories of multiple authorship, the consistency of the poetic voice described by Skeat has loomed large, perhaps most strikingly in the oft-cited debate about the poem's Z-version.[3] As Ralph Hanna has observed, the determining factor of the debate is codicological – if it were copied as early as the Z-version editors suggest, it would have a strong claim for being an early version of the poem – yet the focus of both the introduction to the

---

1 Langland, *Piers Plowman*, ed. Skeat, xxxviii. On Langland's debt to sermon literature, see Wenzel, "Medieval Sermons."

2 Benson, *Public Piers Plowman*, 3–14.

3 On the rise and fall of the multiple authorship theory, see Justice, "Introduction"; Patterson, "Logic." Definitive attributions of the poem to William Langland include Kane, *Evidence*; Chambers, "Robert or William."

Z-version and Kane's famously critical review is the question of the text's "Langlandian" character.[4] Benson has argued that critical focus on the figure of Langland, whose "voice" is made up of the poem's "authorial" readings, has left unasked the larger question of what this apparently large body of imitators wanted to achieve.

Of course, Benson's summary of the field lends somewhat short shrift to the rather large body of scholarship on the readers, scribes, and imitators of *Piers Plowman*, whose interpretations of and interventions into the text have in fact attracted a great deal of critical interest.[5] These studies generally adhere to the A-B-C theory of the text's development, but this has not stopped them from providing ample evidence that the very critical vocabulary of "original" and "copy," "author" and "imitator," "poem" and "fragment" is inadequate for describing the true relationship between the various witnesses of the tradition. The *mouvance* of medieval manuscript traditions is a well-known phenomenon, and the readers of *Piers Plowman* are hardly the only critics in recent years who have engaged with their texts' active and disparate communities of readers.[6] If the versions and imitations of *Piers Plowman* are to be distinguished from other late-medieval textual traditions, it can only be on the impressionistic grounds that their distribution has struck many readers as particularly, perversely bewildering, to the degree that reading the poem and rewriting it appear to have been regarded as one and the same activity.

In his own discussion of the problem, Benson suggests that critics should adopt "such phrases as *the workshop of William Langland* or *the school of Langland*" to describe the authorship of *Piers Plowman*.[7] The proposal is noteworthy, because it is remarkably similar to the terminology long since adopted by Anglo-Saxonists in the face of their own versions of the same

---

4 *Piers Plowman Z-Text*, ed. Rigg and Brewer; Kane, "The 'Z-Version'." On the codicological evidence, see Hanna, *Pursuing History*, 195–202.

5 Particularly important is the work of Kathryn Kerby-Fulton (e.g., Kerby-Fulton and Despres, "Iconography"; Kerby-Fulton and Justice, "Langlandian Reading Circles") and Ralph Hanna (e.g., *Pursuing History*, 203–43, and "Huntingdon"), but they are hardly the only scholars who have written on the audiences, scribes, and imitators of *Piers Plowman*. See also for example Burrow, "Audience"; Middleton, "Audience and Public"; Warner, "Overlooked"; Hailey, "Robert Crowley"; Scase, "Dauy"; Horobin, "Pinkhurst" and "Bodleian."

6 The term *mouvance* was introduced by Paul Zumthor; see his *Medieval Poetics*. For a useful account of authorship and its relationship to manuscript culture in Langland's immediate context, see also Hanna, "Producing Manuscripts," 113–18.

7 Benson, *Public Piers Plowman*, 65.

issues. As in *Piers Plowman*, the relationship between authorship and authority in Old English writing is fluid at best.[8] Certainly the runic signatures of the "school of Cynewulf," for example, provide a productive parallel to the "Long Will" signatures of Langland.[9] In both cases authorship is signalled, but obliquely, and the attribution of the text functions more as a performance of cleverness than an assertion of ownership.

An even closer parallel to Langland's "school" in the corpus of Anglo-Saxon literature is the textual community surrounding the works attributed to Archbishop Wulfstan. Wulfstan's signature was a pen name *"Lupus,"* a correct and yet allegorizing name with similar implications to "Long Will" for distancing the historical person from the authorial voice.[10] As in the *Piers Plowman* tradition, qualities like metre, tone, and diction have been cited to distinguish between "authorial" versions of Wulfstan's homilies and the surrounding body of imitative texts. Moreover, it is a revealing coincidence that one of Wulfstan's most characteristic tendencies is his frequent repetition of the words *georne* and *geornlice*, adverbs that express the same "earnestness" identified by Skeat in the narrator of *Piers Plowman*. In both cases, the narrator authorizes his claims not by clearly defining the actual identity of the person who wrote his words, but by performing an "earnest" trustworthiness in the course of his commentary on "the great problems of life."

As I will argue, this parallel between the "school of Langland" and the "schools" of Cynewulf and Wulfstan discussed by Anglo-Saxonists in fact reveals the formal debt of the *Piers Plowman* tradition to the precedent of Anglo-Saxon textual culture. Simply put, Langlandian authorship more closely resembles Wulfstanian authorship than it does the authorship of closer contemporaries. Ironically, this aspect of Langlandian authorship is easier to see in the non-Langlandian works of the *Piers Plowman* tradition than it is in the versions of *Piers Plowman* itself. As Helen Barr acknowledges in her important study of the *Piers Plowman* tradition, the direct echoes of *Piers Plowman* found in imitative poems and fragments like *Richard the Redeless* and *Mum and the Sothsegger* are not allusions of a kind that implicitly engage in dialogue with an *auctor* predecessor, as when Hoccleve echoes and eulogizes "My maistir Chaucer, flour of eloquence"

---

8 Swan, "Authorship and Anonymity."

9 On the "school of Cynewulf," see Das, *Cynewulf Canon*; Schaar, *Cynewulf Group*. On Langland's signatures, see Middleton, "Langland's 'Kynde Name'."

10 Bredehoft *Authors, Audiences*, 33–4. "Lupus" was first identified as Wulfstan's pen name by Wanley in 1705: Bethurum, p. 25.

in the *Regiment of Princes*.[11] *Piers Plowman* tradition poems like *Richard the Redeless* and *Mum and the Sothsegger* define their relationship to the previous text "not with reference to dead poets with illustrious names but with reference to standards of legal propriety and truth."[12] As I will demonstrate, the difference between authorial practices in *Mum and the Sothsegger* and the poetry of Hoccleve is best characterized as a *generic* one, both in the sense of their different discursive categories, and in the sense of their genetic descent from different predecessors.

Ethan Knapp's important study of Hoccleve, *The Bureaucratic Muse*, provides a terminology for defining this difference more precisely. Reading Hoccleve's bureaucratic work for the Privy Seal in tandem with his poetry, Knapp draws attention to the paradox that "the very same Hoccleve who has been so often described as excessive, rambling, and obsessed with himself was professionally responsible for the endless re-duplication of a language of grave anonymity."[13] Knapp posits a direct relationship between these two facets of Hoccleve's authorship, as he suggests that "bureaucracy and autobiography appear not as opposites but as two sides of the same coin."[14] Knapp's reading of Hoccleve's relationship to Chaucer provides only one example of the ways in which Hoccleve's twin identities interrelate, as Hoccleve's identification of Chaucer as a poetic "father" interrogates legal notions of paternity and inheritance to usurp Chaucer's role.[15]

In contrast, the most remarkable feature of fragments like *Richard the Redeless* and *Mum and the Sothsegger* is that they seem neither to rely on poetic autobiography nor on grave anonymity to justify their central claims. The versions of *Piers Plowman* contain several passages that meditate on the authorial role of the narrator Will.[16] When the themes of authorial

---

11 Line 1962; *Regiment of Princes*, ed. Blyth. Hereafter all poetry will be cited parenthetically by line number in the text. All references are to this edition. On Hoccleve's invocations of Chaucer see Knapp, *Bureaucratic Muse*, 107–27.

12 Barr, *Signes and Sothe*, 9. For other expansions of the *Piers Plowman* tradition "canon," see Somerset, "Langlandian Canon"; Simpson, "Saving Satire"; Grady, "Contextualizing Alexander"; Gayk, "Alliterative Work"; Kerby-Fulton, *Books under Suspicion*.

13 Knapp, *Bureaucratic Muse*, 35.

14 Knapp, *Bureaucratic Muse*, 13.

15 Knapp, *Bureaucratic Muse*, 107–27.

16 On Langland's meditations on his own authorship, see for example Schmidt, *Clerkly Maker*, 7–20. On the poem's "autobiographical" passage see the essays in Justice and Kerby-Fulton, *Written Work*; particularly relevant here are those of Hanna ("Will's Works") and Middleton ("Acts").

self-justification appear in the fragments under discussion (most extensively in *Mum and the Sothsegger*), they are more concerned with the dangers that may be posed to an author who says things that the audience does not want to hear. Their treatment of this issue never interrogates their relationship to Langland, and yet (in the opposite possible extreme) the fragments are not falsely attributed to Langland either. So absent is Langlandian self-construction from these fragments, that it cannot even be conclusively determined if their narrator is meant to be "Will" or some other character. In other words, the opposition with which Knapp begins, between a literary formalism that is "the textual embodiment of aesthetic engagement and interpretive activity" and a bureaucratic formalism that is a "writing denuded entirely of affect and subjectivity,"[17] does not manifest as a formal tension within the *Piers Plowman* tradition. If at least some members of "the school of Langland" were peers of Hoccleve (as Kerby-Fulton and Justice have argued), then this feature of the texts is even more striking.[18]

Similarly, in the Anglo-Saxon period, there was a much more fluid relationship between bureaucratic and poetic formalisms than the mutually oppositional contradiction described by Knapp.[19] In her study of Old English legal formalism, Dorothy Bethurum points out that Sievers himself distinguished between the formal poetry whose lines fall into his famous five types and the more informal *sagvers*, which was "less dignified" and "slightly less regular."[20] The verse forms are distinguishable not only by their style but also by their function; in poetry "form is an end in itself and must be artistic," while in *sagvers* "the content is all-important and must be forcefully impressed on the memory." Hence according to this scheme, the oppositional modes of writing analogous to those employed by Hoccleve's two personas as poet and bureaucrat were not verse and prose, but more formal verse and less formal verse. Bethurum even suggests that both modes were the purview of a single shared persona, an elected expert (called a *laghman* or *asecga* in Old Frisian) who recited law before an assembly of people, performing as he did so a function that "had some similarities to that of the *scop*."[21] Unlike the divided self of Hoccleve

---

17 Knapp, *Bureaucratic Muse*, 4.

18 Justice and Kerby-Fulton, *Written Work*, 73. For a description of Hoccleve's professional context, see: Knapp, *Bureaucratic Muse*, 20–9.

19 See most recently Scott Smith's study of "tenurial discourse" in Anglo-Saxon legal documents and literary texts, *Land and Book*.

20 Bethurum, "Stylistic Features," 269.

21 Bethurum, "Stylistic Features," 266.

the poet / bureaucrat, then, the dual functions of Bethurum's *laghman / scop* were mutually affirming, as they employed different registers of a single mode of formal speech.

But as Bethurum herself points out, the quasi-poetic quality of Old English law cannot be explained by the mnemonic potential of verse alone: the latest written codes like Wulfstan's *I–II Cnut* are also the most strongly alliterative.[22] As Robert Stanton wrote about Wulfstan's contemporary Ælfric of Eynsham, the "oral elements" of the text are in fact "stylistic innovations" authorized with reference to "a shared common heritage, now fully inscribed and institutionalized in a written milieu."[23] Somewhat remarkably, the very inscription and institutionalization of these "oral elements" appears to have made them even more "oral" in appearance than those earlier English texts with a greater claim to preliterate and pre-institutionalized origins. Hence where Hoccleve's writing suggests that the poet wished to partition his poetic formalism from his bureaucratic record-keeping and play the one against the other, Wulfstan's writing suggests rather that he wished to make the two formal modes even less distinguishable than they were in oral pre-history. A similar impulse appears to underlie the imitative fragments of the *Piers Plowman* tradition.

Thus the question with which we began, of defining Langland's relationship to his body of imitators, leads naturally to an analysis of form. Not only are the categories of "poet" and "bureaucrat" difficult to apply to the figures of Wulfstan and Langland, but also the categories of "poetry" and "prose" are difficult to apply to the writings affiliated with their schools. In the case of Wulfstan, Thomas Bredehoft is only among the more recent scholars to argue against the divisions between "high" and "low" levels of metrical formalism in favour of an expanded concept of Old English verse, one that also encompasses homiletic "stressed prose."[24] A particularly pertinent example of this ongoing conversation is the debate between Dorothy Whitelock and Karl Jost over the latter's poetic lineation of Wulfstan's *Institutes of Polity* in his edition, based on Jost's recognition in that text of Wulfstan's "two-beat" stress patterns as identified

---

22 Bethurum, "Stylistic Features," 269–70. For a recent article making a similar claim about Old Frisian laws, see Bremmer, "Dealing."

23 Stanton, *Culture*, 166.

24 Bredehoft, *Authors, Audiences*, esp. 17–98, and *Early English Metre*. See also Zacher, "Rewards of Poetry"; Brehe, "'Rhythmical Alliteration'"; Irving, "Latin Prose Sources"; McIntosh, "Wulfstan's Prose."

by Angus McIntosh.[25] Whitelock does not dispute the appearance of a substantial number of cases of two-beat patterns in Wulfstan's prose, nor does Jost dispute the appearance of a substantial number of exceptions. Rather, their debate hinges on their different opinions about the generalizations that can be sustained through analysis of the borderline cases, and the extent to which those generalizations correspond closely enough with modern concepts of poetry to justify the editorial use of modern poetic formatting conventions. Are the *Institutes of Polity* "high" poetry, "low" poetry, or not poetry at all? However this argument is resolved, the fact remains that the *Institutes of Polity* employ quasi-poetic form to structure a programmatic (and in that sense quasi-legal) description of the duties of the various parts of society, and by doing so it confuses modern editing categories beyond the ability of formatting conventions to finally satisfy.

Another "legal" text bearing some signs of Wulfstan's stressed homiletic prose is the law code *I–II Cnut*. The code is not signed by Wulfstan, and the attribution of this code to the archbishop has been almost entirely on stylistic grounds.[26] *I–II Cnut* appears in its Old English version in three manuscripts: London, BL, Cotton Nero A.I; London, BL, Harley 55; and Cambridge, Corpus Christi College 383.[27] The last of these is dated after the Norman Conquest.[28] The code's Latin translations also appear frequently in post-Conquest collections of Anglo-Saxon law codes, typically at the beginning, in defiance of historical organization.[29] As Patrick Wormald has observed, Wulfstan's legislation "was of much greater importance after 1066 than has almost ever been realized,"[30] and it is not an exaggeration to say that readers from the later medieval period who were at all familiar with genuine Anglo-Saxon law would probably have known some version of Wulfstan's text.

In its organization, *I–II Cnut* more closely resembles an exposition-heavy oratory than it does a rationally organized "code," and only later editors rubricated the text to resemble a reference work.[31] In Mary

---

25 Wulfstan, *Institutes*, ed. Jost; Whitelock, "*Institutes*"; see also Orchard, "Re-Editing Wulfstan," 6; Pons-Sanz, *Norse-Derived Vocabulary*, 28–9.
26 Whitelock, "Wulfstan and the Laws of Cnut" and "Wulfstan's Authorship."
27 *MoEL*, 349.
28 Mary Richards, "Manuscript Contexts," 181–4; *MoEL* 228–36.
29 *MoEL* 240–1.
30 "Introduction," 22. See also Pons-Sanz, *Norse-Derived Vocabulary*, 231–60.
31 *MoEL* 197–210. The text is rubricated in the *Quadripartitus*: Wormald, "Quadripartitus," 125.

Richards's words, Wulfstan's law codes more closely resemble "sources for teaching" than they resemble "records of the past."[32] Even the division of *I–II Cnut* into parts one and two is a later editorial invention; as in the code *Æthelberht* and the similarly divided code *II–III Edgar*, the ecclesiastical law of *I Cnut* is not separate from the secular law of *II Cnut*, so much as it is simply discussed first.[33] The markedly homiletic structure and style of *I–II Cnut* is probably a reflection of the text's original use. M.K. Lawson has argued convincingly that Wulfstan's law codes were orally presented to the king's counsellors or *witan*, probably by the archbishop himself.[34] The implication of Lawson's argument for legal historians is that the text of *I–II Cnut* does not necessarily reflect Cnut's actual program of reform, but rather Wulfstan's "somewhat optimistic" suggestions.[35]

The evidence of Wulfstan's earlier law code, *VI Æthelred*, supports Lawson's argument. The Latin preface to this text describes a legislative session with many preaching interludes, an agenda that leaves readers with the impression that the proceedings were controlled almost entirely by Wulfstan and his fellow archbishop Ælfheah.[36] *VI Æthelred* survives in a Benedictional manuscript with annotations in Wulfstan's own hand, and it looks a great deal like a text from which the archbishop would have preached.[37] Though composed for a particular occasion, then, it appears that Wulfstan continued to preach *VI Æthelred* afterwards also, perhaps in commemoration of its original ratification by the king and the *witan*.

I–II Cnut was probably written and disseminated under similar conditions. In the *Anglo-Saxon Chronicle* entry D 1018, there is a description of a meeting of the king and his *witan* at Oxford, a likely venue for a performance of the *Cnut 1018* code.[38] The entry also makes reference to revisions proposed at the meeting, which presumably led to the later code *I–II Cnut* presented at Winchester; again, Wulfstan appears to have made the requested revisions himself. Given these circumstances, then, it is quite difficult to disentangle the laws actually practised in Cnut's England from

---

32 Richards, "Manuscript Contexts," 176.

33 However in one medieval manuscript a scribal division between *II–III Edgar* is perhaps reflected by an outsize initial appearing at the start of *III Edgar* (*MoEL* 189). On *Æthelberht*, see Oliver, *Beginnings of English Law*, 36.

34 Lawson, "Homiletic Element."

35 Lawson, "Homiletic Element," 581.

36 Lawson, "Homiletic Element," 573–4; *Gesetze* I:247.

37 Lawson, "Homiletic Element," 577.

38 Stafford, "The Laws of Cnut," 173–4, citing Whitelock, "Wulfstan and the Laws of Cnut," 440, and *Saxon Chronicles*, ed. Plummer, I:154.

the laws that Wulfstan merely suggested. The text occupies a wholly different register of documentary commemoration from "law codes" in the modern sense, in that *I–II Cnut* aims not to transparently represent the actual historical circumstances of its production, but rather to evoke the kinds of moral truth discernible in the just laws of earlier kings – in other words, with reference to the same "standards of legal propriety and truth" that pertain to the engagement with *Piers Plowman* in the revisions and interpolations written by the "school of Langland." The authority of Wulfstan's laws is ultimately derived from the same "common sense" of shared values articulated by homilists at the pulpit to encourage righteous living. The text's author is therefore not just a bureaucrat, but also a literary author, who must not only record the law but also convince his audience of his own earnestness.

These similarities between Wulfstan's laws and *Piers Plowman* are obscured in their formative editions. Felix Liebermann took a very different approach to his edition of *I–II Cnut* in his *Die Gesetze der Anglesachsen* than his contemporary Walter Skeat took to *Piers Plowman* in his edition of the latter. Where Skeat enshrined the hypothesis that there are three authorial versions of the text, Liebermann placed the different witnesses and translations of *I–II Cnut* in separate columns, with variations in the substance of the legislation marked in bold.[39] This is particularly ironic because Skeat's thesis of authorial revision is arguably more appropriate to the evidence surrounding the versions of Wulfstan's law code than it is to the manuscripts of *Piers Plowman*. Future editors of the codes *Cnut 1018* and *I–II Cnut* would be well within their rights to rename the texts *Cnut* "A-version" and *Cnut* "B-version," and could do so with a much firmer basis in the historical evidence than Skeat had when he divided up the versions of *Piers Plowman*.[40] That Liebermann did not represent the texts in this way reflects his categorically different concerns: Skeat organized the data to show how it might reflect the evolving work of a particular literary author, while Liebermann looked for continuities and changes in a working legal tradition.

The comparison underscores the fact that if we are to utilize the scholarship based on these editions to compare the textual traditions they summarize, we must translate between the two scholarly methodologies that

---

39 See however A.V.C. Schmidt's columnar edition of *Piers Plowman*: Langland, *Piers Plowman: A Parallel-Text Edition*. For criticisms of Liebermann's editorial decisions, see O'Brien, "*Instituta Cnuti*," 178–82; *MoEL* 22–3.

40 On Langland's authorship, see Middleton, "Langland's 'Kynde Name'"; Kane, *Evidence for Authorship*.

the editions exemplify, looking both for the traces of the literary authors and for the traces of the legal traditions at the same time. In the next two sections of this chapter, I will define the parameters within which my own comparative study will operate, first defining the precise relationship between the methodologies of literary critics and legal historians, and then illustrating through a specific example how Anglo-Saxon documentary culture actively resists the very categorical division that gives structure to each discipline. Disciplinary divisions of medieval texts into "historical records" and "literature" are a major reason that the texts compared in this study have not been compared sooner; hence the presumptions underlying those divisions must be articulated before the comparison may proceed.

Definitions: Orality and Literacy, Law and Literature

It has been accepted for some time among both literary critics and legal historians of the medieval period that the inherited categories of textual criticism insufficiently characterize the complexity of medieval textual traditions. The scribes who produced those traditions do not appear to have been able or willing to impose the standards of quality control now considered essential for the production of genuinely authorial literary texts and authoritatively transparent legal documents. Generally speaking, this is the aspect of medieval legal and literary textual traditions referred to when they are said to reflect the "transitional literacy"[41] or "incipient textuality"[42] of the culture that produced them, in comparison to the more "fully" literate / textual practices that dominate the bureaucratic and cultural institutions of modern nation states. In the term's most basic and inclusive sense, then, "orality" in medieval texts can be summarily defined as the features whereby they resist not only the methods but also the very purposes of modern critical methodologies.

In the remainder of this chapter, I will demonstrate the implications of this observation for Anglo-Saxon legal-homiletic discourse, which is defined in part by its "oral" patterns of resistance to the methodologies of textual criticism. My argument will build on Mary Richards's observation that in the late Anglo-Saxon period and even after the Norman Conquest, law codes "took the force of moral precepts."[43] I will suggest that the kinds

---

41 O'Brien O'Keeffe, *Visible Song.*
42 Foley, "Orality, Textuality," 44.
43 Richards, "Manuscript Contexts," 187.

of formal analysis employed by Anglo-Saxonists to critically analyse sententious literature can provide us with a way of criticizing the legal and literary formalisms of the medieval period simultaneously. Sententious statements and common-sense tropes are among the most pervasive authorizing gestures in all modes and genres, and they lay at the root of the divergent authorizing gestures of literature and law. In the following section I will clarify the distinction between literary and legal authorizing gestures to better frame my analysis of the particular function of sententious statements in Anglo-Saxon legal-homiletic discourse.

Though the "alliterative revival" poems like those in the *Piers Plowman* tradition were clearly written by highly literate poets,[44] the idea that they draw from an oral, alliterative tradition of poetry has maintained its aura of plausibility, in part for reasons identified by Ralph Hanna: "On the one hand, the speakers of these poems personify a hoary wisdom and exemplify it through their reliance upon standard learned texts of Latinate origin ... yet simultaneously, the mode in which such literary communication is not simply marked, but overmarked, as vernacular," so that they "flaunt their own (thoroughly fictive) orality."[45] Alliterative prosody is certainly well suited for "flaunting" a fictive orality. It simultaneously encourages the retention of the oldest words still in the language and the importation of loanwords. Structurally, it responds to the practical needs of the poetic moment to generate a coherence that is better described in temporal rather than spatial terms, a "rhythm" rather than a shape.[46] This loose but identifiable rhythm gives the text a feeling of spontaneity, even when archaic usages and Latin quotations reveal it to be painstakingly composed.

But though the objective qualities of alliteration doubtless played a role in the alliterative poets' choice of metre, it is also likely that alliterative sound-patterning had a specific cultural value in its political context, as a feature of older and therefore more authoritative vernacular texts and documents. Hanna also observes that in alliterative poems, "clerkes" tend to serve bureaucratic roles, as "the lord's secretaries, his recorders, his accountants," and he notes that the narrative forms of alliterative "reckonings"

---

44 Turville-Petre, *The Alliterative Revival*, 15–17; Pearsall, "Origins of the Alliterative Revival," esp. 41–4; and Amodio, *Writing the Oral Tradition*, 182.

45 Hanna, "Alliterative Poetry," 501. On the term "fictive orality," see also D.H. Green, *The Beginnings of Medieval Romance*, 35–47, and "Fictive Orality."

46 On Langland's "rhythm," see also Schmidt, *Clerkly Maker*, 26–7.

often repeat this pattern of listing.[47] These tendencies indicate that the poems aimed to evoke not only oral culture per se, but also written vernacular literature from earlier periods in the "transition" towards literate cultural practice. The contradiction that Hanna identifies between the flagrant orality of Middle English alliterative metre and the learned, sententious, Latinate sources of Middle English alliterative poems was itself a contradiction discernible in the written record of earlier Middle English and Old English literature. The literate communities most likely to encounter those earlier traditions were the secretaries, recorders, and accountants who consulted ancient English legal texts as a part of their professional duties. Hanna has identified the "deeply problematic" nature of Langland's project as "the vernacular appropriation of learnedness."[48] One way this project acquired legitimacy was through its imitation of a pre-existing discourse of vernacular learnedness.

Among the most influential studies of "orality" in the English medieval period are those of M.T. Clanchy and Brian Stock.[49] Both of these scholars draw on the framework for discussing "orality" that was formatively articulated by scholars such as Walter Ong and Jack Goody, who argued that reliance on the written word, or "literacy," in Western Europe has resulted in fundamental changes in the practice of culture itself, which has detracted from our understanding of its pre-literate or "oral" past.[50] In *The Implications of Literacy*, Stock argues that this change in medieval Europe was characterized by an increased tendency to divide and categorize knowledge. He writes that "it was in the fundamental process of categorization, rather than in the content of knowledge alone, that the Middle Ages broke irrevocably with the interpretive patterns of later antiquity and moved towards those of early modern Europe."[51] Of course this change was not uncontested, and in fact Stock observes that "one of the demonstrable signs of a changed environment was the ambivalence with which many

---

47 Hanna, "Alliterative Poetry," 503–4.

48 Hanna, "Alliterative Poetry," 499.

49 Clanchy, *From Memory to Written Record*; Stock, *Implications of Literacy*. See also Rosamund McKitterick's summary of these authors and their contributions to studies of medieval orality: McKitterick, "Introduction."

50 Influential works by Ong and Goody include Walter J. Ong, *Orality and Literacy*; Goody, *The Domestication of the Savage Mind*. For summaries (and criticisms) of these studies focused particularly on their pertinence to medieval European history, see Coleman, *Public Reading*, 1–33; Green, *Medieval Listening*.

51 *Implications of Literacy*, 4.

textual models were greeted by the medievals themselves." [52] As I will argue below, the "ambivalence" about literacy attributed to later medieval thinkers by Stock is not only a secondary "sign" of literacy, but is in fact one of literacy's defining characteristics.

Stock identifies a turning point in medieval European history during the eleventh and twelfth centuries. He says that "up to the eleventh century, western Europe could have returned to an essentially oral civilization," but that "by 1100 the die was cast."[53] In England, this transitional point is almost exactly contemporary to the Norman Conquest and that monumental, categorizing document, the Domesday Book. Thus Stock's argument implies that the traditional disciplinary divide between "Old English" and "Middle English" literature and culture is marked not only by major linguistic changes, but also by a fundamental shift in philosophical outlook, as the later period is characterized by more rigid categories of discourse that were themselves more dependent on categorization as a method for structuring knowledge.[54] In our case, these divisions would have manifested in the greater care taken after the Norman Conquest to distinguish functionally "legal" documents and/or law codes from functionally "literary" accounts of historical events and/or statements of moral principle.

The aftermath of Domesday Book's production is the *terminus a quo* of Clanchy's study, which elaborates on this implicit argument to trace the emergence of lay literacy in England from 1066 to the year 1307. Clanchy summarizes his historical thesis: "lay literacy grew out of bureaucracy, rather than from any abstract desire for education or literature."[55] Clanchy's material-cultural approach to the evidence represents the emergence of lay literacy as a relatively chaotic and almost inexplicable development. He states that "Effective precautions against fraud were not taken [between the Norman Conquest and the fourteenth century], because they demanded extensive professionalism and because writings seemed to have been thought of at first as subsidiary aids to traditional memorizing procedures and not as replacements of them. A new technology usually adapts itself at first to an existing one, camouflaging itself in the old forms

---

52 *Implications of Literacy*, 4.
53 *Implications of Literacy*, 18.
54 On Anglo-Saxon legal literacy, see also Keynes, "Royal Government"; Wormald, "*Lex Scripta* and *Verbum Regis*."
55 *Memory to Written Record*, 19.

and not immediately recognizing its potential."[56] Clanchy's decision to focus on legal literacy after the Anglo-Saxon period in his study had necessarily led him to give short shrift to the impact of Anglo-Saxon documents, as he himself has recently acknowledged in the new edition of his book.[57] He justified his decision by pointing to the relative scarcity of Anglo-Saxon charters, not only in comparison to Norman documents, but also in comparison to contemporary Continental institutions; Cluny's 2532 charters dated before the year 1000 provides a dramatic (if somewhat loaded) point of comparison to the just under 2,000 charters catalogued by *The Electronic Sawyer* for all of England over the entire Anglo-Saxon period.[58] Stock's first chapter and Clanchy's entire book root their sociolinguistic historical claims in precisely this kind of survival evidence, which strongly suggests that England did not produce many documents before the Norman Conquest, but began to produce many more almost immediately afterwards.[59] The trajectory traced by these scholars can be roughly summarized as a shift between the primary reliance on "oral," spoken forms of validation to "literate" written forms, so that the former atrophied as the latter became more complex. The lack of surviving charters implies that sworn oaths and the testimony of witnesses were preferred to written documents in the courts of Anglo-Saxon England. Thus the apparent imitation of specifically Anglo-Saxon poetic form in Middle English alliterative poetry contributes in no small part to modern impressions of their "fictive orality"; any imitation of Anglo-Saxon writing seems by that very fact to evoke the more "oral" cultural practices of the Anglo-Saxon period.

In recent years, studies of orality and literacy in medieval cultures have backed away from Stock and Clanchy's broader narratives, to focus more on the localized "interpenetration, interplay and symbiosis" of oral and written modes of discourse at particular points in history, in service of a "more modest, non-determinist view of literacy as a facilitator of cognitive change."[60] In a recent application of one such adaptable model to both Old and Middle English orality, Mark Amodio has noted that Ong's concept of

---

56 *Memory to Written Record*, 328.
57 On the sophistication of the Anglo-Saxon royal bureaucracy, see Campbell, "Late Anglo-Saxon State"; see also Foot, "Anglo-Saxon 'Nation-State'."
58 Campbell, "The Sale of Land," 227; *ES* accessed 17 March 2011.
59 Stock, *Implications of Literacy*, 12–88; Clanchy, *Memory to Written Record*, 26–32.
60 Chinca and Young, "Introduction," 1–2. The original formulation of this "weak" theory of orality is Finnegan, *Literacy and Orality*, 141, 160.

"primary orality," which posits that orality logically must have preceded the rise of literacy, implies a narrative of progress that cannot be substantiated: "Tying cultural advancement to the rise of literacy is a flawed strategy because many oral cultures manage(d) quite well without ever developing or becoming dependent upon a system of graphemic representation."[61] Indeed, even the presumption that speaking and listening must have preceded reading and writing in prehistoric human cultures can be called into question. For example, J.E. Chamberlin has pointed out that hunters collaboratively use their perceptions about the "signs" of animal tracks, changes in the weather, and the shape of the landscape to develop highly detailed "narratives" of their quarry's movements, "remarkably like the members of the community that gathered in the great library of Alexandria and developed a set of reading practices and interpretive strategies that were dependent on the closed body of texts that were available to them, and the knowledge they shared."[62] Thus the difference between a hunter-gatherer tribe and the English royal court circa 1307 is not that the latter *has* a sophisticated practice of reading, but that it *associates* that practice with listening, as another way of communicating verbally.

If the dichotomy between orality and literacy is thus redefined, from a narrative of technological change to a continuously shifting reschematization of different discursive and interpretive practices, then it provides a more nuanced framework for describing the evocation of Old English orality performed by Middle English alliterative verse. One way of restating Stock's definition of "literacy" is to call it a relatively sophisticated awareness of the extent to which written texts *do not work* as instruments of communication between people. The strategies of reading and writing are fundamentally different from those of speaking and listening, and the analogy connecting them can only be sustained so far. Hence a familiarity with the uses of written texts must also be a familiarity with the precise character of their limitations, as exemplified by the various typical failures of justice with which any denizen of a literate society would be familiar. If early medieval scribes did not take "effective precautions against fraud," as Clanchy claims, it was perhaps because even criminals at the time were not fluent enough in the forms of written documents to realize just how many kinds of fraud they could be used to perpetrate.

---

61 Amodio, *Writing the Oral Tradition*, 2–3.
62 Chamberlin, "A New History of Reading," 82.

The primary difference between literacy and other kinds of technological distrust is that literacy tends to seek out solutions to the known problems by means of a more radical dependence on the faulty technology. When criminals eventually discovered that written documents could be used to perpetrate frauds, societies responded by creating more kinds of written documents, and more complex methods for producing and storing them. In these terms, England's shift from an "oral" to a "literate" society can be more precisely characterized as a shift in the discursive strategies intended to mitigate anxieties about the basic unreliability of *all* linguistic communication, written or spoken, to focus on strategies that aim to correct the problems specifically pertinent to written texts. Medieval English government did not become increasingly reliant on written records *despite* the growing awareness among the populace that such records were fundamentally untrustworthy; it took place *because of* that growing awareness. The dangerous opacity of written documents, whose constitutive convenience is the ease with which they can be taken out of context and adapted to new purposes, inspired the development of specialized strategies intended to increase the difficulty of manipulating the text for uses contrary to the authentic intentions of the texts' authors or transcribers. The processes of categorization identified by Stock, manifest for example in the oppositional categories "literary text" and "legal document," are only among the most pervasive and influential of these strategies.

In this sense the "transitional literacy" of Anglo-Saxon legal-homiletic discourse and the "fictive orality" of Middle English alliterative poetry can both be more precisely defined as the qualities of the traditions whereby they apparently fail to anticipate the particular scepticisms implicit in the methodologies of modern specialist readers. Indeed, as I will demonstrate, alliterative poetry appealed to the school of Langland precisely because it offered this resistance. In the fourteenth century as today, the very strategies employed to curb bureaucratic excess and corruption themselves often lead to the growth of bureaucracy and the creation of new opportunities for corruption. By evoking an earlier model of bureaucratic professionalism, the *Piers Plowman* tradition attempted to create for itself a vantage point from which it could observe the interrelationship between literacy and corruption without inadvertently participating in its processes.

To get a more complex understanding of these "oral" texts, then, we must first re-examine the methodologies of literary critics and legal historians that have thus far proven inadequate for fully describing them. For the present purposes, I will define "literary-critical" methodologies as the various attempts to represent and understand a text's probable authorial version, and the historian's "diplomatic" methodologies as the various attempts to represent the probable circumstances of a manuscript's production. Though these are relatively conservative definitions of the disciplines, they are intentionally so; my goal is not to limit literary critics and historians to certain kinds of analysis, but on the contrary to develop a critical language for describing my own intervention into certain long-standing complaints about traditional methodologies. In my discussions of these methodologies, I will draw on the principles articulated in Will Robins's article "Towards a Disjunctive Philology," where he observes that editions do not "represent" but rather "model" texts: "like any model, [the edition] raises one set of features to visibility by excluding others to serve a heuristic purpose."[63] Because the texts studied here will span both poetic and documentary forms, my readings will have to make a simultaneous application of both "literary" and "diplomatic" strategies for modelling the medieval texts that are their respective objects of study. As such, my readings will be "disjunctive" in Robins's sense, using the two approaches to call attention to the particular features of the text excluded by each of them.[64]

The practices of "literary-critical" reading typically begin with the presupposition that a transhistorical text might be abstracted from many manuscript copies, even if none of those copies exactly represent that text in its totality. "Diplomatic" reading, on the other hand, presupposes that each manuscript witnesses an individual and unrepeatable event; even when two copies are made of a single text to witness a single transaction, the documents have an individual significance that outweighs their common contents. In short, diplomatic reading concerns itself primarily with the strategies by which a text *commemorates*, while literary criticism examines the strategies by which it *creates*.

I define "commemoration" here as a mode of writing employed by legal texts and historical documents, which is authenticated only insofar as it seems to unproblematically or "transparently" transmit historical information from the past into the present, so that it is implicitly directed towards a future in which the commemorated idea will be remembered and repeated. "Transparency" here can be understood in terms of Nancy Partner's description of transparent historical writing, that it pertains to

---

63 Robins, "Disjunctive Philology," 146.

64 Robins's own example of a disjunctive approach is of a facing-page edition of a single-text and a multi-text edition; see also his recent edition in this style: Pucci, *I cantari della Reina d' Oriente*, ed. Robins and Motta.

"the vaguer, affective qualities of scientific knowledge – impersonal neutrality, equability of tone, absence of ornament." [65] Diplomas acquire these vaguer, affective qualities in part because of their similarity to other known transactions from the same time and place, which similarities are typically referred to as their "formulaic" qualities.

The discipline of diplomatics is defined by the Commission internationale de diplomatique as follows: "to examine [written] acts critically, to determine their authenticity, to appraise their textual quality, to extricate from formulaic language all those elements of their contents that may be exploited by the historian, to date them, and finally to edit them."[66] Richard Sharpe summarizes the precise nature of this "exploitation" thus:

> All documents issuing from the same authority in the same period and serving the same function tend to conform to a pattern; a comparison of specimens allows us to identify that pattern. It is then possible, on the one hand, to compare this "form" with those used by the same authority for other purposes, or those used for the same purpose at a different time, or indeed those issued by a different authority. On this basis historians may understand the changing uses of the written word in government, administration, or law.[67]

Hence the transparency of legal documents is determined through a process of formal comparison. How closely does any particular record resemble other records of the same time? Does the state of the archive suggest that these records were produced by a competent bureaucracy? The more it seems that historical events were recorded as a matter of course, the less likely it seems that the version of historical events recorded in a particular document reflects an idiosyncratic political agenda. In brief, a document that seems unusual is a document that seems inauthentic.

"Creativity," on the other hand, is a mode whose claim to self-authentication inadvertently reveals its debt to earlier modes of self-authentication, and in that sense it is implicitly directed towards the prehistory of its influences. As Barthes asserts in an influential formulation: "The Author, when believed in, is always conceived of as the past of his own book: book and author stand automatically on a single line divided

---

65 "New Cornificius," 24; see also "Lost Time." Partner draws in particular from the formative essays of Hayden White, "Rhetoric and History" and "Fictions of Factual Representation."
66 Sharpe, "Charters, Deeds," 230, citing Bautier, *Diplomatica*.
67 Sharpe, "Charters, Deeds," 230. See also Boyle, "Diplomatics."

into a before or after."[68] For literary criticism to situate its object of study, then, it must first set up a perimeter around a text, and eliminate "errors" that may distort the relationship between the text and its prehistory. For example, a critic may ask: what features of the text are scribal interventions? What features allude to earlier authors? What aspects of her source material does the author choose to change, and why? Hence while the idiosyncratic formal features of commemorative texts work against their authorizing procedures, such idiosyncratic formal features are the primary focus of literary critics who "exploit" the unique features of the text to construct arguments about the author's own thought or cultural milieu.

Anglo-Saxon legal-homiletic discourse, which is creative and formulaic even as it is also sometimes commemorative and idiosyncratic, frustrates these traditional methodological presumptions. For example, Anglo-Saxon law codes tend to eschew the author function. There is no evidence that any Anglo-Saxon king personally wrote any law code that bears his name; and indeed, it is striking that Asser's *Life of Alfred*, where we would most expect to find such evidence, does not mention the written legislation of pre-Conquest England's most famous lawgiver.[69] In A.J. Minnis's terms, the *auctoritas* of these laws seems to be dependent on their "intrinsic worth" as statements of correct principle much more than their "authenticity" as an accurate reproduction of the monarch's actual words.[70] Hence the paradox that a law code can be titled "The Laws of King Cnut" though the text is referred to internally as the laws of Edgar,[71] and though it was actually written by Wulfstan. If modern literary critics have identified correspondences between the idiosyncratic features of Wulfstan's homilies and the idiosyncratic features of these laws, and concluded on this basis that Wulfstan wrote them, his authorship is nonetheless an accidental feature of the text itself.

But if the law code *I–II Cnut* is not quite a creative work, neither does it resemble the modern legal documents we would now call "laws," which commemorate the meeting of a legislative body in order to validate certain procedures for adjudicating criminal and civil proceedings. Patrick

---

68 Barthes, "Death of the Author," 145.

69 *MoEL*, 120–1. On Alfred's authorship, see Godden, "Did King Alfred Write Anything?"

70 Minnis, *Medieval Theory of Authorship*, 10–11.

71 *Cnut 1018* 1 reads: "Þonne is þæt ærest, þæt witan geræddan, þæt hi ... Eadgares lagan geornlice folgian" ("Firstly, that witan advised that they ... should earnestly follow Edgar's law").

Wormald has pointed to Bede's statement that the *Æthelberht* code was written "iuxta exempla Romanorum" to argue that the Roman *exempla* were of legal texts that were written down at all. The code may have confirmed Æthelberht's prestige with reference to the standards set by Roman emperors, but it is hardly indicative of a fully realized legal system along Roman lines.[72] Hence even if the law codes are not rooted in the authority of a particular author, the circumstances of their survival indicate that they are nonetheless creative texts, at least insofar as they do not live up to the standards of proof necessary for diplomatic critics to accept that they were enforced as law in the Anglo-Saxon period.[73] In other words, *I–II Cnut* is neither quite a literary text nor quite a legal document, and for that reason it is difficult to analyse it fruitfully with the methods of either literary critics or legal historians.

Of course, no text is ever itself wholly commemorative or wholly creative; both diplomatic and literary-critical methodologies can be applied to virtually any discursive object. Nonetheless, texts tend to lean in one direction or the other, in their formal anticipation of the kinds of questions a reader might most want to ask. "Oral" texts, then, are merely those that tend to sit most squarely in between creative and commemorative modes of writing, in their failure to mark themselves as either strictly formulaic or as strictly innovative. In doing so, they reveal that fundamental weakness of "literate" strategies of textual categorization. The act of dividing commemorative from creative texts may mitigate literate anxieties about the fungibility of textual meaning, but it does not address the underlying cause: whether commemorative or creative in conception and form, any text can be submitted to any critical method, and will ultimately resist final definition according to that method. If the "orality" of any written text is by the very fact of its being written "fictive," so too are all literacies by the same fact transitional, all textualities incipient. As we shall see, Anglo-Saxon-era law codes and documents drew the attention of their late-medieval readers to this ultimate instability of textual categories, simply by retaining political importance in the later medieval period though they failed to conform to the expectations of late medieval diplomatic critics. As a result, imitations of pre-Conquest legal-homiletic form in fourteenth-century alliterative poetry became expressive of cultural anxieties about the literate practices that had come to dominate virtually all aspects of secular life.

---

72 *MoEL* 29. See also Richards, "Anglo-Saxonism," 40–1.
73 See also Frantzen, *King Alfred*, 1–21.

As I said above, the critical division of creative and commemorative writing into mutually exclusive formalisms arose as a particularly literate strategy for mitigating anxieties that in fact pertain to all forms of communication. In the next section I will describe in greater detail the comparatively "oral" strategy for mitigating these anxieties employed in Anglo-Saxon legal-homiletic discourse, which was to frame statements in the context of sententious wisdom. Maxims, proverbs, and commonplace tropes serve the organizing and authorizing function in Anglo-Saxon legal-homiletic discourse that the author would later serve in literary criticism, and that bureaucratic proceduralism would serve in diplomatics. If the poets of the *Piers Plowman* tradition eschewed both the role of the bureaucrat and the role of the literary author in their reworking of *Piers Plowman*, it was because they aspired to the role of the *laghman* and / or *scop*, who enjoyed authority because he had access to the "wordhoard" of shared wisdom. Hence the constant recourse to commonplace structures and sententious statements in *Piers Plowman*, and hence the author's apparent carelessness in citing its proverbs correctly.[74] For the school of Wulfstan as for the school of Langland, England must be protected from those greedy and irreligious interlopers who disrespect the hard work and wisdom of God's true servants, as those servants teach divine law by their words and their example. The more specific political implications of this general claim may change in the different texts surveyed by this study, but the tropes of conventional wisdom used to articulate it are strikingly regular.

Of course the medieval commonplaces that will be cited in the course of this argument are by nature common, and I do not presume to claim that *I–II Cnut* and *Piers Plowman* are connected merely because in both texts old advisers are better than young ones and people are judged by their thoughts, words, and deeds. Instead, the goal of my study is to highlight parallel formal strategies that are particularly representative of the quasi-legal quality of medieval English alliterative formalism. The sententiousness of Anglo-Saxon law codes and Langlandian satire is distinguished from the sententiousness of medieval literature more generally by the fact that in the context of Anglo-Saxon legal-homiletic discourse, generalized references to common sense are used to lend authority to a relatively consistent set of complaints about the abuses of secular government. To illustrate that this is the case, I must first define my term "sententious formalism" more precisely.

---

74 On proverbs and their sources in *Piers Plowman*, see Alford, *Quotations*.

Definitions: Sententious Statements and Proverbial Form

The Old English wisdom poem *Instructions for Christian Living* survives in the first part of the manuscript Cambridge, Corpus Christi College 201, which was joined later in the eleventh century to a collection of Wulfstanian homiletic and legal materials. The manuscript of the poem *Seasons for Fasting*, Cotton Otho B.XI, was heavily damaged in the Cottonian fire, but the poem nonetheless survives in a transcription by Laurence Nowell; the original manuscript also witnessed Old English laws, and in the opinion of Mary Richards this context reflects the legal use value of the poem.[75] Finally, the sententious poems *The Gifts of Men* and *The Fortunes of Men* are both included by Dorothy Whitelock in her English Historical Documents collection, because of their valuable descriptions of Anglo-Saxon material culture. To eleventh-century scribes and to modern editors, then, Old English wisdom poetry served a commemorative function, though its metrical regularity also marks the texts as "poems," and in that sense as creative texts. In the chapters that follow, I will identify the commemorative and creative uses of sententious forms as they manifest in Anglo-Saxon legal-homiletic discourse, starting from the assumption that sententious forms provided a common origin for the authenticating strategies of both modern literary forms and modern documentary formulae.

Because the terminology for discussing "wisdom" literature is notoriously slippery, most of the Anglo-Saxonists who have treated it begin their studies by narrowing the corpus down to a small and manageable size, typically including wholly sententious works such as *Maxims I* and *II*, *The Durham Proverbs*, the Old English translations of the *Dicts of Cato*, and *Instructions for Christians*.[76] In contrast, I will take the most expansive definition possible, to describe sententiousness itself as a feature of Anglo-Saxon writing that is characteristic of its "residual orality." In this discussion I define "sententiousness" as a quality of statements that implies their self-evident truth. My work is not concerned with the origins of particular statements, for example, by distinguishing biblical quotations from pagan proverbs and maxims invented by later authors. Instead, I will aim to define sententiousness solely in terms of the formal qualities of language that conveyed the impression that a statement is wise and widely accepted.

---

75 Richards, "Manuscript Contexts," 174–5. See also more recently "Old Wine."
76 For a recent survey of the field, see Kramer, "Study of Proverbs."

As Thomas Shippey formatively argued, the critical problems of interpreting the sententious qualities of Old English poetry are in a certain sense isomorphic with the problems of Anglo-Saxon England's transitional orality.[77] Sententious statements are highly resistant to the traditional techniques of both literary criticism and legal history. For example, a proverb clearly works to commemorate some idea or nugget of received wisdom, but at the same time a proverb's content is open to manipulation and even reversal. To use a modern example, the East Texan proverb "a bird in the hand causes a big mess" is authorized by its resemblance to the more common proverb "a bird in the hand is worth two in the bush," even though it subverts the sentiment of its source.[78] Both because the transmission of such proverbs is often oral and because their meaning is so generalized – people have both hunted birds and avoided speculative greed in a wide variety of cultural and historical contexts – critics are very limited in their ability to either claim, on the one hand, that any particular poet or homilist or legislator who alludes to a bird in the hand is thereby commemorating a widely known proverb, or on the other hand that she is creatively playing off of a sententious form to express her own ideas. These interpretive difficulties are particularly acute in the Anglo-Saxon corpus of English and Latin literature, which exists at a great historical remove from our own time and imperfectly records the frequency with which certain phrases or proverbs were used in daily life.

Of course, the recognizability of proverbs is not only a problem for modern scholars, but also for the Anglo-Saxons who wished to cite a proverb or maxim to an audience that may not have heard the proverb or maxim before. As Arvo Krikmann observes, one crucial signal to a listener that one is hearing a proverb is the use of speech that is "too regular and ornamental" to be taken literally.[79] For example, "a bird in the hand is worth two in the bush" is a four-beat line, beginning with an iamb and followed by three anapaests, with alliteration falling on the first and last stressed syllables. The regularity and ornamentation of the phrase would help a speaker of English to recognize it as a proverb, even if she had never heard it before. Similarly, the variation "a bird in the hand causes a big

---

77 Shippey, "Maxims."

78 Bowman, *If I Tell,* 54. This collection of sayings is not a scholarly source; however, my point pertains not to the actual popularity of this proverb, but to its successful imitation of a well-known proverb.

79 Krikmann, "Denotative," cited by Deskis, *Beowulf,* 5.

mess" derives its humour from its deviation from the expected form, the proverb reflecting formally the unexpected "big mess" it warns of.

Hence so many critics of Old English wisdom poetry have concluded that in a fundamental sense, form is in fact the "content" of Anglo-Saxon maxims and proverbs. Old English poetic "lists" of sententious statements like *Maxims I* and *II* and *Precepts* are typically read as affirmations of wisdom's constitutive structures rather than the particular nuggets of wisdom recorded for their own sake.[80] Thomas Hill suggests "a series of maxims may be as empty and banal as they seem, but they can serve the purpose of validating one or more problematical maxims that occur in the series."[81] Another modern example will illustrate the point: in the poem "roses are red, violets are blue, sugar is sweet, and *so are you*," the sententious repetition of self-evident facts implies that the concluding compliment is not only true, but also obvious.

Hill's argument can be taken a step further: perhaps the repetition of banal observations in formally consistent patterns has value even beyond its affirmation of the series. The "list" poem also expresses the bare idea that formally patterned speech can be proven true by that formal consistency alone. Not only the contents of the poetic series, but the poetic series itself is validated by poems like *Maxims I*. If we can accept that "a bird in the hand is worth two in the bush" sounds like traditional wisdom because the statement alliterates and falls into a four-beat pattern, it is a short leap to suggest that four-beat lines are by nature sententious, and therefore that metrical poetry "sounds" true in a way that informal language cannot.

Elaine Hansen has claimed that gnomic poems in Old English are "texts 'about language,' in a distinctly structuralist sense of the phrase," and Susan Deskis has remarked that the *sententiae* in *Beowulf* are better described collectively as a "mode of expression" than a coherent set of "actual content."[82] Whatever else sententious poetry may accomplish, then, it provides its audience with evidence that the modes of expression employed in sententious statements are themselves authorizing. In other words, Old English wisdom poems exemplify the ways in which sententious formalism can manifest as a strategy for mitigating anxieties about the possibility that "language" in the structuralist sense may be used to say things that are not true, a possibility that threatens the social fabric itself.

---

80 For readings along these lines see, e.g., Hansen, *Solomon*; Deskis, *Beowulf*; Cavill, *Maxims*.

81 T. Hill, "Wise Words," 172–3.

82 Hansen, *Solomon*, 8; Deskis, *Beowulf*, 142.

If we can at least distinguish statements that sound true from statements that do not, then language will at least seem to function somewhat efficiently as a medium for communicating information. Sententious formalism is aimed at maintaining this uneasy status quo.

Though presumably originating in oral prehistory, this authorizing purpose of sententious language was employed in Anglo-Saxon manuscripts to authorize specifically written literary forms, poetic or otherwise. The arrival of literacy's new technology for linguistic communication not only created its own insecurities, but also brought to mind the insecurities surrounding oral communication that were otherwise ignored out of necessity. Hence, perhaps, the phenomenon noted above, that later Anglo-Saxon writing exhibits a more "oral" dependence on sententious formalism than do earlier texts with a greater claim to oral origins. Before the new technology could develop its own mechanisms for mitigating anxiety about its basic unreliability, it appropriated the mechanisms of the technology that preceded it.

At present, the most sustained effort to define the specific features of sententious formalism in Old English is Paul Cavill's *Maxims in Old English Poetry*. Taking his work a step farther than the "commentary" on proverbial meaning of his peers and predecessors, Cavill describes gnomes, maxims, and proverbs as "linguistic moulds into which observation, experience and thought can be poured in order to clarify, solidify and preserve them."[83] The purposes of these moulds are both social and ethical. Their formulaic structure allows the speaker to address his or her audience not from an individual perspective, but as a mouthpiece of conventional wisdom.

Of particular interest to the present study is Cavill's decision to recast the more traditional distinction between the maxim and the proverb – holding that the former is literal and the latter is metaphorical – into a formal distinction. For Cavill, the defining feature of proverbial regularity is parallelism. The bird in the hand is paralleled with the two in the bush, and this doubling is characteristic of proverbial statements. These parallelisms can be alliterative, as they are for the "bird" and the "bush," but they can also be based on rhyme, assonance, or even on logical association. For example, "life is like a box of chocolates, you never know what you're going to get" is marked as proverbial only by its logical parallel between life and a box of chocolates. Cavill finds that proverbs are much more common in Old English prose than they are in poetry, and he attributes this to the comparative fixity of

---

83 Cavill, *Maxims*, 1, 11.

proverbs, which lose their power when they deviate too far from the syntax of the original parallelism.[84] To go back to my earlier example, the freer adaptation "people who hold birds end up with a mess in their hands" loses its allusion to the better-known proverb and therefore does not register as proverbial. For this reason proverbs are not easily adaptable to the vagaries of metrical necessity, and therefore tend to appear more often in prose, despite their internal and quasi-poetic regularity.

Cavill's "maxims," meanwhile, are dependent on more abstract formal qualities, and so they are much more adaptable to poetry. It is important that in identifying maxims as they recur in the Old English corpus, Cavill does not expect them to be uniform in their strategic employment. He describes formulaic maxims in terms of Anita Riedinger's notion of "sets," which is to say that they are not ideas but merely syntactic patterns that can be applied in different contexts to generate quite different meanings. For example, the maxim *God ana wat* or *Meotud ana wat* ("only God / the Creator knows") tends to appear in verse in the second half-line, where it is followed by at least one full poetic line describing the things that God alone knows.[85] The maxim thus functions on the one hand as a sententious expression of human ignorance, and on the other hand as a rhetorical trope for emphasizing the secrecy of the unknown fact alluded to. Cavill goes on to define the structure of the maxim more precisely as follows: it must have the elements of a complete sentence; it must be in the present tense; its subject may be a disembodied entity (God, the devil) or a particular type (a king, a wise man, "one"), but not a specific individual; and finally there must be no deictic reference to specify a particular time or situation. As Cavill summarizes, "it is clear that the relationship between the poets and their material was a dynamic one, and at the same time can be shown to be a thematically coherent one. They used traditional forms, but they also poured new material into established moulds, thus recreating the tradition."[86]

And so a particularly apt example of a maxim collection from the corpus of Old English literature is the law code *I–II Cnut*. Wulfstan poured his new material into the established moulds of earlier laws, to write conditional present-tense statements with repeating syntactic elements and a dearth of deictic references. Typically, these statements call for persons of particular types to offer certain forms of proof, or to suffer certain

---

84 Cavill, *Maxims*, 20, 68–9.
85 Cavill, *Maxims*, 53–4; Cavill also discusses this maxim in his article "Biblical."
86 Cavill, *Maxims*, 58.

punishments at the hands of disembodied entities. By formulating his laws in the particular way that he did, Wulfstan demonstrated his dynamic relationship with his source material, using traditional forms to recreate the tradition of English law. Listing the laws in the form of a repetitive catalogue – somewhat organized according to theme, but not necessarily – may have allowed Wulfstan to validate one or more of the problematic laws belonging to that series. Finally, the "alliteration, assonance, and parallelism" of Anglo-Saxon law clearly employs the same set of formal strategies apparent in both traditional proverbs and poetic maxim collections, to make legal statements sound not only true, but also conventionally accepted and therefore inarguably true.[87]

Again, the Anglo-Saxons were hardly the first culture to employ the forms of traditional wisdom to authorize their writing, and even in England the practice did not end with the Norman Conquest. Throughout the medieval period, sententious statements were an important aspect of educated discourse, whereby an educated speaker performed his or her fluency in authoritative texts and textual modes. The centrality of proverb and maxim collections to medieval training in reading and translation is well known, and as Deskis points out, "students would be inculcated with the idea of the proverb, in Latin and in the vernacular, as a form of wisdom literature, and would continue to employ this form throughout their lives."[88] Increasingly, however, oral and unattributed proverbs gave way to the greater authority of quotations from recognized authors in philosophical and literary discourse, and the fluid forms of maxim "sets" gave way in documentary and legal discourse to precise formulae and the recitation of legal precedent. In contrast, the sententious wisdom of Old English writing needed neither to be strictly attributable to a particular source nor strictly formulaic in its phrasing of legal claims, though of course correct attribution and formal precision could be practised if one was so inclined. In short, Anglo-Saxon formalism was so informal because the more robust conventions governing the authorization of written texts in later literate discourses – attributing them to authors, noting the time and place of composition, and so on – were not yet widely accepted to be necessary proof for establishing a text's legitimacy.

Of course, the trend described above unfolded over a long period of time, and there is nothing in itself surprising about the fact that late medieval fragments like *Richard the Redeless* and *Mum and the Sothsegger*

---

87 Bethurum, "Stylistic Features," 265.
88 Deskis, *Beowulf*, 144.

should eschew the more robust authorizing conventions of their day. Instead, what is striking about these texts is the fact that they eschew authorizing conventions even though they are clearly concerned with establishing their own authority through internal allusions to their Langlandian source material. These allusions typically take the form of sententious "sets" based on certain passages or themes witnessed in *Piers Plowman*, so that internal evidence reveals clearly the fragments' debt to Langland even though one is generally hard-pressed to identify direct quotations of any length. In other words, the earlier versions of *Piers Plowman* play the role of "source material" that is most safely ascribed in the Anglo-Saxon period to "convention" or (more poetically) "the wordhoard." In *Richard the Redeless* and *Mum and the Sothsegger*, Langland's wordhoard is an authoritative source of political satire, employed particularly to criticize the excessive formalism of Ricardian and Lancastrian government. Therefore it seems that the fragments have returned to the sententious formalism of the Anglo-Saxon period described by Cavill, because the newer modes of literate formalism are implicated in the problems that they wish to criticize.

In the next section, I will historicize my claim that this practice is based on Anglo-Saxon precedent through a reading of the textual tradition of one Anglo-Saxon charter. This charter will provide a concise example of how both literary and diplomatic readings can be self-defeating when they are applied individually to early medieval texts, as the texts do not so much "combine" the features of diplomas and literature as they reflect a coherent and well-established discursive practice that neither modern category can approximate on its own. The later uses of the charter also exemplify the way in which ancient documents came to stand in resistance to newer "literate" procedures in the later medieval period.

The Charter Sawyer 1166

The Anglo-Saxon charter assigned the number 1166 by Peter Sawyer in his 1968 volume *Anglo-Saxon Charters: an Annotated List and Bibliography* (hereafter referred to according to the conventions of Anglo-Saxonists as "S 1166") does not survive in a documentary form, but is transcribed in William of Malmesbury's *Gesta pontificum Anglorum*. The charter is attributed to the Anglo-Saxon poet, bishop, and saint Aldhelm.[89] William transcribed dozens of charters in the *Gesta pontificum,* authentic and forged, and he was not unusual among twelfth-century historiographers for doing

---

89 *GPont*, 201.

so; in fact, the cartulary and chronicle genres in this period occupied a single continuum, narrativizing institutional histories for similar purposes.[90] Despite William's attribution, S 1166 was surely not written by Aldhelm, at least in its present form. The document's long "hermeneutic" Latin proem is first attested in several charters written by a scribe called "Æthelstan A," who worked for the tenth-century king Æthelstan; the proem appears to be the scribe's original composition, written centuries after Aldhelm's death.[91] Below is the charter S 1166 in full, with the proem marked in bold:

Fortuna fallentis seculi procax, non lacteo immarcescibilium liliorum candore amabilis, sed fellita eiulandae corruptionis amaritudine odibilis, filios in ualle lacrimarum fetentis carnis rictibus uenenosis mordaciter dilacerat; quae quanuis arridendo sit infelicibus attrectabilis, Acherontici tamen ad ima Cociti, ni Satus alti subveniat boantis, impudenter est decliuis. Et ideo, quia ipsa ruinosa tanaliter dilabitur, summopere festinandum est ad amena indicibilis letitiae arua, ubi angelica himnidicae iubilationis organa, mellifluaque rosarum odoramina, a bonis beatisque naribus inestimabiliter dulcia capiuntur sineque calce auribus felitium hauriuntur. Cuius amore felicitatis illectus, ego Cenfrithus comes Mertiorum quandam telluris particulam uenerabili abbati Aldhelmo, sub estimatione decem cassatorum, in loco qui dicitur Wdetun ad seruiendam Deo et sancto Petro in perpetuum ius largitus sum, cum consensu domini mei Ethelredi regis. Anno ab incarnatione Domini sexcentisimo octogesimo, indictione octaua.

[The mischievous chances of this fickle world, not to be loved for the milky white of lilies that never fade but to be hated for the bitter poison of lamentable corruption, tear apart its stinking sons in the vale of tears, biting them with venomous fangs of the flesh. Its smile may make it alluring to the unfortunate, but in its impudence it slopes down to the depths of Acherontic Cocytus, were it not that the Son of the High Thunderer comes to the rescue. Because it is in ruins and collapses unto death, one must hurry with all speed to the lovely meadows of ineffable joy, where

---

90 J. Barrow, "William of Malmesbury's Use"; Foot, "Reading"; J. Hudson, "Abbey of Abingdon." On "cartulary-chronicles," see J. Hudson, *Abbey of Abingdon*, 186; Geary, *Phantoms of Remembrance*, 81–5. That chronicle literature was composed for the purpose of preserving ecclesiastical rights and privileges is stated explicitly by John of Salisbury: Gransden, "Prologues," 66.

91 Keynes, *Diplomas*, 44. On this scribe's echoes of Aldhelm, see also Scott, *Land and Book*, 35–47. The charters dated to the reign of Æthelstan in which this proem occurs are S 425, 426, 434–6, 458.

the angelic organs of hymn-singing jubilation and the honeyed scents of roses in all their inestimable sweetness are sniffed by the nostrils of the good and the blessed, and drunk in without end by the ears of the fortunate. Lured on by love for such happiness, I Cenfrith, comes of the Mercians, have with the consent of my lord King Æthelred granted to the respected Abbot Aldhelm a piece of land, reckoned at ten hides, in the place called Wootton, to serve God and Saint Peter in perpetual right. Dated in the year of our Lord 680, the eighth indiction.][92]

This sententious proem is full of unusual Grecisms and utilizes a high degree of alliteration, rhyme, assonance, and other forms of parallelism. Ornate proems like it appear with great frequency in later Anglo-Saxon charters, and Kemble identified the length of a document's introduction as a particularly useful dating criteria.[93] The charters of Æthelstan's reign do not only distinguish themselves by the length and complexity of their proems, but also mark the "highest point of consistency" for documentary formula in the entire Anglo-Saxon period.[94] As Sharpe notes, "consistency of style and form was something to which chanceries have generally aspired, since it enabled subjects to recognize an official document and it inspired the respect due to the authority embodied in such public acts."[95] The ornate rhetoric of the proem thus provides a clue for how exactly this authority chose to represent itself. As good tenth-century Christians, the imagined audience of this proem would surely recognize the self-evident wisdom of the idea that this fickle world is not to be loved – if, indeed, they were able to understand enough of its difficult Latin to recognize that this was the sentiment being expressed.[96] The document S 1166 implies that the recognizable veracity of this conventional wisdom serves as proof of the fact that Cenfrith granted to Aldhelm the ten hides at Wootton, as the gift is framed as an application of that wisdom to a real-life situation. Such a leap may not seem entirely justified according to the standards of

---

92 *GPont*, 201; Winterbottom's translation.

93 J. Barrow, "Chronology of Forgery," 109–11; Kemble, *Codex*, x.

94 H. Hall, *Formula Book*, 3. Though Chaplais argues that in these documents, the consistency is simply an indication of how few scribes were producing royal charters: Chaplais, "Anglo-Saxon Chancery." This argument is insufficient on its own to explain the consistency, as isolated scribes might just as easily have decided to experiment with forms instead of repeating them.

95 Sharpe, "Charters, Deeds," 238–9. The question of Æthelstan's royal writing office is most recently addressed by Sarah Foot: *Æthelstan*, 70–3.

96 On the intelligibility of Æthelstan A's charters to its intended audience, see Foot, *Æthelstan*, 133.

more "literate" bureaucracies, but in Anglo-Saxon England, the proem's homiletic, sententious statement was enough to make the document seem adequate for commemorating a transaction of this kind.

In the case of S 1166, the proem appears to have been selected in part because its style is so strongly reminiscent of the "hermeneutic" writings of Aldhelm himself.[97] A.S. Cook has shown that the charter S 1245, which directly precedes S 1166 in the *Gesta pontificum Anglorum* and is also attributed to Aldhelm, was patched together from words and phrases taken from Aldhelm's homiletic works.[98] In both charters, the densely ornate homiletic proem provides a religious motive for a kingly gift, in order to persuade the charter's readers that the transfer of property is not only legally binding, but morally appropriate. The proems also use a poetic idiom that was particularly associated with the sainted beneficiary of both gifts, and thus it evokes Aldhelm's personal authority as one of the most influential literary authors of the Anglo-Saxon era to strengthen the document's legal claim. The authority embedded in the act by this documentary formula, in other words, is not only that of the form's wisdom nor even that of the royal will that the formula represents, but of the poet Aldhelm whose signature style the formula imitates.

S 1166 takes its formal cues from a combination of the charters S 435 and S 71, the latter of which is Malmesbury's oldest authentic charter.[99] S 435 is the probable source of the *fortuna fallentis* proem. It is also spurious, and was probably not written long before S 1166.[100] Given, then, that the forger had at least two examples of charters to work from, and one was an authentic document and the other a forgery that could have been produced within living memory, we may therefore posit that the Aldhelmian literary qualities of the proem motivated the forger to include it.[101]

---

97 For a full description of hermeneutic Latin, see Lapidge, "Hermeneutic Style."

98 Cook, "Putative Charter." More recently, G.T. Dempsey has argued that the charter is real: "Aldhelm," 61–5.

99 Edwards, *Charters*, 87–90.

100 Keynes, *Diplomas*, 44n.80. Keynes points out that like the similar S 434 and 436, S 435 is dated 21 December. However, all three charters are given different years, even though the indiction, regnal year, epact, and concurrents are all correct for 935. This suggests that they were all copied at a later date from a genuine document from that year.

101 Edwards, *Charters*, 89. Though another possible factor is the fact that both S 1166 and S 435 are for the same plot of land, at Wootton; the only two other charters that mention Wootton in Malmesbury's archives (and that therefore could have served as an exemplar for a forgery) are the problematic charter S 256 and a *pancarta* of Edward the Confessor, S 1038. Of these three, S 435 is the obvious choice as the basis for a forgery.

Aldhelm himself was famous as a poet, and his prose style was "clearly derived from verse," a debt that would have been particularly clear at the time of "Æthelstan A"'s activity, when Anglo-Latin verse was "little more than Aldhelmian pastiche."[102]

Certainly the literary qualities of this charter are the reason that S 1166 was accepted as a valid work of Aldhelm well into the twentieth century, despite the evidence that Malmesbury's legal claim to Wootton was unrecognized in the Domesday Book.[103] S 1166 was edited alongside other, similar forgeries in Ehwald's *Aldhelmi Opera*, where it is included as an accepted work of the author.[104] Even Lapidge and Herren, who hold that "no modern student of Anglo-Saxon diplomatic would consider any of the five [charters edited by Ehwald] to be authentic," included S 1166 in an appendix to their translation of Aldhelm's prose works, finding it of interest "for stylistic reasons."[105] The document thus constitutes both a literary and a legal forgery, and it has proven to be of more interest to scholars as an example of the former than it has as an example of the latter. This state of affairs is all the more problematic to the methodologies of diplomatic and literary criticism because unlike S 1245, S 1166 imitates the Aldhelmian voice by appropriating what was, in the reign of Æthelstan, a highly developed, purely documentary formula. At no point was a literary text appropriated to draft the charter; and yet literary formal qualities, evocative of the creative author Aldhelm, played a role in the document's strategies of commemoration. The proem therefore demonstrates the ways in which sententious statements are adaptable to both creative and commemorative authorizing strategies, sometimes simultaneously, in such a way that exposes the arbitrary nature of the distinctions between literary and legal modes of writing, and by extension the inapplicability of such distinctions to medieval texts.

---

102 Orchard, *Poetic Art*, 239–40. According to William of Malmesbury, Æthelstan had a particular devotion to Aldhelm, which was also perhaps a factor in his scribe's use of the Aldhelmian formula: Kelly, *Malmesbury*, 22, citing *GPont* cap. 246, 247.

103 In Domesday, Wootton is in the hands of private owners: Edwards, *Charters*, 90–1. Finberg and Hart both accept the authenticity of S 1166, the former arguing that S 435 is an imitative forgery whose authentic exemplar is S 1166, the latter pointing out that even though the charter is dated a year before Aldhelm became bishop, he could nonetheless have stepped in to witness the document during his predecessor Hædde's illness. Finberg, *Early Charters*, 31; Hart, *Early Charters*, 383.

104 *Opera Aldhelmi*, ed. Ehwald, 173–5.

105 Aldhelm, *Prose Works*, ed. Lapidge and Herren, 18.

If the role of the *asecga* or *laghman* hypothesized by Bethurum in fact existed in the tribes of pre-Christian Anglo-Saxons, that role was subsumed very quickly in the early Anglo-Saxon period by the function of the bishop. Hence the conflation of legal authority, documentary formula, and literary authorship witnessed in the charter S 1166's performance of Aldhelm's poetic voice is anticipated in the first record of a charter's use, Stephen of Ripon's *Life of St. Wilfrid*. Wilfrid stands at the altar in front of the people and several kings (*ante altare conversus ad populum coram regibus*) and delivers a "sermon" telling them that kings had signed over (*conscripserunt*) many lands to the bishop for the service of God (*Deo ad serviendum pontifici*) with the consent and signature of the bishops and chief men (*cum concensu et subscriptione episcoporum et omnium principum*).[106]

The apparent reference to a witness list in this final phrase suggests that Wilfrid's "sermon" here is a charter.[107] Sermon literature is itself characterized by Beverly Kienzle as a "fluid genre,"[108] and the formal and thematic influence of sermon literature on Anglo-Saxon charters and laws has long been acknowledged.[109] Though the relative influence of monastic and royal authorities has been disputed, it is generally agreed that documents were primarily ecclesiastical instruments throughout the Anglo-Saxon period, and it is not coincidental that so many Anglo-Saxon charters should survive in Gospel books and liturgical manuscripts.[110] The technical competence in reading and writing that underlay ecclesiastical authority over scripture extended to written instruments generally, literary and diplomatic, and analogies between scribal copying and episcopal preaching were quite common in the period.[111] Like the Gospel books, the text of Wilfrid's "signatures" seems to have functioned as a prop in a liturgical

---

106   Stephen of Ripon, *Wilfrid* ed. and trans. Colgrave, 36–7.

107   F.M. Stenton, *Latin Charters*, 32.

108   Kienzle, "Typology," 86.

109   Richards, "Manuscript Contexts."

110   "The Anglo-Saxon diploma was 'essentially an ecclesiastic document' in origin": Thompson, *Royal Diplomas*, 5, citing Kelly, "Anglo-Saxon Lay Society," 43. See especially Chaplais's articles "Origin and Authenticity" (28–42), "Anglo-Saxon Chancery" (43–62), and "Who Introduced Charter into England?" (88–107), all collected in the volume of Chaplais's essays *Prisca Munimenta*, ed. Harmer. See also Whitelock, *English Historical Documents*, 383–4; Ker, *English Manuscripts*, 19–20; Dumville, *Liturgy*, 123–6; Keynes, *Diplomas*, 19–39, esp. 22–8; Smith, *Land and Book*, 22–8.

111   Robinson, "Immediate Context," 24–5.

performance,[112] with a purpose that "resided less in the information it contained than in its function as a potent symbol of ownership."[113] Wilfrid's dominion over the donated regions and Christ's dominion over the entire world were both aspects of the same religious belief, as the political ascendancy of the historical church both validated and was validated by the theological Church.

The interrelationship between literary and legal form in this document persists into the "authentic" context of the *fortuna fallentis* proem's composition, during the reign of Æthelstan. This period is a watershed moment in the evolution of Anglo-Saxon royal charters, but for perplexing reasons. The vernacular boundary clauses of Anglo-Saxon charters, whose emergence marks the moment at which the genre assumed the character of "true written records," had appeared in the early ninth century.[114] Alfred produced very few surviving charters during his reign, and Edward the Elder even fewer; there is a fifteen-year gap between Edward's last charter in 909 and Æthelstan's first in 924.[115] Thus the first charters of "Æthelstan A" follow the rise of the vernacular boundary clause relatively closely, at least in terms of the surviving evidence. This means that not long after the Anglo-Saxon charter's most essential elements came to be written in Old English, its inessential Latin proem swelled into its longest and most difficult form. The documents thus came to more closely resemble modern literary texts and modern legal documents at roughly the same phase in their evolution.

The literary quality of the cartulary form under Æthelstan is represented more dramatically in the "alliterative" charters written by Bishop Cenwald of Worcester.[116] Cenwald's charters fall into a metrical pattern, with alliteration occurring irregularly throughout, and they have been linked to both Cenwald's inscription in the MacDurnan Gospels and the *Anglo-Saxon Chronicle* poem *The Battle of Brunanburh*.[117] Thus the

---

112 On the interrelationship between text and ritual, see Watts, "Ritual Legitimacy"; Gellrich, *Idea of the Book.*

113 Kelly, "Anglo-Saxon Society," 44. On performance and Anglo-Saxon liturgy, see Bedingfield, *Dramatic Liturgy.*

114 Kelly, "Anglo-Saxon Society," 46; Stenton, *Latin Charters,* 57.

115 Stenton, *Latin Charters,* 53.

116 These charters are S 472–3, 479, 484, 520, 544, 548–50, 556–7, 566, 572, 633 and 1606. See Foot, *Æthelstan,* 72, 106–7, 113; Hart, *Danelaw,* 431–5; Keynes, *Diplomas,* 82n.165; and Whitelock, *English Historical Documents,* 372–3 n. 8. On the attribution to Cenwald, see Keynes, "Athelstan's Books," esp. 158–9.

117 Walker, "Context for *Brunanburh.*"

densely ornate *fortuna fallentis* proem is representative of a Aldhelmian quasi-poetic spirit discernible also in Æthelstan's other charters. And in fact a spirit of "antiquarianism" is arguably characteristic of the period's vernacular literature as well, given the number of tenth-century manuscripts witnessing the surviving corpus of classical Old English verse.[118] In the poetry as in the charters, metrical formalism was employed as part of a strategy to invest writing itself with authority, though later assumptions that such forms are inappropriate for documentary contexts would in time transform the documents into evidence for the "orality" of Æthelstan's kingdom.

The explosion in legal documentation at this time appears to have reflected the ambitions of the monarch. Both the alliterative charters and the "Æthelstan A" charters call Æthelstan *imperator* and list several "kinglets" (*reguli*) among the witnesses, a terminology that is thought to indicate the king's imperial ambitions.[119] As I noted above, legal literacy in England has been linked to imperial ambition since Bede's note that Æthelberht's law code was written "following the examples of the Romans." Hence, perhaps, the evidence suggesting Æthelstan was also the most active legislator of the tenth-century kings.[120] By their very existence, written bureaucratic texts symbolize Æthelstan's success in achieving his imperial aspirations.

Æthelstan's ambition also provides a commemorative purpose for the "Æthelstan A" charters' employment of quasi-poetic sententious formulae.[121] The exaggerated homiletic tone of the *fortuna fallentis* proem encodes an anxiety about the shift that has taken place, from a documentary form authorized by the moral authority of the speaker, as it was for St Wilfrid, to a form authorized by its demonstration through rhetoric that the transaction in question was recorded by an educated and literate scribe.[122] "Æthelstan A" is not a saint, but he can read and write well enough to document an exchange of property. By extension, the scribe's formulaic proems functioned irrespective of their moral meaning, in much the way that the phrase "In God We Trust" on a U.S. dollar bill functions in everyday life not as a statement of belief on the part of the transacting parties, but merely as an indication that the bill is authentic and not a forgery. This development is the necessary consequence of centralized

---

118 Bredehoft, *Authors*, 143–4.
119 Walker, "Context for *Brunanburh*," 27–9; *MoEL*, 444.
120 *MoEL* 290.

bureaucracy along Roman lines, but it leads to certain obvious problems. To return to my example, it invites hypocrisy if you force everyone to express a sentiment like "in God we trust" every time they wish to buy something. The formulaic use of the phrase deprives it of its meaning, and undermines the ideology that required its use in the first place.

The formal innovations in Æthelstan's charters therefore encode a response to the ambivalence surrounding this secular *function* to legal literacy. That the texts witnessing the emergence of this secular function should be characterized by abundant and explicit religious rhetoric is not a contradiction, but on the contrary suggests a scribal effort to mitigate the cultural anxieties surrounding the discursive shift that was taking place, away from authorizing modes dependent merely on the trustworthiness of the speaker. The very fact that Æthelstan's legal formulae should seem so exaggeratedly oral indicates that they are a by-product of literacy's growing importance.

The even more explicit fusion of literary and legal authenticating strategies in the "forgery" S 1166 displays the next phase of this evolution. By attributing the proem to Aldhelm himself, S 1166 reinscribes this sophisticated documentary form with the sainted bishop's moral authority as a preacher, even as it reinscribes the authenticity of the bishop's charter by evoking the recognizably Anglo-Saxon formulae of Æthelstan's charters. S 1166 was produced during the "Golden Age" of English forgery, a time when the Anglo-Saxon documentary tradition was subject to challenge by Norman bureaucratic reforms. In Europe generally, this is also a moment of "crisis," as Thomas Bisson describes, wherein a "demonstratively massive multiplication of lay lords and fiefs" fundamentally altered the political landscape.[123] Alfred Hiatt argues that this chaotic period of political and economic reorganization is considered a "Golden Age" of document falsification not because of any verifiable increase in forgery, but because of the particular ease with which modern historians can identify apparent forgeries from the period. There are many spectacularly false documents produced in the hundred years after the Norman Conquest, because in this period there was no clear consensus among the various localized bureaucracies about the procedures whereby legal texts ought to be produced

---

121 See also Lapidge, "Career of Aldhelm," on Aldhelm's relation to the royal family of Wessex.

122 A complementary argument for literary strategies of authentication in pre-Conquest documents is Howlett, *Sealed from Within*. On the secularization of the charter form, see Keynes, *Diplomas*, 39–81.

123 Bisson, *Crisis*, 24.

and stored.[124] Hemming, for example, says openly in the introduction to his well-known Worcester cartulary that he undertook to "repair" the damaged texts of the documents, a term that indicates both his willingness to intervene in the text and his apparent belief that he had no reason to disguise his interventions.[125] Meanwhile, Tinti has identified at least one "forgery" in Hemming's cartulary describing properties that the monastery seems to have actually held, though they had long since lost their claim to the properties listed in the forgery's "genuine" exemplar.[126]

It bears reiterating that forgery during the "Golden Age" was not necessarily an acceptable practice. On the contrary, it appears to have created a kind of "charter inflation" that threatened the efficacy of documents in general and correspondingly placed pressure on the institutions of government, leading them ultimately to standardize their practices.[127] Indeed, the necessity of defending specific claims precedes and even creates the need for standardized formulaic conventions in the documents commemorating claims generally. Institutional reforms create problems in the short term by their very nature, roughly equivalent to the issue of backward compatibility in digital archives: the widespread adoption of consistent and strict formats put the ecclesiastical "early adopters" of the written medium in a difficult position, in that their claims were preserved in forms that were incompatible with the emergent techniques for documentary criticism. Thus the apparent "crudity" of twelfth-century copies of Anglo-Saxon documents indicates only that different monastic "forgers" exploited different ambiguities in their procedural distinctions between correction and distortion, depending on the particular problems presented to them by the particular documented claims they wished to preserve.[128] Begging preservation were not only the particular documented claims, but the larger cultural and historical framework that gave documents themselves both legal efficacy and cultural meaning.

---

124 Hiatt, *Making*, 23–4.

125 Tinti, "Hemming's Cartulary," 242–3. On Hemming, see also Herold, "Memoranda and Memoria," 136–55; Clanchy, *Memory to Written Record*, 103–4; Ker, "Hemming's Cartulary." My use of the designation "Hemming's Cartulary" follows Neil Ker's usage, in which this term refers only to the latter half of the manuscript London, BL Cotton Tiberius A. XIII: Ker, "Hemming's Cartulary."

126 Tinti, "Hemming's Cartulary," 251. The documents in question are S 180 and S 181. See also Stenton, "Supremacy," 445 n. 57; Williams, "Spoliation," 389.

127 Wormald, "Charters, Law," 161. See also Hiatt, *English Forgery*, 22–3.

128 A useful summary of how this problem affects the criticism of Anglo-Saxon documents is Keynes, *Diplomas*, 4–18.

Julia Barrow has observed that the "hermeneutic" Latin in Hemming's cartulary, like that found in the *fortuna fallentis* proem, is "often especially rich" in documents that can be proven on other grounds to have been forged, and she also points out elsewhere that they also are more likely to contain narratives beyond the mere facts of the transaction.[129] Hence the creator of S 1166 was not unusual for falling back on literary strategies to make legal documents seem more authentically Anglo-Saxon. As Julia Crick has argued in her analysis of the charters of St Albans, any post-Conquest modifications to documents might only have continued archival practices that were already well established; after all, the Norman Conquest merely marked the end of centuries of Norse invasion, and each successive wave brought with it new challenges to pre-existing claims for land ownership.[130] Whether licit or not, the interventions in the text by monastic archivists were necessitated by the practical constraints of their situation. In lieu of any other written evidence for the monastery's claim, and in the absence of well-established, universally accepted procedures for creating and maintaining that evidence, "reconstructed" charters were better than no charters at all. In other words, the qualities of the text that we use to date the charters to a particular *period* were perceived by Hemming and the "forger" of S 1166 to be a feature of genuine charters *in their own time*, so that the (necessarily fewer) charters that predated the use of hermeneutic Latin would have seemed less effective for that reason.

Susan Kelly has noted William of Malmesbury's "disinclination" to cite documents from the "generally better-documented tenth and eleventh centuries," and speculates that he is nostalgic for the "cherished independence" of Malmesbury asserted in those early documents and unrecognized in William's own time by Roger of Salisbury.[131] Hence when William of Malmesbury copied S 1166 and in the process attributed the *fortuna fallentis* proem to Aldhelm, he reaffirmed not only the defunct claim of the charter itself, but more crucially he reaffirmed the idea of what a charter ought to be that the document represented. Aldhelm did write texts that sound like S 1166, and thus the historical person Aldhelm himself might well have witnessed the historical events that the charter describes. The authorial prehistory of S 1166 evoked by its attribution to the literary author Aldhelm affirmed the authority of charters resembling it, reinscribing the authority

---

129 J. Barrow, "Forgery in Worcester," 109; "Use of Charters," 69.
130 Crick, "Twelfth-Century Views." See also Crick, *Charters of St Albans*, esp. 56–90; Crick, "Liberty of St. Albans"; Hagger, "Litigation and History."
131 *Charters*, ed. Kelly, 30–3.

of all such documents to legislate for the future. William preserves the charter not only to preserve the claim it documents, but also to preserve the form of its documentation, and by extension the larger principles of government within which that form appeared to operate.

It is highly representative of Anglo-Saxon diplomatic more generally that William of Malmesbury preserved this document on behalf of a monastic institution. Old English legal texts were extremely favourable to cathedrals, priories, and episcopal households, to the degree that maintaining the prominence of ancient ecclesiastical institutions and maintaining the procedures of Anglo-Saxon law were inextricably intertwined after the Norman Conquest. Several circumstances explain this development. William the Conqueror had shut down the "customary" Anglo-Saxon courts in which tenant disputes were traditionally resolved, and transferred their jurisdiction to the monastic courts.[132] The probable flight of the remaining Anglo-Saxon gentry into the church after the Norman Conquest would have meant that many of these formerly secular courts would have been staffed or even controlled by England's former secular rulers.[133] Further, the same formulaic orality of court procedures that ensured the survival into the present of Law French usages such as *voir dire* and "mortgage" similarly appears to have preserved Old English terminology and syntax that would have disappeared elsewhere. This last point can be inferred not only from the continued use of Old English boundary clauses and the survival of Old English legal terms in late medieval monastic contexts,[134] but from the striking fact that the earliest surviving post-Conquest legal dictionaries in England focus almost exclusively on Old English terms.[135] It is therefore natural to presume that post-Conquest ecclesiastical institutions' conservative interest in Anglo-Saxon literature and law

---

132 Janin, *Medieval Justice*, 30. For a thorough survey of ecclesiastical property administration after the Conquest, see Shirley, *Secular Jurisdiction*. On legal advocacy in Anglo-Saxon England, see Rabin, "Old English *forespeca*."

133 Mason, *St. Wulfstan*, 131.

134 For example, the terms "halimote," "hide," and "socone" in the records of St Albans: Levett, *Manorial History*, 134. On boundary clauses, see Herold, "Memoranda and Memoria," 212–14; Tinti, "Hemming's Cartulary," 255–6.

135 J. Baker, *Common Law*, 227. Baker points out here that the dictionaries contained "words still found in Anglo-Saxon charters which might be of contemporary importance, but evidently no one any longer knew their meaning *save by professional study*" (my emphasis). That this study was professional and practical rather than simply nostalgic is argued by James Campbell, "Twelfth-Century Views," and corroborated by Patrick Wormald, *MoEL*, 474.

influenced their contemporaneous interest in keeping Old English literary culture alive, at least until they could adapt their Old English foundational legal documents into newer and more recognizable formats.[136]

Old English literacy does not seem to abate until the turn of the thirteenth century, which is incidentally also the time that manuscripts of Middle English alliterative writing begin to appear. This transition is linked to the shift in England towards what has been called an "administrative" model of kingship.[137] The common law legal system that started to emerge in the Angevin era was heavily dependent on the legal-historical documents used to record and disseminate citable precedent. Bruce O'Brien has stated that "legal literacy, in fact, should be considered the sine qua non of the common law, for without it, the centralization of the courts, which was the catalyst for the emergence of the common law, would have remained a royal fantasy."[138] But as O'Brien also argues elsewhere, it appears that the codification of the common law was designed specifically to undermine the record of Anglo-Saxon law, as the assertion that English law is a *lex non scripta* is a "conscious misrepresentation" of the record.[139] By asserting that English law is not found in written precedent, Ranulf de Glanvill "targets what Brian Stock would call a textual community, the literate critics of Henry II who were capable of using the old treatises in their cause, not literate law in general," and in so doing "tries to eliminate the authority of that community's texts."[140] In the process, Glanvill undermines the laws and charters of Anglo-Saxon kings on the grounds of diplomatic formal criticism, characterizing the remnants of Old English law as fragmentary and untrustworthy. O'Brien argues that compilations like the *Leges Edwardi Confessoris* manuscript London, BL, Additional 49366, which includes Latin translations of genuine Anglo-Saxon law, were copied by Becket and his adherents specifically to refute these arguments.[141] If vernacular poets similarly imitated the formal

---

136 Clanchy, *Memory to Written Record*, 213–17. Abingdon, Ramsey, and Ely had all translated the bulk of their English documents into Latin by the second half of the twelfth century: O'Brien, "Forgery," 4n.14.

137 Hollister and Baldwin, "Administrative Kingship."

138 O'Brien, "Forgery," 1. See also Clanchy, *Memory to Written Record*, 145–83.

139 O'Brien, "Becket Conflict," 14.

140 O'Brien, "Becket Conflict," 13, citing Stock, *Implications of Literacy*, 88–92. On Henry II and English common law, see also Brand, "Henry II."

141 O'Brien, "Becket Conflict," 10. On Becket's involvement in the copying of decretal collections and canon law texts in defence of the same argument, see Cheney, "Origin of Novel Disseisin," 24.

strategies of Anglo-Saxon legal-homiletic discourse to criticize emerging bureaucratic institutions, they only did so after Anglo-Saxon legal texts were deliberately disqualified from legal proceedings by those institutions, who wished to centralize power at the expense of England's most ancient local corporate interests.[142]

Meanwhile, reforms within the church also placed pressure on the local bureaucratic practices of England's ancient ecclesiastical institutions. By the mid-thirteenth century the formal study of Roman law, long considered anathema to the contemplative life, had become a requirement for all Benedictine novices.[143] Evesham's improbable victory in asserting its independence from the see of Worcester in the thirteenth century, at least partially dependent on the Bolognese legal training that Evesham advocate Thomas of Marlborough had at his disposal, is a particularly well-documented example of the shift in the climate.[144] But even though these trends are apparent in the long sweep of English history, the evidence suggests gradual change rather than radical shifts, a process of negotiation rather than decisive victory. Anglo-Saxon charters continued to be preserved until the dissolution as historical reference works, and their model of a legal practice based in homiletic sententiousness rather than regulated formulae persisted.[145]

In the decades leading up to the beginning of the *Piers Plowman* tradition, monasteries were no longer the only corporate interests to use Anglo-Saxon documentary culture to advocate their independence. Comparable legal collections produced by the city of London include the twelfth-century manuscript Cambridge, Corpus Christi College 70,[146] and the "London Collection" manuscripts produced by Andrew Horn in the early fourteenth century.[147] Ralph Hanna, who cites Horn's manuscripts as important predecessors to the fourteenth-century explosion of vernacular manuscript production, observes: "A lesson civic officials learned from monastic cartularies [is that] the fictive forgery may be the truest form of historical remembering and preserving the liberty that should have been

---

142   On these processes of administrative centralization see for example Reynolds, *Kingdoms and Communities*.

143   Brundage "Monk as Lawyer," 428–30.

144   Boureau, "How Law Came." See also Jane E. Sayers, "'Original,' Cartulary."

145   Rumble, "Codex Wintoniensis."

146   Richards, "Manuscript Context," 181–3; *MoEL* 236.

147   *MoEL* 238–9. On Andrew Horn, see Jurasinski, "Alfredian Apocrypha"; Catto, "Andrew Horn."

textually instantiated, even if it hadn't actually been."[148] In some cases Anglo-Saxon charters were even cited to *refute* ecclesiastical claims for autonomous ownership, as the tenants of various manors cited the charters as proof that the crown originally owned ecclesiastical lands, and petitioned the king to take them back.[149] Far from a natural or teleological development in accordance with reason, then, the emerging distinctions between kinds of texts manifest in modern critical methodologies reflect the boundaries imposed artificially on the Anglo-Saxon legal-homiletic discourse as a way of undermining local authority in favour of larger government structures, which boundaries shifted over time in response to the tactics used by both those local authorities and the larger governments. This study will look at only some of the texts wherein such tactics are witnessed, and only some of the political positions they were used to support.

Frank Stenton denigrated the "Æthelstan A" proems for their use of "artificial language employed to the grievous detriment of good sense," and Kemble described them as texts wherein "pedantry and absurdity struggle for the mastery."[150] From the critical perspective of these scholars, the presence of ornate, homiletic formulae in late Anglo-Saxon documents appears to indicate that the people who governed the Anglo-Saxon royal bureaucracy did not understand what legal texts were *for*, and thus could not have been very sophisticated in their "literacy." And yet the very disquiet generated for modern readers by Anglo-Saxon legal-homiletic discourse became itself the operative feature of that discourse, as it was used to articulate literate anxieties about the basic flaws of literate cultural practices. Even if S 1166 has never been a successful document of a legal claim, it remains a powerful challenge to the concept of the "legal document" itself, in its construction of a more virtuous and ostensibly "simpler" time. If taken as an illustrative rather than a unique case, the document S 1166 thus challenges many of the basic disciplinary presumptions of diplomatic scholarship and literary criticism. Similar challenges by similar traditions will be examined in the chapters that follow.

---

148 Hanna, *London Literature*, 44–103.
149 Musson, *Perceptions of Law*, 167; Faith, "'Great Rumour'," 55–7.
150 Stenton, *Latin Charters*, 53; Kemble, *Codex Diplomaticus*, x.

2 *Leges Cnuti, Sermones Lupi*: Homily, Law, and the Legacy of Wulfstan

In the preceding chapter I showed how legal and homiletic modes coexist in the traditions of the Anglo-Saxon charters, so that modern legal-historical and literary-critical methodologies can quickly run into problems when they attempt to rely on a priori distinctions between literary texts and legal documents. I proposed the concept of "sententious formalism" as a way of describing the attributes of medieval texts that are the cause of this critical problem. In this chapter, I will begin my genealogy of sententious formalism in *Piers Plowman* with a study of the Anglo-Saxon legal-homiletic discourse in the writings of Wulfstan. I will also look at Wulfstan's post-Conquest translators and imitators, who continued the archbishop's defining agenda, of preserving the rights and privileges of established English ecclesiastical institutions in an era of political instability. The sententious formalism of Wulfstan typifies the Anglo-Saxon notions of textual authority, and the transmission of his legal texts typifies the preservation of those notions after the Norman Conquest.

Representative of sententious formalism in Wulfstan's lifetime is the charter catalogued by Sawyer as S 956.[1] Wulfstan is one of the document's most prominent signatories, and the document is representative of the kinds of legal texts he would have encountered or produced in his capacity as archbishop.[2] A characteristic example of Cnut's documents that are "more individual literary compositions" than "formula-bound

---

1 On this charter see also Smith, *Land and Book*, 66–7; Foot, "Reading," 62.
2 Wulfstan's influence is suggested by *Charters*, ed. Miller, p. 162. Other charters signed by "Wulfstan archiepiscopus" in Æthelred's reign include S 917, 926, 929, 930, 931b, and 933. For a discussion of them, see Wilcox, "St. Brice's Day."

productions,"[3] S 956 records Cnut's decision to return five hides at Drayton to New Minster that a "headstrong and unstable young man" (*adolescens animosus et instabilis*) had said "with cunning and fraud" (*calliditate et mendacio*) to be Cnut's property, to bestow on anyone he wanted.[4] It is representative of the legal logic encoded in charters from this period that this description of the cunning, fraudulent advisor emphasizes his youth. Old age and wise counsel are literally synonymous in Old English, the term *frod* meaning both "old" and "wise,"[5] and even today the idea that older counsellors are better than younger ones is still conventional wisdom. By calling Cnut's fraudulent advisor "adolescens," then, the charter applies the common-sense distinctions between youth and age to legally justify the charter's resolution of the dispute it records. Indeed, the youth of the young man is the document's primary proof that his claims are spurious, even in the face of "letters contradicting this liberty" (*litteras huic libertati contrarias*) which were "in the possession of the aforementioned young man" (*penes prescriptum adolescentem*). In an oath-based legal system, procedures necessarily centred on determinations of whether or not a particular claimant could be trusted. For this reason, common-sense statements about who is trustworthy and who is not had procedural implications for Anglo-Saxon dispute resolution. S 956's reliance on sententious tropes to invalidate the young man's documented claims is precisely the feature of its composition that makes it seem to be as much a narrative, literary composition as it seems to be a legal text.

A similar sententious legal logic characterizes Wulfstan's Old English legal and homiletic works. As Mary Richards has observed, Wulfstan understood laws "as models for conduct equivalent to Christian precepts."[6] Formalizing laws in this way was a crucial part of Wulfstan's larger plan to give bishops an unprecedented degree of legislative authority.[7] A bishop so concerned with statecraft that his writing recognizes no logical division between spiritual and secular matters, Wulfstan was also the bishop of Worcester who ordered the composition of that institution's (and England's) earliest surviving cartulary.[8] Thus he is a key figure in

---

3 *Charters*, ed. Miller, p. 162.

4 Foot "Reading," 61–2; *Electronic Sawyer*, accessed 14 February 2014.

5 For a discussion of the relationship between old age and good counsel in *Beowulf* see Klein, *Ruling Women*, 90–1.

6 Richards, *Manuscript Contexts*, 180.

7 On Wulfstan's legal authority, see Trilling, "Sovereignty."

8 Baxter, "God's Property."

developing the later monastic practices of document-based legal culture discussed in the previous chapter, as it grew in response to the waves of Danish invasion that culminated in the Norman Conquest.[9]

It is important to note that Wulfstan's appeals to inherited wisdom were by no means "conservative." Wulfstan was remarkably innovative in his efforts to reinvent the formal strategies of Old English Christian precepts in the service of his agenda. Indeed, Wulfstan explicitly disparages actual English proverbs in his homily *De septiformi spiritu* (Bethurum IX). In this homily "wiðerræde" ("hateful counsel," 186, l. 58) and the Devil's "unwisdom ꝺ swicdom" ("foolishness and treachery," 187, l. 72) are exemplified by secular proverbs ridiculing abstinence from food and sex (190, ll. 140–3). As Paul Cavill observes, Wulfstan here rejects not only the sentiment expressed by these proverbs, but also attributes to the Antichrist that whole corpus of common-sense statements that circulated as "guides to action, rules of thumb, approved principles" without clerical permission.[10] In other words, Wulfstan does not imitate the forms of preliterate oral culture out of a wish to preserve traditional wisdom for its own sake. On the contrary, as I will demonstrate, Wulfstan regularizes sententious forms in the service of his ambitious ideological agenda.

The importance of literacy to Wulfstan's construction of sententious clerical authority is manifest in the double valence of the term *gerædnes* itself. Parkes has identified the term *ræd* in Old English with rhetorical *lectio*, or "the process whereby a reader had to identify elements of the text – letters, syllables, words and sentences (*discretio*) in order to read it aloud according to the accentuation required by the sense (*pronuntiatio*)."[11] "Reading" the book and learning the letters are the same activity, the act of interpretation reduced to the reader's recognition of the marks on the page. Similarly, the *gerædnes* of a king ought to constitute a transparent transmission of information; not only the "advisedness" of the traditional wisdom formalized by Wulfstan's writing style, but "that which was read," as the king consults the legislation of earlier kings to ensure that he does not depart from the standard accepted practices of the realm. Hence Wulfstan plays not a dual but a triple role in constructing the *gerædnes* of King Cnut. Wulfstan is a spiritual adviser, a member of the *witan*, and finally a professional reader of texts, who for that reason can speak with neutrality about the laws recorded by Cnut's predecessors.

---

9 Crick, "Twelfth-Century Views."
10 Cavill, *Maxims*, 67.
11 Parkes, "*Rædan, areccan*," 1.

The most immediate imitations of Wulfstan's homiletic style are those manifest in the later Latin legal treatise *Leges Henrici Primi* or *LHP*, which incorporates Latin translations of *I–II Cnut*. The compiler of this work appears to have recognized the power of Wulfstan's efforts to reframe English law as merely a genre of sententious statement. The archbishop's stylistic influence on *LHP* exemplifies the influence that Anglo-Saxon legal-homiletic discourse continued to exert after the Norman Conquest. The imitators of Wulfstan's legislative rhetoric not only drew upon the political and moral authority of his episcopal voice to authorize later political claims, but aimed also to reinscribe that voice's efficacy as a valid documentary form, in order to affirm local corporate authority in response to the increasingly centralized bureaucracies of the crown and the papacy. As such, the *LHP* is a noteworthy counterpoint to the texts examined in the remaining chapters of this book, in which Anglo-Saxon legal-homiletic discourse is similarly reinscribed as a vernacular English poetic mode particularly suited for lamenting lost cultural traditions and satirizing the new institutions that replaced them.

The Problem of Genre I: Sententious Formalism in Wulfstan's Writing

Though his works span many genres, the formal consistency of Wulfstan's sententious formalism is such that it is surprisingly difficult to develop firm criteria for establishing generic distinctions between his legal and homiletic works.[12] As Patrick Wormald has observed, the scribes of two particularly authoritative manuscripts that pair Wulfstan's legal and homiletic materials, London, BL, Cotton Nero A.I (hereafter Nero A.I)[13] and Cambridge, Corpus Christi College 201 (hereafter Corpus 201),[14] make no distinction in their presentation of legal and homiletic materials.[15] Nonetheless, Wormald claims that some texts do remain "identifiable as 'pure' homilies," if "only from the forms of address used."[16] Wulfstan's Old English laws are typically phrased in impersonal constructions and "gif ... ðonne" clauses, while homilies tend to address their audience in the

---

12 One recent attempt to define the corpus is Lionaros, *Homiletic*.

13 On this manuscript, see *Nero A.I*, ed. Loyn; Cross, "Missing Folios"; Cross and Harmer, "Source-Identification"; Ker, "Handwriting"; *MoEL* 224–7.

14 On this manuscript, see *Judgement Day II*, ed. Caie 1–21; Whitelock, "Wulfstan and the Laws of Cnut"; Lawson, "Homiletic Element."

15 *MoEL*, 197–210.

16 *MoEL*, 197–8.

vocative, for example, as "leofan men," or by including them in the first-person plural "uton we."

In fact, only some texts may be identified as "pure" homilies and laws on these grounds. Wulfstan's laws, particularly the ecclesiastical *I Cnut*, have many phrases of the latter, homiletic kind. Nor is the first-person plural in Cnut's pronouncements from *II Cnut* merely royal: as Wormald notes, the sense of *I–II Cnut*'s "we" is "surely more congregational than majestic."[17] This congregational "we" is related to the most homiletic aspect of Wulfstan's legal writing, namely, his tendency to encourage correct behaviour in the subjunctive, instead of issuing commands and describing sanctions. These first-person, subjunctive passages of *I–II Cnut* often appear to be taken directly from extant Wulfstanian homilies, which themselves frequently reuse the same turns of phrase in a manner reminiscent of oral composition.[18] Hence while Wormald's formal distinction between legal and homiletic writing does adequately describe the general trend, the law code *I–II Cnut* in particular combines both the features of law and homily to a degree that the text is not easily defined as one or the other.

As an example, I will quote here a passage that appears in both a homily and a law code. This particular passage comes from homily Napier 59, titled *Sermo Lupi* in its only witness. This homily appears in the York gospel book, alongside religious tracts and the sole surviving copy of Cnut's legislative letter to the English.[19] Lines 16–19 from the passage also appear almost verbatim at *II Cnut* 21, with homiletic stylistic elements intact. My citation from Napier 59 below follows manuscript punctuation to emphasize its structural features:[20]

---

17 *MoEL*, 353.

18 Orchard, "Crying Wolf." On Wulfstan's self-citations, see also Hill, "Authorial Adaptation"; Godden, "Wulfstan and Ælfric"; Wilcox, "Wulfstan and the Twelfth Century," "Dissemination," "Anonymous Works"; Morrison, "Reminiscence of Wulfstan"; Cross, "Wulfstan's *De Anticristo*."

19 *MoEL*, 196–7; Heslop, "Art and the Man"; Keynes, "Additions in Old English." For a study of the manuscript and a full edition and translation of the tracts *Be Hæðendome* and *Be Cristendome*, see also Treharne, *Living*, 17–27, 58–68.

20 The homily is divided into lines following the *punctus* (indicated by ".") or a line break, where it seems to serve as a visual cue to pause. As a *punctus* precedes virtually all instances of tironian "⁊" and the conjunction *oððe*, I have exempted these occurrences from this rule; however, as some tironian "⁊"s are preceded with *punctus* and some with *punctus elevatus*, I have interpreted the latter to indicate line breaks. Lines that are indented and follow "[" are line breaks proposed on the basis of syntax; they are not counted in the lineation of the passage. I have also inserted stanza breaks to mark rubricated capitals, and capitalized "God."

York Gospel Book (f 158 r 1–13) [21]

Eallum christenum mannum is mycel þearf .
þat hy godes lage fylgean ./
˥ godcundre lare geornlice gyman .
  [˥ huru gehadodum is ealra / mæst þearf .
forðam þe hy scylan ægðer ge bodian ge bysnian .
Godes / riht georne oðrum mannum.   5

Nu wylle we læran Godes þeowas georne ./
þat hy hy sylfe wærlice beðencan .
  [˥ þurh Godes fultum clænnesse lufian:/
˥ Gode ælmihtigum eadmodlice þeowian .
  [˥ for eall christen folc / þingian gelome:
˥ þæt hi bocum ˥ gebedum geornlice fylgean .   10
  [˥ bodian / ˥ bysnian Godes riht georne:
˥ þæt hy læran gelome swa hy geornost / magan .
þæt gehadode regollice ˥ læwede lahlice .
heora lif fadian ./
to þearfe hym sylfan: 15

˥ ealle christene men we lærað swyþe georne:/
þat hy inwerdre heortan æfre god lufian
  [˥ rihtne Christendom geornlice / healdan .
  [˥ godcundan lareowan geornlice hyran .
  [˥ Godes lara ˥ laga/
smeagean ˥ spirian .
oft ˥ gelome hym sylfum to þearfe: 19

[There is a great need for all Christian men to attend to God's law and earnestly to heed religious teaching. And especially, there is the greatest need of all for the clergy, because they ought to both preach God's law earnestly to other men, and teach [it to them] by example.

Now we will earnestly teach God's servants to think about themselves carefully, and to love cleanness through God's help, and to humbly serve almighty God, and to intercede frequently for all Christian folk, and earnestly

---

21 The homily is transcribed from a facsimile of the York Minster gospel book, Ker's manuscript 402 (468–9). Abbreviations are silently expanded.

to attend to their books and prayers, and earnestly to proclaim God's law and to teach [it] by example, and to teach frequently as earnestly as they can, so that clergymen conduct their lives according to the rule and lay persons conduct their lives according to the law, for their own needs.

And we instruct all Christian men very earnestly, that they always love God in their inner hearts and earnestly maintain correct Christian behaviour and earnestly obey learned teachers, and often and frequently follow and seek out God's teaching and laws, such as is necessary to them.]

This passage contains many examples of the doubleting and sound-linked, two-stress patterns first identified by Angus McIntosh as the crucial signifiers of Wulfstan's prose style.[22] Besides the three-part injunctions, the passage also features the repetitive use of some of Wulfstan's key lexical preferences, for example, uses of the adverb *georne* or *geornlice* ("earnestly"; in lines 3, 5, 6, 16, and 17), and the envelope pattern based on references to the *þearf* or "need" of Christians (lines 1, 3, 19), and also to God's *lara* (lines 3, 17) and *laga* (lines 2, 17).

Lara and *laga* are only among the most prominent of the sound-linked doublets in the passage; others include *ge bodian ge bysnian, bocum ⁊ gebedum, gehadode regollice ⁊ læwede lahlice*, and *smeagean ⁊ spirian*. Also the lines frequently divide into two-beat patterns, in some cases falling into anaphoric clauses starting with "and." More generally, the passage witnesses the "emphasis through repetition at every level of discourse" identified by Andy Orchard as the "essence" of Wulfstan's style.[23] Wulfstan's structural reliance on parallelisms – both logical and rhetorical, in doublets and in extended catalogues – reveals the origins of his formulaic style in the Old English sententious forms described in the previous chapter. Simply put, Wulfstan writes as if he wishes to revise the "word-hoard" itself, in service of his own ideological ends.

In the passage quoted here, the parallelisms emphasize the reciprocal relationship between the church and the laity. Priests will be judged according to how well they teach, while the other members of society must learn how to listen. The parallelism between *godes lage* and *godcundre lare*

---

22 McIntosh, "Wulfstan's Prose." There have been many attempts since to precisely characterize the Wulfstanian voice, for example, Pons-Sanz, *Norse-Derived Vocabulary*, 26–31; Dance, "Sound, Fury, and Signifiers"; Chapman, "Nominal Compounds"; Orchard, "Crying Wolf."
23 Orchard, "Re-Editing Wulfstan," 320.

in the first stanza underlines the point: the clergy must learn, preach, and live God's law before their flocks can observe it in action. In this manner the passage repurposes the penitential thought/word/deed motif, ingrained in the sacrament of contrition itself, wherein the contrite party must feel contrite, confess, and them perform an act of contrition to be fully shriven.[24]

In an Anglo-Saxon context thoughts, words, and deeds are cited as the three criteria whereby Christians shall all be judged on the Day of Doom, for example, in the following passage from Ælfric: "we sceolon of deaðe arisan, ⁊ agyldan gode gescead ealra ure *geþohta* ⁊ *worda* ⁊ *weorca*" (We shall rise from death, and repay to God the reckoning of all our *thoughts and words and deeds*) (my emphasis).[25] Good thoughts, words, and deeds are also cited as indications of secular virtue by the "homilist" Hrothgar in *Beowulf*, who employs them to identify his beloved counsellor Æschere as "min runwita ond min rædbora, / eaxlgestealla" (my sage and counsel-bearer, shoulder-companion).[26] In another homily, Ælfric elaborates on the traditional formula to explicate the importance of study to the thoughts, words, and deeds of preachers, and by extension for the thoughts, words, and deeds of the congregation who learn from those preachers. The thought/word/deed elements are marked in boldface below:

> Nu sceole we gehyran þæt halige godspell
> mid onbryrdnysse, us to beterunge,
> and eac we sceolon **witan** hwæt ða **word** mænon,
> þæt we magon hi awendan to **weorcum** þe eað:
> for ðan þe se bið **wis** þe mid **weorcum** geswutelað
> þa halgan Godes lage and his halgan lare,
> and se bið unrihtwis þe heorcnað þæra **worda**,
> and nele hi awendan to **weorcum**, him to þearfe.[27]

---

24 Thought/word/deed triads are frequent in Wulfstan's homilies: Orchard, "Re-Editing Wulfstan," 89. For other examples of thought/word/deed in Anglo-Saxon and Celtic texts, see Sims-Williams, "Thought, Word and Deed," and Orchard, *Critical Companion to Beowulf*, 55, 73, 123, 146, 218, 255. For an example from a letter attributed to Cnut, see Treharne, *Living*, 31, 37.

25 Ælfric, *Catholic Homilies*, ed. Clemoes, 227 ll. 100–2.

26 *Beowulf*, 1325–6. On Hrothgar's tendency to homiletic language see Orchard, *Companion*, 155–62.

27 Ælfric, *Homilies*, ed. Pope, 357–8.

[Now let us obey that holy gospel with contrite spirit for our betterment; and moreover we must learn what the word means, so that we may translate it into works the more easily; for he is wise who shows with works God's holy law and his holy lore, and he is unrighteous who listens to their words, and will not translate them into works, according to his need.]

Like Ælfric's preachers and Hrothgar's shoulder-companion, the clergy of Napier 59 are particularly responsible for their thoughts, words, and deeds. Parishioners were expected to learn the wisdom contained in authoritative texts by means of the words and deeds of bishops and preachers. Bishops in particular could serve this role in relation to lay members of the nobility, for whom they served as *runwitan* and *rædboran* along the lines of Hrothgar's Æschere. In other words, these bishops and priests ought to attend not only to the divine teachings of God's *lara*, but also the administration of God's *laga*.

Hence even though his sententious wisdom may implicitly claim for itself great age and wide applicability, Wulfstan's employment of sententious formalism is both innovative and focused on specific political ends connected to the exercise of his own influence. Wulfstan's maxim that bishops must teach *Godes riht* to the people connotes not only "God's law," but also "God's property" or "God's dues"; recognition of ecclesiastical political authority is as much a part of proper Christian behaviour as any more theological articles of faith. To teach *Godes riht* in both of these senses, the bishop must attend to the *bocum* not only of scripture, but also of the written laws and legal documents that preserved ecclesiastical power in the secular realm – hence scripture, law, and legal documents all appear in the York manuscript from which the above passage was transcribed.[28] Virtue in thoughts, words, and deeds guaranteed not only the quality of the clergy's religious teaching, but also the trustworthiness of the law codes and legal documents they recorded on behalf of their secular lords. Not least among these were the documents endowing ecclesiastical institutions with the wealth and administrative autonomy that funded their spiritual mission.

In other words, a major reason that Wulfstan's corpus does not divide easily into religious or secular texts is that such divisions did not serve his interests. The Anglo-Saxon clergy enjoyed a near monopoly on the technology of writing at a time when that technology was growing in importance. The more closely legal and secular documentation resembled

---

28 Described in Keynes, "Additions."

religious writing, the stronger was the argument for maintaining the ecclesiastical monopoly on literacy.

One sententious form found in both Wulfstan's legal and homiletic writing that would enjoy a particularly long afterlife is the alliterative catalogue. In the last chapter I cited the catalogue as one of the sententious forms identifiable in wisdom poetry, which lends authority to each of the individual statements in the series. Given that lists in Old English poetry are sometimes closely parallel to those in eddic verse, the Wulfstanian catalogue therefore has a strong claim to oral prehistory.[29] Wulfstan uses them accordingly, to lend sententious authority to both religious instructions and legal statements.

One example of a Wulfstanian catalogue is seen in *II Cn* 4a:

And gif wiccean oððe wigleras, morðwyrhtan oððe horcwenan ahwær on lande wurðan agitene fyse hig man georne ut of þysum earde, oððon on earde forfaran hig mid ealle, butan hig geswican ʒ þe deoppar gebetan. (my emphasis)[30]

[And if witches or wizards, murderers or adulterous women are found out anywhere in the land, eagerly banish these evildoers out of this land, or in this land they will die altogether, unless they repent and more profoundly atone.]

Variations on this statement appear throughout Wulfstan's legislation, though it is extremely vague even by the loose standards of Old English legislation.[31] For example, we are told that *wigleras* and *horcwenan* should be expelled, but nothing about the standards of proof necessary to identify such individuals.

Similar lists also appear in Wulfstan's homilies, for example, in a passage from Bethurum homily 7 128–33, whose parallels to *II Cnut* 4a I have italicized: "þider scylan *þeofas* ʒ *þeodsceaðan* ... Ðider sculon *wiccan* ʒ *wigleras*, ʒ, hrædest to secganne, ealle þa *manfullan* þe ær yfel worhton ʒ noldan *geswican* ne wið God þingian."[32] This homiletic clustering of

---

29 Jackson, "Lists."

30 *Gesetze* I:310.

31 For example, at *Cnut 1018* 7, *VI Æthelred* 7, and "Peace of Edward and Guthrum" 11; *MoEL* 357.

32 Orchard, "Wulfstan as Reader," 334. His translation: "Thither [to Hell] must [go] thieves and mighty ravagers, ... thither must [go] sorcerers and soothsayers, and to say it quickest, all those evil people who did wickedness before, and did not want to cease nor intercede with God."

criminals resembles and is probably derived from a trope in the Pauline epistles listing the criminals who are to be excluded from heaven.[33] Orchard has noted a further parallel between these lines and a passage from the poem *Christ III* (sometimes called *Christ C*):

Ðær sceolan *þeofas ond þeodsceaþan*,
lease ond forlegene, lifes ne wenan,
ond *mansworan morþorlean* seon,
heard ond herogrim. (1609–12)[34]

[There must [go] thieves and mighty ravagers,
the false and the adulterers, not hope for life,
and perjurers see retribution for crime,
hard and fiercely grim.]

Note that *Christ III*'s *morþorlean* is paralleled in *II Cnut*'s *morðwyrhtan*, though there is no reference to murder in Bethurum 7. The juxtaposition of these relatively unusual words suggests that this recurring catalogue is more than a coincidental imitation of the same biblical motif. As Orchard explains: "It seems unlikely (though not impossible) that Wulfstan had direct knowledge of *Christ C*; both texts, however, may well be drawing on a pre-existing sermon tradition that employed the same trope."[35] Given the prominence of alliterative and rhyming doublets in English law to this day, we might also posit that the motif draws from an oral legal tradition. Perhaps Wulfstan merely recognized the similarity between this oral legal form and the Pauline trope, and adapted it for homiletic use accordingly.

Supporting this hypothesis is another oral-formulaic list found in Anglo-Saxon law, which also demarcates political boundaries. The list is witnessed in a legal formula titled *Hit becwæð* by modern editors, to be sworn by the legal heir of a bequeathed property. This rhythmic and heavily alliterative formula includes a list of rhyming and alliterative doublets defining the rights of the speaker:

⁊ ic agnian wylle to agenre æhte ðæt ðæt ic hæbbe ⁊ næfre ðe myntan *ne plot ne ploh, ne turf ne toft, ne furh ne fotmæl, ne land ne læse, ne fersc ne mersc,*

---

33 Biggs, *Sources*, 38; Orchard, "Wulfstan as Reader," 332–3.
34 *ASPR* 3, 48. Trans. Orchard, "Wulfstan as Rewriter," 332.
35 Orchard, "Wulfstan as Rewriter," 334.

ne ruh ne rum, wudes ne feldes, landes ne strands, wealtes ne wateres, butan
ðæt læste ða while ðe ic libbe /. (my emphasis)[36]

[*And I will own as my own possession what I have, and never intend for you*
neither plot nor plow-land, turf nor homestead, furrow nor footmark, land
nor meadow, fresh water nor marshland, brushwood land or clearing, wood
or field, land or shore, wood or water; *except that it may last as long as I live*.]

Though this formula is relatively late (appearing only in the post-
Conquest manuscripts Cambridge Corpus Christi College 383 and the
Textus Roffensis),[37] there is some reason to believe that it may have been in
use for some time before it was written down. Similar lists of rights are
widely attested in the Anglo-Saxon Latin charters, back to the earliest. A
fairly well-developed example of the formula from Wulfstan's lifetime is
the following clause from the charter S 842, describing a Winchester endowment by Æthelred II: "Sint autem predicta ruricula libera ab omni
mundiali obstaculo cuncteque iugo seruitutis, cum omnibus ad ea perti-
nentibus, *campis, pascuis, pratis, siluis, piscationibus, aquarumque cursi-
bus*" ("The aforementioned lands with all that pertains to them – *fields,
pasture-land, meadow-land, forest, fish, course of water* – shall be free
from any worldly obstacle or yoke of servitude"). The Latin forms *pratis*
and *pascuis* ("with pasture-land" and "with meadow-land") are juxtaposed
as they are here in almost two hundred Anglo-Saxon charters, including
charters of Cnut. The pairing not only has a similar sense to the doublets
"ne plot ne ploh" and "ne land ne læse" from *Hit becwæð*, but also attests
in Latin the alliteration of the Old English.

Both the bequeathment formula and the Pauline list at *II Cn* 4a employ
patterned repetition as a means of defining a territory. In the former, the
territory is defined by the rights of ownership that the oath-taker will
have, and in the latter it is defined by the criminals who have no place in a
Christian community. Given that forfeiture was a common punishment
for crime, the two modes of listing are opposing versions of the same kind
of transfer: one proceduralizes the assumption of ownership, the other
proceduralizes its loss.[38] In both cases the sententious quality of formal
language is employed to convince any listeners that these definitions are

---

36 *Gesetze*, 1:400.
37 See Wormald, *MoEL*, 228–52; Richards, "Manuscript Contexts," 181–6.
38 For an example of forfeiture due to accusations of witchcraft, see Scott, *Land and Book*,
   74–6.

appropriate. Moreover, these alliterative lists are particularly useful for Wulfstan, because they evoke both the authority of scripture and the authority of traditional law. This form can be applied in both homilies and in law codes without feeling out of place in either.

And so the sententious catalogue symbolizes the difficulties created for modern readers of Wulfstan by the very categorical divisions between poetic, homiletic, and legal form that are the basis for dividing their work into the discourses of different scholarly disciplines. These categorical divisions encourage modern readers to emphasize differences between Wulfstanian texts that may well have seemed accidental to the archbishop himself. Indeed, perhaps the most interesting aspect of Wulfstan's legal writing from a formal perspective is its effacement of even the vague generic distinctions that the corpus of Old English literature is otherwise able to sustain. Wulfstan insistently returns to the same authorizing formulae over and over again, regardless of the claims or sentiments he wishes to authorize. The fact that he does so enables him to reassert his own clerical dominance over both the religious and secular uses of the technology of writing. But though this reassertion seems to be his project, he is not entirely successful at achieving it. Despite his efforts, fissures between the homiletic and legal modes are still discernible in his texts. In the next section I will complete my description of Wulfstanian sententious formalism by briefly describing them.

The Problem of Form II: Law, Homily, and Authorship

As I have already suggested above, there is little internal evidence that can help us distinguish between the legal and homiletic texts of the Wulfstan manuscript Corpus 201. Nonetheless, the rubrication of the manuscript suggests that such distinctions were made by Wulfstan's earliest readers. The first half of the manuscript is a collection of diverse materials loosely associated with Wulfstan, which includes his homilies, law codes, poems, and a list of bishop-saints; one of the law codes is *Cnut 1018*. This material seems to have been compiled by Wulfstan for its uses to him in his capacity as archbishop. Wormald identifies a large portion of this section, from folios 8 to 145, as a comprehensive "manual for the drilling of a Christian society,"[39] a phrase that nicely encapsulates the manuscript's survey of legal and devotional topics.

---

39 *MoEL* 207–8.

The majority of these texts are rubricated with titles that begin with the preposition *be* or *de* ("about" / "on") in Old English and Latin, respectively. These titles typically describe the texts' subject matter, rather than their authors or intended audiences. Topic statements of this kind are applied to "homiletic" and "legal" materials alike, and they are similar to the rubrics in the manuscript Nero A.I.[40] In the Corpus 201 manuscript, there is a run of homilies (Ker's articles 7 to 13) that deviate from this convention, titled either *To folce* or *To eallum folce* ("to the people," "to all the people").[41] Working backward in the manuscript provides a possible explanation for this different titling convention. Art. 6 is a pastoral letter of Wulfstan;[42] arts. 4 and 5 are grouped by Bethurum into a single homily in Bethurum's edition (Bethurum 5), and are rubricated *De fide catholica* ("on the Catholic faith") and *Sermo*, respectively. Article 3 is Bethurum's homily 6, titled "Incipiunt sermonis [*sic*] lupi episcopi." Thus the rubrication indicating that these statements are directed "to" the people also indicates that they are "from" Wulfstan himself.

There is some corroborating evidence for this reading of Corpus 201 found in other Wulfstan manuscripts. Many of the "to folce" homilies appear under the same rubrication in two other manuscripts (Oxford, Bodleian Library, Hatton 113, and London, BL, Cotton Tiberius A.III). Several of these homilies also appear in Cambridge Corpus Christi College 419, where their rubrication is more conventional, for example, as *Larspell*. Both Hatton 113 and Corpus 419 witness Bethurum 6, titled "incipiunt sermonis lupi episcopi" as in Corpus 201. In both cases the sermon precedes Corpus 201's *to folce* homilies; thus in all three manuscripts, the homilies fall within the category of "the bishop Wulfstan's sermons." Meanwhile, in Corpus 201 itself, an exception to this grouping that proves the rule is the famous *Sermo Lupi ad Anglos* of Ker's art. 40, titled "the speech of Wulfstan *to* the English."[43] The evidence thus suggests that

---

40 Compare for example the rubrics of homily Bethurum 10c, "her onginneð be cristen-dome" ("here begins 'On Christendom'") in Corpus 201 (56–61) and "be cristendome" ("On Christendom") in Nero A.I (76v–83v) to that of *Institutes of Polity* 23, "Be gehadedum mannum" ("On Ordained Men": Corpus 201 40–2; Nero A.I 72–3). Ker, *Catalogue*, 82–90, 211–5 (MS 49 and 164).

41 Napier homilies 20–3, 25, 27. Napier 23 has analogues in *I–II Cnut* at *I Cn* 12 and 14.1-.2 (*MoEL*, 356).

42 Bethurum 13; actually Wulfstan's reworking of Ælfric's Old English translation of the latter's Latin pastoral letter, discussed in greater detail below (76–7).

43 Bethurum 20 BH. On the *Sermo Lupi*'s rubrication, see also Rabin, "Wolf's Testimony," 404–5; Sharpe, *Titulus*, 34–45; Godden, "Apocalypse and Invasion," 158–61.

Wulfstan's authorship was treated as a significant aspect of his homilies and sermons by the scribes who assembled these compilations.

The same trend does not apply to Wulfstan's legislation. In Corpus 201's rubrication there is a tendency to title legal texts as the *gerædnes* of a particular king. These rubrics are even applied to texts that Wulfstan wrote, such as *The Canons of Edgar* and *Cnut 1018*.[44] The term *gerædnes*, mentioned above, is overwhelmingly associated in Old English with the wisdom particular to kings and often identifies the beginning of a legal pronouncement.[45] Legal texts also appear under this kind of rubrication in Nero A.I, a manuscript that witnesses Wulfstan's own hand, a circumstance strongly suggesting that Wulfstan himself knew this convention.[46] Thus while there is no rubric to tell Corpus 201's readers definitively when the *sermones lupi* end, the legal texts in this collection are clearly attributed to other authors, even when it seems highly likely that Wulfstan himself preached them or even wrote them.

The rubrication thus suggests another way of characterizing the discursive spectrum of Wulfstan's legal and homiletic writing. Though Wulfstan's characteristic sententious *voice* uses the same authorizing formulae in both kinds of writing, the genres nonetheless have different *speakers*. The archbishop can address exhortations to his flock directly in his homilies because addressing them is a part of his ecclesiastical role. Indeed, as the passage from the homily Napier 59 quoted above clearly stipulates, his authority is contingent on his use of it. In contrast, Wulfstan the episcopal legislator claims only to make sure that earlier written legislation is known, and that the king does not fail to uphold the laws of his predecessors because of error or ignorance. Where the sententious parallelisms and catalogues found in Wulfstan's homilies authorize the bishop's exhortations by proving to their audience that the author is well versed in true wisdom, the sententious parallelisms and catalogues of Wulfstan's laws authenticate their strictures by proving to their audience that the laws are drawn from

---

44 See Corpus 201, p. 46, "Her is eadgares cyninges gerædnes" (Here is the *gerædnes* of King Edgar), and Nero A.I p.3, "Ðis is seo gerædnys þe Cnut Cininge ⁊ his witan geræddon" (This is the *gerædnys* that King Cnut and his advisors proclaimed). For the evidence that the *Canons of Edgar* are Wulfstan's, see *Canons of Edgar*, ed. Fowler, xxvi–xxxiv.

45 *OE Web Corpus*, accessed 18 March 2011.

46 For the attribution of this hand to Wulfstan, see Ker, "Handwriting." Though his argument is generally accepted, there has been some disagreement: Tunberg, "Introduction," 45–7; Hohler, "Service-Books," 225n.59.

the wordhoard of shared wisdom that is the source of their society's values. However closely together Wulfstan may try to draw these two different sources of authority, they nonetheless remained distinct to his audience.

Wulfstan's citational practices in his law codes suggest that he deliberately cultivated his poise of legislative neutrality. In *I–II Cnut* the archbishop was relatively scrupulous in his borrowings from earlier law codes, and displayed a decidedly uncharacteristic reticence to either paraphrase or elaborate.[47] Mary Richards has even gone so far as to suggest that on the basis of its unrefined and haphazard internal logic *II Cnut* in its current form was a "work in progress rather than a finished compendium."[48] I will argue that the text witnesses the evolution of Wulfstan's construction of his legislative role, as he began to move from the more oral models of sententious formalism towards the more literate models of quotation to advance his ideological agenda.

Wormald has identified known Old English sources for nearly 75 per cent of the code's clauses.[49] Though this level of borrowing is not necessarily unusual for Wulfstan, it is uncharacteristic that he should make so few alterations to the cited text.[50] The archbishop clearly had access to a large corpus of legal material, and he draws from codes as far back as *Æthelberht*. Of the seventy-one passages in *I–II Cnut* where Wormald has identified a direct source in law codes preceding Wulfstan's, twenty-nine appear to be direct quotations.[51] In total, Wormald identifies 163 direct quotations from known texts in the law codes, and 135 apparent modifications. Virtually all of the twenty-nine unaltered quotations are from the more recent law codes *II–III Edgar* and *I Æthelred*, which together provide over half of the identified citations from non-Wulfstanian legal sources. The *Edgar* codes are quoted directly in twelve passages from *I–II Cnut* and paraphrased in ten, while *I Æthelred* is quoted directly in sixteen passages and paraphrased in six. In both cases, the texts are quoted verbatim more frequently than they are altered.

---

47 This reticence is also commented upon by Patrick Wormald and Pauline Stafford: *MoEL*, 354–5; Stafford, "Laws of Cnut," 173–4.

48 Richards, "*Summa*," 155.

49 *MoEL* 355–61.

50 For an overview of Wulfstan's homiletic practice of citation and modification, see Orchard, "Wulfstan as Reader, Writer, and Rewriter." On Wulfstan's stylistic similarities to the earliest codes, see Schwyter, *Old English Legal Language: The Lexical Field of Theft*, 76–8, 80–1.

51 *MoEL* 361.

This trend continues when we look at Wulfstan's self-citations. The number of direct quotations from his earlier laws or homilies is equal to or greater than the number of modified passages in almost every text. Considering that some of these inconsistencies must be ascribed to the complex transmission history of the texts in question, and particularly in the oldest, this data leaves the impression that Wulfstan was relatively conservative in his use of legal citations, even when they came from legal texts that he had written himself. This conservatism is in sharp contrast to Wulfstan's treatment of other identified sources in his more "purely" homiletic writing.

An illustrative example of Wulfstan's usual practice that will help to explain his deviation from it in *I–II Cnut* can be found in his reworked version of Ælfric's pastoral letter, witnessed in Corpus 201.[52] Internal evidence in other versions of this letter tells us that it is one of two written by Ælfric, who wrote them in a bishop's voice. Joyce Hill details the extensive changes made by Wulfstan to this text, and argues that they indicate his careful reworking of the text in its entirety. She argues further that Wulfstan's responsibility for these amendments is "inherently likely," as the archbishop "would have felt that [Ælfric's letters] were in a profound sense his own property."[53] Though Malcolm Godden has convincingly challenged Hill's supposition that Wulfstan commissioned Ælfric or had otherwise acquired the latter's permission to make his changes,[54] the differences between Wulfstan's treatment of this text and his treatment of the laws are striking. To borrow Hill's phrasing, the relatively light revisions witnessed by *I–II Cnut* suggest that the laws were *not* his property, or at the very least that he had a rhetorical reason to avoid creating the impression that he regarded them as such.

Wulfstan's practice of revision to his legal sources reveals once again the impressive consistency of his ideological agenda. One key change to Ælfric's letter made by Wulfstan is his removal of a section reminding bishops that they are not able to apply the death penalty.[55] Hill has argued that Wulfstan also cut the corresponding passage from the surviving Latin

---

52 Ælfric, "Die Hirtenbriefe," ed. Fehr. See also Ogawa, "Revised Syntax," 3–17; Kubouchi, "Prose Rhythm"; Chapman, "Stylistic Use," 63–71.
53 Hill, "Authorial Adaptation," 64. On authorship and Ælfric, see also Hill, "Changing Text"; Szarmach, "Ælfric Revises."
54 Godden, "Wulfstan and Ælfric."
55 The excised portion is II, 201–13: Ælfric, "Die Hirtenbriefe," ed. Fehr.

version of the *Pastoral Letter*.[56] These substantive omissions bear comparison to one of the most remarkable divergences from his apparent sources in Wulfstan's legal writing, noted by Katherine O'Brien O'Keeffe, that the archbishop's laws generally call for punishment by mutilation where similar laws in earlier codes proscribe the death penalty.[57] Wulfstan's legislation thus accords with the doctrine he twice removed from Ælfric's letter. This suggests that his alteration of the letter need not reflect, as Godden argues, a disagreement between Wulfstan and Ælfric on episcopal functions.[58] On the contrary, the archbishop's reluctance to use the death penalty in his own legislation suggests that Wulfstan recognized the strength of Ælfric's argument. The emendation of the *Pastoral Letter* implies only that Wulfstan made a prudent decision to avoid making statements in his letter that invited criticisms for overstepping his episcopal authority. And in fact his elimination of the death penalty in the law code expanded his authority, by giving secular punishment the pastoral purpose of encouraging sinners to repent their sins. Thus despite the overall pattern in Wulfstan's legislation of faithfulness to the letter of his sources, such faithfulness hardly amounted to an abandonment of his ideological agenda in favour of a position of neutrality. If anything, Wulfstan's conservatism suggests that the texts he drew from were themselves already consistent with his agenda in their unaltered form.

In the next two sections I will examine the interrelationship between Wulfstan's three roles by first looking at the legal implications of his most famous homiletic work, the *Sermo Lupi ad Anglos*, and then looking at the exhortative qualities of *I–II Cnut*. Sententious abstraction in both texts functions as a tool of political expediency, which allowed Wulfstan to argue for the centrality of the church's role in the correct practices of secular government. As I will demonstrate, the favourability of *I–II Cnut* to ecclesiastical institutions will be a major component in the appeal of this text to post-Conquest readers, who read it from their more "literate" perspective not as an archbishop's argument to Cnut about the kinds of laws he ought to have, but rather as a transparent description by Cnut of the laws that he encountered and affirmed.

---

56 Hill, "Authorial Adaptation," 63–4.
57 "Body and Law," 216. See also Marafioti, "Punishing."
58 Godden, "Wulfstan and Ælfric," 361–2.

Wulfstan, Cnut, and the Danes: Text and Context

The *Sermo Lupi ad Anglos* is easily Wulfstan's most famous work, and it is perhaps even the most celebrated work of prose from the Anglo-Saxon era. The sermon enjoys its popularity because of its rare eyewitness account of England in the reign of Æthelred II. Wulfstan cites the Danish incursions into England as evidence for the moral decrepitude of the Anglo-Saxon people, and provides a powerful description of the Viking raids and their consequences. The text (Bethurum 20) survives in five manuscripts, grouped into three rescensions: BH (in Cambridge, Corpus Christi College, MS 419 "B" and Oxford, Bodleian Library, Bodley MS 343 "H"); C (in Corpus 201 "C"); and EI (in Oxford, Bodleian Library, Hatton 113 "E" and Nero A.I "I"). Two of these manuscripts, I and C, also witness versions of Cnut's law codes.[59]

Jonathan Wilcox has compellingly argued that the *Sermo Lupi ad Anglos* was first written to encourage the *witan* to formally accept Swein as king after the death of Æthelred.[60] Wilcox responds to an apparent contradiction in Wulfstan's biography, that he can depict the Danes as murderous monsters in the *Sermo Lupi ad Anglos* only a few years before he became not only a close advisor to Cnut, but one who took particular care to note the different customs of the Danelaw.[61] However, the apparent inconsistency in Wulfstan's allegiances only seems inconsistent when anachronistic concepts of ethnic identity are applied. With regards to his respect for the Danelaw, it is important to remember that even though the inhabitants of northern Britain may have had Danish ancestors and relative autonomy, their laws were a part of English law and they were in this

---

59 The question of whether BH or EI represents the earlier version of the homily has been subject to debate. EI is the longest and fullest sermon, with the most detailed account of the Danish invasions, while BH is the shortest; whether the sermon was expanded or contracted, C appears to be an intermediary point. My citations from the sermon will come from the EI version. For an argument that EI is the earliest version, see Hollis, "Thematic Structure"; Wilcox, "Political Performance"; and Rabin, "Wolf's Testimony," 397–8. For a refutation of Hollis, see Godden, "Apocalypse and Invasion." See also Orchard, "Wulfstan as Reader," 313–14.

60 Wilcox, "Political Performance," 377–8. For a survey of Wulfstan's responses to these raids, culminating in an argument that the *Sermo Lupi ad Anglos* can be dated to 1009, see Keynes, "An Abbot, an Archbishop," esp. 174–89.

61 In the "Laws of Edward and Guthrum": Keynes, "An Abbot, an Archbishop," 177; Hart, *Danelaw*, 47–8; Whitelock, "Wulfstan at York," esp. 224–5; *MoEL* 330–40, 389–91.

sense essentially English.[62] Foreign invaders may be similarly called Danes, but the distinction between them and the local "Danes" did not necessarily pose a conceptual problem: there is a clear difference between occupying a slightly different category within the law, and living under a different law entirely.

Indeed, far from exposing a contradiction in Wulfstan's world view, his contrasting views on Danish invaders and the Danelaw in fact point to the archbishop's unwavering focus on the development of a financially and politically autonomous church. The more autonomous were the regions of Wessex, Mercia, and the Danelaw, the less personal power was held by that monarch who governed all three regions. The less power was held by the king, the more power was held by prominent landholding institutions like monasteries and the dioceses. The limit to royal power set by long-standing local tradition was likely to have been particularly apparent to Wulfstan, whose sees of Worcester and York were in the regions of Mercian law and the Danelaw, respectively. A particularly well-known example of the potential benefits that arose for local churches out of local traditions is the so-called Oswaldslow immunity controlled by Wulfstan's successors to the see of Worcester, an exemption that claimed to derive from the precedent of Mercian law.[63] Even if Wulfstan found the Danes personally repugnant, then, he still would have had ample reason to craft a code that recognized the special cases of their customary laws.

Meanwhile, Wulfstan's castigations of the Danish invaders in the *Sermo Lupi ad Anglos* are revealed to be part of a rhetorical strategy, based in sententious and legal formal precedent. The figure of the Danish invader functions symbolically in the text as a means to a political end. Andrew Rabin's reading of the *Sermo Lupi ad Anglos* provides us with a framework for more precisely characterizing the archbishop's negotiation of legal and homiletic rhetorical strategies. Rabin argues that "For Wulfstan, the documentary nature of *lagu* allows it to do more than merely regulate civic activity; rather, the ordered and permanent nature of the written text imposes a structuring and stabilizing influence on human society itself."[64] The legal "text" evoked by Wulfstan in this case is sworn testimony,

---

62 Hadley, *Northern Danelaw*, 303–4. But see Jayakumar, "'Foreign Policies'," 24n.38. On ethnicity in Anglo-Saxon England, see also Moreland, "Ethnicity, Power"; Harris, "An Overview of Race."

63 See Wormald, "Oswaldlaw Revisited"; Tinti, "Hemming's Cartulary"; Baxter, "God's Property."

64 Rabin, "Wolf's Testimony," 391–2.

reflected in his characteristically precise use in the *Sermo Lupi ad Anglos* of the legal term *gecyðan*, "to make known" or "testify."[65] Wulfstan's "witnessing" of Old English law in the *Sermo Lupi ad Anglos* borrows this testimonial form to produce and express his own moral authority as a historical commentator, which in turn allows Wulfstan to suggest corrective actions.

Hence Wulfstan's sermon witnesses the crimes of heathen invaders only insofar as they provide evidence for the crimes by which the English brought invasion upon themselves. God would never have allowed such atrocities to be visited upon the English had they not deserved them, therefore the punishment is itself evidence for the existence of the sin. As Rabin concludes: "the sins of the English thus become not just a denial of their religious responsibilities but also a negation of those characteristics that invest them with a coherent national identity."[66] The homily's description of a moment in England's political history is thus transformed by its quasi-testimonial genre into a transhistorical exhortation to Christian living, wherein the English people provide both an *exemplum* and an audience, adjudicating on their own crimes.

The precise nature of these crimes bears further elaboration. Audrey Meaney has demonstrated that Wulfstan uses the term *hæðen* and its compounds to refer to criminals who could be either pagan or Christian.[67] Similarly in the *Sermo Lupi ad Anglos*, Wulfstan's criticisms of Danish invaders emphasized not their ethnic difference, but their criminality. This concept of heathendom is the natural extension of the quasi-legal inflection of the Pauline trope listing the criminals banished from the kingdom of Heaven. Pagans from other Germanic cultures and native English criminals are equally worthy of expulsion, because both threaten the ecclesiastical institutions that alone can protect the souls of Christians from eternal damnation in the coming apocalypse.

One of the more interesting rhetorical reversals of the *Sermo Lupi ad Anglos*, then, is that English Christians are found to be more guilty than pagan invaders of attacking the integrity of ecclesiastical institutions.[68] Indeed, this is the first specific abuse mentioned by Wulfstan in his sermon. Wulfstan wryly observes that heathens respect the sanctity of their religious spaces, and do not steal back offerings from their false idols as

---

65 Rabin, "Wolf's Testimony," 396.
66 Rabin, "Wolf's Testimony," 400.
67 Meaney, "*And we forbeodað*," 479–80; see also Meaney, "Penalties."
68 Cowan, "Byrstas and bysmeres," 411.

Christians take back gifts from their church. Wulfstan is unusually early for his use of the Norse word *gridian* to describe the kind of protection that the church ought to enjoy, and one effect of this word choice is that it emphasizes the irony that the law of the Norse "heathens" is more respectful of their gods than is the law of English Christians.[69] In one passage, the failure to provide *grid* is linked specifically to a failure to respect *Godes gerihta*:

Ac soð is þæt ic secge, þearf is þære bote, forþam Godes gerihta wanedan to lange innan þysse þeode on æghwylcan ende, ꝺ folclaga wyrsedan ealles to swwyþe {syððan Eadgar geendode},[70] ꝺ halignessa syndan to griðlease wide, ꝺ Godes hus syndan to clæne berypte ealdra gerihta ꝺ innan bestryte ælcre gerisena […]ꝺ, hrædest is to cweþenne, Godes laga laðe and lara forsawene. (lines 37–49)

[But I say the truth: there is need for remedy, because God's sacred rights (*gerihta*) diminished for too long in this nation in every district, and the people's laws (*folclaga*) have worsened all too greatly {since Edgar died}, and holy places are too widely without protection (*gridlease*), and God's house is ripped bare of old rights (*gerihta*) and stripped within of each fitting thing, […] and as is hardest to say, God's law is hated and his teaching despised.]

The relationship between *Godes gerihta* and the "fitting things" removed from the churches "in every district" implies that the "rights" in question refer not only to a general freedom from molestation, but specifically to the rights of ownership. By extension, the *grid* lacking in the passage above refers particularly to the protection of property from theft or damage. It might also be noted that the term *gerihta* is also used by Wulfstan elsewhere to refer to the sacraments.[71] Wulfstan's insistent repetition of this term thus contains a larger political argument: as the divinely sanctioned rational principle behind the law (*Godes riht*) stipulates, the temporal wealth of the church (*Godes riht* or *gerihta*) is essential to the performance

---

69 On *grid* in Wulfstan, see: Pons-Sanz, *Norse-Derived Vocabulary*, 125–58; Dance, "Sound, Fury," 51n.72; Fell, "*Unfrid*," 90–2.

70 The text in "{ }" appears only in the E manuscript.

71 E.g., *II Cn* 54.1: "ne do him nan preost nan þæra gerihta, þe man Cristenum men don sceal, ærþam he geswice" (nor shall any priest do for him any of those rites which Christian men ought to do unless he refrains [from his crime]).

of its necessary functions (*Godes gerihta*), which protect the souls of Christians and, by extension, protect the nation from divine punishment. The specific cause of divine punishment, then, is the failure of the English to adequately respect the church as a provider of necessary spiritual services. If only the church had been adequately funded and allowed to do its job, the kingdom never would have reached the state of moral decrepitude that necessitated the visitation of divine punishment in the form of heathen invaders. Thus the territorial definitions accomplished by the two kinds of alliterative catalogue cited earlier – one listing criminals to be expelled, one listing property rights to be respected – are revealed to be two aspects of a single composition of national identity: if you wish to keep the heathens and murderers at bay, you must respect the church's rights to meadow lands, pasture lands, and all the wealth derived thereof. In this sense, the apocalyptic rhetoric of the sermon is employed in service of an argument that may be described in modern terms as a resource allocation audit, whose conclusions are derived from the application of generally accepted moral principles rather than the generally accepted accounting practices one would use today.

Wulfstan derives the moral principles applied in his audit not only from biblical precedent, but also from English law. The crimes witnessed by Wulfstan are criminal not only in the eyes of God, but also in the eyes of earlier English kings, who laid down laws that their successors ought to follow. In the E manuscript witness of the *Sermo Lupi ad Anglos*, the failure to respect the property of the church is linked explicitly in a decline in the *folclaga* since the death of Edgar. As I have already noted, the law codes we attribute to Cnut self-identify as the "laws of Edgar," and nostalgia for Edgar's reign is a persistent theme in the Wulfstanian corpus. Wulfstan probably refers to the reign of Edgar as a time of prosperity and peace primarily because Edgar was a supporter of the Benedictine Reform, and endowed a remarkable number of monasteries.[72] Nostalgia for Edgar is therefore the obverse of the popular wisdom in Wulfstan's time, that the death of Benedictine reformer Æthelwold marked a turn for the worse in the reign of Æthelred. Cleansing the monasteries on the advice of reformist bishops caused peace and prosperity, and when the reformist bishops are dead, foreign invasion is inevitable.[73] Despite its name, then, Edgar's

---

72 Keynes, "Edgar, *rex admirabilis*"; Stafford, "Laws of Cnut," 186; J. Barrow, "Ideology," 145–6; Clanchy, "Remembering the Past;" Smith, *Land and Book*, 96–106.
73 Keynes, "Re-reading King Æthelred," 91–3.

folclaga is mourned by Wulfstan not only because it is traditional, but also because of its conformity to the institutional needs and ideological constrictions of English Benedictine monasticism.

Wulfstan holds himself up not only as a witness to the crimes of the English, then, but also as a competent reader of written legal precedent who can adjudicate on those crimes with reference to the written laws of Edgar. Wulfstan himself defines his authority as readerly in the passage from the EI version of the *Sermo Lupi ad Anglos* about the *þeodwita* Gildas.[74] In Nero A.I, the sermon appears immediately before the *Institutes of Polity* section "Be þeodwitan," which in turn is separated out from the other *Institutes* in the manuscript; this section on "nation-counselling" includes a sharp castigation of bishops who fail to preach.[75] In the *Sermo Lupi ad Anglos* also, the cause of the Britons' downfall identified by Gildas is the British *biscopa asolcennesse* or the "sloth of bishops." It is crucial, then, that Wulfstan authorizes this claim by invoking Gildas's text as an authoritative literary antecedent, whose example confirms his own authority as a political commentator in much the same way that the example of Edgar in *I–II Cnut* confers legislative authority on the laws. Certainly the term *þeodwita* carries the connotation of literary authority in the *Enchiridion* of Wulfstan's near-contemporary Byrhtferth, where it refers to the Latin poets Virgil and Caelius Sedulius.[76] In other words, the *Sermo Lupi ad Anglos* is insufficiently authorized as a summary of the state of the nation solely on the basis of its quasi-legal testimonial form; Wulfstan must also evoke the comparable testimony of the similarly literate cleric Gildas. Authoritative written works provide Wulfstan not only with his knowledge of morality, history, and law, but also with a template for putting that knowledge to use, as an author in his own right, who moreover is charged as a bishop to preach against injustice wherever he sees it.

And so in the *Sermo Lupi ad Anglos*, it is apparent that Wulfstan's status as a literate author of homilies is not contrary to or even separate from his political role as a member of the *witan*. On the contrary, his episcopal

---

74 Bethurum ll. 174–84, p. 274

75 Rabin, "Wolf's Testimony," 410. For a further discussion of the specifically episcopal implications of "Be þeodwitan," see Wilcox, "Wolf on Shepherds"; Orchard, "Wulfstan as Reader," 326–7.

76 The term is used to refer to "Vergilius" (2.3.190) and "Sedulius" (3.3.97): *Byrhtferth's Enchiridion*, ed. Baker and Lapidge. The term *þeodwita* is also the Old English translation of the Latin *senator* in the epilogue to the Old English Heptateuch: Crawford, *Heptateuch*, l. 25.

function as a literate *þeodwita* places him in a unique position to be a "witness" of the social document of the law, both because his training as a scholar allows him to accurately read and disseminate the contents of earlier English law codes, and because of his episcopal moral authority to read and preach about the divine truth of holy scripture. The sermon therefore makes the case that Wulfstan can and should serve in the role of legislator that he will take up in *I–II Cnut.* This case is based on his readings of religious principle, legal precedent, and contemporary events. As I will demonstrate, the law code similarly combines these three authorizing principles, even as it seems (in Patrick Wormald's words) that Wulfstan "intended his laws and homilies to be as generic, as general in application, as lacking in *specific* context, as possible."[77]

In the next section I will show how Wulfstan's notion of his role as legislator manifests in his actual legislation, *I–II Cnut.* As I have shown, *Sermo Lupi ad Anglos* presents an example of Wulfstan applying his authority as a prophetic bishop and as a witness of legal precedent: Wulfstan's two kinds of authority are mutually reinforcing, as the literary example of the *þeodwita* Gildas exemplifies. The authorizing function of literary precedent is played in Wulfstan's law codes by his direct quotations from earlier law codes. But even though this practice obscures the more obvious markers of Wulfstan's style, the law code nonetheless constructs kingship in a manner closely analogous to that of the *Sermo Lupi ad Anglos.* In my discussion, I will focus particularly on the peace of the church and on the representation of marriage law, both because Wulfstan's agenda is particularly apparent in these discussions and because they introduce themes of Anglo-Saxon legal-homiletic discourse that will recur in subsequent chapters.

I–II Cnut in Context

The material portion of *I–II Cnut* begins at *I Cn* 2 with a discussion of *cyricgrið*, a term that again uses the unusual Danish term for "church-peace" or "protection of churches." The primary emphasis on this law in *I–II Cnut* has no precedent in its closest antecedents, and the law's apparent source is buried deep in Wulfstan's earlier code *VI Æthelred* at 42.3.[78] The closest parallel to this emphasis on the importance of protecting churches is provided by the *Sermo Lupi ad Anglos*, which evokes crimes

---

77 *MoEL* 14.
78 *MoEL* 356.

against *cyricgrið* as its first example of the crimes of the English that invited divine punishment. Again, the Norse word *grið* may carry special significance, as it alludes to the customs both of Wulfstan's own Danelaw and of Cnut's homeland. This emphasis on *cyricgrið* may also have had particular historical implications for the code's intended audience. The St Brice's Day massacre by Æthelred II, a crime whose victims included Cnut's aunt and thus provided the moral justification for the Danish Conquest, took place in a church, and in that sense was a clear violation of *cyricgrið*.[79] The law therefore reminds the audience that Cnut's ascension was a justified effort to punish an "unready" king for his crime.[80] Hence in this law, as in the code as a whole, Wulfstan maintains the appearance of disinterested objectivity through his scrupulous quotation of his sources, even as he manipulates the structure of those quotations in relation to his political context to encourage Cnut to become Edgar-like in his support of ecclesiastical corporate interests.

The sections of *I–II Cnut* where Wulfstan's political agenda is perhaps most blatantly apparent are those dealing with marriage law. Marriage was undisputedly under ecclesiastical jurisdiction, despite its central importance to almost every aspect of secular life. Stacey Klein has documented how Anglo-Saxon representations of women, and queens in particular, were typically employed "to explore and to express their views on the most difficult and debated issues of Anglo-Saxon society: conversion, social hierarchy, heroism, counsel, idolatry, and lay spirituality" – a set of issues that are also the concerns of Anglo-Saxon law.[81] Medieval commentaries on the book of Esther cited that wise queen's relationship to her people to allegorize the church's relationship to the world,[82] and of course the Virgin Mary's relationship to Christ was (and still is, in modern Catholicism) symbolic of the church's relationship to God. This identification between church and queen was rooted in the long-standing idea, illustrated for example in the figures of St Elene and Bertha of Kent, that the wives and mothers of kings can function as persuasive advocates for the church with their husbands and sons.[83] Laws that attempt to define the

---

79 Wilcox, "St. Brice's Day," 82–3.
80 Keynes, "Cnut's Earls," 44.
81 Klein, *Ruling Women*, 4.
82 On Esther in Anglo-Saxon England, see Klein, *Ruling Women*, 163–89. On the Esther topos in medieval literature, see Huneycutt, "Esther Topos."
83 On positive representations of wifely advice by early medieval clerics, see Farmer, "Clerical Images."

relationship between husbands and wives therefore provide an ideal template for Wulfstan to define by proxy the ideal relationship between king and ecclesiastical advisor. Moreover, the relationships between men and women have always been a major theme of proverbs and maxims, and so discussions of marriage are also good opportunities to utilize the kinds of sententious authorizing procedures that validate longer series of claims.

Though Wulfstan was hardly unique for making wide claims for episcopal authority on the basis of the church's power over marriage, he was particularly persistent in doing so. The sanctity of marriage is a noted theme throughout Wulfstan's writings, both legal and homiletic, and the compound *æwbryce* (adultery) is particularly common in texts bearing signs of his influence.[84] Indeed, Wulfstan's constant discussions of *æw* "marriage" provide a possible explanation for his oft-noted lexical preference for *lagu* to refer to "law." Given his careful use of legal terminology, Wulfstan might simply have thought that using the term *æ* to mean "traditional law" would confuse his listeners.[85]

As Wormald notes, *I–II Cnut* addresses the topic of marriage with unusual thoroughness, "like no other lawmaker since Alfred."[86] This fixation seems daring, given Cnut's own problematic marriage to Emma of Normandy.[87] However, considering that Æthelred II had also fathered children by another woman before marrying the same Emma of Normandy who would later marry Cnut, the issue was a convenient point of comparison between the two kings, and also perhaps a point of contrast with Edgar. To our knowledge Emma was no great benefactress of the church, while Edgar's queen Ælfthryth was an important participant in the Benedictine Reform, who endowed many Benedictine monasteries and priories.[88] In this context, Wulfstan had only to state basic homiletic principles about the importance of marriage and cite long-standing laws against

---

84 Chapman, "Producing and Analyzing," 16–17. Pons-Sanz suggests that Wulfstan invented the term *æwbryce* as a parallelism for *lahbryce*; if true, the echo of *æ* "law" would be emphasized by the juxtaposition: Pons-Sanz, *Norsified Vocabulary*, 90–1.

85 At the very least the similarity between the terms seems to have confused the *Instituta* translator, who makes exactly this mistake in rendering the compound *æwbryce* into Latin: *MoEL* 406.

86 *MoEL* 303–4.

87 That Cnut's extramarital relationship with Ælfgifu of Northampton would have bothered Wulfstan has been often speculated, but rarely argued. See for example Bethurum Loomis, "*Regnum* and *Sacerdotium*"; Lawson, "Homiletic Element," 579.

88 J. Barrow, "Ideology," 146.

adultery to make the point that Cnut was not without sin, and hence that Cnut had need of spiritual advisors like Wulfstan himself.

There are two sections of *I–II Cnut* dealing with marriage – a division and repetition that itself indicates Wulfstan's relative lack of interest in arranging his text for the convenience of legal professionals. Instead, the division suggests a rhetorical effort to introduce and then return to a theme, for the instruction of his audience. The first marriage section is the homiletic passage *I Cn* 24, which reads: "And we laerað, þæt man wið fulne galscipe ⁊ wið unrihthæmed ⁊ wið æghwylcne æwbryce warnige symle."[89] This law concludes a series of sententious statements recognizable as a series of quotations from the York homily Napier 59, cited above, beginning in *I Cn* 20. These clauses constitute one of the most extended parallels to a known homiletic source in the code.[90] The passage addresses several ways of articulating and maintaining promises to God. *I Cn* 22–22.3 asserts the necessity of memorizing the *Pater noster* and the *Credo*, while *I Cn* 22.4–22.6 and *I Cn* 23 describe the importance of Eucharist, baptism, and confession. In sequence, then, marriage in *I Cn* 24 is just one more example of a contract with God that must not be broken.

This homiletic break at the end of the "ecclesiastical" section of the *Cnut* code(s) rhetorically emphasizes both the heroic ideal of keeping one's word, and also the importance of moral advisors like Wulfstan to kings like Cnut. The law describes the bishop's role overseeing the institutional framework necessary to teach young Christians their prayers, to perform the sacraments for them, and ultimately to marry them to good Christian women when they grow up. As a bishop, then, Wulfstan has a particular duty to train young Christians to keep their word, as good citizens should. Wulfstan's citation of a particularly incontrovertible example of Cnut's shortcomings in the process of describing his own trustworthiness reinforces his episcopal authority at a critical juncture in the text. However much Wulfstan may personally like and respect Cnut, he must nonetheless enjoin the king to honour his oaths; by the same token, Wulfstan may be trusted to honour his own.

Wulfstan does not return to the question of marriage until *II Cn* 50–55, but when he does he again makes implicit criticisms of Cnut.[91] This series of laws appears to be largely quoted from existing legal texts. Though the

---

89 "And we instruct, that one should always beware against great lasciviousness and against adultery and against any breaking of the marriage covenant." *Gesetze* I:303–4.
90 *Gesetze* I:300–4; *MoEL*, 356. On Napier 59, see above (64–8).
91 *Gesetze* I:346–9.

progression from law to law in this section of the code again demonstrates little overarching legal logic, the organization nonetheless suggests a similar underlying rhetorical message to that found at the end of *I Cnut*. This time, Wulfstan makes his point with citations rather than homiletic exhortations. The passage begins with a list of punishments for adultery not found in any known law code, suggesting either that the source is obscure or that Wulfstan wrote the law himself. The list begins at *II Cn* 50.1 with a direct value statement that is more descriptive than exhortative: "Yfel æwbryce byð, þæt eawfæst man mid æmtige forlicge, ʒ mycele wyrse wið oðres æwe oððe wið gehadode" (Adultery is evil, if a married person lies with an unmarried one, and much worse with the wife of another or with a member of the clergy).[92] The list concludes in *II Cn* 55 with the only passage from the code identified by Wormald as a direct quotation from a code before *II–III Edgar*, which is also a statement of how foreigners in particular ought to be punished for their indiscretions: "Ælþeodige men, gif hig heora hæmed rihtan nellan, of lande mid heora æhtum ʒ synnan gewitan" (If foreign men will not correct their marital status, let them leave the land with their goods and their sins).[93] Such a statement is clearly applicable to Cnut.

The laws that follow *II Cn* 55 are similarly on the nose. *II Cn* 56 and 56.1, laws with no identified source, continue the discussion of *ælþeodige men* by stating that any foreigner who commits *open morð* ("public murder," in a unique construction) ought to be tried by the children of the murdered person. If the foreigner fails to atone for his crime, he should be judged by the bishop. This law is then followed in *II Cn* 57–9 with a section of Alfred's laws detailing the punishments for killing kings and for breaking into homes.[94]

In this passage, then, Wulfstan groups relatively disparate pronouncements from a variety of obscure sources to address specific crimes related to adultery, murder committed by foreigners, and breaking into a king's home. The juxtaposition of these pronouncements in a law code written on behalf of a foreign king who married the previous king's wife and who took his kingdom as the culmination of a sustained invasion, killing many English people in the process, suggests that the law code's exhortations may not be as lacking in specific context as they might originally appear. Instead the laws provide a preview of the kind of legal argument against Cnut's legitimacy that one could make, if one were a bishop who felt that

---

92 *Gesetze* 1:346–7.
93 *II Cn* 55, *Wihtred* 4.
94 *MoEL* 353, 356. For a list of parallels, see Stafford, "Laws of Cnut," 175–6n.22.

Cnut did not respect the position of the church. Hence while *I–II Cnut* generally and this passage in particular may be less admonitory in tone and homiletic in structure than Wulfstan's earlier legislation, perhaps this only reflects on Wulfstan's increasing skill at sublimating his admonishment under the formal veneer of authoritative Old English law.[95]

The final section of the code, from *II Cn* 69 onwards, is a homiletic rejection of the abuses of lordship that Pauline Stafford has identified as a possible coronation charter.[96] In light of the passages above, the general criticism of kingship appearing in this charter becomes much more pointed, representing the culmination of a comprehensive argument that Cnut should respect the pre-established importance of the church, if he is to duplicate Edgar's successes and avoid repeating Æthelred's mistakes. Wulfstan's citations from Old English law exploit the political tensions of the situation by framing his concerns about Cnut's Christianity as questions about his Englishness, so that the king's sins appear to violate both God's law and Edgar's.

For the remainder of this chapter I will look at the afterlife of Wulfstan's law codes, as a preliminary step towards discussing his influence on post-Conquest remembrances of Anglo-Saxon legal-homiletic discourse. We will look at the *Quadripartitus* and *Leges Henrici Primi,* which are both texts based in part on Wulfstan's laws . In these texts, the translators have reduced the complex negotiations between Wulfstan's homiletic voice and his authoritative legal rhetoric to the single, consistent voice characteristic of more modern forms of legislation. In the process, the text's moral-homiletic tone became reduced to a formal characteristic of genuinely early English legal writing, in much the same way that hermeneutic Latin came to be regarded as a feature of genuine Anglo-Saxon diplomas in the "Golden Age" of English forgery. Below, I will show how imitations of Wulfstan are discernible in certain passages from the introduction to the *Quadripartitus* and the *LHP* that appear to be original to the translator of Q. I will show how these otherwise puzzling departures from legislative rigour in fact play an important legal function, as Wulfstan's homiletic moralizing authorizes political claims on behalf of ecclesiastical authority.[97] This reading will also help to situate the translator "Q" in the intellectual context of Wulfstan's post-Conquest reception.

---

95 On the evolution of Wulfstan's homiletic style, see *MoEL* 330–66.

96 Stafford, "Laws of Cnut." On the fundamentally religious nature of Anglo-Saxon coronation ceremonies, see Bethurum Loomis, "Regnum and Sacerdotium."

97 On the attribution of this text to the author of the *Quadripartitus*, see the introduction to *LHP*, ed. Downer, pp. 42–4.

Quadripartitus and *Leges Henrici Primi*

Though the sermons, homilies and saints' lives of Ælfric enjoyed widespread popularity through the twelfth century, Wulfstan's religious writing virtually disappeared from circulation by the end of the eleventh.[98] Meanwhile the remarkable stability of the *I–II Cnut* textual tradition, in both Old English and Latin, suggests that there was a widely circulated "post-Conquest vulgate" of the code.[99] Thus the post-Conquest readers of the Old English *I–II Cnut* would have had little context for assessing the text as a work of its original author. And yet since the purpose of the text was to influence public policy, this aspect of the law code's survival can be called a success; the legislative advice of Wulfstan to Cnut was accepted a few generations later as the actual legislation of Cnut himself.

M.K. Lawson has argued that *II Cnut* "anticipates the legal compilations of the twelfth century in being to some extent a conscious codification of existing law."[100] This observation can be taken further: Wulfstan's code not only anticipates the later compilations, but influenced them, by modelling the sent-ntious formalism of traditional English law. The homiletic tone of *I–II Cnut* underscored the code's defence of strong, independent ecclesiastical institutions, based in part on the moral authority of the bishops who led those institutions. As this political agenda was shared by church officials of both Anglo-Saxon and Norman descent, the study of Old English in post-Conquest ecclesiastical institutions by both Anglo-Saxon and Norman churchmen was surely related to the preservation of their local legal customs in resistance to expanding royal power.

Post-Conquest manuscripts of Anglo-Saxon law were small and portable compared to their pre-Conquest equivalents, which suggests they were copied for practical use, almost certainly related to the administration of church properties.[101] Wormald has identified the readers of these texts as a "scholarly fraternity" of specialists in Anglo-Saxon law, whose members "were distributed through the cathedrals and episcopal households of the Anglo-Norman realm."[102] As described in the previous

---

98 Cross, "Wulfstan's *De Anticristo*"; Morrison, "A Reminiscence"; Wilcox, "Wulfstan and the Twelfth Century."

99 *MoEL* 349. Wormald's "vulgate" includes the three principal Latin translations of *I–II Cnut*, the *Consiliatio Cnuti*, the *Instituta Cnuti*, and the *Quadripartitus*.

100 Lawson, *Cnut*, 158.

101 O'Brien, *God's Peace*, 5–6.

102 *MoEL* 473.

chapter, the communities who preserved and studied Wulfstan's laws appear to have been participants in the larger, political effort by ecclesiastical institutions to maintain and if possible increase their powers after the Norman Conquest, in response to the institutional reforms begun by Henry I that would culminate in the remaking of English government effected under Henry II.[103]

The *Quadripartitus* translations of English law survive in several arrangements, but it is generally accepted that these different versions represent the work of a single author, typically called "Q," who by his own effort assembled and translated this largest extant medieval collection of pre-Conquest English legal materials.[104] The text has two prefaces, a *Dedicatio* and an *Argumentum*, which are missing from the collection's later redactions. In the former, Q complains at great length to an unnamed colleague about the depravities of his age and submits his work for correction. In the latter, the plan for the work is described. In its current form the text has only two and not four parts, despite the comment concluding the *Argumentum* that inspired Liebermann to give the text its modern editorial title.[105] The two parts do, however, follow the preface by presenting first Latin translations of Old English law and second more modern materials, in a not uncommon old-law / new-law scheme. A second brief preface, directly addressing Henry and his wife Matilda, appears between the first and second sections.

In four of the six surviving versions of the *Quadripartitus* collection (those appearing in the manuscripts London, BL, Cotton MS Domitian VIII; BL, Royal MS 11.B.II; BL, Additional MS 49366; BL, Cotton MS Titus A.XXVII), *I–II Cnut* is the first text in the collection; a fifth (Manchester, John Rylands Library, MS Lat 420) appears to be missing its beginning. Only the sixth, latest version of the text rearranges the codes into chronological order.[106] Similarly Q's later work the *LHP*, which Downer suggested might in fact be the parts three and four of the original work promised by the preface,[107] also relies on *I–II Cnut* more than any other law codes. Hence Wulfstan's code appears to have occupied a

---

103 Hollister, "Anglo-Norman Political Culture," 12–16.

104 *MoEL* 236–44.

105 Liebermann, *Quadripartitus*.

106 Wormald, "*Quadripartitus*," 122–3; *MoEL*, 236–44.

107 Though Wormald agrees with Downer on the close relationship between *LHP* and *Quadripartitus*, he disputes this reading of the *Praefatio*: "*Quadripartitus*," 137–9.

particular pride of place for the compilers and audiences of these texts, as a particularly important witness of Anglo-Saxon law.[108]

Q's editorial preference for the code appears related to what may be called the "optimism" of Wulfstan's "suggestions" to Cnut, particularly as they pertain to the rights of the church. Cnut himself is praised extensively in the *Argumentum* to the *Quadripartitus*, and some of the specific attributes of the king that are admired appear to derive from Wulfstan's code.[109] Most strikingly, Q remarks that "ut purgandis animi uitiis, non inpune gentibus cruciandis, pax quesita uideretur (Peace seemed to be sought by purging the vices of the heart, not by executing people with impunity)."[110] As stated above, the excision of the death penalty from *I–II Cnut* strengthened the claim of ecclesiastical officers to jurisdiction over secular justice. If Q agreed with Cnut on this point, it is probably because he approved of its implications for ecclesiastical jurisdiction.

There is a high likelihood that Q was a native speaker of French, and was thus either first-generation Norman-English or an immigrant.[111] Bruce Brasington's recent study of canon law sources for the *LHP*, connecting the treatise to the libraries of Northern France, provides at least one reason to suspect the latter.[112] It seems unlikely therefore that Q would have been drawn to Anglo-Saxon law because of nationalistic or cultural interest. A more likely explanation is that Q shared Wulfstan's investment in protecting local ecclesiastical authority in the wake of the Norman Conquest. *Quadripartitus* and the *LHP* were thus themselves compilations of extant law into somewhat optimistic suggestions, differing from Wulfstan primarily in their greater attention to the standards of documentary formalism than was necessary in the early eleventh century.

The scholars who have studied the *Quadripartitus* and the *LHP* have devoted a good deal of energy to identifying the exact degree of legal professionalism brought by Q to his task as translator. At the centre of the question is a reference in the texts to "our" profession at *LHP* 8.7, emphasized below:

---

108 Wormald, "*Quadripartitus*," 136.

109 For other accounts of Cnut in the Parker Chronicle and William of Malmesbury's *Gesta regum Anglorum*, see Treharne, *Living Through Conquest*, 38–40, 82–7.

110 *Argumentum* 6, *Gesetze* I:533. All translations of the *Quadripartitus* prefaces were made with reference to Sharpe's translation: Sharpe, "Prefaces," 156.

111 *LHP* 42–4; *MoEL* 473; Schwyter, *Lexical Field of Theft*, 133–58. Animosity between English and Norman religious seems to have been the exception rather than the rule; see Tsurishima, "Rochester Cathedral Priory."

112 Brasington, "Canon Law."

Et si quidem **professioni nostre** congruum precedentium uel sequentium capitula docuerint, si[u]e iure naturali uel legali uel morali gaudeant instituto, et hoc licet multa circumpositorum uarietate minus plene peregerim, bonam saltem uoluntatem ubique pretendo.

[Whether or not the things expounded in the foregoing or following chapters teach anything relevant to **our profession**, or whether or not they show delight in the natural law or the civil law or moral ordinance, and although I may carry out this task less adequately because of the great diversity of relevant matters, at least I offer a universal expression of good will.][113]

The exact nature of *professio nostra* has been a question of some controversy. Liebermann argued that Q must have held an official legal position, but Downer has soundly rejected his arguments for their speculative nature.[114] Downer points instead to a parallel between three other first-person interjections, wherein the speaker appears to be in conflict over the law with certain *professores*. Downer points to similar uses of the term *professor* in the writings of Firmicus Maternus, where it has a sense of "persons claiming special skill or knowledge"; on this basis, he chose to translate the term *professor* (and to identify Q's profession) as "lawyer."[115] Sharpe has also identified similar complaints about *iudices* or "judgment finders" in *LHP* 28.2, whose parallels to the passages about *professores* imply some connection between the two.[116] Wormald contends that Q can't have been in the legal profession, because there was "no such thing"; however, he believes that Q "must have served in some judicial capacity."[117] For similar reasons, Sharpe has suggested the more general translation of *professor* as "practitioner."[118]

Most recently Nicholas Karn, who believes that Q must have worked in the hundreds courts and compiled the *LHP* for that purpose, has posited that the "profession" in the passage cited above refers not to a job, but to an open declaration before a magistrate.[119] Thus the term does not refer to a job title at all. A similar point may be made about the term *professor* in its appearances. In each of the three mentions of these *professores*, the term

---

113 *LHP* 104–5; here and subsequently my translation of *LHP* is based on Downer's.
114 *Gesetze* I:44; *LHP* 38–42.
115 *LHP* 313–14; Maternus, *Mathesis,* vol. 1, 3.8; vol. 2, 30.14
116 Sharpe, "Prefaces," 159n.73.
117 Wormald, "*Quadripartitus,*" 143–4.
118 Sharpe, "Prefaces," 159, 162.
119 Karn, "Rethinking," 217.

is in the plural genitive form *professorum*, also perhaps a form of the passive participle *professus*, translating "of those who are professed" or, because *profiteor* is deponent, "of those who profess [something]."[120] Hence the term might only function as a rhetorical grace note implying that the things stated by ones who profess such are not actually true. We do not need to posit the existence of a nascent legal profession to explain why these "sayers" are always given negative characteristics.

Consider, for example, the third occurrence of *professorum*, in *LHP* 6.3. The preceding passages *LHP* 6.1 and 6.2 describe the division of England into Wessex, Mercia, and the Danelaw, and also into shires and hundreds. In *LHP* 6:3 we are told that shires and counties differ in their practices, but not because of long-standing traditions. Instead, the cupidity (*cupiditas*) and the more oppressive ways of inflicting injury (*graviora nocendi genera*) belonging to the ones who profess such evil, hateful practices (*maligna professorum detestanda studia*) have been added into the legal system (*legalibus statibus adiecerunt*). This statement is followed by an extended homiletic aside, beginning thus:

> 6.4: Tanta quippe rerum peruersitas et malorum affluentia est ut definita legis ueritas uel stabilis medicine prouidentia raro possit inueniri, set ad maiorem omnium confusionem nouus inplacitationis modus exquiritur, noua nocendi fraus inuenitur, tanquam parum noceat quicquid ante fuerit, et pluris esse iudicetur qui pluribus plus nocuerit.

> [6.4: There is so much perversity of [these] things and so much profusion of evil that the precise truth of the law or a settled statement of the legal remedy can rarely be found, but to the greater confusion of all a new method of impleading is sought out, a new trick for inflicting injury devised, as if too little damage follows from what has been done before, and he is judged greatest who most greatly harms the greatest number.][121]

In other words, the methodologies of the courts are not grounded in the written precedent of Anglo-Saxon law as they should be, the "definita

---

120 In *Quadripartitus Dedicatio* 24, the phrase "dum me talia professorum manus impure convenient" can be roughly translated "while the shameful hands of those who profess such prosecute me"; in *Dedicatio* 38 the phrase "venium postulans ne prius hec patiaris grandia professorum debachationibus occupari" can be translated "asking indulgence that you not first allow these great matters to be taken over by the ravings of those who profess [such ravings]." *LHP* 6.3 is discussed in greater detail below.

121 *LHP* 98–9.

legis ueritas" being obscured by the "nouus inplacitationis modus" or "noua nocendi fraus." Wulfstan was an early practitioner of what would become a widespread and vociferous complaint about the criminality of local sheriffs and reeves that this passage appears to continue.[122] The likely cause for this complaint is the fact that these secular officers could complicate disputes between the church and its neighbours by exercising their jurisdiction over them. If Q took Wulfstan's law codes as statements of fact, he may have genuinely considered such abuses to be "new," because they are explicitly forbidden in *II Cnut* 69.1.

In any event, Q employs the same sententious trope witnessed in Cnut's charter S 956, described at the beginning of this chapter. These innovative reeves go one step farther than the young noble who misled Cnut about his property. The young noble may have ignored the legal rights of the true owner of a particular parcel of land, but the reeves ignored the very rules for determining ownership that decide such cases. Like the charter, the *LHP* reasserts the traditional legal truth of the matter with recourse to sententious wisdom. In both cases, the common-sense prejudice that age and tradition are better than youth and change is evoked to make a legal claim in the absence of any specific details.

The remainder of *LHP* chapter 6 employs formally sententious language to drive home its central criticism of bureaucratic innovation. As Downer observes, these statements have "the character of protest against any kind of immoral behavior, not only within the law":[123]

6.5: Illis tantum reuerentiam et amorem stigia simulatione pollicemur quibus carere non possumus.

[6.5: With odious hypocrisy we proffer respect and love only to those whom we cannot do without.]

6.5a: Quicquid nostre crudelitati pari congressione non respondet nobis natum non reputamus.

[6.5a: Whatever does not answer our own cruelty with matching accord we consider to be of no concern to us.]

6.5b: Induimus animos tyrannorum, et o! rabiem nobis induxere diuitie.

---

122 Bisson, *Crisis*, 177–8; O'Brien, *God's Peace*, 102.
123 *LHP* 42–3.

[6.5b: We assume the disposition of tyrants, and, alas, greed for riches has brought a frenzy upon us.]

6.5c: Nemo quantum potest set ultra modis omnibus appetit insanire.

[6.5c: No one strives to his fullest capacity, but pursues madness beyond all measure.][124]

Three of the four phrases are built around pairs of verbs that alliterate on stressed syllables (*pollicemur* and *possumus*, *induimus* and *induxere*, *potest* and *appetit*), and the fourth pair shares the same prefix (*respondet* and *reputamus*). This structure echoes Wulfstan's signature two-beat phrase, and also his larger tendency towards repetition. More generally, it echoes the tendency of English proverbs to link their parallel elements by alliteration rather than rhyme. Besides these formal qualities, the content of the passage also echoes the complaints of the *Sermo Lupi ad Anglos* against the laziness and greed of the English nation, as a way of witnessing the crimes of its inhabitants. In all of these ways, it appears that the notion of traditional law that Q would hold up to refute the innovations he criticizes is based not in the particular strictures of that law – Q offers no example of the hateful practices in this passage – but in its formal qualities, which signal his own trustworthiness.

The political implications of this critique are spelled out in *LHP* 6.6: "Tot denique sunt et tantis occupata sollicitudinibus, tot circumductionibus inuoluta sunt infortunia seculorum ut uitande potius uideantur exactiones et incerta penitus alea placitorum" (Finally, the misfortunes of secular affairs are overtaken with so many great anxieties, and are wrapped around by so many tricks, that its exactions and thoroughly unpredictable hazards of pleading seem more preferably to be avoided). Of course the more predictable legal venue for ecclesiastical servants is the ecclesiastical court system; hence the "avoidance" of secular alternatives proposed in this digression verges on an outright rejection of royal jurisdiction. This overtly homiletic passage therefore applies vague moral criticisms of secular authority not because its purpose is vague, but because its homiletic rhetoric enables an assertion of ecclesiastical independence from that secular authority. Such claims are authorized not only by the moral truth claim of the text's homiletic content, but the sententious, homiletic form itself,

---

124 *LHP* 98–9.

whose employment here has clear precedent in the legal language of authentic Anglo-Saxon law codes like those written by Wulfstan.

The extended use of the first-person plural in *LHP* 6.1–6, alongside the appearance of the word *professorum* in *LHP* 6.3, is the reason that Q's *professores* are identified with the first-person plural of the phrase *professio nostra* in *LHP* 8.7, cited above. In context, however, the "curious habit" of using the first-person plural found throughout *LHP* seems based in the precedent of *I–II Cnut*. Like Wulfstan's "we," the "we" of *LHP* chapter 6 is more congregational than majestic. The crucial difference is that Wulfstan's authority as a homilist and archbishop was vested in him by the "we" of the church, but Q's authority to criticize his contemporaries is given to him by the "we" of Wulfstan's text, where it appears as a formal convention. *LHP*'s debt to Wulfstan's sententious, homiletic style in this chapter provides one of the clearest indications that Q found in Wulfstan's laws not only a record of legal precedent that supported his particular political position as a servant of the church, but also as a strategy for authorizing critiques of the innovations in royal administrative practices already under way in the early twelfth century.

Hence in an irony characteristic of legal history, the sententious legal-homiletic mode crafted by Wulfstan in order to advocate for innovative reforms was employed by Wulfstan's chief translator in order to criticize innovation and reform as being intrinsically suspect. Further, this very alteration to Wulfstan's text may be best described as a consequence of the innovations and reforms it criticizes, as Q unselfconsciously applied to Wulfstan's codes his own anachronistic notions of what laws were and the reasons that they were written down. As we shall see, this irony only increases as Anglo-Saxon legal-homiletic discourse moves out of the realm of legal practice and into the realm of authoritative social critique. Though codified by highly literate men who were clearly invested in the promulgation of literacy through the expansion of the church, Anglo-Saxon legal-homiletic discourse would manifest in the *Piers Plowman* tradition as a performance of pre-literate English legal principles, derived from the folk practices of the people and recorded in the features of the landscape itself. The next two chapters will look at representative moments in that evolution, to sketch the contours of its trajectory.

The *Quadripartitus* manuscript London, BL, Additional 49366 contains a gloss claiming that the law code was copied from an old Worcester book. There is little reason to believe that this is accurate,[125] but the statement is

---

125 Wormald, "*Quadripartitus*," 113.

rendered plausible by the disproportionate survival of vernacular Old English texts from the region. The remaining chapters of this book will focus on representative texts that come from the Worcester region, not because Anglo-Saxon legal-homiletic discourse only survived in that area, but because the evidence of its survival is both particularly robust and particularly pertinent to the *Piers Plowman* tradition. In the next chapter, I will draw the connections between the Worcester community's well-known interest in vernacular literacy and its well-known institutional reliance on Anglo-Saxon laws and documentary culture. In the same way that homiletic style in S 1166 and *LHP* perform an "orality" defined by its resistance to innovations in literate secular administration, so also did the "orality" of vernacular alliterative poetry in the thirteenth century derive from its origins in a system of education that had lost its practical purpose.

3 Ecclesiastical Anglo-Saxonism in Thirteenth-Century Worcester: *The First Worcester Fragment* and *The Proverbs of Alfred*

In the last two chapters I have shown how formal authentication in Anglo-Saxon legal texts is dependent on sententious formulae and wisdom motifs found also in Anglo-Saxon poems and sermons, rather than the formulaic patterned language that came to dominate legal discourse in later ages. By implication, the "literary" formal qualities of these texts were central to their ideological purposes. Because these texts were continuously copied and studied at the same time and in the same places that "Middle" English literature first emerged, they ought to be integrated into existing critical narratives about the evolution of vernacular English literature after the Norman Conquest. For the remainder of this book, I will take the first steps towards such an integration.

In this chapter and the next, I will examine three texts that appear to have been written in either the late twelfth or the thirteenth century. In this chapter I will look at *The First Worcester Fragment*, *The Proverbs of Alfred*, and in the next chapter, I will turn to Laȝamon's *Brut*. The texts all date to roughly the same period that monastic scribes stopped copying Anglo-Saxon homilies and law codes in the vernacular, as governmental reforms diminished the procedural viability of Anglo-Saxon charters and legal precedents. In this sense the texts mark the culmination of a long-term trend, wherein English legal discourse became increasingly "formulaic" in the diplomatic sense of the term, and the quasi-literary legal texts of earlier eras began to seem less trustworthy. Legal statements written after Henry II were not so easily confused with literary performances of educated authority, and so legal professionals came increasingly to regard with suspicion those texts that did not conform to the new standards. Written in this historical context, the alliterative poems discussed here capture with particular clarity a crucial moment of transition in English literary production. Not only a written language of local conservative bureaucracy, thirteenth-century English was already finding wider circulation as a written language of lay instruction. Nonetheless, in certain contexts the older administrative uses of English were still remembered, and the authors who worked within those contexts employed the sententious formalism of Old English legal writing in their verse.

To strengthen my claims for continuity between the Middle English poems under consideration, I have chosen to focus on medieval alliterative poems associated with Wulfstan's old diocese of Worcester, either because they appear to have been written there (Laȝamon is from Areley Kings) or because they were copied there (as is the case with *The First Worcester Fragment* and *The Proverbs of Alfred*). Worcester has long been identified as an important centre for early Middle English vernacular literacy, and in particular for continuity with Anglo-Saxon vernacular literacy. As Elaine Treharne summarizes, English in the West Midlands was used "to protect the interests of the dioceses, their churches and their congregations."[1] Well over half of surviving Old English manuscripts dated to the period of the Norman Conquest and after come from either Worcester or Exeter.[2] The bishop of Worcester and abbot of Worcester priory at the time of the Norman Conquest was St Wulfstan, the last "Anglo-Saxon" bishop; and from quite an early date it has been supposed that he was personally resistant to Norman reforms.[3] Later, in the thirteenth century, Worcester would also be home to the so-called Tremulous Hand of Worcester (henceforth "the Tremulous Hand," discussed below), whose Old English manuscript glosses provide the best surviving evidence for the study of Old English before the early modern period.[4] Scribes and texts from Worcester also influenced later medieval book production in the London area, as Ralph Hanna attests.[5] Finally, the mention of Malvern

---

1 Treharne, *Living Through Conquest*, 112.

2 J. Barrow, "Chronology," 106; Treharne, "Worcester and Exeter," 19. On early Middle English literacy, see also Hahn, "Early Middle English."

3 On St Wulfstan's life and writing, see Mason, *St. Wulfstan*; Treharne, *Living Through Conquest*, esp. 105–21.

4 Franzen, *Tremulous Hand*; see also Frankis, "Regional Context"; Collier, "Englishness," 43; Stanley, "Antiquarian Sentiments."

5 See the many examples of western/Worcester influence identified in Hanna, *London Literature*, 1–38. To cite one example particularly illustrative of this book's larger thesis, the first English-language manuscript to use the documentary anglicana hand as a book hand, Oxford, Bodleian Library, Digby 86, was written by a scribe from Worcester: *London Literature* 50.

Hills in the opening lines of *Piers Plowman* and the dialects of the fragments *Richard the Redeless* and *Mum and the Sothsegger* tie the *Piers Plowman* tradition to the region as well.[6] Hence while Worcester is hardly the only region where Anglo-Saxon legal-homiletic discourse was preserved, it is a convenient locale for historicizing the parallels between the vernacular English literature of the Anglo-Saxon period and Middle English alliterative poetry.

Worcester's tradition of vernacular English writing is also a particularly appropriate locale for this discussion, because it is relatively easy to establish that the local interest in vernacular literacy was tied directly to the administration of episcopal and monastic lands. Administrators in Worcester relied on vernacular literacy in the Anglo-Saxon era, and their practices do not appear to have been changed much by the Conquest. Written records of ownership could make all the difference in legal conflicts, and changes in bureaucratic practices threaten to invalidate those records that precede the new practices; hence the diocese and its monasteries had a strong motive to keep things as they were.[7] It is worth reiterating that this fact in itself provides a sufficient explanation for the twelfth-century practice of producing relatively conservative copies of Anglo-Saxon homilies. Though the archaisms in the text may have posed problems to would-be preachers, the inconvenience would have been more than offset by the training readers would have received in Old English language, directly pertinent to the criticism of ancient legal texts and documents. Elaine Treharne has quite rightly pointed out that one ought not mistake the formal conservatism of post-Conquest Old English manuscripts for passive copying; these texts were copied with a purpose, and "new" English writing only became more popular when the ideal means for achieving that purpose had changed.[8]

The figure of St Wulfstan personifies the pragmatic value of English literacy to Worcester's ecclesiastical institutions in the twelfth century. St.Wulfstan ordered not only the copying of penitential and religious texts, but also the production of a cartulary under the direction of his subordinate Hemming, which recorded both Latin charters and vernacular boundary clauses.[9] William of Malmesbury's *Vita S. Wulfstani*, itself based on a

---

6 *Piers Plowman* A.Prol 5, B.Prol 5, C.Prol 6. On the dialect of *Piers Plowman*, see M.L. Samuels, "Dialect." On the dialect of *Richard the Redeless* and *Mum and the Sothsegger*, see most recently Horobin, "Dialect and Authorship."

7 Treharne, *Living Through Conquest*, 113.

8 See, e.g., *Living Through Conquest*, 91–121.

9 See also Barrow, "Chronology of Forgery."

(probably vernacular) saint's life by St Wulfstan's contemporary Coleman,[10] praises the saint's success at litigation more than once.[11] If it is accepted that Hemming's cartulary aided Wulfstan in this litigation, then the text also exemplifies the practical purpose of reading Old English: without a certain degree of fluency in the language, one cannot convince a judge that any Old English document is legitimate, or even that it says what one thinks it says. In brief, then, St Wulfstan's stewardship of Anglo-Saxon culture goes hand in hand with his diligence as an archivist and his success as an administrator. Indeed, given that monasteries had such a strong incentive to manipulate the record (exemplified perhaps by the invention of "Oswaldslow"), it may well be the case that we have unconsciously adopted a view of history carefully cultivated by St Wulfstan and his successors when we characterize Norman efforts to assert control over monastic lands as "innovations."[12]

This context is important, because it counteracts the tendency to read the texts under consideration here as merely the idiosyncratic work of isolated antiquarians. One of the great ironies of the texts under discussion here is that their very elegiac tone is one of the strongest indications that the "lost" traditions they mourn in fact continued to survive. From the translations of Alfred to the homilies of Wulfstan, Old English literature has persistently predicted its own imminent demise; and just as one is always injured on the last run down the ski slope, so also was it inevitable that eventually one of the texts employing this motif should prove to be correct. This does not mean, for example, that we should take the speaker of *The First Worcester Fragment* at his word when he suggests that all knowledge of Anglo-Saxon literary traditions have utterly vanished.

Insofar as they necessarily resist scholarly interpretive methodologies, wisdom poems like *The First Worcester Fragment* and *The Proverbs of Alfred* are, in the broad terms defined in chapter 1, "oral" texts, which perform their orality in their appeal to the shared cultural authority of common sense.[13] Again, this "orality" appears to derive from the nominally or apparently oral traditions of Anglo-Saxon legal-homiletic discourse. In essence, these poems take Anglo-Saxon legal forms derived from oral precedent and leave out the legal content, to reinvent those forms as a

---

10 On the vernacular characteristics of William's source, see Orchard, "Parallel Lives."
11 Giandrea, "Recent Approaches," 97; citing *Vita S. Wulfstani* I.§13, II. §1.
12 Wormald, "Lordship."
13 On orality and proverbs, see also Frank, "Proverbs."

vernacular literary mode appropriate for articulating dissatisfaction with the institutionalized literacy of the high and late medieval periods. If the connection between these poems and Anglo-Saxon legal traditions has never been noted, it is because the dissatisfaction expressed by this mode is necessarily vague: the texts are rejecting precisely the sorts of formulaic discursive practices that make commemorative writing seem specific to literate historians. Hence, for example, the fact that the poems are so studied and mannered, though at the same time they are so metrically informal. The former attribute betrays their origins in a literate discourse, while the latter exemplifies the particular discourse's performance of orality-as-critical-resistance. As we shall see, the formal echoes of Old English legal texts apparent in these poems demonstrate the kinds of authenticating strategies that will manifest also in the *Brut* and in the *Piers Plowman* tradition.

But even though alliteration is a particularly obvious feature connecting these Middle English poems to Wulfstan's homilies and laws, it is worth reiterating that my arguments for continuity between the texts are not based solely or even primarily on prosody. Just as the absence of alliteration from early English poems need not prevent those texts from participating in Anglo-Saxon legal-homiletic discourse, so also is the mere presence of alliteration in a Middle English (or Latin) text insufficient evidence in itself for that participation. In the present study, alliteration in itself provides relatively weak evidence for a connection between the texts under consideration. *The First Worcester Fragment, The Proverbs of Alfred*, and the *Brut* all follow discernible stress patterns, but those patterns do not entirely overlap with patterns of alliteration, and not infrequently their structures even rely on rhyme.[14] As Ralph Hanna puts it, the alliteration in these poems represents "merely one motivated selection from a more fluid and various menu" of formal possibilities; there are a "relatively vast" number of rhymed English poems from the same period that inhabit the same metrical continuum despite the absence of alliteration.[15] Further, as David Lawton in particular has demonstrated, there are closer analogues to the metre of Langland in Middle English rhymed verse and even in Latin than there are in the verse forms of Laȝamon.[16]

---

14 On the *Brut*'s prosody, see Moffat, "Intonational"; Allen, "Nv Seið."

15 Hanna, "Alliterative Poetry," 492.

16 Lawton, "Gaytryge's Sermon," "Unity," "Middle English Unrhymed," "Idea." See also Ian Cornelius's work on the *ars dictaminis*, e.g., "Rhetoric."

But if Laȝamon and Langland are not connected by the mere fact that alliteration occurs in their poems, the two authors do both participate in the same mode of English sententious formalism, which has its origins in the writings of the Anglo-Saxon era. The authors employ their formal strategies with the specific aim of critiquing the secular governments of their day, and especially of critiquing the refusal of those governments to submit to ecclesiastical moral authority. Because Anglo-Saxon legal-homiletic discourse was generally preserved by local ecclesiastical institutions in conflict with expanding secular authorities, ecclesiastical moral authority came to be modelled by both authors as a local, traditional kind of law, which saw itself in conflict with a rapacious and invasive secular authority indifferent to legal precedent. All of the texts discussed in the remaining chapters of this book operate within this same symbolic framework, and their disparate alliterative metres constitute different efforts at different times to renovate the forms of traditional law to authorize their historical and political claims.

In this chapter, I will look at *The First Worcester Fragment* and *The Proverbs of Alfred.* In these two alliterative English poems, the older sententious formalism of Anglo-Saxon law is reborn as a literary mode that operated within vernacular English writing. This mode abandoned the more specific legal claims that sententious formalism previously authorized – for example, that Malmesbury Abbey owned Wootton, or that Cnut should punish breaches of *cyricgrið* – to function more self-reflexively, claiming merely that alliterative and/or antiquated English writing continued to sound true. This claim is implicitly political: if Anglo-Saxon legal forms remained viable, then by implication the reformed bureaucratic practices of more recent vintage were unnecessary and even harmful. Hence each of the texts studied here encodes its own critique of institutional novelty, and for this reason they are important forebears of the homiletic alliterative satire of the *Piers Plowman* tradition.

The First Worcester Fragment

The First Worcester Fragment survives in a unique manuscript, copied by the Tremulous Hand of Worcester, alluded to above. This scribe is so called because he seems to have had a degenerative condition, so that his later letterforms are more erratically composed than the earlier ones. As Christine Franzen has demonstrated in her classic study of the Tremulous Hand, the changes in the glosses allow us to chart one scribe's evolution as a scholar of Old English literature, and to hypothesize about the familiarity of earlier written English dialects to his community of thirteenth-century readers.[17] Franzen speculates that the Tremulous Hand annotated Old English manuscripts in order to prepare a vernacular "handbook for priests, or a collection of homilies for their use."[18] This possible goal reminds us that the glosses need not reflect the Tremulous Hand scribe's own ability to understand the text, but only his presuppositions about what would work best for his intended purpose of reaching an audience that was not composed of legal specialists.[19] Franzen herself identifies glosses made purely on the basis of interest (as the scribe is not likely to have glossed the word *englisc* because he found its meaning difficult to understand), and she observes that it is difficult to distinguish between words glossed for interest and words glossed because they were unintelligible in the Tremulous Hand's dialect.[20]

Certainly in his few glosses of Wulfstan's Old English law codes, the Tremulous Hand provides us with some evidence that the contents of the texts were not overly difficult for him to understand. Three Tremulous Hand glosses appear in the Wulfstan law manuscript London, British Library, Harley 55.[21] In one, the Tremulous Hand glosses the Old English *ðolige* as *perdat* ("let him lose"), a word choice corresponding to the legal meaning of the term, and corresponding also to the *Quadripartitus* translation of it at *II Cn* 61. Meanwhile, the term *ðolian* also appears in the Tremulous Hand's transcription of Ælfric's *Grammar*, where it translates the more abstract Latin *carere*, meaning either "to lack" or "to absent oneself."[22] The verb *tholen* also persists in Middle English, where it continues to have both the specialized legal meaning and the more general meaning (*MED* s.v. *tholen*). Thus to the extent that the scant glosses tell us anything about the Tremulous Hand's ability and interests, they suggest that the scribe was able to understand the text well enough to know that the legally precise meaning of *ðolian* was appropriate in the law code, and that a Middle English speaker having difficulty with the text might accidentally read the word in its more common sense of suffering or doing without.

---

17 Franzen, *Tremulous Hand*.

18 Franzen, *Tremulous Hand*, 193.

19 The preaching focus of the Tremulous Hand is also discussed by Collier, "Tremulous Worcester Hand."

20 Franzen, *Tremulous Hand*, 141–2.

21 *MoEL*, 188; Franzen, *Tremulous Hand*, 70.

22 OE Corpus, accessed 5 March 2009.

The First Worcester Fragment is one of the few complete works copied by the Tremulous Hand of Worcester. The poem uses a loose, two-stress homiletic prosody reminiscent of Wulfstan's homilies. Its manuscript also includes Ælfric's *Grammar* and *Glossary* (the last of the sixteen known witnesses of this earliest Latin grammar in a European vernacular) and a didactic *Soul's Address to the Body*.[23] Franzen speculates that the manuscript might have been produced by the Tremulous Hand to teach both Latin and Old English together, in an apparent effort to renew the educational program codified during the Benedictine Reform.[24] Though these efforts apparently failed, they nonetheless anticipate subsequent efforts by vernacular poets to renovate Old English legal-homiletic forms as an authoritative discourse of political critique.

S.K. Brehe has characterized *The First Worcester Fragment* as evidence "that the English viewed the cultural rupture they suffered after the Norman Conquest as a spiritual loss."[25] This "cultural rupture" appears to be specifically the result of a decline in Old English literacy in ecclesiastical institutions. Christopher Cannon has pointed out that the poem need not refer to the Norman Conquest as a cause of this decline, as Anglo-Saxon England had experienced cultural rupture caused by wave after wave of Danish invasion long before 1066.[26] I would go further than Cannon, and add that foreign invaders need not have created the rupture at all. As I discussed in the last chapter, "lawbreaker" and "heathen" are overlapping categories in Anglo-Saxon jurisprudence. If you did not follow the laws that were the basis of English identity, you no longer participated in that identity. And so the cultural rupture in *The First Worcester Fragment* can also be attributed to native Englishmen, who did not sufficiently respect the wisdom passed down to them by their ancestors.

Indeed, given the similarity of the poem's lament to many other similar laments witnessed in Old English literature, one may even argue that the speaker's complaints about the ignorance and sinfulness of his

---

23 Worcester, Worcester Cathedral MS F.174, f. 63r; for a full summary of contents, see: Ker, *Catalogue* 398, 466–7. On Ælfric's grammar, see Law, *Grammars*, 200–3; J. Hill, "Grammatical Tradition."

24 Franzen, *Tremulous Hand*, 84–5; on English and Latin study in the later Anglo-Saxon period, see Chapman, "Uterque Lingua." A thorough survey of linguistic change as represented in these texts, presumably copied from an Old English exemplar, is Moffat, *Worcester Fragments*.

25 Brehe, "*First Worcester Fragment*," 535.

26 Cannon, *Grounds*, 38–9. For a critique of this argument from another angle, see Treharne, *Living Before Conquest*, 95–6.

contemporaries are themselves evidence that the rupture imagined by Cannon need not have been terribly severe. The commonplace in the poem's final lines is widely paralleled in Old English, resembling not only the *Sermo Lupi* but the works of virtually every Anglo-Saxon author since King Alfred:

> [Nu is] þeo leore forleten.   and þet folc is forloren.
> Nu beoþ oþre leoden   þeo læreþ ure folc,
> and feole of þen lorþeines losiæþ   and þet folc forþ mid. (17–19)[27]

> [Now is that learning abandoned and that people [*folc*] lost.
> Now there is another people / language [*leoden*] that teaches our folc,
> And many of the teachers dead and those folc with them.]

Among the most striking aural features of this passage is its threefold repetition of the word *folc* to refer to the people who have suffered because this learning has been abandoned. These folk are contrasted with the new *leoden* who have taken over, and who do not teach what they ought. *Leoden*, of course, could be "language" (as it may also be in the poem's lines 3 and 9, quoted below), in which case the lament would best be read as a post-Conquest reference to the French language that has replaced Old English.[28] However, the context is ambiguous, and in particular line 9's phrase "ilærde ure leoden on Englisc" uses *leoden* more specifically in the sense of "people" or "nation." But if we cannot assign a specific meaning to the term *leoden* in line 18, it is not only because of the ambiguity of the word, but also because the offending people are given no cultural identity at all. Whether Normans or Danes or the English themselves, these "other" people are criticized not for being foreign or even ignorant, but only for failing to teach *leore* to "our" folk. Certainly the different terms carry weak class connotations – OE *folc* can often imply specifically "common people," while *leod* means "nobleman" in some heroic poetry[29] – but there is no particular reason to align the *leoden* with a specifically Norman

---

27 All citations of the poem come from Brehe's reconstruction of the text, and follow his lineation: Brehe, "*First Worcester Fragment*," 530. Characters in square brackets are obscured by manuscript damage; the emendations are those proposed by Brehe.

28 See for example Tiller, *Brut*, 17–18.

29 On the class connotations of *folc*, see OED definition 2; on the class connotations of *leod*, see Klaeber, "Textual Notes," 130.

aristocracy and the *folc* with a specifically Saxon peasantry. The passage need not refer to a conquered nation, but only a mismanaged one.

Leading us further from the theme of conquest is the implicitly religious nature of the lost lore. Seth Lerer notes that the components of the unique compound *lor-þeines* ("teachers") are synonyms for the components of the common compound *leorning-cnihtas* ("students"), but he does not point out that in the Old English translations of the Gospel, the latter term referred specifically to the disciples.[30] ME "thein" on its own is similarly defined as "apostle" in MED definition 2.c., and according to the sample quotations in the entry, this meaning of the term is particularly prominent in early vernacular homilies. In other words. these "teachers" clearly exercise spiritual and even episcopal authority. Hence while the "other" *leoden* who have forgotten their *leore* may or may not be foreign, they are certainly irreligious.

To return to Brehe's argument, then, perhaps the "spiritual loss" lamented in the poem is not so much a "cultural" rupture as it is an institutional one. Again, law codes were among the most commonly circulated and read Old English texts in the post-Conquest period, and manuscripts like the *Textus Roffensis* were compiled specifically to protect church property from spoliation. In contrast, as I have said in chapter 1, Ranulf de Glanvill's codification of English common law appears to have been undertaken with the specific aim of invalidating Anglo-Saxon legal precedent. Whether foreign or not, then, the "other" *leoden* who have hidden tradition from the *folc* are innovators, and the most obvious "spiritual" consequence of their abandonment of English learning was the diminishment of ecclesiastical legal authority.

This more specific and political implication of the poem's lament is strongly indicated by the specific examples of teachers it evokes. The first two are Bede and Ælfric:

Sanctus Beda was iboren   her on Breotene mid us,
And he wisliche   [bec] awende
Þet þeo Englise leoden   þurh weren ilerde.
And he þeo c[not]ten unwreih,   þe questiuns hoteþ,
Þa derne diȝelnesse   þe de[or]wurþe is.
Ælfric abood,   þe we Alquin hoteþ,

---

30 See, e.g., Ælfric's translation of the Latin *discipulos* as *leorningcnihtas*: *Catholic Homilies*, ed. Godden, 223, ll. 55–60.

he was bocare,   and þe [fif] bec wende:
Genesis, Exodus, Leuiticus,   Numerus, Vtronomius.
Þu[rh] þeos were ilærde   ure leoden on Englisc. (1–9)

[Saint Bede was born here with us in Britain,
And he wisely translated books
Through which the English nation/language [*leoden*] was taught.
And he untied the knots that are called Questions,
That hidden secret which is precious.
Ælfric abode, whom we call Alcuin,
He was a learned man, and translated the five books:
Genesis, Exodus, Leviticus, Numbers, Deuteronomy.
Through these our people [*leoden*] were taught in English.]

If the "Questions" of Bede refers to a specific work, it is almost certainly his *Thirty Questions on the Book of Kings*, though the potentially misattributed *On Eight Questions* is another possibility.[31] This sententious work is referred to in several of its manuscripts as *parabolas Salomonis*, or "the proverbs of Solomon," and this association with sacred history's wisest king is clearly implied by line 4–5's description of Bede's work "untying the knots" to arrive at a "hidden secret."[32] In other words, the opening lines suggest that the poet is less concerned with specifically English-language learning than he is with a kind of sententious wisdom he attributes to great English scholars.

Of course the poem's next example of a teacher, Ælfric, is identified specifically as an important vernacular author, as is exemplified by the Old English translations of the Old Testament cited by the poem. However, the juxtaposition of these texts with Bede's *Thirty Questions on the Book of Kings* places greater emphasis on Ælfric's adaptation of Old Testament wisdom to an Anglo-Saxon context. This subject matter has clear political implications. Indeed, the Pentateuch's Mosaic law is explicitly cited as an important precedent in the preface of Alfred's law code.[33] The apparent confusion of Ælfric with Alcuin in line 6 further underscores the specifically political nature of his translated wisdom. As Brehe argues, the poet is probably using an honorific to distinguish the translator of Alcuin from

---

31 On both texts, see Bede, *Biblical Miscellany*.
32 King and Lainster, *Handlist*, 62.
33 For further discussion of Alfred's laws and their preface, see *MoEL*, 265–86; Stanley, "Laws of King Alfred." On Ælfric's translation of the Heptateuch, see Marsden, *Text*, 402–6.

other Ælfrics.[34] This honorific ties Ælfric, the author of the grammar appearing in the same manuscript as the poem, to another grammarian who was also one of the premier *þeodwitan* of Charlemagne's court. Ælfric "Alcuin" and Bede are therefore cited as authors of teachable texts in English and Latin that emphasize the important political role that the church ought to play in Christian kingdoms, and particularly England.

Already, then, we can see that the central lament of the *The First Worcester Fragment* contains a certain irony. The speaker claims that the learning of Bede and Ælfric has been abandoned, even as he demonstrates through his own citation of their works that in fact he knows the authors quite well. Not all of the *lorþeines* are dead; at least one is still around. The speaker's own authority on these matters is reiterated further in a list of bishop-saints:

> Þet weren þeos biscop[es]   [þe] bodeden Cristendom,
> Wilfrid of Ripum,   Iohan of Beoferlai,
> Cuþb[ert] of Dunholme,   Oswald of Wireceastre,
> Egwin of Heoueshame,   Æld[elm] of Malmesburi,
> Swiþþun, Æþelwold   Aidan, Biern of Wincæastre,
> [Pau]lin of Rofecæastre,   Dunston and Ælfeih of Cantoreburi. (10–16)

> [These were the bishops that taught Christendom,
> Wilfrid of Ripon, John of Beverley,
> Cuthbert of Durham, Oswald of Worcester,
> Ecgwine of Evesham, Aldhelm of Malmesbury,
> Swiþun, Æthelwold, Aidan, Birinus of Winchester,
> Paulinus of Rochester, Dunstan and Ælfheah of Canterbury.]

This list is geographically ordered and resembles many contemporary lists of Old English saints' resting-places.[35] Eight of the thirteen had, at some point in their career, occupied positions in the immediate vicinity of York (Wilfrid of Ripon, John of Beverley, Cuthbert of Durham, Aidan, Birinus of Winchester, Paulinus of Rochester), Worcester (Ecgwine of Evesham and Dunstan of Canterbury), or both (St Oswald).[36] Again, Worcester and

---

34 Brehe, "*First Worcester Fragment*," 531.

35 Brehe, "*First Worcester Fragment*," 532–3.

36 Though Dunstan was most famous for being archbishop of Canterbury, he was previously bishop of Worcester, from 958–9: *Dictionary of National Bibliography On-line*, accessed 4 February 2014.

York were sees occupied in plurality by Archbishop Wulfstan. Hence the poem's survey of Anglo-Saxon teachers is concentrated in particular on the sainted churchmen who were particularly venerated in dioceses once governed by a man who did more than anyone to preserve English-language law, and whose legacy includes the Worcester archive that preserved a remarkable number of early English laws, documents, and literary texts – including *The First Worcester Fragment* itself.

The five saints in the list who are not affiliated with York and Worcester suggest that the compiler of the list tended to choose saints who were associated both with major works of Anglo-Saxon literature and with the protection of "God's rights." As was discussed in chapter 1, Aldhelm was an influential author in his own right, whom William of Malmesbury claims to have been a vernacular poet. Lives of Sts Æthelwold and Swiþun are attributed to Wulfstan "Cantor" of Winchester, an accomplished and widely read Anglo-Latin author. [37] Æthelwold was also responsible for translating the relics of Swiþun and Birinus to Winchester, and hence the two saints are associated with his cult. Further, the cults of Birinus, Aldhelm, Swiþun, and Æthelwold are each affiliated with the foundations of ecclesiastical institutions: Birinus founded Winchester, Swiþun was the patron of Winchester Cathedral, Aldhelm is sometimes called founder of Malmesbury,[38] and Æthelwold was, with Dunstan, a major architect of the Benedictine Reform who refounded institutions such as New Minster by delivering them from the Augustinians and into the hands of Benedictines.

The final and most frequently discussed saint in the list is Ælfheah of Canterbury, cited along with Æthelwold in Ælfric's preface to the *Catholic Homilies* as an instigator of that major work,[39] and (as alluded to in chapter 1) a co-instigator with Wulfstan of the meeting of the *witan* that resulted in the law code *VI Æthelred*.[40] Another important vernacular reference to Ælfheah appears in the E version of *Anglo-Saxon Chronicle*, which says that he was murdered in 1012 by Viking raiders for his refusal to be ransomed.[41] I would argue that the inclusion of Ælfheah in *The First Worcester Fragment* is misread if it is assumed that the archbishop personified an ideal loyalty to English ethnic identity. After all, the ransom that would have paid for Ælfheah was a "Danegeld," a term that later came to

---

37 Lapidge and Winterbottom ed., *St. Aethelwold*; Lapidge et al., *The Cult of St. Swithun*.
38 *Malmesbury*, ed. Kelly, 1–5.
39 *Catholic Homilies* I, ed. Clemoes, 174, ll. 44–8.
40 See chapter 1 (25).
41 *Anglo-Saxon Chronicle E*, ed. Irvine; Cannon, *Grounds*, 39.

describe a national tax levied by the king (e.g., at *LHP* 15.1). The refusal to pay such a "ransom" is therefore more broadly symbolic of the archbishop's rejection of overweening secular authority. Hence, perhaps, the legend that Thomas à Becket prayed to Ælfheah just before his own murder by Henry II's knights.[42] But though the citation of St Ælfheah may have had this specifically anti-royal resonance, in the context of the poem's list, the saint is only one among several highly successful administrators of ecclesiastical institutions. Indeed, Ælfheah may only have warranted mention because of his brave refusal to authorize unnecessary expenditures. Hence the saints listed in *The First Worcester Fragment* appear to have been selected in part for their local interest in Worcester and York, in part for their aptitude as administrators, and in part for their interest to students of Anglo-Saxon literature in Latin and Old English. Where Bede and Ælfric merely adapted the texts of Old Testament law for an Anglo-Saxon readership, the thirteen Anglo-Saxon saints put that law into practice.

A final aspect of this list that reveals its debt to Anglo-Saxon legal-homiletic discourse is its very form as a catalogue. Lists of saints are highly conventional and widely attested in the manuscript record throughout the medieval period. The Old English list that most closely parallels *The First Worcester Fragment* appears in the Wulfstan manuscript Corpus 201, a parallel that may indicate the poet's direct knowledge of Wulfstan's writing.[43] Indeed, since Corpus 201 contains both an excerpt from Ælfric's translation of Genesis (chapters 37 to 47) and also Bede's poem *De die iudicii*, the manuscript is a remarkably apt example of the tradition whose loss the fragment laments.[44] I have observed in chapter 2 that alliterative catalogues are commonly employed in Old English legal writing, and that they appeared to have served the particular legal function of demarcating specific territories. Similarly, it appears that the saints listed in *The First Worcester Fragment* inscribe the rights of the church over the jurisdiction of England, as authorized by its employment of a formula derived from English *folclagu* itself. By repeating the list, the poet therefore suggests not only that he is a learned reader of English-language texts, but also that he has a specialist's knowledge of important English ecclesiastical institutions.

---

42 First recorded in William Fitzstephen's *Life and Death of Thomas Beckett*: see *Materials for the History of Thomas Beckett*, ed. Robertson, III, 141.
43 Brehe, "*First Worcester Fragment*," 532.
44 On Corpus 201, see chapter 2 (63, 72–4).

In addition to its symbolic function, the list may even have had a practical mnemonic function in legal contexts. One scrap of evidence to this effect is found in the Wulfstanian law fragment *Norðhymbra grið*,[45] appended to the treatise *Grið* in the Wulfstan manuscript Nero A.I. *Grið* itself contains a lament for the decline of English learning parallel to *The First Worcester Fragment*, in its complaint that "some men" do not listen to the bishops that would teach them the law.[46] In *Norðhymbra grið* Wilfrid of Ripon and John of Beverley are cited in rhythmic apposition, in a poetic breaking of the syntactic flow of the sentence: "on Norðhymbra lage is sanctus Petrus [cyric]frið ꞇ *sanctus Wilfriðus* ꞇ *sanctus Iohannes* binnan ciricwagum þreo hundred æt cwicum men, ꞇ æt deadum botleas" (In Northumbrian law, the penalty for violating the church peace [*cyricfrið*] within the church walls of Saint Peter, Saint Wilfrid and Saint John is three hundred for living men, and unpardonable for the dead) (my emphasis).[47] In this context, the saints are named to designate a legal jurisdiction, which has its own particular way of dealing with the violations of *cyricgrið* that were such a major preoccupation of Wulfstan. In post-Conquest England, then, John and Wilfrid are worth remembering not only because they provide a moral example for Christian living, but also because their names denote meaningful political entities that enforce their own traditional laws.

The popularity of saint lists between the twelfth and fourteenth centuries and their continued association with legal texts – from the *Textus Roffensis* to the updated, fourteenth-century version of Nero A.I's list appearing in a Breviate of the Domesday Book – suggests that if the lists had such a mnemonic jurisdictional function, it survived the Norman Conquest by centuries.[48] Certainly the later survival of these lists reinforces the irony of the poem, that its lament for the loss of a literary tradition is in fact a sign that the tradition was not lost at all. Indeed, laments for the decline of English literacy are among the oldest genre of English literature, beginning with the works of King Alfred himself. But if Old English had not truly disappeared, it certainly had lost its procedural relevance as a basis for practising law.

---

45 *MoEL*, 394–5. Fowler identifies *Norðhymbra grið* as a work written by Wulfstan, but his arguments have been disputed by Wormald and Pons-Sanz: Wulfstan, *Canons of Edgar*, ed. Fowler; *MoEL*, 208–9, 396–7; Pons-Sanz, *Norse-Derived*, 16–17; Treharne, *Living Through Conquest*, 119.

46 *Grið* 21; *MoEL* 457.

47 *Norðhymbra grið* 1–5: *Gesetze* I:473.

48 Blair, "Local Cults," 465. Another tradition that may contain echoes of this list is the *South English Legendary* (*SEL*); see chapter 5 (158–9).

In the next section I will turn to another memorial of Anglo-Saxon legal-homiletic discourse, *The Proverbs of Alfred*. Like *The First Worcester Fragment*, this poem applies the forms of Anglo-Saxon legal-homiletic discourse to make fairly broad claims about the wisdom of English historical figures. In particular, *The Proverbs of Alfred* applies the narrative structure of the law code to organize a catalogue of sententious statements. Nonetheless, the particular maxims chosen indicate that the clerical refiguration of English traditional wisdom had taken hold in English poetry, as the figure of Alfred in the poem looks less like an Anglo-Norman king than he looks like a Wulfstanian bishop.

The Proverbs of Alfred, MS Oxford, Jesus College 29

The poem *The Proverbs of Alfred* survives in four independent recensions.[49] Of these, the most important here is the version found in Oxford, Jesus College 29, a late thirteenth-century manuscript that also witnesses the brief alliterative lyric *On Serving Christ*, and also *The Owl and the Nightingale*. *The Owl and the Nightingale* in turn shares a manuscript with Laȝamon's *Brut* (London, British Library, Cotton Caligula A.IX), and *The Proverbs of Alfred* also resembles the *Brut* in its loose stressed metre, which recalls Old English verse; hence by association, it seems that the two texts both derive from the same textual community.[50] Though the provenance of the original poem is undetermined, J's language shows signs of originating in the Worcester region.[51] Thus I will focus primarily on the J-text of *The Proverbs of Alfred* because it is the most representative of Worcester's vernacular readership in the century after the Tremulous Hand of Worcester, and hence it makes the best point of comparison to *The First Worcester Fragment* and the *Brut*.

Like any proverb collection, *The Proverbs of Alfred* is a difficult text to date and its sources are difficult to identify. Some of the poem's proverbs appear to derive from Old Testament wisdom and from the *Disticha Catonis*, but these texts are widely taught and widely cited throughout the Middle Ages.[52] Nonetheless, the attribution of the text to Alfred and its English language, alliterative form both strongly suggest that the text is connected to the large corpus of proverb collections in Old English poetry.

---

49 *Proverbs*, ed. Arngart, I.
50 On the metre of *The Proverbs of Alfred*, see Minkova, "Credibility."
51 *Proverbs of Alfred*, ed. Arngart, II:37–8.
52 Cox, "Old English Dicts"; Mann, "He Knew Nat Catoun"; Baer, "Cato's Trace"; Brunner, "Distichs."

Some context for assessing the influence of Old English proverb literature on *The Proverbs of Alfred* is provided by the Old English *Dicts of Cato*. These translations appear in three post-Conquest manuscripts, and modify the text to emphasize the "spiritual and intellectual" over the "temporal and practical," an attribute of the collection that suggests to Elaine Treharne that the intended audience of the texts was monastic.[53] The earliest copy of the Old English *Dicts of Cato*, in Cambridge, Trinity College R.9.17 (c. 1100), is preceded by a copy of Ælfric's *Grammar*, and followed by a brief tract on the importance of hierarchy in government; thus the manuscript in general appears directed towards "an audience that is interested in acquiring a sense of political know-how."[54] Already, then, it seems that Old English proverb collections were affiliated with both vernacular education and practical legal knowledge in twelfth-century monastic contexts. *The Proverbs of Alfred* shows signs of similar affiliations.

The other two manuscripts of the Old English *Dicts of Cato*, London, British Library, Cotton Julius A.II and Cotton Vespasian A.XIV, appear to be directed towards contemplative religious and preaching audiences, respectively.[55] The latter manuscript also includes a poem in Wulfstan's honour, which appears (like the legal and homiletic manuscript Nero A.I) to be glossed in Wulfstan's own hand.[56] Hence Worcester in particular was a place where Old English proverb collections were continuously studied after the Norman Conquest alongside more obviously "legal" texts. This manuscript context also provides us with a basis for connecting the formal, alliterative list of self-evident truths in *The Proverbs of Alfred* to the alliterative catalogue of bishops in *The First Worcester Fragment*. In both cases the catalogue flaunts the speaker's knowledge of the kinds of wisdom stored by Old English literary and documentary traditions.[57] Alfred is revealed to be wise not only by the wisdom of his individual proverbs, but also by the fitness of the catalogue he uses to organize them.

The self-conscious form of *The Proverbs of Alfred* is most clearly revealed in the poem's introduction, which is the section of the text that changes the least in its various recensions. All versions of the poem begin with a description of Alfred surrounded by his advisors. The preface of *I–II Cnut* is markedly similar and provides a helpful point of comparison:

---

53 Treharne, "Form and Function," 471–2.
54 Treharne, "Form and Function," 475.
55 Treharne, "Form and Function," 476–8.
56 Ker, "Handwriting."
57 Jackson, "'Not Simply Lists,'" 339.

I Cnut, "Prologue": Ðis is seo geræednys, þe Cnut ciningc, ealles Englalandes ciningc ⁊ Dena cining mid his witena geþeaht geræedde, Gode to lofe ⁊ him sylfum to cynescipe ⁊ to þearfe; ⁊ þæt wæs on ðæere halgan midwintres tide on Winceastre.

[This is the geræednys that King Cnut, king of all England and king of Danes, determined with the advice of his counsellors, for the glory of God and for his own royal power and need; and this took place during the holy midwinter season at Winchester.]

In *The Proverbs of Alfred*, we are told that Alfred is surrounded by his advisors, including "fele Biscopes / and feole bok-ilered / Eorles prute" (many bishops and many proud Earls, taught by books) (3–5).[58] Alfred is "of þare lawe swiþe wis" (very learned in the law) (8), and for that reason he is characterized as a "hurde" (10) or shepherd. Like Cnut's *witan*, this assembly is situated in a particular geographic locale, in Alfred's case Seaford.[59] The term "shepherd" and the emphasis on the bishops draw attention to the poem's episcopal model of kingship that the *Proverbs of Alfred* will espouse.[60] Such is reinforced when Alfred is said to be both a king and a clerk (19) and to be "wis on his word / And war on his werke" (wise in his words and knowledgeable in his work) (21–2).[61] This emphasis on Alfred's thoughts, words, and deeds repeats the same formulaic trope used by Wulfstan and Ælfric to describe the authority of their own clerical training.

Once Alfred's authority is established, Alfred begins with a command to love and worship God over all things (25–60). He begins: "wolde ye mi leode / lusten eure louerde" (Would that you, my people, obey your lord) (27–8). Alfred seems to imply that he wishes his people to obey him, until he goes on to explain that he is not himself the "lord" he's referring to: "þat ye alle a-drede / vre dryhten crist / luuyen hine and lykyen" (so that

---

58 All citations from *The Proverbs of Alfred* come from Arngart's appendix, which presents the J-text individually: *Proverbs*, ed. Arngart, 2:135–50.

59 On the location of Seaford see *Proverbs*, ed. Arngart, 1:15–19; Rouse, *Idea*, 16–18, 31–2. Though Arngart discounts Borgström's identification of the poem's *Seuorde* as Shifford in Oxfordshire, the possibility is worth citing, because it would place *The Proverbs of Alfred* in the same vicinity as the original performance of the law code *Cnut 1018*, as was recorded in the Worcester version of the *Anglo-Saxon Chronicle*: see chapter 1 (35–6).

60 For example, Wulfstan refers to bishops as shepherds in *I Cn* 26.3.

61 Rouse, *Idea*, 20; Crépin, "Mentalités," 57.

you all honour our lord Christ, praise and worship him) (41–3). A similar command to praise God is expressed in *I Cn* 1.1:

> *I Cn* 1.1: Ðæt is þonne ærest þæt hi ofer ealle oþre þingc ænne God æfre woldan lufian ꝺ wurðian ꝺ ænne Cristendom anrædlice healdan, and Cnut Cingc lufian mid rihtan getrywþan.

> [Firstly, that over all other things, they forever love and worship one God, and persistently hold one Christendom, and love king Cnut with appropriate faithfulness.]

Again, the love and worship of the lord God is linked to the love and worship of the secular lord. In both texts, the assertion of this basic Christian precept establishes the authority of the speaker, both because he is himself a secular lord, and because he knows his place in the divine political order.

The parallel to *I Cnut* continues in lines 72–97. The proverb stipulates that "lawelyche" (77) or "lawful" behaviour is required of both knights and the clergy, and in particular the knights are charged "For to werie þat londe / Wiþ hunger and wiþ heriunge / Þat þe chireche habbe gryþ / And þe cheorl beo in fryþ" (to protect that land from hunger and from devastation, so that the church should have protection and the peasant live in peace) (88–91). This statement of knightly duty echoes the parallelism of *grið / frið* in *I Cn* 2: "And Godes cyrican griðian ꝺ friðian ꝺ gelomlice secean saulum to hæle ꝺ us sylfum to þearfe" (And maintain peace and protect and frequently provide for God's church, for the health of the soul and the need of ourselves). Given the pride of place occupied by the Cnut codes in the post-Conquest study of English law, the parallel appearances of *grið* and *frið* here suggests that the opening lines of *The Proverbs of Alfred* may well have been based directly or indirectly on some version of the *I Cnut* prologue. At the very least, the poem holds quite closely to the formal conventions of Old English legislation, and it therefore represents Alfred's pronouncement of proverbs as a spectacle of lawgiving analogous to the lawgiving practices of actual Anglo-Saxon kings.

In between these parallels, from lines 60 and 71, *The Proverbs of Alfred* discusses the importance of kingly literacy. We are told that no king may be "ryhtwis" unless "he beo / In boke ilered; / And he his wyttes / Swiþþe wel kunne" (he is learned in books, and masters his senses very well). The former skill gives him the latter quality, as consulting books will tell him "How he schule his lond / Laweliche holde" (how he should lawfully hold his land) (63–71). This statement makes explicit the rhetorical effect of Alfred's adherence to the conventional opening of an Anglo-Saxon law code. Alfred's familiarity with the conventions of written Old English law indicate that he has read Old English law, and hence that he is qualified to dispense wisdom. It is striking, then, that he does not proceed to pronounce on legal matters, but simply gives generally applicable advice about living a virtuous life. The addition reflects a difference in context: King Alfred addressing his *witan* in English no longer registers as a historical political authority making enforceable legal claims, but as a mythic figure speaking to more abstract truths. He is not only Solomon, but also Bede commenting on Solomon, to adapt the wisdom of Israel to the context of Anglo-Saxon England.

The political subtext of the poem is most clearly demonstrated by the misogynistic proverbs near the end of *The Proverbs of Alfred* (225–360). These provide an instructive parallel to the laws about marriage from *I–II Cnut* discussed in the last chapter.[62] In the law text, Wulfstan's discussions of sexual ethics encode an argument in favour of episcopal intervention in secular affairs. The audience of the code knows that Cnut is guilty of certain shortcomings, and hence the laws against those shortcomings imply that he will need the continued guidance of legal professionals like Wulfstan. In *The Proverbs of Alfred*, the king is not so concerned with the legality of various sexual practices, but rather with the wisdom of getting married in the first place. He particularly rejects the idea that a wife may serve as a trusted counsellor. For example, Alfred states: "Ne wurþ þu neuer so wod / ne so wyn-drunke / þat euere segge þine wife / all þine wille" (never become so crazy nor so drunk that you ever say all of your intention to your wife) (268–71). Note that this example of a familiar misogynistic trope employs a version of the thought / word / deed motif, with "wod" and "wyn-drunke" referring to thoughts, "segge" referring to words, and "wille" referring to intended actions. The sentiment is repeated shortly thereafter in even balder terms: "Evre þu bi þine lyve / Þe word of þine wyve / To swiþe þu ne arede" (While you are alive never be advised [*arede*] too quickly by the word of your wife) (319–21).

In *The Proverbs of Alfred* (and, as we shall see, in Laȝamon's *Brut* as well), the text's representation of wicked wives reflects a change in the status of the Anglo-Saxon legislator. Alfred's proverbial rejection of wifely advice – which moreover presents that advice as a parodic inversion of

---

62 Discussed in chapter 2 (86–8).

priestly and virtuous thoughts, words, and deeds – asserts the narrator's clerical authority over sexual matters, much as Wulfstan asserted his own in his laws about marriage. The correct use of the thought / word / deed commonplace in the poem not only describes ideal clerical wisdom, but also signals the wisdom of the clerical king that employs it. However, the very fact that Alfred must contrast his authority with that of a foolish wife marks a diminution of his influence. Alfred speaks not with the single, unified voice of the English law that Wulfstan is at least able to assume temporarily; he addresses his audience with the voice of one advisor among many, who must compete with them if his ideas are to be heard.

The precise nature of that advice is manifest in Alfred's various exhortations to young men. Young men should work hard so that they may rest when they are old (150–4), and they should leave any money that they have left to the church for the good of their souls (155–8). Men do not know how long they are going to live (160–78), they should not be proud of their wealth because it belongs to God (181–94), and in fact anyone who neglects his own soul for the sake of his wealth would be better off if he were never born (195–210). One does not have to read far between the lines of the poem to interpret Alfred's proverbs as an exhortation to secular lords to endow the church. According to these proverbs, men of middle age and older ought to give whatever wealth they have to the church and live out their final days in contemplation, whatever their wives may think of the idea, if they are to atone for the follies of their youth. The clerical king Alfred therefore serves not as a legal authority whose precedent must be obeyed, but as a pitchman who personifies the Church's ideal version of a righteous secular lord. Hence though the figure of the Anglo-Saxon lawgiver in *The Proverbs of Alfred* may have diminished in authority since Wulfstan's day, that authority's exhortations on behalf of the church have correspondingly become more explicit.

In the next chapter, I will continue my discussion of Anglo-Saxon legal-homiletic discourse in the thirteenth century with a reading of the alliterative *Brut* chronicle. Laȝamon's home at Areley Kings lay within the diocese of Worcester, a fact that has inspired much speculation about possible connections between the chronicle-poet and the Tremulous Hand scribe.[63] There is a good deal of circumstantial evidence that a priest like the one described in the introduction of the *Brut*, who called himself "Law man" and lived in the vicinity of Worcester, would have encountered Old

---

63 See Frankis, "Regional Context."

English literary culture through contact with its large and powerful community of monastic bureaucrats, for whom the continued use of that textual culture was identical to their right to self-governance. In the next chapter I will examine some of the evidence for this influence, and apply it to present a new reading of some of the text's more difficult aspects.

4 Laʒamon's *Brut*: Law, Literature, and the Chronicle-Poem

The thirteenth-century *Brut* is a poetic retelling of Geoffrey of Monmouth's legendary history of pre-Saxon Britain, the *Historia regum Britanniae*. The poem follows the Anglo-Norman *Roman de Brut* by Wace so closely it is essentially a translation, though Laʒamon appears to have used supplementary sources as well.[1] The *Brut* is of key importance to philologists and literary scholars as an unusually late witness of many Old English words and poetic conventions. As a result, studies of the poem have generally looked backwards to identify its origins in post-Conquest Old English literature.[2] In one such study, particularly relevant for the current discussion, Scott Kleinman shows how Laʒamon's Old English vernacular legal terminology may have derived in part from Wulfstan's writing.[3] The *Brut* also shares a strikingly similar confluence of themes, tropes, and formal qualities with Wulfstan's law codes and homilies, most obviously its two-beat metre, which makes a similarly omnivorous use of sound linkages to connect its half-lines. All of these aspects of the poem mark it as yet another effort to reinvent Anglo-Saxon legal-homiletic discourse for the Angevin era. In this chapter, I will argue that the *Brut* translates Wace's poem into an Old English legal-homiletic idiom in order to reinvest that idiom with historical authority.

My reading of the text builds on Daniel Donoghue's argument that the style and vocabulary of the *Brut* act "as a common middle term that never lets Laʒamon's contemporary reader forget that the role of victims has

---

1 For the full study of the sources of the *Brut*, see Le Saux, *Poem and Its Sources*.
2 For a recent survey of the Old English language in the *Brut* manuscripts, see England, "Two Manuscripts."
3 Kleinman, "Friŏ."

shifted from the Britons to the post-Conquest Anglo-Saxons and that the role of victors has shifted from the Anglo-Saxons to the Normans."[4] I will argue that the poem's style and vocabulary also have political implications for the institutions of English government, as the "victims" in the poem also allegorize those local ecclesiastical institutions founded in the Anglo-Saxon era, who had to contend with the Norman institutional reforms enacted by the monarchs and royal bureaucrats who occupied the "role of victors." As I have described in the previous chapters, Anglo-Saxon ecclesiastical institutions were particularly successful at preserving Old English poetry, homilies, and legal texts, and they did so precisely in order to maintain and invent exceptions for themselves under the Norman system of law. In the *Brut*, the text aims to reinvest the forms of (Anglo-Saxon) ecclesiastical charters and practices with an authority they had lost to the new forms of administrative practice implemented by the growing (Anglo-Norman) institutions of principality and aristocracy.

Following a recent trend in Laȝamon scholarship, then, I will focus not on the text's linguistic attributes, but rather on its historiographic intervention into the chronicle form.[5] In the process, I will tease out the legal implications of what Kenneth Tiller calls the poem's "layering" of different histories.[6] The complex, ambivalent, layered quality of the *translatio imperii* in Tiller's account of the *Brut* is best read as the poet's fundamentally pragmatic response to the state of the historical evidence documenting those changes. As in *The First Worcester Fragment* and *The Proverbs of Alfred*, the apparent nostalgia and vague sententiousness of the *Brut* in fact encodes a defence of local ecclesiastical institutions from the procedural innovations that had excluded English writing from legal discourse. More than those other poems, however, the *Brut* undertakes to reinvest the forms of English writing with historical authority.

Perhaps more than any other medieval genre, the chronicle exposes the limitations of literary criticisms that eschew questions of historical veracity, and historical analyses that eschew questions of literary authorship. Twelfth-century chronicles in particular are both the most highly developed literary productions and the richest sources of historical detail written in England during that period. They also first arose because ecclesiastical institutions needed to narrativize and maintain legal precedent if they were

---

4 Donoghue, "Ambivalence," 561.
5 See also Tiller, *Brut* and "Truth"; Galloway, "Gift"; Wickham-Crowley, *Writing*; Bryan, "Truth"; Le Saux, *Poem and Its Sources*; Rider, "Merlin"; Shichtman, "Gawain."
6 Tiller, *Brut*, 145.

to protect themselves from legal challenge.[7] This is reflected not only by their inclusion of legal documents, as in "Aldhelm's" charters from the *Gesta pontificum*, but also by the large section of the *Instituta Cnuti* that appears in version 5B of Henry of Huntingdon's *Historia Anglorum*, a text that was in turn one of Wace's sources for the *Roman de Brut*.[8] Hence while the *Brut* may register for modern readers as a poetic text recording a romance narrative, it is important to remember that generically speaking, the *Brut* is not far removed from its origins in institutional record-keeping.

In the more immediate background of the *Brut* is Geoffrey of Monmouth's explosive intervention into the chronicle genre, the *Historia regum Britanniae*. This text exploited the basic formal ambiguity of chronicles to narrate a past so distant that in it, "history joined hands with prophecy."[9] Geoffrey's vision of English history profoundly influenced the emergent secular traditions of English common and constitutional law, as it provided lay authorities with a more amenable narrative of national origin than an Anglo-Saxon history recorded in written laws and legal documents that endowed the Church with enormous power. In Francis Ingledew's words, Geoffrey's history is constructed from the alternate "social starting point" of "the institutions of principality and aristocracy, with their interests in an emergent sense of nation" – interests that were directly opposed to the interests of ancient ecclesiastical institutions, who generally claimed that they wished for things to stay as they were.[10]

The quasi-historical authority of Geoffrey's text helps to explain the "persistent slippage between romance thinking and the formulation of legal ideas" identified by Ralph Hanna in the centuries following the *Historia regum Britanniae*'s composition.[11] For example, Geoffrey's work was cited directly by Edward I as legal historical precedent, in the course of his argument that he had ancient rights to Scotland.[12] Even more

---

7 See chapter 1 (39–51).

8 O'Brien, "Legal Treatises," 188n.24; Liebermann, *Quadripartitus*, 105. A large portion of the "London Collection" revisions of *Quadripartitus* appears also in Roger of Howden's *Chronica*: Hanna, *London Literature*, 70–1; citing Plucknett, *Legislation*, 30 and *MoEL* 142, 430.

9 Southern, "Classical Tradition," 27.

10 Ingledew, "Book of Troy," 680. Le Saux lists the evidence that Laȝamon directly consulted the *Historia regum Brittanie* itself: Le Saux, *Poem and Its Sources*, 94–117.

11 Hanna, *London Literature*, 96.

12 For a helpful summary of the dispute and its implications for the connections between law and romance, see Hanna, *London Literature*, 89–91. See also Clanchy, *Memory to Written Record*, 154–5; Prestwich, "England and Scotland," 182–5.

strikingly, passages from Geoffrey's *Historia* made their way into the articles on London that appear in the *Magna Carta*, via the *Leges Anglorum* collection that was itself interpolated into the *Leges Edwardi Confessoris* alongside excerpts from *Quadripartitus*.[13] Despite the expectations of modern readers, then, the obviously legendary quality of Geoffrey's history did not exclude it from the legal realm of citable precedent. If the text was not quite historical enough to change the accepted narrative of English history, it was certainly enough to muddy the waters, and discredit contrary claims. Hence there is nothing in itself innovative about Laȝamon's decision to mix Old English legal forms with Anglo-Norman historical content. By the thirteenth century, the "true" record of Anglo-Saxon law and the "false" record of post-Norman invention had long since become indistinguishable.

This historiographic context will have important implications for my reading of the "ambivalence" of the *Brut*'s depiction of the Saxons. It has seemed strange to many readers that Laȝamon should use an Anglo-Saxon poetic idiom to tell a story in which the Saxons are the villains. But like Wulfstan's apparent ambivalence about the Danes, the apparent ambivalence in the *Brut* in fact reflects the text's legal theory of ethnic identity. As in Wulfstan's laws and homilies, it is clear throughout the *Brut* that the "folklaw" of England resides in the land, and therefore that "Englishness" adheres in obedience to that law and not ethnic origin. Foreign invasion is not only a punishment, but a consequence that naturally follows from inefficient stewardship of legal institutions that will always manage to reassert themselves. My reading of the Saxons in the *Brut* will demonstrate that the Saxons are precisely such inefficient stewards, who exploit their proximity to the monarchs Vortigern and Vortimer for their own profit. Such a representation of the Saxons need not reflect any ambivalence on the author's part about the ethnic origins of his own Anglo-Saxon legal-homiletic discourse; indeed, the poem's criticisms of overweening and greedy Saxons are wholly consistent with that discourse, as Anglo-Saxon princes and secular lords are likely to have been the intended audience of the many Old English texts criticizing overweening and greedy pagan princes.

In this chapter's second section, I will argue that the Saxons in the poem typify the secular lords and wicked women who have long been accused of falsely advising kings, and whose wicked counsel has long been contrasted in Anglo-Saxon legal-homiletic discourse with the learned counsel of

---

13 Musson, "Appealing to the Past," 169; Ullmann, "Influence of Geoffrey." On the *Leges Anglorum*, see Catto, "Andrew Horn," 386–7; *MoEL* 238.

bishops and educated men. Even if Hengest and Horsa introduced the poem's own English language and accompanying forms of legal practice to the island of Britain, they also hypocritically abused those forms, and for that reason they are subject to criticism. As I will demonstrate, Laȝamon's "ambivalence" about the origins of his "archaic" vernacular literacy is best explained as an innate distrust of legal innovation.[14] Again and again in the *Brut*, the Saxons introduce new cultural precedents so that they may take something that is not theirs. The text's criticism of the Saxons on the grounds of their hypocritical formalism marks it as a closer cousin to the satires of the *Piers Plowman* tradition than has ever been acknowledged.

I will conclude the chapter with a reading of the figure of the wicked queen Rowenna. Rowenna is both a pagan invader and a hypocritical abuser of formulaic oaths; she exemplifies the ways in which Laȝamon reworks Gildas's wisdom to make a point about procedural innovation. Rowenna's corruption of the "wassail" ceremony exemplifies the ways in which the Saxons employ formally correct signs of fealty to conceal their hypocritical and self-interested efforts to undermine the nation. Not only a pagan invader, the Saxon queen is also a type of the king or royal advisor whose misleading advice invited the foreign invasion in the first place.

The Lawman

There have been many efforts to find parallels between Laȝamon's metre and Old English metre since J.P. Oakden first noted the similarities in his formative survey of alliterative verse.[15] For example, Mark Amodio has identified several features of the *Brut* indicating the influence of a surviving oral-performative matrix.[16] Though many compounds in the *Brut* are extremely unusual in Middle English, they do not appear in either manuscript of the poem with anything close to the frequency of their survivals in the Old English corpus.[17] The paucity of compound words in the *Brut* has been acknowledged since Oakden, and Charlotte England is right to remind us that this fact in itself already compromises any arguments that the poem's "Old" English either reflects the poet's "antiquarian" sentiments or

---

14 On Laȝamon's "antiquarianism," see Stanley, "Antiquarian"; England, "*Brut*."

15 Oakden, *Alliterative Poetry*. For a comprehensive survey of this historiography, see Allen, "Loft-Songe," 251n.1. On the disappearance of classical Old English poetry after the Conquest, see O'Brien O'Keeffe, "Death and Transformations."

16 Amodio, *Oral Tradition*, 101–9, 113–28.

17 Compounds occur in 2.5 per cent of lines, as opposed to 33 per cent of lines in the Old English poetic corpus (Amodio, *Oral Tradition*, 103).

provides evidence of a continuous oral tradition of alliterative poetry.[18] Still, the compounds are numerous enough to suggest more knowledge of Old English literary conventions by thirteenth-century poets and scribes than we might otherwise have reason to expect.

To date, the attempts to identify parallels between Laȝamon's poetry and Old English literature have found themselves on the firmest ground in discussing the similarities between the *Brut* and the works of Ælfric, whose homilies are among the most common works of Old English literature found in post-Conquest manuscripts. One recent effort to establish continuity between the two is the concluding chapter of Thomas Bredehoft's *Early English Metre*.[19] But though Wulfstan's writing is not as consistently metrical as Ælfric's, Bredehoft's arguments nonetheless point the way towards a connection between Laȝamon and the archbishop. Building on the original hypothesis of N.F. Blake and the metrical analysis of Brehe, Bredehoft argues that the scansion of the *Brut* is not only a descendant of the "rhythmical prose" of Ælfric and Wulfstan, but also suggests first-hand knowledge of the poems of the *Anglo-Saxon Chronicle*.[20] For one thing, Wulfstan himself interpolated poems into the *Anglo-Saxon Chronicle*. For another, as Scott Smith has recently demonstrated, the *Anglo-Saxon Chronicle* is deeply concerned with what he calls "tenurial discourse," as it "incrementally records and affirms dynastic *anweald* over an expanding realm and its various peoples."[21] Needless to say, royal dominion is a subject that greatly concerned Wulfstan in his law codes. As we shall see, the thematic parallel extends to the *Brut* as well.

There are also some more local indications that Wulfstan's influence on the *Brut* might have exceeded the Ælfrician. Out of Jost's list of nineteen lexical preferences used to distinguish Wulfstan's style from Ælfric's, fifteen of the pairs involve words that appear in Laȝamon's *Brut*, so that the

---

18 Of 411 compounds in the *Brut*, 228 do not occur in Old English, and 200 of these are unique to Laȝamon in Old or Middle English: Oakden, *Alliterative Poetry*, 2:130. See also Le Saux, *Poem and Its Sources*, 192.

19 Bredehoft's larger argument, which asserts that common metrical rules govern late Anglo-Saxon verse, Ælfric's stressed prose, and Laȝamon's metre, has not found wide acceptance; see for example the reviews by Cable (*JEGP* 107, no. 3) and Minkova (*Speculum* 83, no. 3).

20 Blake, "Rhythmical Alliteration"; S.K.Brehe, "'Rhythmical Alliteration'." See also McIntosh, "Alliterative Verse," 26, and "Wulfstan's Prose," 130n.11; Turville-Petre, *Alliterative Revival*, 8; Salter, "Alliterative Revival," 56–7.

21 Smith, *Land and Book*, 152–89, quoting 153. See also his discussion of vernacular documents narrativising dispute resolution: 70–107.

similarities of usage can be assessed.[22] As Table 1 indicates, my count indicates that the preponderance of word use in the Caligula *Brut* follows Wulfstan's preference over Ælfric's in ten of the fifteen indicators, goes against Wulfstan in three, and shows no clear preference in two.

Table 1

Wulfstanian (# in Brut)	Preference	Ælfrician (# in Brut)
dryhten (20+)	>	hælend (1)
gebeorgan, gemiltsian (4)	>	arian (0)
gebetan (4)	>	cennan, acennan (1)
lagu (20+)	>	æ (2)
gesælig (6)	>	eadig (3)
gecnawan (8)	>	oncnawan, tocnawan (0)
gegenge (14)	>	þreat, heap (5)
lac (2)	>	onsægdness (0)
geþolian (5)	>	forberan (0)
synn, misdæd, gewhyt (20+)	>	gylt (4)
werian (7)	<	gescyldan (9)
namian (12)	<	hihtan (20+)
tallian (2)	<	tellan (20+)
aginnan, onginnan (6)	=	beginnan (5)
gesamnian (20+)	=	gegaderian (20+)

Like Laȝamon, Wulfstan's rate of compounding is extremely low; like Wulfstan, Laȝamon shows a preference for doublets over compound words. Both authors have a small active vocabulary, especially considering their penchant for unusual words.[23] And whatever his knowledge of Ælfric

---

22 Jost, *Wulfstanstudien*, 155–7; Dance, "Sound," 43–5.

23 By turning a .TXT file of the Caligula-text (downloaded from University of Virginia Electronic Text Center, 14 September 2006) into a word list and eliminating exact repetitions, I have identified 10,236 individual words in the Caligula *Brut*. Presuming that two out of three of these words are different forms, variant spellings, or proper names (a conservative estimate on the basis of my samplings), then Laȝamon's active vocabulary includes roughly 3,400 individual headwords. Orchard and Dance put Wulfstan's vocabulary in the vicinity of 2,000: Dance, "Sound"; Orchard, "Wulfstan as Reader," 321.

might have been, Laȝamon never uses the Ælfrician word *gelaþung* in his many references to churches, though he uses dozens of words that are at least as obscure in Middle English. The non-occurrence of this word in Wulfstan's homilies is also a key distinguisher between his style and Ælfric's.[24]

Though this evidence contradicts the idea that Ælfric is Laȝamon's primary source for Old English words, it does not therefore suggest that Laȝamon wrote in self-conscious imitation of Wulfstan, or even in imitation of any particular Wulfstanian text. Rather, it instantiates the larger trend, that Wulfstan's word choices tended to be ahead of the linguistic curve. As I noted in chapter 2, *griđ* and the related verb *griđian* are Norse loanwords, commonly used in Wulfstan's writing; the words do not appear frequently in other Old English contexts.[25] Laȝamon uses *griđ* many times, particularly in a formulaic phrase *ȝirne griđ* that appears fourteen times in the poem, typically when a ruler desires to end a conflict with a truce.[26] But as with the poet's preference for *lagu* over *æ* to refer to "law," this trend is actually weak evidence for Wulfstan's influence, because Wulfstan's own preference prefigured the usage that would become common after the Conquest. In both instances, Laȝamon might simply be following standard Middle English practice, and the parallel to Wulfstan may suggest only that late Anglo-Saxon legal vocabulary had an important influence on early Middle English generally.

More specific evidence for Laȝamon's familiarity with Old English law is found throughout the *Brut*. Perhaps the most striking is a parallel to the formulaic oath *Hit becwæð*, discussed in chapter 2.[27] The person who swears the oath claims right to lands, waters, marshes, woods, fishing, and so on, in lists that alliterate in both the English version of the formula and in the closely parallel lists found in Anglo-Saxon Latin charters. A strikingly similar list of territorial features appears in both Wace and Laȝamon's version of the narrative, in a passage where the English corresponds to the French with unusual exactitude.[28] The English version is as follows:

---

24 Dance, "Sound," 48–9.

25 On *griđ* in Wulfstan's writings, see Fell, "*Unfriđ*," 90–2; Pons-Sanz, *Norse-Derived Vocabulary*, 157–8.

26 At Caligula lines 3644, 4219, 5135, 5377, 5917, 5935, 7365, 7503, 9275, 11111, 12010, 13141, 13959, and 14455.

27 See above (70–1).

28 Wace ll. 1209–16, Laȝamon cited below. See LeSaux, *Text and Tradition*, 28; and Tiller, *Brut*, 133–4 for alternative readings of this passage.

Brutus hine biðohte and þis folc bi-heold
Bi-heold he þa muntes feire and muchele.
Bi-heold he þa medewan þat weoren swiðe mære.
Bi-heold he þa wateres and þa wilde deor.
Bi-heold he þa fisches biheold he þa fuȝeles.
Bi-heold he þa leswa and þene leofliche wode.
Bi-heold he þene wode hu he bleou bi-heold he þat corn hu hit greu.
Al he iseih on leoden þat him leof was on heorte. (1001–8)

[Brutus thought to himself and beheld the people.
He beheld the fair and great mountains.
He beheld the meadows that were very broad.
He beheld the waters and wild beats.
He beheld the fish and the birds.
He beheld the grasslands and the lovely plains.
He beheld the plains, how they flowered. He beheld how the corn grew.
He saw entirely in the people that love for him was in their hearts.]

The list of Britain's bounty underscores with procedural exactitude the
rights to the island that Brutus now enjoys. His "beholding" implies not
only seeing, but also possession. This list of Brutus possessions begins and
ends with his people: at first, he "beholds" them, and in the end he "sees"
in their hearts that they love him, as Cnut wished for his people to love
him in *I Cn* 2. Brutus' ownership of the land and his right to rule the
people are therefore both asserted here in a form apparently derived from
Anglo-Saxon legal-homiletic discourse.

Laȝamon's debt to Anglo-Saxon legal forms helps to explain some of the
stranger features of the highly unusual preface to the *Brut*.[29] Below is the
passage in its entirety, quoted from the Caligula manuscript of the poem:[30]

An preost was on leoden. Laȝamon wes ihoten.
he was Leouenaðes sone. liðe him beo Drihten.

---

29 Here and throughout I will quote the Caligula-text of the poem because it is the fullest,
   and mention any substantial differences between this manuscript and the Otho-text in
   the notes. The fullest study of the difference between the two manuscripts is England,
   "Brut." See also Stanley, "Antiquarian"; Cannon, "Style and Authorship"; Bryan,
   Collaborative Meaning; Perry, "Origins."
30 On the differences between the two versions of the prologue, see my forthcoming
   article "Diplomatic Antiquarianism and the Manuscripts of Laȝamon's *Brut*."

He wonede at Ernleȝe. At æðelen are chirechen.
vppen Seuarne staþe. Sel þar him þuhte.
on-fest Radestone. þer he bock radde.   5
hit com him on mode. ꒳ on his mern þonke.
þet he wolde of Engle. þa æðelæn tellen.
wat heo ihoten weoren. ꒳ wonene heo comen.
þa Englene londe. ærest ahten.
æfter þan flode. þe from Drihtene com.   10
þe al her a-quelde. quic þat he funde.
buten Noe. ꒳ Sem. Iaphet ꒳ Cham.
꒳ heore four wiues. þe mid heom weren on archen.
Laȝamon gon liðen. wide ȝond þas leode.
꒳ bi-won þa æðela boc. þa he to bisne nom.   15
He nom þa Englisca boc. þa makede Seint Beda.
An-oþer he nom of Latin. þe makede Seinte Albin.
꒳ þe feire Austin. þe fulluht broute hider in.
Boc he nom þe þridde. leide þer amidden.
þa makede a Frenchis clerk.   20
Wace wes ihoten. þe wel couþe writen.
꒳ he hoe ȝef þare æðelen. Ælienor.
þe wes Henries quene. þes heȝes kinges.
Laȝamon leide þeos boc. ꒳ þa leaf wende.
he heom leofliche bi-heold. liþe him beo Drihten.   25
Feþeren he nom mid fingren. ꒳ fiede on boc-felle.
꒳ þa soþere word. sette to-gadere.
꒳ þa þre boc. þrumde to are.
Nu bidde[ð] Laȝamon alcne æðele mon.
for þene almiten Godd.   30
þet þeos boc rede. ꒳ leornia þeos runan.
þat he þeos soðfaste word. segge to-sumne.
for his fader saule. þa hine for[ð] brouhte.
꒳ for his moder saule. þa hine to monne iber.
꒳ for his awene saule. þat hire þe selre beo. Amen.   35

[A priest was among the people, who was called Laȝamon.
he was Leovenath's son, the Lord be merciful to him.
He lived at Areley Kings, at a noble church
on the banks of the Severn – it seemed well to him –
just beside Redstone, where he read his book.
A thought came into his mind and his pure thoughts
that he would tell of England's noble men,

what they were called and from what places they came,
those who first possessed the land of the English
after the flood that came from the Lord,
and that killed everything here that it found alive
except for Noah and Shem, Japhet and Ham,
and their four wives, who were with them on the ark.
Laȝamon went travelling far through this nation
and acquired the noble book that he took as his model.
He took the English book that Saint Bede made;
another in Latin he took, made by Saint Alban
and Saint Augustine, who brought baptism here.
He took and set between the others a third,
made by a French clerk
named Wace, who knew well how to write;
and he gave it to the noble Eleanor,
who was the queen of Henry the high king.
Laȝamon laid out these books and turned the leaf;
he gazed at them gratefully, the Lord be merciful to him.
He took quill pens in his fingers and composed on the parchment,
and set together the truer words,
and those three books he pressed into one.
Now Laȝamon begs every noble man
for almighty God's sake
who might read this book and learn its secrets
that he say together these true words,
for the soul of his father, who first gave him being,
and for the soul of his mother, who bore him as a man-child,
and for his own soul, that it might be better.
Amen.]

The poem begins by indicating who its author is and the location in which he's working, in a third-person description (1–3). He then goes on to describe several authoritative sources, discussed below, in a fairly typical historiographic gesture, before concluding with a prayer for his family.[31]

The most unusual component of this introduction for the present argument is its description of the poem's composition.[32] The poet's description of his work as the assembly of a book is strikingly material-cultural, and it

---

31 Gransden, "Prologues," 71–2.
32 For another take on the physicality of the passage, see Tiller, *Brut*, 103–16.

is appropriate that the historiated initial of the Caligula manuscript, displaying Laȝamon at his lectern, is both the earliest artistic representation of an English vernacular poet and a relatively rare medieval illustration of scribal practice.[33] The poet's act of writing proceeds from his act of reading, as he redocuments stories about the heroes and lawmakers who lived in Britain's remote past (5–13). A close parallel to this representation of the author's craft is provided by Hemming's cartulary, whose composition is described in similarly material terms in its *Enucleatio Libelli*. Like in the *Brut*, Hemming's introductory phrase "Hunc libellum ... composui" implies not only a historian's compilation of relevant materials, but a scribe's assembly of a physical manuscript.[34]

This act of assembly is also important because it forms the third term of the passage's triadic structure of thoughts, words, and deeds. We are told that Laȝamon thought and read until "hit com him on *mode* ˥ on his *þonke* / þat he wolde of Engelond þe riȝtnesse *telle*." Once he has made this decision to write the truth in words, he travels through the world to take or hold ("nom," in 16, 17, and 18) the books, after which "feþere he nom mid fingres / and wrot mid his honde" (26). The emphasis on Laȝamon's hands, which seize the book and the quill before they begin writing, makes it clear that writing his book is a deed, and not merely an extension of his thoughts and words. The introduction concludes by asking the reader to turn the words written in the book into their own speech, so that "alcne æðele mon" (each noble man) will "þeos soðfaste word. segge to-sumne (say these true words together)," ensuring in this way that the poet's thoughts, words and deeds will have the desired proselytizing effect.[35] Laȝamon thus combines several sententious, homiletic formulae from Old English law (such as the thought / word / deed triad, the connection between literacy and good counsel, and a homiletic allusion to Noah's flood) with the kinds of authorizing gestures that literate audiences had already come to expect from a competent historian (such as statements of his name, profession, and location, and a list of his primary sources). His work is described not only as an act of writing, but also as a scribal work of manuscript assembly; this draws attention to the documentary quality of the book produced. The introduction thus nicely encapsulates the tension in the poem, between the formal expectations of thirteenth-century

---

33 On Laȝamon's portrait, see Hilmo, *Medieval Images*, 102–5.
34 *Hemingi chartularium*, ed. Hearne, 282. See also Tinti, "Hemming's Cartulary," 241.
35 The passages referred to are cited above (130).

scholastic readers for a work of history, and the much looser and more sententious formal expectations witnessed in the genuine historical documents that a "law-man" in Worcester would have encountered.

The version of the preface cited above also provides a clue about the rhetorical purpose behind the poem's echoes of Anglo-Saxon legal-homiletic discourse. In the Caligula manuscript of the poem, the preface includes the detail that Wace presented his text to Queen Eleanor, to be given in turn to Henry (31–3). Historical and legal texts of the twelfth and thirteenth centuries are frequently dedicated to queens. For example, *Quadripartitus*, as I noted in chapter 2, is dedicated to Matilda as well as Henry I. Dedications were yet another strategy employed by the Church's representatives to encourage queenly intercessions in their favour, and there is every reason to believe that they were founded in the legitimate expectation that queens could exercise such power.[36] But as Paul Strohm has documented, the actual power of the queen diminished after the twelfth century, as she was supplanted in her advisory role by the same bureaucrats whose new practices threatened ancient ecclesiastical institutions.[37] This account of Wace's dedication to Queen Eleanor nostalgically evokes a world order wherein queens and clergymen exercised moral authority in this way, in a practice that was already vanishing in the face of the crown's ever-increasing dependence on documentary literacy. As we shall see, the collaboration between Wace and the "good" queen Eleanor foreshadows the later representation of the "bad" Saxon queen Rowenna, who personifies the hypocritical formalists who came to replace the wise men and good queens who had advised kings in the past.

In his own reading of this introduction, Donoghue argues that the "soþere" words set together in this poem articulate a theory of pre-Saxon British history that is not terribly different from that articulated by Laȝamon's predecessor Gildas: namely, that the sinfulness of a nation invites divine punishment, in the form of foreign invasion.[38] According to Donoghue, the ultimate conquest of the British by Saxon invaders is deserved, and Laȝamon's recognition of this fact tempers his distaste for them. In the following section I will reconcile Donoghue's reading of the poem with Noble's counter-argument, that Laȝamon distinguishes

---

36 See Strohm, "Queens as Intercessors"; Parsons, "Queen's Intercession"; and Huneycutt, "Esther Topos." On medieval concepts of feminine virtue generally, see Blamires, "Case for Women."

37 Strohm, "Queens as Intercessors," 138.

38 Donoghue, "Ambivalence."

between the Germanic conquerors at the end of his narrative from the tribes of Hengest and Horsa, and that he is unsparingly critical of the latter.[39] Noble is quite right to identify an analogy between the (Norman) Saxons of the *Brut* and the heathen Danes of the *Sermo Lupi ad Anglos*. [40] Indeed, the Normans were relatives of the Danish invaders, as is reflected in the name "North men," and Henry of Huntingdon conflates the two periods of invasion as a continuous 230-year exercise in divine retribution.[41] But as in the *Sermo Lupi ad Anglos*, Gildas's logic of divine retribution functions in the *Brut* as a part of a relatively pragmatic argument about secular administration. As I will demonstrate, Hengest and Horsa are singled out not only as pagan Saxons, but also as corrupt royal advisors. The figures therefore conflate the Danes of the *Sermo Lupi ad Anglos* with the English nation that is the true target of that sermon's criticisms. The status of Hengest as both ethnic forebear and barbarian invader is decidedly convenient for Laȝamon, as it enables him to employ the tropes of Anglo-Saxon legal-homiletic discourse to criticize a kind of institutional reform for which that discourse has no vocabulary.

Laȝamon's Saxon "Ambivalence" Reconsidered

My argument that the *Brut* is situated within a tradition of vernacular legal literacy complicates Christopher Cannon's argument in *The Grounds of English Literature* that Laȝamon and his contemporaries chose the English language as a poetic medium only to differentiate themselves from existing Latin and Anglo-Norman literary norms. Cannon writes: "In their splendid isolation from vernacular inspiration, early Middle English writers learned to see the creative potential in the rich world of *all* forms," not only literary and documentary, but also in the physical and natural world (his emphasis).[42] On this basis Cannon argues that the *Brut* is "chorographic," or more concerned with mapping the territory of Britain than it is with telling a story; the chaotic history of Britain merely demonstrates, by contrast, the stability of the island's landscape itself.[43] As it states plainly in the Caligula manuscript: "laȝen beoð an ærde" (laws are in the land) (9676).

---

39 Noble, "'Ambivalence' Reconsidered."
40 See also Wickham-Crowley, *Writing the Future*, 53–5.
41 Gransden, "Prologues," 78.
42 Cannon, *Grounds*, 11.
43 Cannon, *Grounds*, 54–5.

Another possible inspiration for the poem's theme is found in the vernacular, "chirographic" boundary clauses of Anglo-Saxon charters. Many early medieval legal practices proceduralize the notion of law residing in the earth itself, as can be seen in the ritual recorded in Byrhtferth's *Life of St. Ecgwine* wherein one plants a scythe in the ground while swearing that one owns the land,[44] or in the widely attested practice of presenting a clod of earth as livery of seisin. In both of these cases the "law" residing in the land is specifically the right of ownership – a major preoccupation of the *Brut*. Hence the splendid isolation of the *Brut*'s vernacular form manifests in the text as a problem it wishes to solve: Old English law and legal procedures ought not to have been forgotten, and the poem aims to ensure that they are remembered.

Cannon notes the number of times that the *Brut* appears to expand on Wace's mentions of law and land. There are only six references to "law" in the *Roman de Brut*, compared to seventy-six in the *Brut*.[45] Eighteen of the "new" mentions of law occur in the Caligula-text between 6947 and 8461, or roughly 40 per cent of the occurrences in less than 10 per cent of the poem.[46] These fifteen hundred lines correspond to the portion of the *Brut* describing the invasion of Hengest and Horsa. Laȝamon's deviations from his source in these lines tend to be quite critical of the Saxons, particularly in the passages that describe the deeds of Hengest and Horsa. Thus the poem's thematic concern with law and legality centres around these figures, who incidentally first brought into England the language in which the earliest English laws would one day be written.

Noble argues that the poem's critical "ambivalence" towards the Saxons manifest in these tendencies reflects the poet's ambivalence about the Normans.[47] Hengest and Horsa are invaders before they are ethnic forebears; conversely, the arrival of the Anglo-Saxons to Britain at the end of the poem is not a conquest at all, but rather an acceptance of an invitation to settle. Part of the evidence offered by Noble in service of his argument

---

44 Byrhtferth, *Lives*, 294.

45 Twenty-seven of these new occurrences do not appear in the Otho-text. The lines omitted are Caligula-text lines 1404–5, 3117, 3506, 3569, 5022, 5057, 6021, 6947, 7041, 7071–2, 7210, 7278, 8378, 8388, 8461, 9676, 11046, 11470, 14083, 14171, 14275–6, 14351–2. Lines for which the reading in the Otho-text is impossible to determine because of manuscript damage are 14717, 15599, 15818, 15964, 16089.

46 The same pattern follows the Otho MS's omissions: 36 per cent of the law references missing from the Otho-text occur between 6947 and 8461.

47 Noble, "'Ambivalence' Reconsidered," 178–9.

is his reading of a passage from the *Brut* at lines 1019–36, where he lists the various names that have been held by the city of London. In Noble's account, one would expect an heir of Gildas to use this passage as an occasion to point out that each new generation of inhabitants was sent there by God to punish their predecessors. Instead, the narrator merely observes: "þus is þis eit-lond i-gon from honde to hond" (thus this island has gone from hand to hand) (1033).[48]

Noble contrasts this passage with a later meditation on the same subject, which is somewhat harsher in tone:

Seoðöen comen Sæxisce men & Lundene heo cleopeden.
þe nome ileste longe inne þisse londe.
Seoðöen comen Normans mid heore nið-craften.
and nemneden heo Lundres þeos leodes heo amærden.
Swa is al þis lond iuaren for uncuðe leoden.
þeo þis londe hæbbeð bi-wunnen and ef[t] beoð idriuen hennene.
And eft hit bi-ȝetten oðeræ þe uncuðe weoren.
ꝺ faldene þene ælden nomen æftre heore wille.
of gode þe burȝen ꝺ wenden heore nomen.
swa þat nis her burh nan in þissere Bruttene.
þat habbe hire nome ælde þe me arst hire on-stalde. (3545–55)

[Then came the Saxon men and they called it London.
The name lasted long in this land.
Then came the Normans with their hateful arts
And named it Londres; these people made it famous.
So is all this land changed by ignorant people,
Who have won this land and are after driven hence.
And after it, others were born who were ignorant,
And forgot the old names according to their intention.
They grow in wealth and their names go forth,
So there is no city in this Britain
That has the old name that was first established.]

---

48   Cannon adds that the couplet employed here, *lond/hond*, is used by Laȝamon 192 times in contexts not paralleled by Wace. On this basis, he argues that the pairing "neutralizes the sense that conquest causes change": *Grounds*, 62.

Noble argues that Laȝamon represents the Normans here "as modern-day equivalents of the Saxons."[49] I will return to this argument in a moment. First, I would observe that this passage also happens to occur roughly thirty lines before the arrival of Julius Caesar to Britain (3588), which is also the event that begins Laȝamon's other extant cited source, Bede's *Historia ecclesiastica gentis Anglorum*. Tatlock has argued that Laȝamon used Bede's text to correct the place names found in Wace, though Le Saux is right to remind us that this kind of evidence is "notoriously inconclusive."[50] However, if Tatlock's hypothesis were correct, then this passage occurs immediately before Laȝamon has an authoritative basis for corroborating Wace's spelling for the various names of places like the city of London. Given the context, the lament is perhaps more indicative of the historian's anxiety about the quality of his scholarship than it is of the Englishman's anxiety about his ethnic identity. After all, the *nið-craften* ("hateful arts") of the Normans are specifically identified with the *uncuðe* ("foreign," but also "ignorant") renaming of a city that already had several names.[51] At the very least, Laȝamon seems worried that his readers might believe that he could make the same mistake.

Second, it is worth noting that elsewhere, Laȝamon omits a specific reference to place names occurring in his source. In lines 14736–56, Wace lists several examples of place names in British that were changed by the Saxon king Athelstan; for example, he observes that *Kaer* became *Cestre* and *Suiz* became *Sire* or "shire." Thus Wace's Athelstan engages in precisely the sort of renaming that Laȝamon criticizes in lines 3545–55. In the corresponding passage of the *Brut*, Laȝamon describes Athelstan's linguistic intervention quite differently:

> Me dude him to understonde of al þisse londe
> Hu Aðelstan her com liðen ut of Sexlonden,
> And hu he al Anglelond sette on his aȝere hond;
> And hu he sette moting, and hu he sette husting,
> And hu he sette sciren and makede frið of deoren,
> And hu he sette holimot, and hu he sette hundred,
> And þa nomen of þa tunen on Sexisce runen;
> And ȝilden he gon rere mucle and swiðe mære,

---

49 Noble, "'Ambivalence' Reconsidered," 178.
50 Tatlock, *Legendary History*, 488; Le Saux, *Poem and Its Sources*, 17.
51 For some context on the word *nið*, see Tiller, *Brut*, 146–7.

And þa chirchen he gon dihten after Sexisce irihten,
And Sexis he gan kennen þa nomen of þan monnen,
And al me him talde þe tiden of þisse londe. (15968–76)

[One made him [King Cadwaḷader] understand with regard to all this land
how Athelstan had come out of Saxony, and how he had set all England in
his hand; and how he established the *gemot*, and how he established *husting*,
and how he established *scire* and *frið* for deer, and how he established the
haligemot, and how he established *hundredes*, and set the names of the town
in Saxon writing; and how he established many great guilds, and Saxon rights
in all the churches, and changed the names of the men into Saxon; and one
told him [Cadwalader] completely the news from this land.]

Athelstan's practice of translating place names is mentioned only briefly in
15974, and the change is accounted for as a different convention of writing. The passage focuses instead on the king's establishment of Anglo-
Saxon legal terms, presented in their original Old English form in my
translation above.[52] Hence it seems that Laȝamon wishes to exempt
Athelstan from the "ignorant people" he has criticized some eleven thou-
sand lines earlier; instead of introducing new names for cities that were
already named, Athelstan introduces new legal institutions that, as
Laȝamon's audience knew, would stand the test of time. The most obvious
difference between Athelstan and the ignorant conquerors of London is
that Athelstan does not enrich himself at the expense of his new subjects,
as the conquerors are said to have done in line 3553. On the contrary, we
are told that he makes a point of re-endowing guilds and churches with
charters written in Saxon English – assertions that incidentally connect
him to the ninth-century king Æthelstan, who wrote many charters endowing churches and whose code *VI Æthelstan* established the duties of
the London peace guild.[53] Hence it seems that Laȝamon's complaint was
not as abstract as it seemed, but instead targeted the kinds of theft that can
occur when a new conqueror comes in and chooses to ignore both the
established rights of ownership and the good of the people that he has
conquered.

Laȝamon's particular sympathy for ancient institutions faced with reforms is also manifest in the poem's treatment of an episode from Bede,

---

52 On this list see also Kleinman, "Frið"; Stein, "Making History English," 109.
53 On Æthelstan's charters, see chapter 1 (39–51).

describing a conflict between Augustine of Canterbury and the monks of Bangor. Laȝamon's sources depict the incident in markedly different ways, as the monks are described by Bede as heretics and by Geoffrey and Wace as martyrs.[54] Laȝamon's own take on the episode is largely sympathetic to the monks, though his account de-emphasizes the theological aspects of the conflict to focus instead on the episode's political and legal aspects. As Tiller notes, the story plays as an allegory of episcopal overreach at the expense of established local ecclesiastical institutions.[55] In the *Brut*, the monks write a thorough and reasoned explanation for their denial of Augustine's visitation rights (14843–63), in which they echo Laȝamon himself by calling Augustine *uncuðe* (14850) and cite the precedent of three hundred years to justify their autonomy (14860). The letter thus casts the founder of the English church as a target of criticism, and more-over as an ally to the "hundes heðene / þa comen of Sexlonde" (heathen hounds that come from Saxony) (14855–6).

More damningly, the clergy of Bangor are ultimately betrayed by their Saxon opponents, in a clear violation of the king's *grið*. Laȝamon describes the "monekes and heremite and canunes white / bischopes and clærkes and preostes mid Godes mærkes" (monks and hermits and white canons, bish-ops and clerks and priests with God's signs) (14898–9) who went to the king and "his grið geornden" (asked for his *grið*) (14900). The king asks the clergymen to come out into a field and await his reply; again, the clergy are listed: "Ut wenden munekes and þa masse-preostes. / Ut wenden clærkes, ut wenden canones, / alle ut wenden þa þer icumen weoren, / þes kinges grið to wilnien for lufe of Godd seolfne" (Out went the monks and the mass priests, out went the clerks, out went the canons, they all went out that had come there, to ask the king's *grið* for the love of God himself) (14907–11). The king then sends out five hundred knights, who "[mid] unrihtes sloȝen al þat heo neh comen" (slew with injustice all that came near them) (14919).

The alliterative lists of clergy emphasize that the victims here are not merely a group of heterodox monks. Representatives of the entire church asked the king for *grið* on two separate occasions, but their requests were denied. The resulting episode allegorizes the institutional reforms of the twelfth and thirteenth centuries from a decidedly English and ecclesiasti-cal perspective. Bangor's clergy wish simply for things to continue in peace as they had before, but a reform-minded foreign bishop stands in

---

54 Tiller, *Brut*, 147–60.
55 Tiller, *Brut*, 164.

their way. This bishop's wrong-headedness enables secular authorities to attack and pillage the church. Such a narrative is highly consistent with many monastic histories of the Norman Conquest, both chronicle and cartulary. Again, Hemming's Worcester cartulary provides a helpful point of comparison. The *Codicellus possessionum* section of the cartulary mirrors the Saxon portions of the *Brut*, in that its narrative describes the theft of land rightfully belonging to Christians who had held it for a long time before.[56] As one would expect, both Danish and Norman interlopers are cited by Hemming as thieves; but alongside them are the corrupt reeves and tax-collectors who were the subject of complaints in the *Institutes of Polity* and the *LHP*.[57] Similarly the treacherous Saxons of the Bangor episode, working at the behest of king and bishop, act both as foreign invaders and as the kinds of corrupt reeves and tax collectors that were the bane of semi-autonomous religious institutions.

Of course, such a view of Norman institutional reform is almost wholly out of sync with the way this period is remembered in modern histories of English law. Generally speaking, the "crimes" perpetrated by reeves and tax-collectors against institutions like Worcester in the twelfth and thirteenth centuries are regarded in the modern era as bumps along the road towards an England unified under a single "common" law. In contrast, the rhetorical association between heathen invaders and royal servants witnessed in Hemming's cartulary encodes a larger political claim, as it implicitly argues that the centralizing reforms of the Normans and Angevins were intrinsically "un-English." Reformers have ignored the precedent of Old English law, and in so doing they have abandoned their English identities. To return, then, to Noble's argument, the modern-day equivalents of the Saxons are not only "the Normans," but they are more specifically the agents of the secular, Anglo-Norman and Angevin institutions of government whose very existence worked to deprive ecclesiastical institutions of their long-standing administrative autonomy.

One particularly striking example of the Saxons' depiction as land-grabbing royal servants is that describing Hengest's acquisition of his first estate. Hengest asks the British king Vortigern to give him as much land as a cow's hide can cover (7079), and Vortigern agrees (7084). Hengest then finds a particularly strong hide (7091), and has it cut by a particularly

---

56 *Hemingi chartularium*, ed. Hearne, 248–91.
57 Tinti, "Hemming's Cartulary," 239.

crafty man into an extremely long thong (7092–6). He then uses this thong to encircle a large estate, named "Thong-chester" after its origins. As Tiller observes, Laȝamon's expanded account of this episode not only emphasizes the Saxon's legalistic treachery, but also provides a "mytho-poetic origin" for the term "hide" to connote a unit of land.[58] As Tiller also observes, Hengest's clever "stretching out" of an animal skin recalls the physical production of parchment, and hence of a legal document conferring ownership. Read in this way, the episode is a darkly ironic origin story for English land measurement and documentation of land ownership. Hengest technically obeys the precise wording of the king's original promise, but he uses craftiness and trickery to subvert its intent, literally cutting up the parchment in the process. In this way Hengest's methodology for acquiring Thong-chester bears a striking resemblance to the legalistic treacheries of reeves and tax collectors, lamented by Hemming and so many other monastic historians.

This political allegory implicit in Laȝamon's depictions of the Saxons is discernible in two other themes in their representation, identified by Noble. The first of these is the tendency in the *Brut* to refer to the Saxons as not only heathen, but "hæðene hundes"; the second is Laȝamon's tendency to linger over the Saxon practice of poisoning their enemies.[59] In the remainder of this section I will look at each of these attributes of the Saxons in turn, in order to demonstrate how they derive from the conventional tropes of Anglo-Saxon legal-homiletic discourse.

I will begin with the phrase "hæðen hund." This alliterative phrase echoes the motif of dog-like pagan criminals common in Old English literature, most pertinently in the vivid passage of the *Sermo Lupi ad Anglos* where criminals who share a woman as a sexual slave are said to be "most like dogs" (*hundum geliccast*) in their indifference to "filth."[60] Wulfstan's writing also features the unique Old English occurrence of the word *werewulf*, which he uses to describe the Antichrist from whom a bishop must protect his flock.[61] This imagery recalls the long-standing association between wolves and criminals in pagan North Atlantic

---

58 Tiller, *Brut*, 136.
59 Noble, "'Ambivalence' Reconsidered," 172–4. The "heathen dogs" formulae appear in Caligula-text lines 8261, 8296, 9182, 9749, 10248, 10564, 10929. Crimes of poisoning appear in lines 7429–96, 8765–8905, 9790–9892.
60 Bethurum XX (EI) l. 85–9.
61 For example at *I Cn* 26.3.

contexts, represented for example in the Old English word *wearg* ("criminal") and its Icelandic counterpart *vargr* ("werewolf" or "outlaw"). The same imagery appears also in Old English poetry, where *wulf-x* compounds often refer to pagan or subhuman criminals, for example the "wulfheort cyning" Nebuchadnezzar of the poem *Daniel*, and the description of Holofernes as a "heathen hound" in *Judith*.[62] In other words, the trope arises from a poetic description of treacherous and immoderate foreign invaders that reveals in its semantic origins the same association between heathens and native criminals (*weargas*) discernible in Wulfstan's writing.

It is also crucially important that that the "heathen hounds" Hengest and Horsa begin their sojourn in Britain as corrupt royal servants, who gave the king advice that suited their own selfish ends instead of the larger good of the kingdom. Similarly, the poison motif reimagines the biblical link between pestilence and foreign invasion as a personal crime against the king committed by a treacherous advisor. In this way the Saxons who poison kings are precisely contrary to the confessor priests described in *Institutes of Polity* 18 ("Ad sacerdotes"), who remove poison from sinners by the act of confession: "Ne ænig man ne mæg synna butan andetnesse wel gebetan, þe ma þe se mæg wel hal weorðan, þe unlibban gedruncen hæfð, butan he þæt attor aspiwe."[63] The false Saxon "confessors" not only fail to remove the poison from the bodies of their kings, but they add further poison.

In the next section, I will look at the poem's most dramatic example of a Saxon poisoner. Rowenna's murder of her stepson Vortimer by poison is described in a hundred-line passage of the *Brut* that covers two lines in Wace; the addition of the episode is therefore a key moment for understanding Laȝamon's depiction of the Saxons.[64] In another deviation from Wace (and also every other attested source), Laȝamon's Rowenna poisons Vortimer herself, in a scene whose closest analogue is arguably the episode in Norse myth where Sinfjötli (or Fitela in Old English) is poisoned with

---

62 *wulfheort* appears in *Daniel* at lines 116, 134, 245: *OE Web Corpus*, accessed 1 February 2008.

63 "Nor can any man fully amend sin without confession, no more than he may become fully healthy, who has drunk poison, unless he spit out that venom." See also Jost, *Wulfstanstudien* 170–1. This passage is found in Oxford, Bodleian Junius 121, a Worcester manuscript (Jost, *Wulfstanstudien*, 12–13).

64 My citations of the passage below are from the Caligula-text, as there are few differences between the two versions.

wine by his aunt and / or stepmother Borghild.[65] Laȝamon's account of Rowenna's crime follows logically from an earlier and more famous *wassail* scene from Geoffrey's narrative, in which Rowenna seduced Vortimer's father Vortigern and in the process introduced him to the customary exchange "wæs hail," "Drinc hail" (7152). By poisoning her son-in-law according to precisely this traditional display of fealty, Rowenna reveals her utter faithlessness, not only to the bonds of marital duty (OE *æw*) but also to the formal customs of Anglo-Saxon traditional law (OE *æ*). She is for this reason an archetypal example of a wicked royal counsellor, as constructed in Anglo-Saxon legal-homiletic discourse.

Formalism, Hypocrisy, and the Wicked Queen

As I observed earlier, Laȝamon first represents ideal queenship as an advisory role in the poem's opening lines, when he describes Wace's presentation of his metrical chronicle to the queen Eleanor. Laȝamon picks up this theme again much later, when he departs from his source to repetitively emphasize the role of the good queen Marcia in the original codification of Alfred's "Mercian" law (3143–50).[66] Laȝamon's expansion of his source emphasizes the virtuous thoughts, words, and deeds that went into her composition of the law, parallel in structure to the prologue's description of the author's own process for composing the *Brut*. The operative words are indicated by italics: first Marcia "wes a boken wel *itaht*" (was well taught by books) (3139), then "of hire wisdome sprong that *word* wide" (word of her wisdom spread widely) (3141), and then "*makede* heo ane læȝe and *læide* ȝeon þat leode" (she made a law and laid it on the nation) (3143). Like Laȝamon, Marcia began by consulting books and thinking about what she read. Also like Laȝamon, she performed an emphatic act of publication when her work was finished, not merely proclaiming the law but "laying" it down, as the poet laid his history down upon the manuscript page. The primary difference between Marcia and Laȝamon is that word of the latter's wisdom had not widely spread at the time of his writing, though in the prologue of the poem the narrator clearly hopes that it will.

---

65 Fitela appears in *Beowulf*, line 879. On Fitela and Sigmund in *Beowulf*, see Orchard, *Companion*, 109–13; Earl, "Forbidden."

66 Cannon, *Grounds*, 69–71; Le Saux, *Poem and Its Sources*, 226.

La3amon's identification with Marcia – along with his curious emphasis on the fact that she and not Alfred was the original author of Mercian law (3150–3) – again suggests that the poet's moralization of history demonstrates a greater concern for local politics than it does for questions of ethnic identity. Mercian law lay behind Worcester's Oswaldlow immunity, discussed in chapter 2; hence the question of its authorship had important political implications for La3amon's own diocese.[67] La3amon's particular interest in Marcia provides yet more evidence of his particular interest in the parts of English history that pertain to the survival of small, autonomous ecclesiastical institutions.

The "good" queen Marcia also serves as a productive point of contrast to the "evil" queen Rowenna. Both the British queen and the Saxon queen codified English traditional practices, of law and ceremonial friendship respectively. But where the former introduced a secular law that would later establish the dominion of the servants of Christ, the latter introduced a custom that she herself would pervert in defiance of both religious and secular law. These women are therefore positive and negative examples respectively of the wifely role as advisor and intercessor, who moreover illustrate the ways in which traditional cultural practices can be appropriately conserved on the one hand or corrupted by innovation and wickedness on the other.

Given that the "wassail" custom is a vehicle for Rowenna's treachery, it is introduced to the poem with surprising reverence: Vortigern's trusted adviser Keredic, "a cniht swiðe sellic" (a very excellent knight), tells the king that "þis beoð sele la3en inne Saxe-londe" (this is the excellent law in Saxony) (7145, 7156). Shortly thereafter the "excellent" Saxon law is implicitly contrasted with Vortigern's corrupt British law, which allows him to marry Rowenna: "Þ an kinge hit was [icweme] he imaked heo to quene. / al after þan la3en þe stoden an hæðe[ne] dæ3en" (Then it was pleasing to the king that he make her the queen, after the laws that stood in heathen days) (7178–9). As the narrator observes here, the Christian laws that would have prevented Vortigern's inappropriate marriage in the first place were not yet practised at the time.[68] Ironically, then, Vortigern succumbs to the crimes of both apostasy and lechery in part because he honours his

---

67 As I discussed above, Worcester's dominion over "Oswaldslow" was based in Mercian customary law (89). For a somewhat parallel pair of positive and negative exempla, see Stacey Klein's readings of Ælfric's representations of Jezebel and Esther: *Ruling Women*, 16.

68 A noteworthy parallel to the criticisms of Vortigern's allowance of heathendom is found in the *Anglo-Saxon Chronicle* poem in the entry for 959 DE, which uses similar language to criticize King Edgar: Bredehoft, *Early English Metre*, 118.

oath of fealty to his pagan guests more strongly than he honours the true Christian laws his kingdom ought to have. This error is symbolized by his inappropriate marriage to the heathen Rowenna. The problem is not the *wassail* custom itself, then, but rather the larger legal context within which it was performed.

Vortigern's illegal marriage is the circumstance that makes Rowenna's treachery to Vortimer possible, as it promotes Rowenna's family members to positions of authority within the royal household. It is with considerable irony that Hengest says to Vortigern:

> Þu hæuest mine dohtor þæt me is swiðe deore.
> ⁊ ich æm þe an folke swa ich þi fader weore.
> *Hærcne mine lare* heo sculleð þe worðen leofue.
> for ich wulle hæhliche to helpen þe *ræden*. (7211–15, my emphasis)

> [You have my daughter who is very dear to me,
> And I am your own folk, as if I were your father.
> *Listen to my lore*, and it will become dear to you,
> For I intend greatly to help you *govern*.]

By submitting himself to the *lar* and *ræd* of heathens rather than religious authorities, Vortigern undoes himself and his three children, who are said to suffer from the lack of a positive female role model: "Heore moder was þa dæd þer-uore heo hafden þe lasse ræd" (Their mother was then dead, therefore they had less wisdom) (7195). The poisoning of Vortimer is a long-term consequence of this state of affairs, as his *unræd*ness is the reason the king is taken in so easily by his stepmother's lie that she wishes to be baptized. Not only is he unaware of his kingdom's true law, but he is ignorant of the more conventional *ræd* about the untrustworthy nature of women, and especially stepmothers. Vortimer's actual poisoning is thus only a delayed reaction to the metaphorical "poison" allowed into the body politic by Vortigern, in the form of his lawless intermarriage with the Saxons that allowed heathen criminals to participate in government.

One important feature of the passage describing the poisoning itself is its repetition of the word *swike*. The word is attested in the Caligula-version of the poem alone or in compounds seven times, clustering in the lines immediately before the poisoning itself.[69] The word appears with

---

69 Caligula lines 7446, 7462, 7468, 7470, 7471, 7475, 7485. Wickham-Crowley identifies Laȝamon's persistent use of this term as symptomatic of his relatively oral concept of law, and the importance of trustworthiness: Wickham-Crowley, *Writing the Future*, 36–55.

great frequency in the writings of Wulfstan, particularly his legal texts, and it appears to be an example of a word he prefers to use in a technical legal sense: not only "trickery," but "fraud" or "treason." For example, in *Sermo Lupi ad Anglos*, Wulfstan thematically links a catalogue of crimes to the failure of the nobility to observe the bonds of *comitatus*, as the nobles choose instead to betray (*beswican*) their lords. I have marked the forms of the word in bold:

> Forðam syn on lande ungetreowða micele for Gode and for worulde, ꝺ eac her syn on earde on mistlice wisan **hlafordswice** manige. And ealra mæst **hlafordswica** se bið on worulde þæt man his hlafordes sawle **beswice**; ꝺ ful micel **hlafordswica** se bið on worulde þæt man his hlaford on life **beswice** oððon of lande lifigende drife, ꝺ ægðer is geworden on þyssan earde: Eadweard man forrædde ꝺ siððan acwealde ꝺ æfter þam forbærnde; ꝺ Æþelred man dræfde ut of his earde.[70]

> [Thus here in this land are great treacheries, concerning Godly and worldly things, and also there was here in this land many **treasons** [done] in several ways. And it is the worst of all **treasons** in the world, that one **tricks** his lord's soul; and it is a very great **treason** in the world, that one **tricks** his lord from his life or drives him, living, from the land; and both have happened in this land: Edward was tricked, and then killed, and after that he was cremated; and Æthelred was driven out of his land.]

In this passage, we are told of false advisors, both spiritual and political, who tricked their lords in order to bring about the loss of land (as is repeatedly invoked throughout the passage) and the corruption or murder of a king. Rowenna is guilty of both of these crimes. The compound *hlafordswice* also appears at *II Cn* 64, where it is called a *botleas* crime that cannot be resolved by monetary compensation.[71] As a perpetrator of *hlafordswice*, then, Rowenna is a British criminal whose fraud is beyond legal remedy and invites divine punishment in the form of pagan invasions. The irony that she is also a pagan invader herself is a direct consequence of Vortigern's foolish decision to marry her in the first place.

It is therefore crucial here that Rowenna's "swikedom" (treachery) is both *for Gode and for worulde*, as the occasion of the banquet was her

---

70 Bethurum XX (BH), 257, ll. 78–83; my emphasis.
71 *Gesetze* I:352; *MoEL* 462–4.

expression of a desire to convert to Christianity. The *Vita Merlini's* characterization of Rowenna as "protectaque fraude" is the closest that any other version of the story comes to accusing Rowenna of false baptism.[72] The representation of Rowenna's false baptism oath adds a third, spiritual crime to her two earthly crimes of false counsel and murder. These three crimes correspond to thought, word, and deed, and constitute a parodic inversion of the three duties of Wulfstan's *godcundre lareowan* – to hold the Christian faith, to teach the law correctly, and to act in accordance with Christian principle – taken up by La3amon himself in the preface to the poem.

This tripartite structure of her crime is emphasized in the passage itself. When Rowenna tells the king she wishes to see him, the narrator interjects to comment on her thoughts: "Wale þat þe gode king of hire þonke nuste na-þing / þat he nuste þene swikedom þe þohte þa luðere wimman" (It is sad that the good king knew nothing of her thoughts, that he did not know the treachery that the hateful woman thought) (7445–6). Ten lines later, the idea is repeated in slightly different terms, but focused particularly on her treacherous words: "wæs Uortimer þe king bliþe þurh alle þing / he wende þat hit weore soð þat þo scaðe sæide" (Vortimer the king was happy throughout the event, he thought it was truth that the harmful one said) (7455–6). Then, finally, after ten more lines, the poisoning itself is described, with a clustering of finite, active verbs, describing each individual action that leads to Vortimer's death:

> & heo gon scenchen; on þas kinges benche.
> Þa heo isæh hire time; heo fulde hir scale of wine.
> & at-foren al þan dringe; heo eode to þan kinge.
> & þus hailede him on; þe swic-fulle wimman. (7465–8)

> [And she went to bear the cup to the king's bench.
> Then she saw her time; she filled her cup with wine
> And poured out all that drink; she went to the king,
> And thus raised it to him, the treacherous woman.]

This passage of the *Brut* thus expands on the misogynistic folktale motif of the wicked stepmother to represent Rowenna's relationship to her stepson as a parody of the ideal retainer / lord relationship. As in *The Proverbs of Alfred*, a triad of thoughts, words, and deeds ironically contrasts the

---

72 Le Saux, *Text and Its Sources*, 173; Geoffrey, *Vita Merlini*, 108–9.

advice of a woman with the preferable advice of priestly, spiritual advisors. Instead of drinking the poisoned wine given to him by a wicked queen like Rowenna, Vortimer should have drunk the sacramental wine of a priestly *þeodwita* like Laȝamon. And so again, it seems that Rowenna's ethnicity is an incidental aspect of her representation within the poem. First and foremost, she is a treacherous royal advisor, who moreover demonstrates her treachery through her perversion of a ceremony that is intended to document trust and fellowship.

The emphasis in this passage on formula and ritual – the ritual of baptism, the ritual of "wassail," and the thought/word/deed triad – reveals that the true anxiety expressed in this episode circles around the value and threat of formalism itself. The insistence throughout the *Brut* that the law resides unchanged in the land is by necessity a criticism of thirteenth-century legal institutions, which were not unchanging and deliberately excluded early precedent in determining who, by law, owned particular plots of land. If there is an ambivalence in the *Brut*, then, it manifests because the poem's very effort to reinvigorate older legal forms in a new literate context carries with it the real danger that one will merely repeat earlier mistakes, or worse, create new opportunities for wicked counsellors to distort and pervert precedent for their own ends. As we shall see, this is precisely the anxiety that manifests in *Richard the Redeless* and *Mum and the Sothsegger*, as they attempt to enshrine Langlandian sententious formalism as an alternative mode of legal discourse.

Before moving on to these texts, I will conclude this chapter with a quick look at the *Brut*'s one brief comment on its own form. There are two occurrences of the word *loft-songe* in the *Brut*, both particular to the Caligula-text.[73] The first is a reference to the poem as a whole, made in a transition from the prologue to the narrative: "Nv seið mid loft-songe þe wes on leoden preost./al swa þe boc spekeð þe he to bisne inom" (Now the priest says, with the *loft-songe* that was in the people/language, everything the book said that he took as an example) (36–7).[74] The second describes how "mid muchele loft-songe" (with great *loft-songe*) Vortimer returned to England to reclaim it from Hengest and Horsa (7308). Brehe argues that these two references to archaic songs associate the term with specifically poetic, alliterative metre, particularly of a kind appropriate for "important and dignified contexts."[75] However, there is also a more

---

73 Allen, "Loft-Songe," 253–6.
74 The Otho-text in this line uses the term "louesange."
75 Brehe, "Rhythmical Alliteration," 78.

context-specific reading of this word suggested here: the *loft-songe* of Vortimer accompanied the triumphant return of legitimate royal authority to a land that had been overrun by heathen criminals, whose crimes also happen to be a primary narrative focus of the larger *loft-songe* of the poem. If the *loft-songe* of the *Brut* is similarly written on behalf of rulers like Vortimer, who were vulnerable to poisoning at the hands of treacherous heathen advisors, then the recurrence of the word becomes all the more loaded. Like good alliterative poems, good laws are not only able to stand the test of time, but prove their quality by their ability to do so. Both laws and *loft-songes* exist in order to teach their readers that it is the duty of Christian citizens to live in accordance with truth, and resist the criminals who derive their authority not from divine right (as sanctified by the ecclesiastical order) but from their *swikedom* and *unræd*.

In the next chapter I will turn to the *Piers Plowman* tradition. The titular figure of this tradition, Piers, personifies a law that resides in the land. His poems are deeply concerned with defining the role of kingship, and the later imitations of those poems pick up on this theme. More to the point, he is deeply concerned with the identification and rejection of criminals, and in particular criminals who abuse formulaic procedures and bureaucratic training for their own selfish gain. The *Piers Plowman* tradition will strike many readers as being quite different from the early Middle English alliterative poetry, legal documents, and law codes I have examined so far. I will begin the next chapter by demonstrating that these changes reflect the role of Anglo-Saxon legal precedent in the later medieval period. On the one hand, Piers and the alliterative mode of his poems will present an idealized alternative to those fourteenth-century administrators who exploited the bureaucracies of church and royal household for their own ends, and whose exploitations were still characterized pejoratively as "innovations." On the other hand, the notion of the law that Piers represents was itself a nostalgic construct created by those very administrators, who indeed sometimes disguised their innovations by claiming that they originated in "time out of mind" – a claim difficult to disprove for the very reason that time out of mind is by definition imperfectly recorded.

5 Defining the *Piers Plowman* Tradition

In chapter 2, I cited the bequeathment formula *Hit bicwæð* as an example of the repetitive, alliterative lists characteristic of Anglo-Saxon poetry, homily, and law. As I noted then, the formula's alliterative catalogue of territorial rights has parallels in early Anglo-Latin charters, and therefore its basic structure has some claim to oral antiquity.[1] However, the appearance of the word *ploȝ* in *Hit bicwæð* suggests that its precise phrasing of the formula is relatively late. The only other pre-Conquest texts in Old English attesting the Norse loanword *ploȝ* date to the reign of Cnut, and originate in the diocese of York.[2] In Old English, the word *ploȝ* does not refer to the farm implement "plow" (in Old English this is a *sylh*), but is more precisely translated as "plow-land," a Danelaw unit roughly equivalent to the hide. The "carucate" unit of the Domesday book appears to derive from OE *ploȝ*, and it is correspondingly frequent in the records of Domesday's sixth circuit, covering Yorkshire and the Danelaw. Because Domesday was cited frequently in the later medieval period to prove ancient demesne, ME *plouȝ* continued to connote land measurement and administration well into the fourteenth century, not only in York but across England. The Middle English "plowman," then, is not only "a man who drives a plow," but also "a man who inhabits a *ploȝ*." The etymology of the word reminds us that the plowmen of the fourteenth century evoked not only the allegorical agrarian labour of the

---

1 See *MoEL* 228–52; Richards, "Manuscript Contexts," 181–6.

2 *OE Corpus*, accessed 9 December 2012. The other pre-Conquest texts are the document S 968 and the list of York's possessions copied in the back of the York gospels. S 968 survives in volumes 1 and 2 of York's *Magnum registrum album* (c. xiv) and London, BL, Cotton Claudius B.III (c. xiii); Electronic Sawyer, accessed 9 December 2012. On the York gospels, see chapter 2 (64–6).

Bible, but also the legal framework of land ownership within which agrarian labour took place – which is to say, in more senses than one, "the law of the land."[3]

In the next two chapters, I will demonstrate that the poetic tradition surrounding the figure of "Piers the Plowman" utilizes Anglo-Saxon legal-homiletic discourse to set itself in authoritative opposition to fourteenth-century discourses of power.[4] Late medieval bureaucracies consolidated their power by imposing certain formal requirements on historical and legal claims. Past events had to be properly documented if they were to be considered by a court of law. This is the phenomenon that Andrew Galloway describes when he observes that in late medieval England, "tradition itself ... became increasingly clearly a legal construction."[5] Legal and political claims had always been historical claims by implication, operating in relation to the formal, bureaucratic parameters developed for the purposes of recording history. The spread of literacy in the fourteenth century meant that more people were more adept at criticizing the documents mediating history, and more cognizant of the fact that those documents were often untrustworthy or subject to manipulation. In Galloway's terms, they knew that legal tradition had been constructed, and they knew that it could be manipulated. As a result, parties that wished to advance political claims that were inconsistent with "tradition" could still make persuasive arguments, if they challenged the efficacy of the parameters governing the documentation of tradition. Langlandian discourse renovated the sententious formalism of Anglo-Saxon legal-homiletic discourse precisely in order to frame such challenges, in the service of larger legal and political claims aimed at exposing the immorality of fourteenth-century bureaucracies, religious and secular.

In this discussion, I will focus in particular on the formal strategies employed by the Langlandian voice to address its "twin themes of hypocrisy and formalism."[6] As Burrow argues, it is highly relevant that the narrative(s) of *Piers Plowman* circles back over and over again to the triad of will,

---

3 For a parallel study of plows and plowmen, see Morey, "Plows, Laws." On biblical agrarianism and the figure of the plowman, see Barney, "Plowshare." One particularly striking parallel to Piers is the *arator* from the prophecies of Bridget of Sweden: Kerby-Fulton, *Reformist Apocalypticism*, 108. For other readings of Piers's symbolism, see Watson, "Pastoral"; Griffiths, *Personification*; Troyon, "Who"; Raw, "Image."

4 On the law and legal professionalism in *Piers Plowman*, see for example Anna Baldwin, *Theme* and "Historical Context"; Galloway, "Making History Legal," 10.

5 Galloway, "Making History Legal," 9.

6 Burrow, "Words, Works, Will."

words, and works – which is to say thought, word, and deed – while attacking the hypocrisy and formalism of fourteenth-century government. Readers of the *Piers Plowman* tradition have long noted the structural importance of repeated maxims and commonplaces, and starting with the medieval scribes themselves, many have applied them to organize the texts' progress.[7] More recently, however, a critical consensus has emerged that the various *Piers Plowman* poems seem to work and rework the schemes as they go along.[8] In these accounts, the *Piers Plowman* tradition is not only sententious, but fundamentally concerned with its own sententiousness. Indeed, the very refusal of the poem to finally reach any conclusions – its restless circling around its own process – appears to be central to its religious, philosophical, and political claims. Perhaps, then, the texts of the *Piers Plowman* tradition do not aim to say the final word on the various problems of the late fourteenth century, so much as they aim to establish the Langlandian mode as an authoritative vocabulary for discussing those problems.

Richard the Redeless and *Mum and the Sothsegger* are among the most explicit commentaries by members of the "school of Langland" on the process of discourse modelled by *Piers Plowman*. They provide a useful entry point for examining the uses of *Piers Plowman* for three reasons. First, their relationship to the source tradition of the poem's three versions is relatively stable. *Richard the Redeless* and *Mum and the Sothsegger* are thought to share an author who is manifestly not the author of the original poems.[9] Second, the fragments are dated quite late in the evolution of the *Piers Plowman* tradition, and we can assume that they rewrite and rework the versions of *Piers Plowman*, and not the other way around.[10] Third, *Richard the Redeless* and *Mum and the Sothsegger* are manifestly concerned with legal, documentary authority, and discuss these issues with a degree of specificity unmatched by the other texts of the *Piers Plowman* tradition, including those attributed to Langland himself.

In my readings of *Richard the Redeless* and *Mum and the Sothsegger*, I will demonstrate that they treated the versions of *Piers Plowman* as a

---

7 See introduction (9).

8 Carruthers, *Search*; Kirk, "Langland's Plowman"; Alford, "Design"; Salter, *An Introduction*, 47–8; Newman, "Redeeming"; Smith, "Negative"; Fletcher, "Essential (Ephemeral)."

9 Barr, "Dates"; Horobin, "Dialect and Authorship."

10 For a summary of the scholarly consensus about the dates of *Piers Plowman* A, B, and C, see Kerby-Fulton, "*Piers*," 515.

repository of authorizing formulae. In both form and content, the fragments do not respond to their source tradition in a literary way, which is to say that they neither construct new creative texts nor interpolate forged passages into the creative work of another author. Rather, they treat *Piers Plowman* as a legal tradition commemorating certain claims about a political moment. Like legal texts, Langland's various political statements are subject to clarification and elaboration by professionals, who demonstrate their professionalism through their mastery of the poems' appropriate rhetorical forms. Christopher Cannon and others have written about Langland's constant recourse to the forms of grammar and school texts – including, incidentally, the *Disticha Catonis*, which is quoted more frequently in *Piers Plowman* than is any other single source.[11] These grammatical sources and school texts mark the Langlandian voice as educated, even as it also projects a model of education that is markedly different from the kinds of training that were given to the professionals who governed the realm. The poets of the *Piers Plowman* tradition took up the educated voice of Langlandian "traditionalism" because it provided an alternative form of literate, educated professionalism to the traditionalism more dominant at the turn of the fifteenth century. The Langlandian narrator may be eccentric, but he is no fool, and he cannot be dismissed as such.

My argument about this formal practice in *Richard the Redeless* and *Mum and the Sothsegger* is predicated in part on the remarkable continuity that exists between these texts and the versions of *Piers Plowman* itself, discernible in the manuscript evidence. The fragments were printed together in Mabel Day and Robert Steele's 1971 EETS edition *Mum and the Sothsegger*, in response to the evidence that they shared a transmission history. John Bale, following Nicholas Brigham, cites a poem in his *Index Britanniae Scriptorum* called "*Mum, Soth Segger*," and provides a Latin translation of its first two lines, which actually corresponds with those of *Richard the Redeless*.[12] Meanwhile, on the back cover of the *Mum and the Sothsegger* manuscript, there is a fifteenth-century inscription labelling it "the lyff off kyng Rychard the ij."[13] Though scholars have since

---

11 Cannon, "Langland's *Ars Grammatica*." On Cato and *Piers Plowman*, see Alford, *Quotations*. On Langland's education, see also Hanna, "Ymaginatif"; Galloway, "Schools"; Alford, "Langland's Learning"; Schmidt, "Scholastic"; Middleton, "Two Infinites."

12 This was first observed by Bradley, "Misplaced Leaf," 481. See also *Mum and the Sothsegger*, ed. Day and Steele, ixn.3.

13 *Mum and the Sothsegger*, ed. Day and Steele, ix.

abandoned the idea that this evidence proves the two texts to be fragments of a single poem, the evidence nonetheless suggests that the two fragments were grouped together by at least some of their medieval scribes, and perhaps in some cases (if Bale's note is not merely erroneous) presented as a single text.[14]

Richard the Redeless survives only in Cambridge University MS Ll.4.14, where it appears directly following a copy of the B-version of *Piers Plowman*. Both texts are written in the same scribal hand, and the scribe made no great effort to distinguish the end of *Piers Plowman* from the beginning of *Richard the Redeless*.[15] Walter Skeat included *Richard the Redeless* in his edition of *Piers Plowman* as an appendix, and argued that it was the work of Langland in his old age.[16] There are six blank pages in this manuscript after the end of *Richard the Redeless* that could have been intended for at least part of *Mum and the Sothsegger*. Meanwhile, the codicological evidence suggests that the *Mum and the Sothsegger* fragment could have been preceded by as many as 1,104 lines of poetry, 247 lines more than *Richard the Redeless* in its current form.[17] Thus if the ambiguous interrelationship between the two fragments suggests that *Richard the Redeless* and *Mum and the Sothsegger* might have been sometimes treated as parts of the same text, the circumstances of their survival further suggest that this text might itself have been treated as a continuation of *Piers Plowman*, analogous perhaps to other scribal efforts to "finish" the poem.[18]

The "tradition" connecting *Mum and the Sothsegger*, *Richard the Redeless*, and the other various versions and fragments of *Piers Plowman* is therefore most precisely defined as an interrelated *textual* tradition, of manuscripts witnessing identifiable Langlandian discourse characterized in part by its use or reuse of existing Langlandian verse. These texts are not

---

14 Following the conclusive arguments of Dan Embree, "Mistaken Identity."

15 Though the end of *Piers Plowman* in Cambridge MS Ll.4.14 is rubricated "Explicit hic Dialogus Petri Plowman," *Richard* is nonetheless presented "like a continuation of *Piers Plowman*.": Benson and Blanchfield, *Manuscripts*, 47.

16 Skeat's argument is highly subjective: "An imitator of William might have copied his phrases, but how was he to attain his genius?": Langland, *Piers the Plowman*, ed. Skeat, vol. 2, lxxxv.

17 Benson and Blanchfield, *Manuscripts*, 46; *Mum and the Sothsegger*, ed. Day and Steele, xviii.

18 Kerby-Fulton, "*Piers*," 516. See in particular the passus 12 added by "John But" to the end of the A version: Middleton, "Making"; Rickert, "John But"; Scase, "First to Reckon"; Warner, "John But."

only inspired by *Piers Plowman*, but in fact they rewrite its totality in the process, elaborating on particular themes or rewriting particular scenes to encourage particular interpretations of the larger whole. Configured such, the "social document" of the poem must remain finally unwritten, in much the same way that English common law is unwritten; it may be edited, compiled, excerpted, or elaborated upon according to the needs of a particular moment, as long as editor, compiler, or continuator demonstrates his or her own skill in the text's formal strategies of authentication.

Such new writing is neither quite a continuation of the earlier text, nor quite an interpolation into it. Like "the law," the "original" text of *Piers Plowman* circulated in too many different versions for the evidence to sustain such distinctions. In *Piers Plowman*, the text is not authoritative because it transparently records the coherent vision of a particular author, but because it performs certain formulaic authenticating strategies to make claims about different aspects of private and public life. Paradoxically, this constitutive lack of final definition functions in its own right as a formal guarantor of authority, as it reflects the amorphous, ambiguous formal precedent of "traditional" English law, and particularly the "transitional orality" of early English methods for recording legal principles and devising policy on their basis.

In the next section I will situate the *Piers Plowman* tradition more precisely in the context of other fourteenth-century memorials of the Anglo-Saxon period, and in particular the apparent interest in Anglo-Saxon legal precedent expressed by the revolutionaries during the Peasant's Revolt. I will then turn to the fragment *Richard the Redeless*. In its very title, this fragment uses the same nickname already applied to "Æthelred the Unready," the king with whom Wulfstan had such a vexed relationship.[19] The fragment probably plays off of Richard's veneration for Æthelred's son, King Edward the Confessor, himself mentioned by name in versions B and C of *Piers Plowman*. As we shall see, *Richard the Redeless* reworks the formal features of the *Piers Plowman* tradition's "social document" to make the tradition itself an example of the "rede" that Richard failed to understand. By connecting Richard's inability to understand sententious statements to his forfeiture of the throne, *Richard the Redeless* employs the same legal logic displayed by Wulfstan in his exhortations of Cnut: a king who does not listen to conventional wisdom is unfit to rule, however technically "legal" his claim may otherwise appear to be.

---

19 On Wulfstan, Æthelred, and Cnut, see chapter 2 (78–89).

As I will demonstrate, the "transitional literacy" of Anglo-Saxon documentary culture provided a textual precedent for the performance of "fictive orality" witnessed in the *Piers Plowman* tradition texts. These texts display "literate" anxieties about the inherent limitations of written texts themselves, and in particular their openness to corruption and misrepresentation.[20] *Piers Plowman* provided its imitators and continuators with both an authoritative precedent for discussing these problems and also a proven method for avoiding them in one's own writing. Whether or not Langland himself chose the plowman figure with the specific intention of using him as a quasi-legal authority, the author(s) of the fragments *Richard the Redeless* and *Mum and the Sothsegger* certainly regarded *Piers Plowman* as a quasi-documentary source, which they drew from as a kind of authoritative wordhoard for structuring legal and political claims about the injustices of current practices and the hypocrisies of royal and ecclesiastical bureaucrats. In the next section I will identify some of the evidence that this wordhoard had its origins in the fourteenth-century memorials of Anglo-Saxon legal-homiletic discourse.[21]

Langland's Immediate Contexts

Kathryn Kerby-Fulton has argued that one may see in the versions of *Piers Plowman* evidence suggesting that Langland felt an affinity for the Benedictine order. First, Langland seems to distinguish between the endowments of regular clergy and secular clergy, and he seems to be far more critical of the latter.[22] Second, there is some evidence that Langland studied in a Benedictine abbey as a boy, and the apocalyptic allegory witnessed by the versions of *Piers Plowman* betrays its origins in monastic traditions of exegesis.[23] Finally, criticism of the surviving manuscripts of *Piers Plowman* has suggested that monastic houses made up a significant

---

20 For a fuller discussion of the terms "fictive orality" and "transitional literacy," see the introduction (27–33).

21 My examination of later Middle English alliterative writing is by no means comprehensive; for fuller surveys, see for example Salter, "Alliterative Modes"; Hanna, "Alliterative."

22 Kerby-Fulton, "Piers," 530. On Langland's distinctions between regular and secular clergy, see Lawler, "*Secular Clergy*," esp. 95. On *Piers Plowman* and disendowment, see also Galloway, "Making History Legal," 21–3; Scase, *New Anticlericalism*; Baldwin, "Historical Context," 75.

23 Kerby-Fulton, "Piers," 530–1, citing Kaske, "Local Iconography"; Bryer, *Little Malvern*, 24. On *Piers Plowman*'s "monastic philosophy-theology" (45), see also Bloomfield, *Apocalypse*.

percentage of Langland's early readership.[24] Taken together, this evidence suggests that Langland's choice of alliterative verse may well have been influenced by the monastic traditions of vernacular English literacy surveyed in the preceding chapters, and that his work appealed to audiences who were themselves trained in those traditions. In the first part of this section, I will briefly summarize some of the more compelling evidence for continuity between Anglo-Saxon legal-homiletic discourse, early vernacular alliterative verse, and the *Piers Plowman* tradition. I will then go on to contextualize Langland's particular employment of alliterative verse as a quasi-documentary form.

As I said in chapter 3, Langland's highly innovative mode of writing appears to derive from the scribal and intellectual culture of the West Midlands, not far removed from the scribes and audiences of *The First Worcester Fragment*, the *Brut*, and the Jesus 29 manuscript of the *Proverbs of Alfred*.[25] Among the best evidence for this connection is the so-called Harley lyrics, appearing in the manuscript London, BL Harley 2253. The scribe of the Harley manuscript appears to have been a legal scrivener, who likely worked in the vicinity of Hereford Cathedral.[26] In William of Malmesbury's *Vita Wulfstani* it is clear that Robert de Losinga, bishop of Hereford, was a close friend and ally of St Wulfstan, and the dioceses maintained this connection for some time thereafter; hence the Harley scribe's work falls into the general orbit of Worcester book production.[27] The Harley lyrics have been often cited as important antecedents to Langland's own mode of alliterative satire, though it is generally agreed that their basic formal elements are reworked considerably in the versions of *Piers Plowman*.[28]

Though the lyrics do strongly suggest some direct continuity between St Wulfstan's literate community and the first versions of *Piers Plowman* (and hence they help to justify my decision to limit my study to the West Midlands), it should not therefore be inferred that later medieval legal-homiletic discourse survived only in the vicinity of Worcester, or that Langland could only have encountered it there. Even the lyrics themselves appear to be written in a larger number of regional dialects.[29] Evidence that

---

24 Kerby-Fulton, "*Piers*," 531.

25 Kerby-Fulton, "*Piers*," 531; Pearsall, "Origins," 14.

26 On the scribe and his context, seek Birkholz, "Harley."

27 On the history of Hereford cathedral from the eleventh to the thirteenth centuries, see Barrow, "Athelstan."

28 Hanna, "Alliterative," 494, and *London*, 259–61; Kerby-Fulton, "*Piers*," 531; Salter, "*Simonie*." On alliterative style in the Harley lyrics, see Osberg, "Alliterative Technique."

29 Hanna, "Alliterative," 509.

alliterative traditions existed outside the vicinity of Worcester is provided by the two alliterative poetic fragments in the manuscript London, BL MS Arundel 292.[30] The fourteenth-century fragments are copied into a thirteenth-century manuscript of *The Bestiary*, a text that has itself been identified as a possible "missing link" between alliterative Old English and alliterative Middle English.[31] The additions were made while the manuscript was kept in the Benedictine priory of Norwich, though neither appears to have been written by a local author; one text appears to come from York or Beverley, the other from London.[32] Norwich was founded in 1096 by Herbert de Losinga, who had previously been abbot of Ramsey. Ramsey was founded in turn by St Oswald of Worcester and York, and its most famous denizen in the late Anglo-Saxon period was the author Byrhtferth, who died roughly seventy years before Herbert left for Norwich. Among Byrhtferth's works are lives of St Oswald and St Ecgwine that paraphrased and recorded monastic charters attributed to those men, commentaries on Bede's scientific works, and most famously an *Enchiridion* or "Manual" in both Latin and Old English on *computus*.[33] Hence there are not many degrees of separation between the dense, learned fragments copied into Arundel 292 and the learned tradition of Anglo-Saxon Latin and English writing exemplified by Byrhtferth. Further studies of the Arundel fragments and other poems like them – in particular the texts surviving only on legal documents – may narrow the gap even further, offering still more proof that the West Midlands was far from unique for its continuous legal-homiletic traditions of English literacy.[34]

But though there is plenty of work to be done fleshing out these specific narratives of local continuity in alliterative verse traditions, not all survivals of Anglo-Saxon legal-homiletic discourse in fourteenth-century English writing are as unusual as those cited above. Anglo-Saxon legal-homiletic discourse also survived in the mainstream of widely circulated vernacular texts, for example, in the *South English Legendaries* and *Lay*

---

30 Shrader, "Inharmonious," 2; Hanna, "Alliterative," 509–10; Salter, "A Complaint." The poems are titled respectively "The Chorister's Lament" and "A Complaint Against Blacksmiths."

31 Duncan, "Bestiary."

32 Hanna, "Alliterative," 510.

33 Byrhtferth, *Lives, Enchiridion*.

34 Hanna, "Alliteration," 46. One poem is "A Bird in Bishopwood," appearing on a rent roll from St Paul's: Kennedy, "Bird." Another poem appearing on a commission is "A Lament for Sir John Berkeley": Turville-Petre, "Lament."

Folk's Catechism. In the first instance, it is striking that manuscripts witnessing Görlach's "E" redaction of the *SEL* preserves legends of so many of the Anglo-Saxon saints listed in the *First Worcester Fragment*, especially since several of these saints are relatively obscure.[35] Görlach even connects this redaction to the West Midlands, and posits that it marks a relatively early stage in the *SEL*'s dissemination. Even more striking evidence of Anglo-Saxon legal-homiletic discourse in the *SEL* may be found in the *Life of St. Kenelm.* The text focuses on a central miracle, in which a dove brings a "writ" to the pope documenting the martyrdom of the boy saint and identifying his resting place. The text of the writ deviates from the normal rhyme of the *SEL* to take the form of an alliterative couplet.[36] The couplet is powerfully associated with the legend for centuries to follow, and it appears in its original English form in Higden's Latin *Polychronicon*; John Trevisa also leaves the text unaltered in his English translation.[37] The dissemination of this "writ" provides yet another indication that alliterative metre, documented truth, and the Anglo-Saxon period continued to be linked in the English imagination after the thirteenth century.

Closer in date and purpose to *Piers Plowman* than the *SEL* is *The Lay Folk's Catechism.*[38] The text is a 1357 translation and expansion of six topics for lay instruction issued at the 1281 Council of Lambeth.[39] The translation was written by John Gatrynge, a monk of St Mary's Abbey, perhaps at the behest of York's archbishop John Thoresby.[40] The text is written in an alliterative quasi-metrical form that poses problems for the critic similar to those posed by Anglo-Saxon stressed prose, leading David Lawton to suggest that its form is based in part on the *ars dictaminis.*[41] It is also clearly a legal-homiletic text, which relies upon the listener's faith in the

---

35 Görlach,*Textual Tradition*, 32–7; Lapidge, *St. Swithun*, 712–3. Eight of the twelve saints listed in the *First Worcester Fragment* have *SEL* lives in surviving manuscripts; and though Aidan does not have his own poem, he dominates the brief "Life of Oswald the King," and can be added as a ninth. See also Frederick, "National Identity"; Blanton, "Counting Noses"; and my articles "Documents, Poetry" and "St. Egwine."

36 Wogan-Browne, Evans, and Johnson, "Locating Saint's Lives," 257–9.

37 Wogan-Browne, Evans, and Johnson, "Locating Saint's Lives," 252; Higden, *Polychronicon* 6.306–7. For a list of the couplet's occurrences, see *Landboc*, ed. Royce, pp. vii–viii.

38 Lawton, "Gaytryge's Sermon"; Powell "Transmission." On the similar impulses behind *The Lay Folk's Catechism* and *Piers Plowman*, see Watson, "Pastoral," esp. 89–90.

39 *Councils & Synods*, ed. Powicke and Cheney, 2:900–5.

40 Lawton, "Gaytryge's Sermon," 330.

41 Lawton, "Gaytryge's Sermon," 343. See also Salter, "Alliterative Modes," 173–7.

Christian teachings it summarizes to authorize specifically legal and political claims.

The legal-homiletic quality of *The Lay Folk's Catechism* is apparent, for example, in its description and gloss of the tenth commandment. The passage begins with a statement of the commandment itself (237–43), and it then continues to stipulate that anyone who breaks the commandment by theft must return the stolen goods as part of the penance (244–7).[42] The text then goes slightly off topic to assert ecclesiastical jurisdiction over the crime of perjury, enjoyed by the bishops of England since at least the reign of Æthelstan (*II Æthelstan* 26):

> And in cas that we have thurgh fals athes,
> Als in assizes or othir enquestes
> Wittandly and willfalli gere our euen cristen
> Lese thaire patrimoyne, or thair heritage,
> Or falsly be desesed of land or of lithe,
> Or fals diuorce be made, or any man dampned,
> Of all we do, that we may, unto the party,
> Yit may we noght be assoiled of our false athe,
> Bot of our bisshop or him that has his power,
> For swilk cas is riuely reserved til him seluen. (248–57)

> [And in case through false oaths we have
> In assizes or in other inquests
> Knowingly and wilfully caused another Christian
> To lose their patrimony or heritage,
> Or to be falsely deprived of land or limb,
> Or to make a false divorce, or any man to be damned,
> No matter what we do to the party
> We are not cleansed of that false oath
> Except by the bishop or someone acting in his stead,
> For such a case is typically reserved to him alone.]

Needless to say, this repetitive, alliterative list of perjury's possible consequences is not closely related to the topic of the tenth commandment. Indeed, one may rather expect it to appear in a description of the eighth commandment, against bearing false witness. The appearance of this

---

42 All citations from the EETS edition, *Lay Folk's Catechism*.

passage in a description of the commandment against coveting a neigh
bour's property emphasizes in particular the bishops' jurisdiction over false
claims of ownership, asserted also in *I Cnut*'s survey of oaths that bishops
must oversee.[43] It is especially striking that this Wulfstanian assertion of
episcopal jurisdiction over oath-taking should be written by a monk of
Wulfstan's former diocese, at a time when the archbishop's gospel book
discussed in chapter 2 was still used as an oath-book for the chapter.[44]

And so even though my examination of these examples has been brief,
we can nonetheless draw certain provisional conclusions. It seems that
certain formal strategies of Anglo-Saxon legal-homiletic discourse – and in
particular, alliterative sound-patterning – persisted in medieval English
monasteries and in nearby ecclesiastical bureaucracies even after Old
English homilies and law codes were no longer being copied into new
manuscripts. When authors trained in these monasteries and bureaucracies
wrote or compiled newer English-language texts, they sometimes used
those same formal strategies to give those texts a kind of self-evident, sententious authority. In this manner Anglo-Saxon legal-homiletic discourse
went on to influence Middle English vernacular literary production more
generally, though it tended to do so either in minor texts circulated in local
literate communities, or in popular works of lay religious instruction.

Below, I will argue that the marginal status of alliterative, sententious
formalism places the *Piers Plowman* tradition in authoritative opposition to the clerical establishment, framing the Langlandian narrator as a
voice that may have spoken from the wilderness, but that was nonetheless situated well enough to see what was happening behind the city
walls. The Langlandian narrator is clearly educated enough to document
bureaucratic abuses with specificity, even as he clearly operates far
enough outside the actual bureaucratic discourse of his day to avoid being implicated in those abuses. It is precisely the liminality of Langland's
sententious formalism that makes it so efficacious as a mode of religious
and political satire.

The thing, then, that most clearly separates "the school of Langland"
from its most obvious forbears is the extent to which that school seemed
to recognize the potential of Middle English alliterative satire to serve as
an extra-literary and quasi-documentary formal mode. Not content to
be poems about the abuses of the law, *Richard the Redeless* and *Mum*

---

43 See chapter 2 above (86–7).
44 Treharne, "York."

and the Sothsegger modelled *Piers Plowman* as a new, old kind of legal document, which based its authority not on its precise imitations of the accepted models – never strictly necessary in Anglo-Saxon documents – but instead on its employment of sententious forms reflecting the apparent inner virtue of the text's speaker. Indeed, this virtue is configured in later Anglo-Saxon legal-homiletic discourse precisely by the flagrant rejection of accepted models, in favour of homiletic and even poetic assertions of proverbial truth. The fourteenth-century memorials of Anglo-Saxon law and legal documents were similarly renovated and remembered in a kind of "anti-formalist" gesture, as they enabled various interests to comment both on specific injustices of their day and on the forms of official justice themselves.

As I will demonstrate, then, my claim that the alliterative poetry of the later medieval period originated in the legal-homiletic discourse of ancient English monasteries does not contradict the long-standing scholarly consensus, that the turn to English literacy in the fourteenth century was a radical reinvention of administrative precedent. Old English legal documents clearly predated the legal traditions of common and constitutional law, and hence their authority could not be wholly suppressed; better still, they were sententious, vague, and easily adapted to a wide variety of claims. For these reasons, Anglo-Saxon law and legal documents served as a kind of contestable ground on which the relationship between ideal principle and administrative practice could be negotiated and redefined. In the next section I will survey this contestable ground in more detail.

Alliteration, "Documentary Poetics," and Anglo-Saxon Legal-Homiletic Discourse

As I said in the introduction, my reading of *Piers Plowman* as a kind of quasi-documentary tradition owes a debt to Emily Steiner's reading of Middle English "documentary poetics." Steiner compares fictive legal documents like the Lollard charters of Christ to the *Piers Plowman* tradition, arguing that these texts all "used documentary culture both to challenge orthodox notions of textual authority and to construct an oppositional rhetoric."[45] Steiner's perceptive reading of these texts is influenced by the work of scholars such as Steven Justice, Susan Crane, and Richard Firth Green, whose explorations of literacy's impact are perhaps best summarized by

---

45 Steiner, *Documentary Culture*, 194.

the title of Justice's influential book: *Writing and Rebellion*.[46] The massive social disruptions of the fourteenth century coincided with the widespread proliferation of English-language texts, both legal-documentary and literary. As these scholars have demonstrated, the very fact of these texts' existence was itself a major cause of the social disruption they witness, as the various powers that be sought to control written English and define its purposes.

The authors, compilers, and critics of written English texts in the fourteenth century were well aware of the Old English precedent for their activities. For this reason Anglo-Saxon legal-homiletic discourse constituted a third term that sat between Steiner's "orthodox" and "oppositional" notions of textual authority. On the one hand, Anglo-Saxon charters and legal documents continued to play a vital role in the government of ancient and well-established corporate interests. On the other, the homiletic character of those documents was so alienated from contemporary practices by the fourteenth century that their forms provided a compellingly authoritative basis for social critique, which exposed the reliance of latter-day bureaucratic practices on "empty" form over moral "content" – which is to say, diplomatic formulae over sententious commonplaces.

In her own take on the amorphous structure of *Piers Plowman*, Steiner demonstrates that the text "portrays spiritual pilgrimage as the work of the chronicler or legal clerk as well as the contemplative reader, and as the careful copying, justification, and reinterpretation of a series of legal instruments."[47] Here, I will supplement her findings to argue that the poem's construction of "true" record-keeping in these terms harks back to the old presumptions of Anglo-Saxon clerical literacy. As I argued in chapters 1 and 2, it is clear that Anglo-Saxon clerics based their administrative authority on simultaneous claims of technical competence in writing and moral excellence in thoughts and deeds. The poem's refiguring of Anglo-Saxon "oral" precedent is not so much nostalgic as it is formulaic, implicitly criticizing the professionalism of fourteenth-century clerks by means of older and more homiletic authenticating strategies.

One of the clearest manifestations of Langland's formulaic dependence on Anglo-Saxon authority appears in an oft-cited passage from the prologue of *Piers Plowman* B-version:[48]

---

46 Crane, "Writing Lesson"; Justice, *Writing and Rebellion*; Green, *A Crisis of Truth*.

47 Steiner, *Documentary Culture*, 142.

48 See for example Scanlon, "King, Commons," 204–12; Crane, "Writing Lesson," 211–13; Baldwin, *Theme of Government*, 12–15; Donaldson, *Piers Plowman*, 88–91.

> The kyng and knyghthod and clergie bothe
> Casten þat þe commune sholde hire communes fynde.
> The commune contreved of kynde wit craftes,
> And for profit of al þe peple Plowmen ordeyned
> To tilie and to travaille as trewe lif asketh.
> The kyng and þe commune and kynde wit þe þridde
> Shopen lawe and leute, ech lif to knowe his owene. (Prol. 116–22)

> [The king and both the gentry and clergy
> Judged that the commons should find its sustenance.
> The commons devised skills, according to natural wisdom,
> And ordained plowmen for the profit of all the people
> To till [the earth] and work, as the true life asks.
> The king and the commons and, third, natural wisdom
> Shaped law and justice, for each creature to know his own.]

This narrative of English legal history repeats the same basic authorizing structure found in the opening lines of Anglo-Saxon law codes, and also *The Proverbs of Alfred*.[49] A king calls together the knights and clergy so that they may draft a description of legal practices and principles for the benefit of the people. The B prologue elaborates on the basic narrative, to subtly redefine the role played by the king and his *witan*. These powerful men intervened in the commons not for their own "royal power and need" (as Cnut did in his law code) nor to ensure that the people obeyed their lord (as Alfred did in his poem), but with the specific, practical aim of ensuring that the people should be able to find their sustenance. We are told further that the commons had applied their innate intelligence to figure out the kinds of jobs that were necessary, and in particular they had ordained plowmen to fulfil the basic functions of agriculture. By implication, then, the king in the B prologue invents law and justice specifically to manage the distribution of food among the people, to ensure that no person among the commons will be denied his or her *communes*.

The most striking aspect of this passage's appropriation of legal-homiletic formal precedent is its emphasis on the centrality of property law to the principles of justice in general. The king ensures that everyone will have sustenance by forcing "ech lif to knowe his owene" – "place,"

---

49 On the parallels between this passage and Richard II's coronation oath, see Bennet, "Date."

perhaps (as Donaldson translates), but certainly "property" or "due" as well.[50] In other words, the passage asserts that the very purpose of law and justice is to advertise the true principles of ownership, so that each individual is able both to protect his own property and to respect the property of his neighbours. In this narrative, the labour of the plowmen is given its purpose not only by the "true life" it exemplifies, but also by the legal framework demarcating the property and dues of the commons, necessary to distribute the fruits of the plowmen's labour. Indeed, the B prologue implies that "law" as a feature of human society exists primarily in order to regulate the work of the plowmen and the distribution of their products, according to the dictates of "kynde wit."

Some fourteenth-century occurrences of the English word "plow" provide context for the passage's emphasis on the roles of property and plowmen in the foundation of English law. Though the "plow-land" meaning of ME *plouȝ* cited at the start of this chapter is an archaism, it is frequently attested in later Middle English as part of the alliterative doublet *park and plouȝ*. This doublet appears to be derived from some later version of the formula recorded in *Hit bicwæð*, where the similar doublet *ne plot ne ploh* initiates a list of a whole series of rights: "⁊ ic agnian wylle to agenre æhte ðæt ðæt ic hæbbe ⁊ næfre ðe myntan ne plot ne ploh, ne turf ne toft, ne furh ne fotmæl (And I will own as my own possession what I have, and never intend for you neither plot nor plow-land, turf nor homestead, furrow nor footmark)."[51] In Middle English poetry, the doublet *park and plouȝ* appears to have been a proverbial shorthand phrase summarizing the traditional rights of ownership, in much the same way that the proverbial doublet "to have and to hold" taken from traditional English wedding vows serves in the present to summarize the duties of marriage.

The proverbial meaning of the *park and plouȝ* doublet is suggested in its three appearances in John Gower's *Confessio Amantis*. In the first, from book I, Florent is attempting to buy his way out of his agreement with the loathly lady, so that he "behihte hire good ynowh / Of lond, of rente, of park, of plowh, / Bot al that compteth sche at noght" (promised her enough of land, of rent, of parks, of plow-lands; but all that she counted as nothing) (I.1565–7). The "park and plow" offered here is a restatement of the offer to give the loathly lady land and rent, summarizing an implicitly much longer list of rights to the land that she would have if she accepted

---

50 Donaldson, *Piers Plowman*, 89.
51 See chapter 2 (70–2).

his offer. The second occurrence is in book V, when the Confessor speaks against those lovers who choose their beloveds "Noght for the beauté of hire face, / Ne yit for vertu ne for grace (not for the beauty of her face or for her virtue or grace)," but on the contrary, "for the park and for the plowh, / And other thing which therto longeth" (for the park and the plow-land and the other things belonging thereto) (V.2520–5): which is to say, for their wealth, derived from tenurial rights to arable land. Shortly thereafter Amans asserts in reply: "I axe nouther park ne plowh: / If I hire hadde, it were ynowh" (I ask for neither park nor plow-land, if I had her it would be enough) (V.2846–52), rejecting the value of such wealth. In all three of these occurrences, then, "park and plow" serves as shorthand for a whole host of transferrable rights and privileges.

In alliterative poetry, *park* and *plouȝ* appear together in catalogues of possessions and rights remarkably like the *Hit bicwæð* formula. In *Awntyrs of Arthur*, a ghost describes the greatness of her former property as follows: "Gretter then Dame Gaynour, of garson and golde, / Of palaies, of parkes, of pondes, of plowes, / Of townes, of toures, of tresour untolde" (Greater that Lady Guenivere in treasure, gold, palaces, parks, ponds, plow-lands, towns, towers, treasure untold) (47–8). In *Parlement of the Three Ages* lines 140–5, Middle Elde counts his parks and plow-lands in the course of obsessively going over his accounts:

> One his golde and his gude gretly he mousede,
> His renttes and his reches rekened he full ofte,
> Of mukkyng, of marlelyng, and mendynge of howses,
> Of benes of his bondemen, of benefetis many,
> Of presanttes of polayle, of pufilis als;
> Of purches of ploughe-londes, of parkes full faire.

> [He thought a great deal about his gold and his wealth,
> He counted his rents and his riches very often:
> of fertilizing and mending houses,
> of services from his bondsmen, of many benefits,
> of presents of poultry, of small parcels of land,
> of purchases of plow-lands and very nice parks.]

And so the *park and plouȝ* doublet is yet another example of a formula from Anglo-Saxon legal-homiletic discourse that found an afterlife in Middle English alliterative poetry. It is also representative of the particular applicability of the legal traditionalism embodied by the "plowmen" of

Piers Plowman. After all, disputes over tenurial rights to "park and plow" provided the occasion for most late medieval citations of Anglo-Saxon law and history. This centrality of land law to the late medieval construction of legal traditionalism is surely part of the reason that Piers the Plowman, cited as the author of *Piers Plowman* in virtually all early accounts of the poem, came also to serve as a personification of traditional law's disembodied and decontextualized authority.[52] In the B prologue's origin story of English law, the "true life" of the plowmen not only precedes but provides the model for the *lawe and leute* governing ideal land ownership.

The importance given to the plowmen in this passage is indicative of the major changes in Anglo-Saxon legal-homiletic discourse between the reign of Cnut and the reign of Richard II. For example, it is difficult to imagine that Wulfstan, who so frequently asserted the importance of class distinctions, would feel comfortable investing so much symbolic power in a common labourer like Piers. This difference between the schools of Wulfstan and Langland reflects the changing status of English literacy in relation to the institutional discourses of power. Though Wulfstan reinvigorated and regularized the conventions of Anglo-Saxon homily and law, the mere fact that he wrote in English could not have been more formally conservative. Royal law codes were among the oldest known examples of English writing, and in Wulfstan's lifetime they had been copied and improved upon for four hundred years. By the fourteenth century, this legal tradition had long since been eclipsed, and its remnants were bracketed off from mainstream legal discourse as uncitable survivals from so-called time out of mind.

But even though pre-1189 legal precedent was theoretically exempt from legal proceedings, references to Anglo-Saxon history enabled late medieval authors to provide a veneer of conservatism to exceptional cases and even large-scale innovations. A particularly illustrative example for our present purposes appears in Trevisa's translation of Higden's *Polychronicon*. Like Wulfstan, Trevisa holds up King Edgar's Benedictine Reform as a model for secular lords in relation to the church, but unlike Wulfstan he does so to argue that "seculer lordes schulde take awey the superfluyte of here [i.e., the church's] possessiouns, and ȝeve it to hem þat nedeþ" (secular lords should take away what is left over from their [i.e., the church's] possessions and give it to those in need).[53] Needless to

---

52 E.g., Middleton, "'Kynde Name'," 16.
53 Higden, *Polychronicon* vol. 6, 465–7. See also Scase, *Anti-Clericalism*, 111.

say, this is a sentiment that contrasts quite strongly with the major themes of Wulfstan's writing.

Trevisa's rather more radical reading of Edgar's Anglo-Saxon precedent is related to his rather more liminal status as a vernacular author. Elsewhere, Trevisa cites Anglo-Saxon precedent to justify his activities as a translator of Latin texts into English – a kind of justification that Wulfstan never had to make. In the *Dialogue Between the Lord and the Clerk on Translation*, the Lord observes that King Alfred "translated the best lawes into Englisshe tonge, and a grete del of the Sauter out of Latyn into Englisshe, and made Wyrefrith, Bysshop of Wyrcestir, translate Seynt Gregories bokes Dialoges out of Latyn into Saxoun" (translated the best laws into the English tongue, and a great deal of the Psalter out of Latin into English, and made Werfrith, bishop of Worcester, translate Saint Gregory's book *Dialogues* out of Latin into Saxon).[54] Alfred was the king most commonly evoked in such arguments, but he was not the only one; for example, one (potentially Wycliffite) defender of biblical translation makes a similar allusion to Sts Aidan and Oswald, king of Northumbria, as they are memorialized in Bede's *Historia ecclesiastica*.[55] These memorials of Anglo-Saxon kings and saints are paralleled by the similar memorials in *The First Worcester Fragment* and *The Proverbs of Alfred*, but they have a markedly different character from the poems of the thirteenth century. Instead of performing their direct formal continuity with Anglo-Saxon literary traditions, fourteenth-century English texts cited Anglo-Saxon precedent to justify the novelty of their work.

The most radical late medieval appropriations of Anglo-Saxon precedent are those found in the records of the 1381 Uprising. In the revolts at Bury St Edmunds and St Albans monasteries, for example, the peasants demanded the abbots to show them the Anglo-Saxon charters they believed to be hidden, even as they destroyed other, "newer" charters.[56] At Bury St Edmunds they specifically demanded documents dating to the reign of Cnut, which may suggest a popular memory of his reign reflecting the centrality of his law code to post-Conquest Anglo-Saxon legal-homiletic discourse.[57] Similarly, Wat Tyler demanded that Richard II reinstate "the law

---

54 Wogan-Browne, *Idea of the Vernacular*, 233–4.

55 Wogan-Browne et al., *Idea of the Vernacular*, 147.

56 Justice, *Writing and Rebellion* 47–8; Faith, "'Great Rumour'," 64; Strohm, "Introduction," 4–5; Galloway, "Making History Legal," 36.

57 Musson, "Appealing," 175–8. Also relevant are the claims that Cnut founded Bury St Edmunds: Gransden, *Legends*, 11–12.

of Winchester," an apparent reference to the traditional seat of government in the Anglo-Saxon era. Whether it refers specifically to Cnut's Winchester law code *I–II Cnut*, to the Domesday Book, or to some other specific legal text, Tyler's phrasing almost certainly indicates that popular memories of Anglo-Saxon kingship were highly nostalgic, equivalent perhaps to contemporary American memories of the "founding fathers."[58]

Again, the popular nostalgia among Tyler and his followers for the Anglo-Saxon era is particularly conditioned by the applicability of Anglo-Saxon precedent to land law. As I mentioned in chapter 1, a specific reason that the Anglo-Saxons would be particularly favoured by the people is that ancient precedent could sometimes persuade judges to invalidate the rights of local lords and ecclesiastical institutions, by reverting land ownership to the king.[59] Trevisa's evocation of King Edgar was not merely rhetorical; if an old king's authority had first validated an Anglo-Saxon charter, then perhaps a new king's authority could invalidate it, as Edgar himself had done. Of course, such arguments were not always successful in court, and the endowments of Anglo-Saxon kings remained major sources of monastic power and wealth until the Reformation. Still, the threat of legal challenge lead to the copying of many late thirteenth- and fourteenth-century witnesses of Anglo-Saxon legal documents and law codes, appearing in monasteries all over England.[60] The example of St Albans is particularly instructive. The chronicler Thomas Walsingham ordered the production of a new St Albans cartulary within a few years of the likely date for *Richard the Redeless* and *Mum and the Sothsegger*.[61] In this work Thomas followed in the footsteps of his illustrious predecessor, Matthew Paris, who ordered Anglo-Saxon charters to be copied in Dublin, Trinity College MS 177, and London, BL Cotton Nero D.i.[62] As Julia Crick has documented, the abbey continued to draw upon these Anglo-Saxon documents to incrementally redefine concepts of *libertas* according to their own benefit.[63] Thus the very same documents could be cited either

---

58 Musson, *Medieval Law*, 252; R. Green, *Crisis*, 201–2, 412; Galloway, "Making History Legal," 19.

59 See pp. 58–9.

60 See chapter 1 (39–51). The *Electronic Sawyer* lists over one hundred individual manuscripts dated to the fourteenth century that witness one or more Anglo-Saxon charters: accessed 18 July 2013.

61 In the manuscript Chatsworth House, Library of the Duke of Devonshire, St Albans Cartulary: Crick, *Charters of St. Albans*, 51–2.

62 Crick, *Charters of St. Albans*, 45–51.

63 Crick, "*Pristina Libertas*," "Liberty and Fraternity." See also Hagger, "*Gesta abbatum*."

as a way of denying the local autonomy of ecclesiastical institutions, or as a way of maintaining and even increasing that autonomy.

In the *Piers Plowman* tradition itself, this negotiation takes place most dramatically in the famous letters by the revolutionary preacher John Ball. These letters evoke Piers to justify explicit calls for revolutionary action, and Helen Barr calls them an "incipient *Piers Plowman* tradition."[64] Emily Steiner describes their function in this regard quite well: "the rebel letters [of John Ball] put into circulation the very text that Langland advertises as a model of public writing but never acknowledges as his own," which is to say "the fictive legal document, the legal document as poetic form."[65] Ann Astell has argued convincingly that the Langlandian imagery of Ball's letters is intended to evoke a higher moral authority for the extra-legal activities of the revolutionaries.[66] Thus the letters commemorate a validity that has yet to be authorized by the hypothetical or "fictive" legality of any revolution, which can only become truly legal when the revolution is complete.

At the same time, however, the letters strongly imply that their moral authority would in fact have conformed to the record of written law, if that record had itself been properly maintained. A major authorizing impulse in the letters is their recourse to traditional sententious statements, for example, in the rhyming pair of alliterative couplets in London, BL, Royal MS 13. E. ix: "Be war ye be wo, / Knoweth your freend fro your foo" (9–10). Ball's letters are also preoccupied with uncovering a documented "trewthe" that has been hitherto ignored or hidden by corrupt authorities.[67] As I have already demonstrated, it appears that this notion was not merely metaphorical, and that the hidden "truth" was sought by Ball's followers in documents dated to the Anglo-Saxon era. Indeed, if Ball's letters are read as replacements for those "lost" documents, then we may even classify these "fictive" documents as forgeries. Not unlike the forged charters copied in monastic chronicles, Ball's letters aim to

---

64 Barr, *Signes and Sothe*, 12–13. The fullest study of these letters is Justice, *Writing and Rebellion*. Justice includes the full text of the letters (13–15) and discusses their relationship to *Piers Plowman* at length (102–39). See also Gellrich, *Discourse and Dominion*, 151–91; Crane, "Writing Lesson," 201–11; and Astell, *Political Allegory*.

65 Steiner, *Documentary Culture*, 173.

66 Astell, *Political Allegory*, 44–72.

67 See Justice, *Writing and Rebellion*, 124–5 for how Ball reappropriates for political ends Langland's more theological concept of "trewthe." Hudson tentatively identifies the use of this word as a part of the language of Lollardy: Hudson, "Sect Vocabulary," 16–17.

reinscribe the "lost" precedent that had been hidden by corrupt bureaucrats, who did not respect the traditional sententious formalism of older, "oral" texts. In these letters, then, the new law of revolution represented itself as a return to the old law of ancient England, the unassailable justice of Final Judgment linked in this way to the uncitable precedent of time immemorial.

Hence Ball's letters are inspired not only by the apocalyptic imagery of *Piers Plowman*, but also by the tradition's renovation of the ancient legal forms "hidden" in the (alliterative) laws of Winchester and (homiletic) charters of Cnut. Andrew Galloway has written that in *Piers Plowman*, history is "thoroughly hollowed out, both by demands for a justice that pay no heed to tradition as such, and by self- or institution-serving presentist manipulations of tradition that accomplish the same ends."[68] The fact that history has been hollowed out in this way does not deprive that history of its rhetorical power or political force. Indeed, the "documentary poetic" of Ball's letters and the *Piers Plowman* tradition takes up the hollowed-out shell of early English history and incorporates it into an alternative narrative of law's origin. In the process they abandon the vexed authority of Anglo-Saxon precedent for the even more vexed authority of the apocalyptic vision.

Like Ball's letters, the fragment *Richard the Redeless* renovates the allegorical genre of *Piers Plowman* to retroactively justify a change in power: in this case, the rise of Henry IV to the throne of England. The parallel between the nickname "Æthelred the Unready" and the fragment's title *Richard the Redeless* indicates that fragment's debt to Anglo-Saxon legal-homiletic discourse.[69] I argued in chapter 2 that the dual meaning of *ræd* as both reading books and offering counsel aligned clerical literacy with traditional wisdom; *Richard the Redeless* operates within the same field of presumptions, as the king's "redelessness" is evoked through his inability to read and understand the meaning of the written text *Piers Plowman*. In this manner the poem does not merely imitate Langland's verse, but reclassifies it, as a text documenting the kind of wisdom that a king must have, if he is to protect law and justice and ensure that each of his subjects knows which things are his or her own.

---

68 Galloway, "Making History Legal," 30.

69 On the trope of the ill-advised king in Ricardian literature, see Embree, "King's Ignorance." On Æthelred and his counsellors, see Damon, "Advisors"; Sheppard, "Noble Counsel"; Keynes, "Declining Reputation." On some of the shifting connotations of the words *ræd* and *rædan*, see above (61–2).

The King's *geræednes* and *Richard the Redeless*

Andrew Horn's "London Collection" manuscripts, which contain the latest witnesses of the *Quadripartitus* and *Leges Henrici Primi*, juxtapose these texts with the *Mirror of Justices*, a book of advice for judges that purports to record practices dating to the reign of King Alfred.[70] The title of the *Mirror of Justices* is only one of the clearer examples of the intersections between the documents and law codes of the Anglo-Saxon era and the themes, concerns, and discursive methods of the "mirror literature" genre of the later Middle Ages, of which *Richard the Redeless* is an important example.[71] In the remainder of this chapter I will identify the ways in which *Richard the Redeless* frames its representation of kingly virtue in direct response to the *Piers Plowman* tradition, as the fragment's discussions of Richard's ability to understand the poem's allegory are themselves allegorical for Richard's ability to rule wisely. In the process, *Richard the Redeless* reframes the entirety of *Piers Plowman* as a mirror text, capable of instructing would-be royal advisors in the moral principles necessary to do their jobs correctly. As I will demonstrate, the fragment employs the sententious forms derived from Anglo-Saxon legal-homiletic discourse in the process of this transformation.

As I stated earlier, the title of the poem *Richard the Redeless* connects Richard II to the last king of England to have been forced from his throne, Æthelred the Unready. There is some context for this allusion in *Piers Plowman* itself. Æthelred's son, Edward the Confessor, is cited by name alongside Edmund the Martyr in both the B-version and C-version of Anima's speech, as examples of true royal charity (B.15.223–4, C.16.348–9). It is worth pointing out that the most compelling historical evidence for their charity is found in the documentary record of their royal gifts: in the almost 2,000 Anglo-Saxon charters catalogued in the *Electronic Sawyer* website, 167 date themselves to the reign of Edward the Confessor and 57 to the reign of Edmund, so that collectively the kings account for roughly one in ten of surviving English legal documents dated between the arrival of Augustine in Canterbury and the Battle of Hastings. The fact that many of these documents are considered forgeries by scholars only underscores the powerful symbolism of these figures in post-Conquest English law.[72]

---

70 Catto, "Andrew Horn," 386–7.

71 For a survey of this genre, see Ferster, *Fictions of Advice*.

72 The names Edmund and Edward are also connected through the juxtaposition of the law codes *I–II Edmund* and *I–II Edward* in a "mini-collection" of legal texts attested in Cambridge, Corpus Christi College 383 and the *Quadripartitus*: in Corpus 383 the

The royal saints Edmund and Edward the Confessor also appear alongside Richard II in the Wilton Diptych. Richard was particularly fond of comparing himself to Edward the Confessor, and Richard built a Westminster tomb for himself and Anne of Bohemia in Edward's chapel. Edward the Confessor had inspired Henry III to name Richard's great-great-grandfather Edward – a name then passed on to Richard's great-grandfather Edward II (whom Richard sought to canonize), grandfather Edward III, and father Edward "The Black Prince."[73] The allusion to Edward in *Piers Plowman* is in this sense a surprisingly topical one.

In *Richard the Redeless*, then, the titular allusion to Anglo-Saxon precedent signals that the poem will assess Richard not only in terms of abstract, ahistorical notions of kingship, but also in terms of more historically contingent notions derived from the post-Conquest memories of the house of Wessex. According to Bruce O'Brien, the example of Edward was "wielded" rhetorically, "from the Angevins onward, principally as a political rod to chastise monarchs who, according to baronial opinion, had overstepped their authority."[74] By assigning to Richard the same unfortunate sobriquet given to Edward's ill-counselled father, *Richard the Redeless* obliquely participates in this long tradition.

Richard the Redeless follows the end of *Piers Plowman* B-version in its manuscript with an echo of the opening lines of Passus B 19:

And as I passid in my preiere ther prestis were at messe,
In a blessid borugh that Bristow is named
In a temple of the Trinité the toune even amyddis,
That Cristis Chirche is cleped amonge the comune peple,
Sodeynly ther sourdid selcouthe thingis,
A grett wondir to wyse men, as it well myghth,
And dowtes for to deme for drede comynge after.

[And as I passed in my prayer where priests were at mass,
In a blessed town named Bristol
In a temple of the Trinity, in the middle of the town,
Called Christ's Church among the common people,

---

collection also attests the formula *Hit becwæð*, cited above. Edward in this instance is Edward the Elder; but then again, Anima may be referring to this earlier Edward. *Gesetze* I:138–44, 184–90.

73 Schiefele, "Visual Arts," 259, 262. On Richard II and Edward, see also Astell, *Political Allegory*, 102–6.

74 O'Brien, *God's Peace*, 48.

> Suddenly there arose many things,
> A great wonder to wise men, as it ought to be,
> And also fears for judgment of dreadful things]. (Prol.1–7)[75]

There are two major differences between this opening and the beginning lines of Passus B 19 that are relevant here. First, the church is placed in a particular location; Bristol is important in the conflict between Bolingbroke and Richard II, and the locale emphasizes the political immediacy of the vision. Second and perhaps more importantly, the narrator does not fall asleep. Frank Grady has argued that the principal difference between Lancastrian and Ricardian poetry is that the former "trades dreams for documents,"[76] an argument that will be explored in more detail in the next chapter; for now, it can merely be observed that *Piers Plowman* provides a formal model for metre, narrative structure, and sententious content, but the tradition's dream-vision genre is almost deliberately eschewed at the very moment that the poem's specific political focus is signalled by the allusion to Bristol. The narrator of *Richard the Redeless* explicitly rejects the claims to mystical truth implicit in the dream-vision genre, to extract a more documentary mode of writing from his poetic model.

Helen Barr argues that in this prologue, *Richard the Redeless* positions itself "as if the narrator were adjudicating a dispute between Richard and Henry," so that the form of *Piers Plowman* is therefore employed in the fragment as a venue in which the trial takes place.[77] Barr's reading can be productively compared to Andrew Rabin's reading of the *Sermo Lupi ad Anglos*, discussed in chapter 2. In both texts, legal language is employed by an authoritative witness to attribute contemporary unrest to the "redelessness" of the realm's rulers. In both texts the failure is represented in ontological terms, as a disruption of the natural order of the universe that invites the mechanisms of divine punishment. As we shall see, however, the mechanisms have shifted. The *Sermo Lupi ad Anglos* describes two distinct categories of people: first, the English sinners who invite punishment and, second, the heathen hordes who punish them. In the last chapter, I discussed how the two groups are merged in the poem in its representation of the Saxons, who are both treacherous advisors and

---

75 All quotations from *Richard the Redeless* and *Mum and the Sothsegger* are from Dean's edition, consulted with reference to *PPTrad*.
76 Grady, "Generation of 1399," 206.
77 Barr, *Signes and Sothe*, 159–60.

heathen invaders. *Richard the Redeless* similarly describes corrupt royal servants as both the causes and agents of divine retribution, as they hypocritically observe the correct forms of fealty to the king only so that they may ravage the kingdom behind his back.

The poem begins its criticism of Richard as follows: "Now, Richard the redeles, reweth on you-self, / That lawelesse leddyn youre lyf and youre peple bothe" (Now Richard the Redeless, pity yourself, who leads your life and your people both lawlessly) (Prol. 88–9). The poem addresses Richard directly, but its advice is directed more generally to "every Cristen kyng" with the following promise: "So he were lerned on the langage, my lyff durst I wedde, / Yif he waite well the wordis and so werche therafter" (So long as he was learned in the language, I would dare wager my life, if he considers these words and works well therafter) (Prol.42–5). It is crucial here that the poem claims to teach not only administrative skills and moral rectitude, but the very "langage" it uses to express its message. As we shall see, this language is not only English, but the sententious formulae of the poem's Langlandian discourse.

The poet tells Richard that if he "fynde fables or foly" in the poem, he should let his "conceill" and "clerkis" correct it: "For yit it is secrette and so it shall lenger, / Tyll wyser wittis han waytid it overe, / That it be lore laweffull and lusty to here" (Prol. 57–63). The assertion that the poem does not have any "fables," "foly," or "fantasie" is difficult to reconcile with the several beast fables that appear in the poem that follows. The misdirection perhaps suggests that this statement of modesty should be read with an edge of sardonic sarcasm. The poem will go on to make quite clear that the king's clerks and counsellors need to "amende" not the poem, but their own behaviour, so that if the poem seems fabulous or fantastic to them it is only because they do not understand it. Further, given the status of *Richard the Redeless* as a continuation of *Piers Plowman*, this defence applies to the entire text.

Another sarcastic defence of the poem's allegory is apparent later in the text, in an aside following a discussion of two partridges, one of which personifies Richard and the other of which personifies Henry:

"What is this to mene, man?" maiste thou axe,
"For it is derklich endited for a dull panne;
Wherffore I wilne, yif it thi will were,
The partriche propurtés by whom that thou menest?"
A, Hicke Hevyheed, hard is thi nolle
To cacche ony kunnynge, but cautell bigynne! (III.63–7)

[You may ask, "What does this mean, man?
For it is obscurely written for a dull head;
Thus I ask, if it be your will,
Who you mean by the partridge's qualities?"
Ah, Hick Heavy-head, hard is your head
To catch any knowledge, unless it starts with trickery!]

The "you" here is implicitly King Richard, to whom the text was addressed at the beginning. Richard is referred to by the diminutive "Hicke" and given the nickname "Hevyheed," which speaks to the broader scepticism expressed throughout the poem that its ostensible target is learned enough in its symbolic language to understand its meaning. If Richard cannot be taught by the complex allegory of the *Piers Plowman* tradition, the problem is not the allegory, but Richard's thick head.

In his explication of the partridge analogy, the narrator refers back to an earlier passage where Henry in the form of an eagle is praised for his clear-sightedness, which helps him to hunt down criminals (II.176–92). The eagle is also a traditional image of contemplative wisdom and philosophical learning;[78] eagle-like Henry is "well-read" in every sense of the term, and he therefore understands both the allegory of the partridges and the state of his kingdom. Richard, in contrast, is so far from understanding the state of his kingdom that he cannot even comprehend the meaning of the simple metaphor intended to explain it to him. Implicitly, then, for Richard to become a good king, he must first become a more sensitive reader of Langlandian sententious allegory.

Richard's inability to interpret words correctly is precisely the cause of his susceptibility to the rampant misuses of speech among his counsellors:[79]

Whane ye were sette in youre se as a sir aughte,
Ther carpinge comynliche of conceill arisith,
the chevyteyns cheef that ye chesse evere,
Weren all to yonge of yeris to yeme swyche a rewme. (I.86–9)

[When you were set in your throne as a lord ought,
Where the common discussions of counsel arise,

---

78 Steadman, "Chaucer's Eagle."
79 Barr, *Signes and Sothe*, 69–70.

The main advisor that you always chose
Were all too young in years to govern such a realm.*]*

Richard's chief advisors were too young and inexperienced, and hence they lacked the seriousness necessary to provide correct counsel. In Richard's case, the young counsellors were not up to the difficult task of correctly interpreting the inherited "reule of realles kynde" (91), either because they were not sufficiently trained to understand it, or because they wilfully distorted it. Richard accepts the portrait of the kingdom presented to him by self-interested advisors because he is a surface reader, who cannot discern a text's deeper and more important levels of meaning.

The young, malicious counsellors are contrasted with the great age of Wit (III.211–31), the poem's first allegorical personification, who plays a role in the poem closely analogous to the *witan* and *þeodwitan* who counselled the Anglo-Saxon kings.[80] Wit's age provides an occasion for expounding a model of three degrees of society, roughly equivalent to the three estates, but in fact divided according to age, with the greater power going to the old and the greater labour going to the young (III.250–3).[81] The narrator goes on to say that it is not appropriate for young men "To usurpe the service that to sages bilongith, / To become conselleris er they kunne rede" (to usurp the service that belongs to wise men, and become counsellors before they can read / advise), concluding with a reduction to the absurd: "For it fallith as well to fodis of twenty four yeris, / Or yonge men of yistirday to geve good redis, / As becometh a kow to hoppe in a cage!" (For it is befitting for young men of twenty-four years or one day to give good advice, as it befits a cow to hop in a cage) (III.258–62). The pun of line 259, that the young men "become conselleris er they kunne rede," suggests both that these young men are too young to counsel, and that they never finished school.

This pun on the two meanings of *ræd* is underscored by the remainder of this passage, which stresses the importance of learning from the example of history:

It is not unknowen to kunnynge leodis
That rewlers of rewmes around all the erthe

---

80 *MED* def. 5 and 6
81 *PPTrad*, 281–2. This same scheme appears in *The Proverbs of Alfred*: see chapter 3 (117–18).

> Were not yffoundid at the frist tyme
> To leve al at likynge and lust of the world,
> But to laboure on the lawe, as lewde men on plowes. (III.263–7)

> [It is not unknown to knowledgeable people
> That rulers of the realm all over the Earth
> Were not endowed at the start of time
> To live in pleasure and lust for the world,
> But to work on the law, as unschooled men on plows.]

As I have already discussed in this chapter, the passage's parallelism between "law" and "plow" is implied elsewhere in the versions of *Piers Plowman*, but never stated as explicitly as it is here.[82] The passage particularly echoes the repeated phrase in *Piers Plowman* that an ideal ruler would "make of lawe a laborer" (e.g., B.3.300). As I argued earlier in this chapter, the "plow" in Middle English referred not only to the farm implement, but also to traditional divisions of the land. This allusion to the "lewde" plowmen refers not only to the titular character of the poem that precedes *Richard the Redeless* in its only manuscript, but more generally to the traditions of law that first divided the land up into *plouȝes*.

This passage's suggestion that laws and plows are in some sense equivalent is therefore a clear manifestation of the tropes of Anglo-Saxon legal-homiletic discourse, with specific implications for the *Piers Plowman* tradition. Perhaps recognizing in Langland's text the same abundance of grammar-school material commented upon by Cannon, the poet concluded that *Piers Plowman* was itself sufficient to provide a would-be advisor with an education.[83] Young, "lewde" men, called labourers in *Richard the Redeless* III.253, should learn to "read" through "labouring" on not only plows, but on the text *Piers Plowman*, while the older and better-informed advisors should apply their knowledge of history to labour on the law. In an inversion of this book's title, then, such advisors would transition from "plowmen" to "lawmen." In this formulation, Langlandian discourse is framed as a style of writing that teaches royal servants to perform their duties in accordance with ancient customs, "yffoundid at the frist time."

---

82 Most explicitly when "Law" and "plow" appear in two successive lines in the A-version and B-version (A.VII.154, B.VI.169); there is also a passage in the B-version and C-version about Piers's "new" and "old" plow that evokes the trope of the "old" and "new" laws (B.XIX.426, C.XXI.426).

83 Cannon, "Langland's Ars Grammatica."

This model of traditional, Langlandian legal education is directly contrasted in the poem with the newer kinds of bureaucratic professionalism that rely only on formal exactitude to decide points of law. At the beginning of Passus II (1–9), Richard's failures as a monarch are connected to the abuses of livery.[84] In the poem's allegory, the hart image on Richard's livery literally transforms Richard's followers into a pack of harts that trample his realm. Though this livery should symbolize the faithfulness of liveried servants to Richard, it symbolizes instead the abuses that the servants carry out in his name. The "hearts" of his people are traded for the "harts" of the livery. Thus the poem's criticisms of livery take the theme of allegorical exegesis and apply it in the political realm. Like Rowenna's "wassail" ceremony in the *Brut*, the form of the livery appears to signify fealty, when in fact it signifies only the gap between signs of fealty and true fealty itself. Thick-headed as he is, Richard is unable to read the signs well enough to tell the difference.

Richard the Redeless also echoes the poison motif of the *Brut* in a passage when the narrator discusses the relationship of the liveried harts to poisonous snakes (III.17–25). In nature, we are told, harts kill snakes and drink their poison in order to live for a long time. So, too, under natural law the true hearts of loyal servants ought to root out the poison of treachery that threatens the kingdom for their collective benefit. Contrary to the natural activities that might eliminate poison, however, the liveried harts attack and kill other animals. As we may expect, their crimes are described in an anaphoric, alliterative list:

> This is clerlie hir kynde, coltis nat to greve,
> Ne to hurlle with haras, ne hors well atamed,
> Ne to stryve with swan, though it sholle werre,
> Ne to bayten on the bere, ne bynde him nother,
> Ne to wilne to woo that were hem ny sibbe,
> Ne to liste for to loke that her alie bledde;
> This was ageins kynde, as clerkis me tolde –
> Propter ingratitudinem liber homo reuocatur in seruitutem ut in stimulo
>   compunccionis et in lege ciuili. (III.26–32a)

> [This is clearly their nature, not to hurt colts,
> Nor to run at stallions or well-trained horses,

> Nor to fight the swan, though it intends war,
> Nor to bait the bear nor bind him either,
> Nor to desire misfortune for those that are close kin,
> Nor to wish to see his allies bleed;
> This was against nature, as clerks told me –
> For unfaithfulness a free man is called into servitude, as in the prick of conscience / compunction and in civil law.]

These three animals all allegorize the victims of the Merciless Parliament. All of them were either imprisoned or executed by Richard; these actions were "ageins kynde," which is to say contrary to natural law.

There is a source for the legal concept here, that freemen guilty of "ingratitude" should be deprived of their legal status, in the civil law collection *The Institutes of Justinian*; however, no such statement appears in the Middle English poem *The Prick of Conscience*.[85] The apparent choice of *stimulus compunctionis* as a Latin title for this work rather than *stimulus conscientiae* evokes the doctrine of compunction, which is defined as a kind of spiritual pain that comes from the sufferer's knowledge of his or her own sinfulness.[86] Indeed, *ut in stimulo compunccionis et in lege ciuili* might not refer to the popular Middle English poem at all, but could be translated "as in a goad to compunction, and in civil law." Either way, punishment according to civil law is ascribed the same purpose of producing compunction articulated in the preface to *The Prick of Conscience*, as freemen lose their legal status to provoke the "drede" that leads to moral improvement.[87] In context, then, the Latin quotation argues that the harsh punishments enacted by Richard and his parliament are against "kynde" because they do nothing to improve the souls of the punished parties. Even if death may provide sinners with a motive to repent, it also takes away their ability to do so.

In chapter 2, I suggested that Wulfstan avoided the death penalty in *I–II Cnut* because he wished for the church to play an active role in all sorts of criminal punishments.[88] The implicit association of the death penalty with the secular state persisted throughout the Middle Ages, as ecclesiastical

---

85 *PPTrad*, 272.
86 McEntire, "Compunction"; Palmer, "*Compunctio*."
87 See the introduction to "The Prick of Conscience" in Wogan-Browne, Evans, and Johnson, eds, *Idea of the Vernacular*, 242–4.
88 Discussed in chapter 2 above (77).

courts continued to advocate for punishments aimed at moral correction.[89] Hence the Latin quotation cited above demonstrates both the poet's familiarity with civil law and his sympathy for the ecclesiastical court system.[90]

The narrator's interest in legal procedures comes up again at the end of Passus III, in a sustained attack on the "chyders of Chester":

> For chyders of Chester where chose many daies
> To ben of conceill for causis that in the court hangid,
> And pledid pipoudris alle manere pleyntis.
> They cared for no coyffes that men of court usyn,
> But meved many maters that man never thoughte,
> And feyned falshed, till they a fyne had,
> And knewe no manere cause, as comunes tolde. (III.317–23)

> [For brawlers of Chester were chosen many days
> To be counsel for legal actions that hung in the court,
> And they played piepowders with all manner of complaints.
> They did not care for the coifs that men of court use,
> But brought up many matters that man never thought of,
> And feigned falsehoods, until they had a fine,
> And they understood no kind of legal action, as the commons reported.]

The "piepowders" were informal courts convened around fairs and markets that dealt predominantly with petty theft; to "play piepowders" is therefore to ignore the correct rules of procedure observed in more formal courtrooms.[91] The brawlers of Chester would take sides in legal proceedings and influence them, until things reached a settlement that benefitted them or the king, but was not necessarily just. Such corrupt practices are brought to an end by divine intervention, when "oure Sire in His see above the seven sterris / Sawe the many mysschevys that these men dede" (when our Lord in his throne above the seven stars saw the many mischiefs that these men did) and then "sente for his servauntis that sembled many, / Of baronys and baccheleris, with many brighth helmes, / With the comunes of contres they cam all at ones" (sent for his servants that assembled, many barons and knights, with many bright helmets, they came all at once with

---

89 Gauvard, "Justification," esp. 206.
90 On the representation of civil law in *Mum and the Sothsegger*, see my article "Lollardy."
91 *PPTrad*, 285n.319; see also Giancarlo, *Parliament*, 233.

the people of [their] districts) (III.352–9). In other words, Lancaster's "invading" armies were sent by God in direct response to the corrupt practices of the Cheshiremen, just as Wulfstan's Danes came to punish the English and Gildas's Saxons punished the British. In an almost complete reversal of the divine justice recorded by the *Sermo Lupi ad Anglos*, however, the invading army here is not the "heathen" Danes, but rather the English victims of corruption. If Richard is a new Æthelred, then Henry is a new Cnut.

Just as Wulfstan's sermon recorded the "un-Englishness" of the English, then, *Richard the Redeless* reveals a certain un-Englishness of English royal government. Richard's reign is criticized specifically because its strict adherence to form and procedure gives it an ethical and moral neutrality inconsistent with Christian values. Though in the strictest sense formally correct, Richard's heavy-headed practice of government is ultimately divorced from the hidden, moral meaning that gives government purpose; no amount of procedural innovation could hope to correct for his original misinterpretation of his royal office. All of these problems could have been avoided if Richard had only read and understood *Piers Plowman*, which both articulates the principles of good governance that Richard ought to know, and trains its readers in the difficult task of interpreting counsel.

Barr observes that the final passus of *Richard the Redeless* breaks off in the middle of a parliamentary debate, "almost as if in mimesis of the breakdown of institutional resources to redress grievance and corruption (and inspired perhaps by the narrative schemes in *Piers Plowman*)."[92] It is representative of the poem's technique that one cause for the breakdown in parliament is its abuse of written documents (IV.24–30). In contrast, *Richard the Redeless* exemplifies the kind of document that can benefit both the king and the commons, which is to say the continuously unfolding document of the *Piers Plowman* tradition.

---

92 Barr, *Signes and Sothe*, 43–4. See also Giancarlo, *Parliament*, 237; Grady, "Generation of 1399," 225.

6 Documents, Dreams, and the Langlandian Legacy in *Mum and the Sothsegger*

If *Richard the Redeless* criticized the king's ability to understand the *ræd* of wise counsellors, *Mum and the Sothsegger* is focused instead on the ability of would-be counselors to provide it.[1] Jon Whitman has noticed the tendency of allegorical modes towards self-exposition, as characters that personify wisdom necessarily provide commentary on the appropriate method for reading the allegory in which they appear.[2] If we apply this observation to the titular *sothsegger* of this poem, then the commentary of "sothe-saying" in the text is implicitly a comment on the *Piers Plowman* tradition as a whole. In this sense *Mum and the Sothsegger* is perhaps the most "literate" of all the texts examined in this study, as it goes beyond merely expressing or modelling anxiety about the commemorative functions of literacy to explicitly address that anxiety as its subject matter.

In this fragment the problem of remaining silent or speaking the truth is fundamentally a problem of text and its interpretation. Anglo-Saxon legal-homiletic discourse provides the poem both with a language for describing this problem and with a way of performing its resolution. The irony of using highly ornate poetic conventions to frame a criticism of bureaucratic formalism threatens to overwhelm the text, until in its final section it can only reauthorize Langlandian poetry as a documentary form by listing a series of documents, containing them within the form of the alliterative, sententious list.

The term *sothsegger* itself is the first clue that the fragment's notions of "truth" derive from the language of Anglo-Saxon legal-homiletic discourse.

---

1 On the representation of counsel in this poem, see also Ferster, *Fictions of Advice*, 36–8; Simpson, "Constraints of Satire," 11–30.

2 Whitman, *Allegory*, 8.

The word *soð* appears in two key contexts in Old English: first, in the common homiletic formula "soð is þat ic segge" appearing in the first line of the *Sermo Lupi ad Anglos*,[3] and second in the formula "soð is gecyþed" that frequently introduces citations of proverbs.[4] Andrew Rabin suggests that these phrases evoked a specifically textual, biblical authority, as versions of both phrases appear in Old English translations of Christ's *Amen dico vobis*.[5] We may even trace the origins of the *sothsegger* all the way back to the Old Frisian *asecga*, cited by Bethurum as a synonym for the term *laghman*: hence, perhaps, Laȝamon's desire for noble men to read his books and learn his counsel so "þat he þeos *soðfeste* word *segge* to-sumne" (that he should say together these true words) (32, my emphasis). Certainly the *sothseggers* in the poem teach God's lore and law to kings by using their thoughts, words, and deeds, just as Mum exhibits the *asolcennesse* that afflicted Britain's bishops before the Saxon and Danish invasions.[6]

In this chapter I will begin by arguing that the commonplace trope of text and gloss frames a larger discussion in the text about literacy and its discontents. Though the "text" may contain the truth, the difficulties of applying the text in everyday life mean that Mum is able to make a more compelling case for adherence to the "gloss" than one would expect. The brief dream vision that divides the text is necessary to enable the narrator's escape from this problem. This dream not only precedes, but it also initiates the catalogue of hidden books whose description reveals certain injustices in the kingdom. The poem's reliance on Langlandian dream vision to authorize itself as an example of "sothe-saying" exposes an irony that underlies its satire: the poem manages only to articulate anxieties about bureaucratic culture, not to present a viable alternative.

Text, Gloss, and the Book of Life

The most striking evidence that *Mum and the Sothsegger* draws from the traditions of Anglo-Saxon legal documents appears in an echo of *Piers Plowman* found in an anti-fraternal passage:

---

3 See also Orchard, "Re-Editing Wulfstan," 65, on occurrences of this phrase in Wulfstan.
4 Deskis, "*Beowulf*" and *Medieval Proverb Tradition*, 15.
5 Rabin 2006, 41 n104. Rabin does not provide examples; see, however, the Lindisfarne *Gospel of John* verses 3:3, 3:5, 3:11, 5:19, 5:24, 5:25, 5:32, 6:26, 6:32, 6:47, 6:53, and 8:14. *Four Gospels*, ed. Skeat; OE Corpus accessed 9 April 2009.
6 See chapter 2 (67–8, 83).

I cannot reede redily of what reule [the friars] been,
For hooly churche ne hevene hath not thaym in mynde,
Save in oon place thaire office and ordre is declarid:
I sawe hit in a ympne and is a sentence trewe,
And elleswhere in hooly writte I herde thaym ynempnyd.
Auferte gentem perfidam. Credentium de finibus;
Deleantur de libro vivencium, et cum iustis non scribantur. (516–20b)

[I cannot explain easily the rule that the friars are from,
For neither holy church nor heaven has them in mind;
Their office and order is declared in one place.
I saw it in a hymn and it is a true statement,
And elsewhere in holy writ I have heard them named.
Expel the deceitful people from the territories of the believers;
Let them be blotted out of the book of the living, and let them not be written
with the lawful [ones].]

The first of the two Latin quotations at the end of the passage comes from
the hymn for the Vespers of All Saints, "Placare Christi servulis," and the
second is from the Latin Vulgate version of Psalms 68:29. The operative
phrase of the latter quotation, *Deleantur de libro vivencium*, appears frequently in the Anglo-Saxon charters as an anathema, or clause threatening
to punish anyone who fails to respect the rights and privileges granted by
a document.[7] This line from Psalm 68 was only one of many biblical quotations given this "maledictional" force in early medieval legal documents,
and the phrase appears in such contexts across Europe; but because maledictions start to disappear from sanction clauses by the twelfth century, in
England their appearance is particularly a feature of Anglo-Saxon legal
records.[8] As we have seen, there are many ways that this legal use of proverbial quotations from the Psalms may have survived into the alliterative
poetry of the fifteenth century.

More directly antecedent to *Mum and the Sothsegger*, the same Latin
quotation from Psalm 68 appears in all three versions of *Piers Plowman*
(A.VII.67–9, B.VI.75–7, C.VIII.77–9), in a passage where Piers lists the
various criminals and wasters exempted from tithing – a clear instance of

---

7 Harmer, *Writs*, 68.
8 Little, *Benedictine Maledictions*, 54–7, 63.

the same Pauline trope witnessed in Wulfstan's homilies. The longest version of the list is in the C-version:

> Y shal fynde hem fode þat fayfulleche libbeth,
> Save Iacke þe iogelour and Ionet of the styues
> And Danyel the dees playere and Denote þe baude
> And Frere Faytour and folk of þat ordre,
> That lollares and loseles lele men holdeth,
> And Robyn the rybauder for his rousty wordes.
> Treuthe tolde me ones and bad me telle hit forth:
> Deleantur de libro viuencium; y sholde nat dele with hem
> For holy chirche is holde of hem no tithe to aske,
> Quia cum iustis non scribantur. (C.VIII.70–78a)

> [I will find food for those who live faithfully,
> Except Jack the Juggler and Jane of the sties,
> And Daniel the dice-player and Denny the pimp,
> And Friar Cheat and folk of that order,
> That Lollards and rogues consider to be loyal men,
> And Robin the ribald for his foul words.
> Truth told me once and ordered me to pass it on:
> They shall be deleted from the book of life; I should not deal with them,
> For Holy Church is obligated to ask no tithes of them,
> Who are not written with the just.]

The quotation has the same punitive, legal inflection in *Piers Plowman* that it has in Old English documents. By implication, *Mum and the Sothsegger* draws not only on the authority of the psalm, or only on the authority of the anathema form, but also on the authority of *Piers Plowman*, where this same anathema also appears.

A central irony in *Mum and the Sothsegger* is that the character of Mum or "silence" speaks extensively throughout the poem, while a *sothsegger* appears only briefly and says nothing at all. For this reason Mum seems to represent not a literal but an essential silence, the failure to communicate meaningfully rather than the failure to speak. The result of this silence is that Mum selfishly promotes local and personal interests, while the *sothsegger* speaks for the collective welfare. In the context of the poem's political critique, Mum is an allegorical representation of the social forces that fragment administrative practice, by preventing cooperation between its constitutive forms of communication (spoken, written, heard, or read) and thereby reducing the practice of government to a competition between self-interested parties. A *sothsegger*, on the other hand, is someone who attempts to unify government, so that all of the various hands that operate the machinery of justice can know what all of the other hands are doing, and coordinate their efforts accordingly. In other words, the "sothe" is not only the written text, but the text as it appears in the context of its proper use, transcendent and eternally true on the one hand but specific and politically apt on the other.

This historically contingent notion of written truth poses immediate problems for the notions of textual authority encoded in the ancient documents of Anglo-Saxon England, which are extremely difficult to apply in context. For example, it is challenging to expel interlopers from a particular territory on the basis of a six-hundred-year-old document stating that the boundary of that territory runs "of sceorten dic in to langen dic (from the short ditch into the long ditch)."⁹ And yet, as I have suggested throughout this study, the very vagueness of Anglo-Saxon legal-homiletic discourse was constitutive of its authority as a critique of latter-day bureaucratic abuses. This disconnect between the vague, affective truthfulness of Langlandian discourse and the ideally neutral, historically precise truthfulness encapsulated by the term "sothe" is the principle topic of *Mum and the Sothsegger*.

The problem is first raised in the fragment at its very beginning with Mum's interruption:

But I dreed me sore, so me God helpe,
Leste covetise of cunseil that knoweth not hymself
(Of sum and of certayn, I seye not of alle)
That of profitable pourpos putteth the king ofte,
There his witte and his wil wolde wirche to the beste –
"Nomore of this matiere," cothe Mum thenne,
"For I mervaille of thy momeling more thenne thou wenys." (227–33)

[But I fear sorely, God help me,
That the covetousness of a counsellor who does not know himself
(as is true of some certain [ones], I would not say all)
that often sends the king from profitable purpose,

---

9 This phrase is taken from the boundary clause of S 1208: *Electronic Sawyer*, accessed 10 December 2012.

that his wits and his intention would work to the best –
"No more of this matter," Mum then said,
"For I marvel at your mumbling more than you know."]

This thought, word, and deed triad describes a relationship between king and advisor. The false, spoken counsel of Henry's untrustworthy royal advisors prevents the king from having the correct disposition of wit and will, which would allow him to work as he ought. The narrator's speculation about the negative consequences of such a scenario occasions the interruption of Mum, which distracts the narrator from providing the corrective counsel that would, by implication, lead to the appropriate thoughts and deeds that would manifest in wise policy decisions. More damningly, Mum criticizes the narrator specifically for his "momeling," which is to say for speaking in a manner that is not only foolish but also incoherent and vague.

The narrator responds to Mum's interruption as follows:

"Now to this altercacion," cothe I, "an answere behoveth,
For I fele by thy fabelyng thou art felle of werkes
And right worldly wise of wordes and deedes,
And ever kepis thee cloos for casting bihinde." (263–6)

[Now to this argument," I said, "an answer is fitting,
For I feel because of your fable-making that you are evil in works
And skilled in words and deeds in a worldly way,
And you keep yourself close so you do not fall behind."]

The "wisdame and witte" of Mum described above translates into "worldly" words and deeds, because his silence is selfishly motivated. In the last line, Mum's lack of moral fortitude is associated with his desire to keep up with the most recent trends, lest he fall behind. And yet Mum's very currency is itself a problem, as of course the "profitable pourpos" that the king ought to pursue can only be defined in response to circumstances as they evolve. Mum is therefore not merely malicious, but a personification of the basic problem constitutive of literate authority itself: the meanings of even truthful texts are very difficult to maintain when their truths are applied in any particular context, and the formal strategies for composing texts that aim to correct this problem not only fail to prevent abuse but in fact generate new abuses.

It is noteworthy in this regard that Mum first interrupts the narrator immediately after he expresses his "dreed" for what will happen. "Dreed" is itself personified later in *Mum and the Sothsegger*, after the narrator does finally locate a *sothsegger*. Unfortunately, as he is told by "a eldryn man," the *sothsegger* in question has given up his efforts:

> ... the Sothesigger
> Dyneth this day with Dreede in a chambre,
> And hath ydrunke dum-seede, and dar not be seye
> Sith Mum and the mayer were made suche frendes. (837–40)

> [The sooth-sayer
> Dines this day in a room with Dread,
> And has drunk dumb-seed, and he does not dare to be seen
> After Mum and the mayor were made such friends.]

Here, Dreede's poison does not kill the *sothsegger* so much as it prevents him from speaking. The association between silence and poison here is related to a "venom" or disease motif occurring throughout the fragment in the metaphor of the body politic:[10]

> For as I herde have, [boils] helen wel the rather
> Whanne th'anger and th'attre is al oute yrenne,
> For better were to breste oute there bote might falle
> Thenne rise agayne regalie and the royaulme trouble. (1125–8)

> [For as I have heard, [boils] heal well, rather,
> When the poison has all run out,
> Because it would be better to burst out so a remedy might occur
> Than it would be to rise again to trouble the king and the kingdom.]

Like the harts of *Richard the Redeless* who ought to kill the poisonous snakes but instead commit unnatural acts, so this *sothsegger* who ought to drain poison from the body politic is instead poisoned himself by Dreede. The remarkable aspect of this fairly typical description of fearful advisors

---

10 Appearing in line 1035, where the franklin explains that the king of the bees has no stinger, because "venym doeth not folowe hym, but vertue in alle workes."

is its enormous sympathy for the fallen *sothsegger*. Under the circumstances, it seems that his silence is only to be expected, and it is no wonder that the narrator sincerely considers following suit.

At the centre of the titular debate between Mum and *sothsegger* is an extended metaphor between the words of the *sothsegger* and the true text, and between the counsel of Mum and the false gloss. Amanda Walling has traced the origins of the text/gloss trope in *Piers Plowman* back to the hermeneutic controversies arising at the foundation of the fraternal orders, and specifically their use of illustrative "fables" in their preaching.[11] Walling notes that this trope becomes symbolically aligned with flattering courtiers in *Piers Plowman*, and cites *Mum and the Sothsegger* as a text in which this imagery is applied to secular satire.[12] This satire is witnessed for example in lines 158–64:

> But the king ne his cunseil may hit not knowe
> What is the comune clamour ne the crye nother,
> For there is no man of the meeyné, more nother lasse,
> That wol wisse thaym any worde but yf his witte faille,
> Ne telle thaym the trouthe ne the texte nothir,
> But shony forto shewe what the shire meneth,
> And beguile thaym with glose, so me God helpe,
> And speke of thaire owen spede and spie no ferther,
> But ever kepe thaym cloos for caicching of wordes.

> [But neither the king nor his counsel may know
> Of what is the clamour and cry of the commons,
> For there is no man of the king's retinue, greater or lesser,
> Who will tell them any word unless his wits fail,
> Nor tell them neither the truth nor the text;
> Instead they avoid showing what the shire says,
> And beguile them with gloss, God help me,
> And speak of their own wealth and look no further,
> And always keep themselves close to overhear words.]

The king and his counsellors do not know "the trouthe ne the texte" of what is happening in their kingdom, because there is no one in their

---

11 Walling, "Flatterer."
12 Walling, "Flatterer," 58.

employ who will tell them; instead these advisers "beguile thaym with glose." This contrast does not fit neatly into the common satirical trope of the virtuous text and the sinister gloss, but rather provides a way of thinking through certain practical difficulties pertinent to the enactment of social justice. The "text" kept from the king in the passage above is not the Gospel, but more generally the state of the kingdom, just as the "boils" on the body politic are not a divine plague but only a set of problems that should be taken care of sooner rather than later. Religious imagery is employed, but scriptural interpretation is not the topic.

The text / gloss division is explained further immediately after the narrator's conversation with Mum, when he looks over the textual authorities available to him for arguments against Mum's position:

> I bablid on thoo bokes that thoo barnes made,
> And waitid on thaire wordes aswel as I couthe,
> But of the matiere of Mum might I nought finde,
> Ne no maniere nyceté of the newe jette,
> But al homely usage of the olde date,
> How that good gouvernance gracieusely endith.
> But glymsyng on the glose, a general reule
> Of al maniere mischief I merkid and radde:
> That whoso were in wire and wold be y-easid
> Moste shewe the sore there the salve were. (308–17)

> [I studied in the books that those men made,
> But I could not find anything on the matter of Mum,
> Nor any niceties of the latest style,
> But only homely usages from a long time ago,
> How good governance ends favourably.
> But looking at the gloss, a general rule
> Of all kinds of mischief I noted and read,
> That whoever wanted to be eased in their perplexity
> Must take the sore to where the salve was.]

Though the analogy between Mum and the "nyceté of the newe jette" is clearly intended as a criticism, the "homely usage of the olde date" is not necessarily a preferable alternative. Good governance is obviously good, but how specifically should Henry IV govern well at his particular historical moment?

The question leads the narrator to turn to the "glose," which employs the metaphor of disease to suggest that the narrator "shewe the sore to where the salve was." This is the gloss that inspires him to make his journey through the secular world, looking for a salve. The implication, perhaps, is that the narrator's quest was doomed from the start. The world simply does not work in such a way that speaking the truth about social injustice could ever be profitable or even sustainable. And yet at the same time, the very record of corrupt practices that proves so compellingly that one can never say the "sothe" is itself a revelation of hidden sores. Hence merely by considering the question of whether or not to become a *sothsegger*, the narrator had already become one, and his own "text" is a continuation of the same "gloss" on the text he read in his books. In a paradoxical gesture, then, the fragment's very acknowledgment of its own inadequacy is itself the proof of its authority.

The poem is able to arrive at this solution to its constitutive problem by gesturing beyond itself towards the authority of a dream, in which a "franklin" uses an allegory of bee-keeping to explain the importance of *sothseggers* to the body politic, before he goes on to urge the narrator to write the poem that will turn him into a *sothsegger*. This character provides the narrator with the external validation for saying the *sothe* that the world itself could never offer. Matthew Giancarlo has suggested that the identification of this interlocutor as a franklin suggests that he "stands for exactly the kind of seigneurial figure whose political identity has coalesced in the fairly exclusive bourgeois club of the 'shire-men'," and even suggests that the character may be an allusion to Chaucer's Franklin in the *Canterbury Tales*.[13] To this point I would add that Chaucer's Franklin is not only a member of Parliament, but also "a shirreve" (I.359),[14] and in this capacity he is also a representative of the class of secular legal professionals that is so frequently a target of criticism in Anglo-Saxon legal-homiletic discourse. In these terms, the most ironic aspect of the franklin is that his very membership in Mum's class of secular legal professionals is itself the source of his authority to criticize that class.

But the symbolism of the franklin extends beyond this basic irony. If this franklin resembles Chaucer's Franklin, he also resembles the figure of the *procuratour*, appearing in the alliterative sermons edited as *Lollard*

---

13 Giancarlo, *Parliament*, 244–5.
14 Chaucer, *Canterbury Tales*.

Sermons by Gloria Cigman.[15] Shannon Gayk has observed that preachers are often called "procuratouris" in these texts, in a probable reference to the Vulgate version of the Gospel of Matthew's parable of the labourers in the vineyard.[16] In the parable, the lord of the vineyard communicates with his labourers through a *procurator* (Matt 20:8) who gives them their wages and chastises them when they complain. The ancient, wise franklin of *Mum and the Sothsegger*, who oversees a garden full of fruit and leads the narrator to eschew earthly monetary reward in exchange for the eternal reward of heaven, certainly resembles this biblical figure. Commonly, the *procurator* of the parable is read as an allegory of the preachers who mediate between God and Christian believers, though of course his job was not terribly different from the mediating role played by secular officials or estate managers. Hence the franklin is both a secular figure and a religious symbol at once, as his representation recalls a certain well-established biblical trope.

One likely explanation for the preference among "Lollard" homilists for the term *procuratour* to refer to this trope is that they wish to avoid the more common English translation of Latin *procurator* as "reeve." The parable of the vineyard had a long history of being translated in this way. *Procurator* in Matt 20:8 is glossed in the Old English Lindisfarne Gospels as *giroefæ*,[17] and in the retelling of the parable in *Pearl*, the character is similarly called a *reue* (542).[18] The word "reeve" was therefore readily available to vernacular preachers who wish to make an analogy between their own role and that of the biblical figure from the parable, and yet they chose to use the original Latin word instead. John Alford's legal glossary makes a distinction between the role of *procuratour*, who is as an agent allowed to serve as a lord's legal representative, and the reeve who more specifically collects rent.[19] Though there is no real contradiction between those two roles, one would imagine that a vernacular preacher would rather wish to be considered a representative of a higher power than a tax collector. A similar motive may explain the choice of the still more ambiguous term "franklin" to describe the *procurator*-like dream

---

15 On the question of whether these sermons are actually Lollard, see Gayk, "Alliterative Work," 48–9.

16 Gayk, "Alliterative Work," 50–1.

17 *Four Gospels*, ed. Skeat; OE Corpus, accessed 23 March 2011.

18 *Poems of the Pearl Manuscript*, ed. Andrew and Waldron.

19 Alford, *Glossary*.

figure in *Mum and the Sothsegger*. In any event, the juxtaposition of the sustained anticlerical satire of the poem's first section and the idealized franklin of the dream is not easily cast in terms of a church / state dichotomy.[20] On the contrary, the dream-space inhabited by the franklin serves a figurative purpose like the ideal reign of Cnut in the *Argumentum* of the *Quadripartitus* and the reign of Edgar in the writing of Wulfstan, as it allows the poet to imagine an idealized figure who takes care of both ecclesiastical and secular interests.[21]

It should perhaps be no surprise, then, that in this regard the franklin is strongly reminiscent of Piers the Plowman himself. Piers the Plowman is assigned the roles of both procurator and reeve in *Piers Plowman* B 19 (260), and similarly seems to serve in the versions of that poem both as an ideal preacher and as an ideal secular administrator.[22] Like Piers, the franklin appears to the narrator in a dream; but unlike Piers, the franklin specifically asks the narrator to write the poem in which he appears:

Sith thou felys the fressh, lete no feynt herte
Abate thy blessid bisynes of thy boke-making
Til hit be complete to clapsyng, caste aweye doutes
And lete the sentence be sothe, and sue to th'ende;
And furst feoffe thou therewith the freyst of the royaulme,
For yf thy lord liege allone hit begynne,
Care thou not though knyghtz copie hit echone,
And do write eche word, and wirche thereafter. (1280–8)

[While you feel fresh, let no faint heart
Stop the blessed business of your book-making
Until it is complete to the binding. Cast away doubts
And let the meaning be true, and continue to the end;
And first invest with the freest of the realm,
For if your lord liege along begins it,
Do not care whether other knights copy it,
And write each word and work afterwards.]

---

20 See my fuller discussion of these issues: "Lollardy."
21 Giancarlo, *Parliament*, 246.
22 Baldwin, "Historical Context," 69.

This passage consists of two parallel four-line commands: first, that the narrator not allow inward faintness of heart slow his book-making process, and second, that he give his book to the most powerful person that he can find, to make sure that it has the desired effect. The juxtaposition between the private act of composition and the public act of presentation demonstrates the poet's relatively "literate" anxiety about the unbridgeable gap between a writer's intention and a reader's interpretation. Both of these four-line injunctions conclude with a reference to the act of writing itself: "lete the sentence be sothe" (1284) and "do write eche word and wirche thereafter" (1288). With the poison of dread removed, the narrator can now actively write his truthful words and bring his thoughts and deeds into alignment, so that he may take upon himself the role of *sothsegger*.

This passage bears comparison to the description of book-making in the Caligula preface to the *Brut*, cited again below:[23]

> Laȝamon leide þeos boc. ꝛ þa leaf wende.
> he heom leofliche bi-heold. liþe him beo Drihten.
> Feþeren he nom mid fingren. ꝛ fiede on boc-felle.
> ꝛ þa soþere word. sette to-gadere.
> ꝛ þa þre boc. þrumde to are.
> Nu bidde[ð] Laȝamon alcne æðele mon.
> for þene almiten Godd.
> þet þeos boc rede. ꝛ leornia þeos runan.
> þat he þeos soðfaste word. segge to-sumne. (24–32)

Again, a description of a truth-telling book's production is bisected into a description of composition (24–8) and a description of audience reception (29–32), almost exactly equal in length to the passages in *Mum and the Sothsegger*. In particular, Laȝamon's "þa soþere word sette to-gadere" at the end of the *Brut*'s description of book production is very similar to *Mum and the Sothsegger*'s "lete the sentence be sothe, and sue to th'ende." So also does the "æðele mon" that Laȝamon asks to read his book anticipate the "lord liege" who is the narrator's ideal audience in *Mum and the Sothsegger*. Both the *Brut* and *Mum and the Sothsegger* call attention to the documentary status of their texts before they describe their intention to shape the actions of noble men. In this manner the franklin's injunction

---

23 See also chapter 4 for translation and discussion (130–1).

to the dreaming narrator serves as an authorizing formula paralleled by Laȝamon's preface, except that the "book" authorized by the franklin is already over twelve hundred lines long by the time the formula appears. Hence while we can say that the dream of the franklin resolves the tension of the poem's first part within the poem's narrative, it can only do so by falling back on formulaic statements of authority derived from Anglo-Saxon legal-homiletic discourse, put in the mouth of a dream authority who manages to be even more amorphous and ambiguous than Piers Plowman himself. While such recourse does not present a genuine resolution to the conflict between text and gloss framing the poem's treatment of the problem of literacy, it nonetheless presents a strategy for framing irresolution that is itself symptomatic of not only Anglo-Saxon legal-homiletic discourse, but all literacies that acknowledge implicitly the fact of their own inability to deliver the fixity of meaning that their authenticating strategies promise.

In his insightful study of *Mum and the Sothsegger* and other texts of the Generation of 1399, as he calls them, Frank Grady argues that the poem makes a "decisive turn away from the dream vision; the answer to the dream's own uncertain calls for reform and for an authoritative, written cultural criticism lies not in visionary poetics but in the documents and instruments of the workaday, wide-awake world."[24] In the next section, I will build on Grady's work to argue that the distinction between the world of the dream and the world of documents and instruments is not in fact so stark as it first appears. The Langlandian dream vision is itself a kind of document, as the dream does not so much mark the end of the first section of the text as the beginning of the second, not preceding the bag of books section but presenting the poem itself as the first of the documents it examines.

How to Solve a Problem Like Genghis Khan: The Return to the Dream Vision

Frank Grady's reading of *Mum and the Sothsegger* echoes Richard Firth Green's argument in *A Crisis of Truth*, that the "material solidity" of the documents in the narrator's bag of hidden books provides an "ironic counterpoint" to the larger social problem that the poem addresses,

---

24 Grady, "Generation of 1399," 229. See also Giancarlo, *Parliament*, 237–52, who reads the dream as an allegory of idealized parliamentary procedure.

namely, the "unholy alliance between unprincipled authority and literate technology."[25] Green sees the introduction of literate technology to England as having the disastrous effect of allowing "litigation to be removed from its context"; the impartiality of professional judges can only be considered an advantage when the court brings "superior forensic techniques to bear on a case."[26] Green's formulation therefore presumes that the poet of *Mum and the Sothsegger* would have privileged the forensic techniques of modern courts as being inherently more just, and more recognizably so, than the practices of medieval courts.[27] For both Grady and Green, the distinctions between truthful text and beguiling gloss in *Mum and the Sothsegger* are ultimately impossible to transform into valid poetic practice, because no methods had yet been devised for correcting the unworkable bureaucratic system of the poem's political context. This description of the poem ably describes the aspects of its form that appear to have left it at the end of one of literary history's many blind alleys, as alliterative verse diminished in subsequent decades to a largely local and nostalgic metrical form.

Contrary to expectation, however, it appears that in its own formalization of its concerns, the very lack of forensic rigour in older forms of government is the aspect of earlier English law for which the narrator of *Mum and the Sothsegger* is so nostalgic. As I have argued throughout this study, the alternative to the royal bureaucracy that most directly concerned the school of Langland was provided not by actually oral practices, but by the *nominally* or *apparently* oral practices of ancient corporate entities. These practices seemed relatively "oral" only insofar as they based their political claims in the religious and moral authority of documentary forms that were difficult to criticize according to the literate methodologies of later bureaucratic procedures. The counterpoint to Green's "unholy alliance" offered by the poem is the *holy* alliance between *principled* authority and literate technology, modelled in the ancient legal records of Anglo-Saxon England.

This alternative model has important ramifications for Grady's argument about the "decisive turn" away from the dream vision in *Mum and the Sothsegger*. Grady argues that for the Lancastrian poets, "the apparent fixity and unalterable archival persistence of legal documents, chronicles, and statutes would have had an undeniable appeal."[28] This formulation

---

25 Green, *Crisis of Truth*, 281.
26 Green, *Crisis of Truth*, 127.
27 Giancarlo similarly privileges parliamentary democracy over earlier models of government in his own reading of *Mum and the Sothsegger*: Giancarlo, *Parliament*, 237–52.
28 Grady, "Generation of 1999," 222–3.

ignores the fact that documentary permanence in general was not necessarily considered desirable. Fixity and persistence are not themselves sufficient guarantors of documentary truth; if anything, they are the foremost causes of documentary abuse, as even authoritative texts can be damaged by the "gloss," which is able to deceive readers despite its newness precisely by means of its juxtaposition with authoritative text in the manuscript. The "appeal" of such records is perhaps better characterized as an ambivalence about them, manifest here in the poem's obsessive reworking of the same themes.

Representative of the ambivalence about historical records in *Mum and the Sothsegger* is a digression about Genghis Khan that emerges in the course of his examination of twenty-four "comunes of culmes" (1388). The digression suggests that Genghis Khan's order to his nobles that they kill their firstborn children and give up their lands was a good kingly decision (1414–43). Grady argues that this passage's approval of such a monstrous action reveals the poem's appeals to history to be "fundamentally ironic."[29] What worked for the pagan despot of thirteenth-century Mongolia could never work for the Christian king of fifteenth-century England, and suggesting the Khan as a model of kingship only draws attention to the Lancastrian crisis of legitimacy. The Genghis passage is therefore exemplary of the poet's failure to create "a new 'documentary poetic' that does not simply tell truths but endows them with the formal properties and performative powers and 'material solidity' of rolls and testaments."[30] The fact that he must rely on the dream vision's outmoded and deliberately enigmatic narrative form to initiate the bag of books section draws the reader's attention to the fact that the narrator does not literally represent the actual contents of the obscured texts, but only gives us his poetic "gloss" of them.[31]

This reading of the poem provides a compelling account of the poem's more specific political implications at its probable date of composition. However, there is more to be said about the poem's various failures. As Emily Steiner notes, the "comunes of culme" occasioning the digression are themselves spurious, in the sense that they served private rather than public interests. Steiner argues that the narrator is "very careful" in this passage "to distinguish documentary poetry from the unsubstantiated

---

29 Grady, "Generation of 1399," 221.
30 Grady, "Generation of 1399," 227.
31 Grady, "Generation of 1399," 214–22.

complaint of the commons. It is as if he is worried that broadsides and documents, because they disclose the condition of the realm, might *seem* to be issued by the commons at large" (her emphasis).[32] Thus the narrator glosses the "comunes of culme" so problematically because the documents themselves are quite problematic. As records of gossip, they *are* gossip, and are therefore both evidence of abuse and instances of abuse themselves. In other words, they are emblematic of the far more profound failure of authoritative documents to prevent injustice. Indeed, the *comunes of culme* are themselves a cause of social unrest rather than a solution to it.

The Genghis story resolves the tension created by the documents by providing an alternative, "oral" model for communication between king and subject. This is apparent in the passage describing the results of his decree:

> Thus proved this prince his peuple and thaire hertz,
> And to feil of thaire fiance ful felly he wroughte.
> And whenne he wiste that his wil was not encountrid,
> But that he had thaire hertz al hoole at his wil,
> He forgafe thaym thaire graunt and goodely thaym thanked.
> Thenne clepid he to cunseil knightz and other,
> And wroughte alle with oon wil as wise men shuld. (1446–51)

> [Thus this prince proved his people and their hearts,
> And to feel their allegiance he worked very direly.
> And when he knew that his will was not contradicted,
> And that he had their hearts completely at his will,
> He forgave them their gift and thanked them.
> Then he called the knights and others to council,
> And they worked together with one will as wise men should.]

Through his harsh decree, the Khan learns the true "hertz" of his followers. Knowing this, he is able to assemble a "cunseil" of the knights he can trust, so that they "wroughte alle with oon wil as wise men shuld."

The severity of the injunction is thus dramatically important, because it underscores the basic point that the Mongolian nobles cannot possibly have been motivated by selfish reasons when they agreed to follow the

---

32 Steiner, *Documentary Culture*, 185.

Khan's orders. If impracticable for a Christian king, the story of an arbitrary ruler demanding the sacrifice of children and property nonetheless has Old Testament analogues, in both the book of Job and the story of Abraham and Isaac in Genesis. The passage also calls to mind a similarly sensational (and "hysterically funny") passage of the *Mirror of Justices*, where King Alfred hangs forty-four judges within a single year for failure to properly perform their duty.[33] As Seipp argues in his reading of that text, the narrator does not necessarily condone Alfred's barbaric measures, and perhaps he only wanted "to make his points more memorable by putting them in the form of fables set in the distant past."[34] A similar pedagogical motive is probably behind the Genghis passage. After all, the precedent recorded here is impracticable not only because Genghis' actions are barbaric, but because no royal servant in the world described in *Mum and the Sothsegger* would ever sacrifice even a small part of his wealth and comfort, much less the entirety of it, because his king asked him.

This leads us back to the poem's unresolved tension between truthful text and specific gloss. One early indication of the strength of Mum's argument is his citation of Cato in service of his cause:

> And cleerly Caton construeth the same,
> And seyth soethly, I saw hit in youthe,
> That of "bable" cometh blame and of "be stille" never –
> Nam nulli tacuisse nocet, nocet esse locutum. (289–92)

> [And clearly Cato construes the same,
> And says truly (I saw it as a youth)
> That from babbling comes blame, but never from "Be still" –
> For to be silent harms no one; it is harmful to speak.]

This correct citation of a known authority is so disruptive because it signals the generalized applicability of textual authority, so broad that it can even be applied to prove that it has no applicability at all. Mum actually *does* have a point, and Cato confirms it. Though the text here is true, then, the necessity of applying and interpreting it – in other words, of glossing it – also gives it the potential to be false.

---

33 Hanna, *London Literature*, 89.
34 Seipp, "Mirror of Justices," 105.

The next time that Cato appears in the poem, in a passage about the authenticity of dreams that follows the dream's final rejection of Mum's argument, the pagan *auctor* is superseded by the greater authority of the prophet Daniel:

But sum of the silde-couthes I wol shewe hereafter,
For dreme is no dwele by Danyelis wordes,
Though Caton of the contrarye carpe in his bokes. (875–8)

[But some of the wonders I will show hereafter,
For according to Daniel's words, a dream is no illusion,
Though Cato says otherwise in his books.]

This subversion of a secular, pagan authority to a religious, prophetic one signals a larger bracketing-off of the poem's central paradox by the sudden interruption of a dream vision. Daniel correctly identified the hidden text of one king's dream before interpreting it, and later he read the original writing on the wall. The passage quoted above goes on to cite also the authority of Joseph, who foresaw in a similar vision that he would reveal the treachery of his brothers, and provide for the sustenance of his people. Thus the living, speaking text of scripture validates the text of the poem's dream, in which the franklin gives him spoken advice, that he should not only write a book but make it, "til hit be complete to claspyng," creating in this sense a direct line of validation from the stories in scripture to the specific volume that we are either reading from or having read to us (1282).

This retreat to scriptural authority may be read as an abdication of the poem's original question, about the applicability of truthful text in latter-day political contexts. But the source of validation evoked here is not merely the Old Testament, but more specifically *Piers Plowman*. These exact same allusions to Cato, Daniel, and Joseph appear in a similar justification of the dream vision form witnessed in all three versions of *Piers Plowman* (A.VIII.133–47; B.VII.155–72; C.IX.303–17).[35] In just one verbal echo between the texts, both *Piers Plowman* and *Mum and the Sothsegger* use the language of testimony to claim that "the bible bereþ witnesse" to the precedent of Daniel and Joseph (B.VII.157, *Mum and the Sothsegger* 1314). Emily Steiner has demonstrated that many of the representations of documents within *Mum and the Sothsegger* echo the

---

35 On this passage, see Schmidt, "Visions and Revisions."

representations of similar documents in *Piers Plowman*.[36] The juxtaposition of Cato, Daniel, and Joseph is another such echo. The difference here is that the "document" in question is not an image from an allegorical fiction, but the social document *Piers Plowman* itself, and in particular a formula provided within that document to justify its participation in the dream-vision genre, with reference to the authoritative text of scripture. The authority to write granted by the franklin is an authority derived not only from that franklin's resemblance to the figure of Piers the Plowman, but also from *Mum and the Sothsegger's* formal resemblance to the poem(s) *Piers Plowman*.

Like the quotation from Psalm 68 discussed at the beginning of this chapter, the sequence of biblical allusions at the end of the dream are a kind of documentary formula used to authorize a claim. The passage citing Cato, Daniel, and Joseph not only imitates the versions of *Piers Plowman* but procedurally repeats the original passage to validate the new claims made in the dream-vision section of *Mum and the Sothsegger*. Thus the dream vision does not *precede* the document analysis of the bag of books, but rather *initiates* it, as the dream performs the poem's debt to *Piers Plowman* in order to assume the authority necessary to revivify the books' contents without devolving into mere gloss. The nostalgia for the Old Testament implicit in these allusions anticipates the similar nostalgia for Genghis Khan apparent many lines later. The dreams interpreted by Joseph and Daniel made the truth of justice apparent to the pharaoh and emperor, just as the sacrifice of the Mongolian lords made their loyalty apparent to the Khan. If these principles were impracticable in the actual world of fifteenth-century England, it is because of the fallen state of English society, not because of any flaw in the principles themselves. In other words, Grady and Green are both quite correct to read *Mum and the Sothsegger* as a failure; the poem does not ultimately manage to gain for itself the authority and transparency of contemporary historical and legal documents. It does, however, manage to show quite effectively that its contemporary historical and legal documents were hardly as authoritative and transparent as they advertised themselves to be.

I will conclude this reading with a brief look at the last item to be described from the bag of books, which is a document from the recent present that reminds the narrator of the distant past:

---

36 Steiner, *Documentary Culture*, 177–90.

Yit sawe I there a cedule soutelly indited
With tuly silke intachid right atte rolle-is ende,
Ywrite ful of worde of woundres that han falle,
And fele-folde ferlees wythynne these fewe yeris,
by cause that the clergie and knighthoode togedre
Been not knytte in conscience as Crist dide thaym stable.
For who so loketh on the lawe may lerne, yf hym like,
Thayre ordre and office and how thay ought wyrche.
For thay folowe no foote of thaire forne-fadres,
I do hit on thaire deeth-day, and deme no ferther,
For seurly sumtyme I saw hit not late
Yn cronicle of clercz and kingz lygnées
How prelatz of provinces pride moste hatid
For the theme that they taughte was tachid on thaire hertz.
Thay preched the peuple and provyd hit thaymself
And were lanternes to lewed men to lyve thaym after. (1734–49)

[I saw there a schedule subtly written
With red silk attached at the roll's end,
Writ with words of many wonders that had befallen,
And many different marvels within these few years,
Because the knighthood and clergy
are not bound in one conscience as Christ established them.
For whoever looks on the law may learn, if he likes,
Their order and office and how they may work.
For they follow no footsteps of their forefathers,
I do it on their deathday and judge no further,
For recently I saw it
In chronicles of clerks and royal lineages
How prelates of the provinces hated pride
Because the theme that they taught was attached to their hearts.
They preached to the people and proved it themselves,
And were lanterns to unschooled men, that they may life like them.]

In light of the preceding discussion, the narrator's twin evocations of "the lawe" on the one hand and of a "cronicle of clercz" on the other, in a lament that "the clergie and knighthoode togedre / Been not knytte in conscience," allude to the traditions of law and history represented by *I–II Cnut* and the *Brut*, respectively. Though perhaps only an accident of the text's survival, it is appropriate that *Mum and the Sothsegger* concludes with an acknowledgment of these predecessors, in its lament for a past when leaders were virtuous in thought, word, and deed, and improved the lives of their subjects through personal example: "For the theme that they taughte was tachid *on thaire hertz,* / Thay *preched* the peuple and *provyd hit thaymself* / And were lanternes to lewed men to lyve thaym after" (my emphasis). The narrator does not specify that the history described here is specifically the history of England; however, the parallel between this identification of virtuous leadership with not only the knowledge of history, but also specifically with the examples of "prelatz of provinces" (like the bishop-saints evoked in the *First Worcester Fragment*), encourages a reading of this passage as a thematic treatment within the poem of the parallel texts identified above. But more than this, the feature of this passage that most closely aligns it with Anglo-Saxon legal-homiletic discourse is its performed nostalgia for an era when Christian truths were held self-evident, and not concealed by ignorance as they are in the narrator's present. The *sothsegger* of *Mum and the Sothsegger* aims to continue the process of interpretation and renewal that forms the crucial connection between the texts of the past and the scholarship of the present, as each deepens our understanding of how the other attempts to "teche treuly the texte as hit standeth" (477).

Conclusion

In a recent study of Piers's pardon in passus B7, Alistair Minnis has provided a compelling account of the document's symbolic function in terms of the conventions governing indulgences in the fourteenth century.[1] The one lacuna remaining in Minnis's study is an explanation for the pardon's highly unconventional text. The document contains only a Latin quotation from the Athanasian Creed: "Et qui bona egerunt, ibunt in vitam aeternam; qui vero mala, in ignem aeternum (he who does well will go to eternal life and he who does poorly will go to eternal fire)." As Minnis observes, the "utter simplicity and uncompromising rigor" of this statement means that "Piers' Pardon is no pardon at all."[2] The unpardoning text of this pardon is all the more remarkable because it marks the first occurrence of the phrase "do well" in the poem, which will serve as the basis for the triad "do well, do better, do best" that will reoccur throughout the remainder of the B-version. And yet when this poem was revised for the C-version, the pardon scene itself is drastically curtailed. Hence it seems that the same symbolic document whose disruptive potential generated so much of the poem's additional length in the B revision ultimately proved too disruptive for the poem, and had to be contained in the C revision.

I conclude this study by pointing towards the problem of Truth's pardon, because the document described in the poem is also formally reminiscent of late Anglo-Saxon charters, to the degree that the pardon may be characterized as a distillation of the documents' features that were emphasized in post-Conquest forgeries. Certainly there is an analogy between

---

1 Minnis, "Letter and Spirit."
2 Minnis, "Letter and Spirit," 234.

the function of the pardon and the function of most Anglo-Saxon charters: both documentary forms commemorate ecclesiastical acceptance of goods and services as a contribution towards the remission of sins. More to the point, the pardon specifically grants Piers the right and obligation to remain within a certain plot of land, and to either plow that land or use it in some other profitable way (B VII.5–8). Also like the Anglo-Saxon charters, this particular pardon is relatively informal by the standards of fourteenth-century bureaucratic culture.

Truth's pardon is not only uncompromising in its rigour, but it also lacks virtually all of the basic elements anticipated in late medieval documents, so that Minnis's own analysis of the pardon in material-cultural terms must rely on the context of its uses in the narrative rather than its actual text.[3] The pardon does not specify the date of its production, the names of its recipient or issuing officer, the circumstances under which it could be invalidated, or any of the kinds of detail that would allow it to commemorate a particular transaction or decision. The only thing it does contain is a proverb, whose first half states briefly the sentiment of many proems to Anglo-Saxon charters, "one should do well while one is alive" (and so I grant this land to a monastery), and whose second half states briefly the sentiment of many sanction clauses, "one will suffer eternal fire" (if one does not respect the terms of this charter). Truth's pardon does not function as a commemoration of a past event or transaction, but on the contrary is an article of faith in its own right, and one that a Christian must continually reaffirm. In this sense the main thing documented by this pardon is its own inability to finally perform any of its necessary functions, except perhaps the documentation of its own inadequacy.

For these reasons, Piers's pardon is emblematic of the larger ambivalence about documentary formalism that is constitutive of the larger project of the *Piers Plowman* tradition. As I have said, the text satirizes the formalistic bureaucracy of its historical moment, and its alliterative, sententious form claims an authority based in earlier English forms of governance. But at the same time, the earlier English forms of governance cannot be resuscitated except by formulaic imitation of their authorizing procedures. Moreover, their authority derives from the very sententious generality that makes them subject to doubt by sceptical critics. In the terms described in *Mum and the Sothsegger*, the "text" of Truth's pardon cannot

---

3 Minnis, "Letter and Spirit," 219–29.

be applied in life without passing through the mediation of interpretive "gloss," even though "glosing" by its very nature invalidates truthful texts.

But if *Mum and the Sothsegger* provides us with a language for articulating the problem of the pardon, it also exemplifies the solution, such as it was. As I have observed in chapter 6, the defence of dreams in *Mum and the Sothsegger* functions as a formulaic imitation of Langland's own defence of dreams, which originally appears in the B-version directly following the vision of the pardon. Hence the very same retreat to authoritative, sententious abstraction employed in B-version to close off the disruptive potential of documentary symbolism is employed in *Mum and the Sothsegger* in precisely the opposite way, to justify the text's indulgence in the conceit of the bag of books. Read in comparison to the B-version, then, *Mum and the Sothsegger* exemplifies the strategy that literacies have always employed when confronted with the problem of their necessary failures: that is to say, they rearticulate the problems of literacy as formulae in their own right, whose self-evident status as genuinely good questions can provide an authoritative basis for further writing, even though further writing can never solve the underlying problems articulated by the formulae. If Piers's pardon managed to successfully document its own untrustworthiness, then the author of *Mum and the Sothsegger* may authenticate future documents on its basis.

And so it is no accident that one of the most persistent themes I have identified in *Piers Plowman*, the *Brut*, the manuscripts of the Tremulous Hand, *The Proverbs of Alfred*, the writings of Wulfstan, and the earliest charters of the Anglo-Saxons is their shared dissatisfaction with the state of English literacy itself. This dissatisfaction is not only a feature of the written traditions of literature and law that they all draw from, but it also marks the texts as corrective measures against the state of affairs they describe. When Æthelberht writes his law code *iuxta exempla Romanorum*, he is not laying claim to greatness on the level of the Romans; rather, he signals his aspirations towards the status of a Caesar, aspirations which necessarily suggest dissatisfaction with the status quo. And whatever the original reasons for writing his laws in English, his choice created a symbolic connection between the aspirations of English kings and the formalization of English-language literacy, so that the latter also became similarly aspirational. This symbolic connection between English writing and English nation never disappeared, even after the English-language law of the Anglo-Saxons was rendered invalid by the institutional reforms of the Angevin era. When the English language returned to English government in the fourteenth century, it came in at the ground level, to be reformalized on the basis of later documentary models. And yet at the same time, the older, more "oral" formalism of Anglo-Saxon precedent persisted, in documents and in popular memory, proving by its very existence that the "common" law's claim to antiquity and commonality was a revisionist fiction. To put it another way: if Truth's pardon is the problem that generated the second half of *Piers Plowman* B-version, then perhaps the Anglo-Saxon prehistory of English literacy is the problem that generated the corpus of Middle English literature, as Middle English writers worked either to adapt or to erase the various memorials of Anglo-Saxon legal-homiletic discourse still circulating in the late medieval period, in the service of constructing a new, secular English identity.

As I have said, this book's genealogy of the legal-homiletic discourse manifest in the *Piers Plowman* tradition aims to serve only as a first enquiry into this much broader historical thesis about the connections between the Old and Middle English literature. There are many other sites with great potential for further investigation; for the remainder of this conclusion I will identify some of the more obvious. The first, so vast that it can be mentioned only briefly, is the corpus of Anglo-Norman literature. Q, after all, was an Anglo-Norman author, and some of Laȝamon's imitations of legal-homiletic discourse have their roots in Wace. Indeed, the Anglo-Norman translation of the Cnut law codes is the earliest known French-language legal text. There are surely many more such intersections between Old English law and the dialect that would one day be called "law French."

Among the corpus of early Middle English texts in the Worcester region, the most notable are the *Ancrene Wisse* and the *Ormulum*. Since Tolkien's formative study, the critical consensus has been that the six remarkably similar manuscripts of the thirteenth-century *Ancrene Wisse* and the associated "Katherine Group" of hagiographic and devotional materials, called the "AB" tradition, were assembled by an Augustinian canon who lived near Worcester in Herefordshire.[4] These texts use alliterative Middle English prose to define both the virtues of the ascetic life and also to limit and contain the public roles of women, both themes treated at great length in Anglo-Saxon homily and law, and Christopher Cannon has noted the implicit analogy to political boundaries implied by the texts' careful construction of feminine, devotional space.[5] Surely, then, the actual

---

4 Tolkien, "Ancrene."
5 Cannon, *Grounds*, 143.

language used to construct such boundaries in the political sphere must play some role in these texts. The *Ormulum*, meanwhile, contains a direct echo of Wulfstan's lists of criminals, and therefore may have been directly influenced by one or more of Wulfstan's homilies.[6] Meg Worley has theorized that its standardized spelling marks it as a text for preaching designed to be used by francophone preachers – the text perhaps serving as an example of what the Tremulous Hand's collection of vernacular preaching materials might have looked like had he finished it.[7]

Another locale requiring further study is Wulfstan's other former diocese, of York. Prominent alliterative texts associated with northern England include *Wynnere and Wastour*, *Parlement of the Thre Ages*, and the alliterative *Morte Arthure*, all appearing in manuscripts copied by the Yorkshire gentleman Robert Thornton.[8] The "York realist" playwright of the York Cycle wrote in alliterative verse,[9] and even further north Scottish court poets continued to write with alliteration until well into the sixteenth century.[10] Nor is York the only other region that merits this sort of analysis. As Ralph Hanna observes and I have demonstrated, "narratives of interregional penetration (and apparent appreciation)" provide more compelling accounts of alliterative poetry's transmission than narratives of regional isolation.[11]

Indeed, this polyvocality appears to reflect not only the complexity of the evidence, but also the ideological purposes behind much alliterative writing. Indeed, the highly idiosyncratic nature of late medieval alliterative writing indicates just how polyvocal was the model of traditionalism provided by Anglo-Saxon legal-homiletic discourse. Nor was this polyvocality simply for its own sake. I have already suggested that Wulfstan's careful distinctions between West Saxon law and its Mercian and Danish counterparts was intended to construct a narrative of English history based on interregional penetration and appreciation, as a way of resisting the eventual consolidation of power around the single, "common" law of the king. The more pluralistic was England's *folclagu*, then the more practical importance was given to *Godes lagu* as a consequence. Hence even if alliterative romances like *William of Palerne*, the alliterative *Morte Arthure*,

---

6 Meaney, "Hæðenscipe," 479–81; Wilcox, "Twelfth Century"; Morrison, "Reminiscence."
7 Worley, "Using."
8 Hanna, "Alliterative Poetry," 509.
9 For example in "The Conspiracy": *York Mystery Plays*, 125–37.
10 Hanna, "Alliterative Poetry," 497.
11 Hanna, "Alliterative Poetry," 509.

Sir Gawain and the Green Knight, *Awntyrs of Arthur*, *The Parlement of the Thre Ages*, and *The Wars of Alexander* have appeared to most readers to be secular, courtly texts that are connected by little more than their individualistic employment of a difficult and endlessly adaptable verse form, their very refusal to conform to predictable expectations in itself signals the fungibility of the traditional model provided to them by Anglo-Saxon legal-homiletic discourse. Christine Chism observes that alliterative romances "stage a drama of revival, creatively, strategically, and spectacularly revising insular traditions rather than faithfully reconstituting them."[12] As I have shown, the irony of this characterization is that the spectacular revisionism is itself a kind of faithful reconstitution, in a way that slavish imitation would not be.

I will bring this study to a close with a brief consideration of the responses to the Anglo-Saxon legal-homiletic tradition found in two other major canonical authors of the Ricardian era: the Pearl Poet and Chaucer. Of the two authors, the Pearl Poet may seem at first to be the more likely candidate for a connection to Anglo-Saxon legal-homiletic discourse, because of his alliterative metre. Certainly *St. Erkenwald*, sometimes attributed to the Pearl Poet, is the late medieval alliterative poem that engages most explicitly with the themes of Anglo-Saxon history and ecclesiastical power that have dominated this study. And yet the most widely read works by this poet (and best-known examples of "alliterative revival" verse), *Sir Gawain and the Green Knight* and *Pearl*, are so deeply invested in the idiom of noble courtly culture that their alliterative metre seems to be merely one part of a larger and highly original project, whose complexity is also signalled formally by the poems' sophisticated stanzaic and narrative structures. In order to account for the creative and unusual redeployment of alliterative verse in these works, I will turn briefly to the related poem *Patience*. As I will demonstrate, the Pearl Poet's works do not merely recapitulate Anglo-Saxon legal-homiletic discourse but present a sophisticated response to the ideology coded within it.[13]

In the original book of Jonah, the storm that besets the prophet's ship causes each of the sailors to pray to his own God (1:5). The men then discover Jonah asleep in the hold and wake him (1:6), and then decide to cast lots to identify the culprit who has angered the Gods (1:7). In *Patience*,

---

12 Chism, *Alliterative Revivals*, 16.

13 The most succinct evidence for this context is *Sir Gawain and the Green Knight*'s conclusion, where it is revealed that the poem is an origin story for Edward III's Order of the Garter (2505–30). *Works*, Andrew and Waldron.

meanwhile, a catalogue of the sailors' false Gods (164–8) culminates in the statement by the *spakest* ("wisest") man on the ship: "I leue here be sum losynger, sum lawless wrech, / Þat hatz greued his god and gotz here amonge vus" (I believe that here is some lawless wretch that has aggrieved his God and hidden here among us) (171–2). The man proposes that they cast lots to determine who the lawless wretch may be. Only then is Jonah roused from the hold (182–92) and the lots actually cast (193–4).

This poem's addition of a wise pagan counsellor to the story, who moreover comments on the "lawlessness" of the only man on the ship who worships the true God, employs the same manoeuvre witnessed in the *Sermo Lupi ad Anglos* and the *Brut*. Damned though they may be, the heathens at least respect their own laws, and the wise heathen's very existence is a reproach to Jonah's own failure to obey the true "law" that he ought not only to know, but also to enforce. Jonah's exaggerated snoring and slobbering (186) indicates the precise nature of his crime: he is an example of the "lazy" bishops castigated at such length in Wulfstan's sermons, who similarly ought to preach to a laity on the verge of catastrophe. To drive home the legal implications of this scene, the casting of lots itself and Jonah's exchange with the sailors (Jonah 1:8–14) is rendered in the poem as a trial, as the poet adds a formal accusation and proposed remedy to the statement by the sailors ("Lo, þy dom is diȝt, for þy deds ille / Do gyf glory to þy godde, er þy glyde hens" [Lo, your judgment is ruled; give glory to your God for your ill deeds before you go hence] [203–4]) and a confession by Jonah ("Alle þis meschef for me is made at þys tyme, / For I haf greued my God and gulty am founden" [All this mischief is made for me at this time because I aggrieved my God and am found guilty] [209–10]). The reduction of this appeal to God's divine intervention makes the lot-casting into a kind of ordeal, and as such the scene reflects a highly traditional form of legal logic. In other words, the biblical scene is recast so that it functions within a symbolic framework that draws from the conventions and procedures of Anglo-Saxon law and homily. In particular, the poem drives home the notion that preaching is a legal obligation of bishops, and also the related notion that the bishop's failure in those duties will invite divine intervention and punishment.

The most striking thing about *Patience*, then, is the way it employs a symbolic framework strongly reminiscent of Wulfstan's legal and homiletic writing to argue precisely the opposite side of Wulfstan's overarching point. Though Wulfstan certainly acknowledges the potential for bishops to fail in their prophetic duties, he typically does so only in order to stress the importance of episcopal oversight in the secular realm. Here, the episcopal Jonah does not function as the lawgiver: a nameless pagan sailor does. Where Wulfstan's case for ecclesiastical power hinges in part on his characterization of bishops as repositories of cultural knowledge, *Patience* critiques ecclesiastical power, and provides a scriptural case in which a righteous lay pagan is able to arrive at a spiritual, legal truth that has evaded a divinely appointed prophet.

In particular, the poem appears to employ its Anglo-Saxon legal-homiletic discourse as a critique of ecclesiastical endowment. The critique is signalled most strongly in the poem's final scene. In the poem as in the Bible, Jonah has fallen asleep under a woodbine after his argument with God over His decision to spare the Ninevites. God causes the woodbine to wither and die, and Jonah awakens with a sunburn. In Jonah 4:9, God asks Jonah about the loss of the woodbine: "putasne bene irasceris tu" (do you think it well that you should be angry)? In *Patience*, *bene* is translated as "ry3twis" (490), not only "well" or "appropriate" but also "just." Similarly, the poem's translation of Jonah's reply "bene irascor ego usque ad mortem" (It is well that I be angry until death) is rendered: "Hit is not lyttel ... bot lykker to ry3t" (it is not insignificant, but closer to justice) (492). The debate about the woodbine that flourished and disappeared is thus cast in *Patience* as a debate about Jonah's "rights": is it unjust that Jonah is deprived by God of property that God had given to him for his comfort? The answer, of course, is no, as the reader of *Patience* already knows from the discussion of poverty in the poem's opening lines (35–58). In this way, the figure of Jonah appears to be a satire of those lazy ecclesiastical figures that imagine they can lead comfortable lives without having to perform their clerical duties. *Patience* witnesses many of the same tropes that we have seen before in alliterative Anglo-Saxon legal-homiletic discourse, but it employs them in service of a statement precisely contrary to the agenda they originally served. Where Wulfstan wished to maintain and even increase ecclesiastical wealth and power, *Patience* implies that the church is already more wealthy and powerful than it deserves, given the poor quality of the services provided by its slothful representatives. Such a view is certainly typical of the courtly milieu within which the poet apparently operated.

If we can read in *Patience* a coded connection between the figure of the recalcitrant prophet and the figure of the recalcitrant English bishop, the poem makes a far more explicit parallel between Jonah and the poet himself, who like Jonah serves a "lege lorde" who sends him on fruitless quests without sufficient compensation (51). Any aspersions cast by the poet on Jonah are in this sense self-directed. Though the poet may criticize the ideology implicit in the alliterative idiom, he is nonetheless highly cognizant of his own complicity in that idiom as an author of alliterative poetry. As I have said, the poet's employment of that idiom has long been identified as a marker of the poet's regional identity. Whether or not this is the case, it is certainly true that the poet was not successful at recuperating alliterative metre for the tastes of secular bureaucrats, however he may have tried.

Perhaps the most dramatic proof of his failure in this regard is found in the poet Chaucer. *The Canterbury Tales* contains one of the most famous references to alliterative verse in Middle English, in the passage where the Parson dismisses alliterative verse as follows: "I am a Southren man; / I kan nat geeste 'rum, ram, ruf,' by lettre, / Ne, God woot, rym holde I but litel bettre" (I am a Southern man; I cannot say "rum, ram, ruf" by letter, and God knows I can rhyme only a little better) (X.42–4). It should be noted first that the Parson's rejection of alliteration in these lines is more probably an allusion to alliterative sermons, like those identified by Shannon Gayk, than it is a reference to narrative poems like *Sir Gawain and the Green Knight* or even *Piers Plowman*. The Parson has already made it clear that he will not tell "fables and swich wrecchednesse" (X.34); he is talking about alliteration and rhyme in "moralitee and virtuous mateere" (38). Hence the Parson implies that his audience would be within their rights to anticipate that a virtuous churchman about to speak on moral topics would use structural alliteration.

Second, when the Parson refers to himself as "a Southren man," he lays no claim to the sophistication of cosmopolitan London in contrast to the country bumpkins and alliterative poets of the North. On the contrary, he rejects alliterative verse by means of the classic sentiment of the country bumpkin: "that's not how we do things around here." Ironically, there is evidence interpolated into *The Canterbury Tales* itself disproving even this claim: southern men could and did *ram, rum, ruf* on occasion.[14] Hence the Parson does not so much assign a regional identity to alliterative verse as he makes the (unsupportable) claim that alliterative verse operates outside of his own regional identity – which is, not coincidentally, Chaucer's identity as well.[15] The Parson's retreat from the foreignness of alliteration reveals the difference between Chaucer's response to Anglo-Saxon

---

14 In the manuscript Oxford, Bodleian, Bodley MS 686, ff. 54v–55v. See Morse "Man of Law," 29–31.

15 On London's regional identity see Hanna, *London Literature*.

legal-homiletic discourse and the Pearl Poet's. Where the Pearl Poet attempts to work within that idiom and reinvent it, Chaucer works to repress and reject it as "un-English." In its place we are presented with a prose form utterly unbeholden to the alien, "Northern" forms of Anglo-Saxon legal-homiletic discourse.

And yet Chaucer's very repression of Anglo-Saxon legal-homiletic discourse from *The Canterbury Tales* also occasions its return. The first evidence to this effect is provided by the metafictional joke running throughout the frame narrative that Chaucer is a poor poet, echoed by the Parson's claim that he is unskilled at rhyme in the lines cited above. Particularly relevant here are two similar claims made by Chaucer himself in *The Canterbury Tales*. Chaucer's own skills as a poet are disparaged in an offhand aside by the Man of Law that Chaucer "kan but lewedly / On metres and on rymyng craftily" (II.47–8), and again in Harry Bailly's direct address to Chaucer the pilgrim following *Sir Thopas*: "pleynly, at a word, / Thy drasty rymyng is nat worth a toord!" (VII.929–30). Because Chaucer has already exhausted the medium of poetry, the Man of Law promises to tell a tale in prose, and so it is generally assumed that he was originally assigned the prose *Tale of Melibee*. Like the Parson's own assertion that he cannot alliterate or rhyme, then, the two other jokes about Chaucer's inability to write verse both initiate a turn to non-metrical prose.

In his response to the Host's interruption, Chaucer prefaces the *Tale of Melibee* with the warning that his listeners will here in it "somewhat moore / Of proverbs than ye han herd bifoore" (VII.955–6). Chaucer the pilgrim thus retreats from the forms of poetry in exchange for the forms of sententious statements, rendered not in verse but in prose. And so Chaucer the poet who so effectively satirized the vagueness of sententious wisdom in the character of Pandarus from *Troilus and Creseyde* also made his character Chaucer the pilgrim fall back on proverbial wisdom when his rhymes have failed, because only in proverbs may he eliminate "difference" from his "sentence."[16] Hence while Chaucer's Parson will reject the sententious formalism of Anglo-Saxon legal-homiletic discourse in fragment X, Chaucer the pilgrim in fragment VII is anxious about the forms that his proverbs take, and feels compelled to assert that they will nonetheless remain authoritative even if that form is unfamiliar to his English-speaking audience. Taken together, the two prologues to prose tales point to Chaucer's

---

16 The words "difference" and "sentence" end rhyming couplets in VII.947–8 and 961–2. On Pandarus and the satirical use of proverbs, see McDonald, "Proverbs."

anxiety about form in the text, implicit already in the fact that *The Canterbury Tales* is both one of the most influential poems in the English language and also a text that contains too much prose to be referred to in the singular as a "poem." A southern, London man such as Chaucer may not want to *ram, rum, ruf,* but at the same time abandoning alliteration runs the risk of depriving his verse of true sententious authority.

But even though the sententious *Melibee* enables Chaucer to think through a new relationship to sententious form, it does not address the related problem of establishing a new relationship to English history. Hence in the place of the prose, sententious *Melibee,* the Man of Law tells a tale that is the only work in the Chaucerian corpus to be set in Anglo-Saxon England. The tale of Custaunce presents not only an alternative account of the conversion of the English to Christianity, but also a fable of the invention of English law, modified by Chaucer so that the pagan king Alla serves as a naive lawgiver along the same lines as the pagan sailor in *Patience.* Though Chaucer emphasizes the ludicrous and improbable elements of his source's conversion narrative, the tale nonetheless is appropriate to serve as a second beginning to *The Canterbury Tales,* by introducing the very prehistory of English writing that the Parson will later suppress in his non-alliterating prose.

Ultimately, then, Chaucer and the Pearl Poet both seem to be responding to the same problematic history. Though these authors may eschew the formal conventions of Anglo-Saxon legal-homiletic discourse that influenced their contemporary Langland, their work nonetheless demonstrates the continued authority of that discourse within vernacular English poetry. The continuities traced in this book between the law codes of Anglo-Saxon lawmen and the tradition of Piers Plowman is only one small part of this much larger story, to be fleshed out in future investigations.

Bibliography

Abbreviations

Anglia	Anglia: Zeitschrift fur Englische Philologie
ASE	Anglo-Saxon England
EHR	English Historical Review
JEGP	Journal of English and Germanic Philology
MAe	Medium Ævum
MLR	Modern Language Review
PMLA	Publication of the Modern Language Association
YLS	Yearbook of Langland Studies

Primary Sources

Anglo-Saxon Chronicle: A Collaborative Edition. MS E. Ed. Susan Irvine. Cambridge: D.S. Brewer, 2004.

Awntyrs off Arthur. Sir Gawain: Eleven Romances and Tales. Ed. Thomas Hahn. Kalamazoo: Medieval Institutes Publications, 1995.

British Library Cotton Nero A.I: A Wulstan Manuscript. Ed. Henry R. Loyn. Early English Manuscripts in Facsimile, 17. Copenhagen: Rosenkilde and Bagger, 1971.

Charters of Malmesbury Abbey. Ed. Susan Kelly. Oxford: Oxford University Press, 2005.

Charters of the New Minster, Winchester. Ed. Sean Miller. Oxford: Oxford University Press, 2001.

Councils & Synods with Other Documents Related to the English Church: A. D. 1205–1313. Ed. Frederick Maurice Powicke and Christopher Robert Cheney. 2 vols. Oxford: Clarendon Press, 1964.

Daniel and Azarias. Ed. R.T. Farrell. London: Methuen, 1974.

English Wycliffite Sermons. Ed. Anne Hudson. Oxford: Clarendon, 1983.

The Four Gospels in Anglo-Saxon, Northumbrian, and Old Mercian Versions. Ed. Walter W. Skeat. Cambridge: Cambridge University Press, 1871–87.

Hemingi chartularium ecclesiæ Wigorniensis. Ed. Thomas Hearne. 2 vols. Oxford: University Press, 1723.

Klaeber's Beowulf. 4th ed. Ed. R.D. Fulk, Robert E. Bjork, and John D. Niles. Toronto: University of Toronto Press, 2008.

Landboc sive Registrum monasterii beatae Mariae virginis et sancti Cenhelmi de Winchelcumba. Ed. David Royce. 2 vols. Exeter: William Pollard, 1892, 1903.

The Lay Folk's Catechism. Ed. T.H. Simmons and H.E. Nolloth. EETS os. 118. London: Oxford University Press, 1901.

The Old English Poem Judgement Day II: A Critical Edition with Editions of 'De Die Iudicii' and the Hatton 113 'Homily be Domes Dæge.' Ed. Graham D. Caie. Woodbridge, UK: D.S. Brewer, 2000.

Materials for the History of Thomas Becket. 7 vols. RS 67. Ed. James Craigie Robertson. London: HMSO, 1875–85.

Mum and the Sothsegger. Ed. Mabel Day and Robert Steele. EETS os. 199. Oxford, New York: Kraus Reprint, 1971.

The Poems of the Pearl Manuscript: Pearl, Cleanness, Patience, Sir Gawain and the Green Knight. Eds. Malcolm Andrew and Ronald Waldron. London: Arnold, 1978.

The Proverbs of Alfred: An Emended Text. Ed. Olof Sigfrid Arngart. Lund, Sweden: GWK Gleerup, 1978.

Richard the Redeless and Mum and the Sothsegger. Ed. James Dean. Middle English Text Series. Kalamazoo, MI: Medieval Institute Publications, 2000.

Select Charters and Other Illustrations of English Constitutional History From the Earliest Times to the Reign of Edward the First. Ed. William Stubbs. Oxford: Clarendon, 1874.

Textus Roffensis, Part I. Ed. Peter Sawyer. Early English Manuscripts in Facsimile 7. Copenhagen: Rosenkilde and Bagger, 1957.

Two of the Saxon Chronicles in Parallel. 2 vols. Ed. C. Plummer. Oxford: Clarendon Press, 1892, 1899.

The Vulgate Bible. 5th ed. Ed. Roger Gryson. Stuttgart: Deutsche Bibelgesellschaft, 2007.

Wynnere and Wastour and Parlement of the Thre Ages. Ed. Warren Ginsberg. Kalamazoo: Medieval Institutes Publications, 1992.

York Mystery Plays. Ed. Richard Beadle and Pamela M. King. Oxford: Oxford University Press, 1984.

Adam of Usk. *The Chronicle of Adam of Usk, 1377–1421.* 2 vols. Ed. Chris Given-Wilson. Oxford: Clarendon, 1997.

Aldhelm. *Aldhelmi Opera*. Ed. Rudolf Ehwald. Monumenta Germaniae Historica Auctores Antiquissimi 15. Berlin, 1919.

– *Aldhelm, The Prose Works*. Ed. Michael Lapidge and Michael W. Herren. Cambridge: D.S. Brewer, 1979.

Ælfric of Eynsham. *Ælfric's Catholic Homilies: The First Series Text*. Ed. Peter Clemoes. EETS ss. 17. Oxford: Oxford University Press, 1997.

– *Ælfrics Grammatik und Glossar*. Ed. J. Zupitza. 2nd ed. Intro. Helmut Gneuss. Berlin: Max Niehans, 1966.

– "Die Hirtenbriefe Ælfrics in Altenglischer und Lateinischer Fassung." In *Bibliothek der Angelsächsischen Prosa*. Ed. Bernhard Fehr. Darmstadt: Wissenschaftliche Buchgesellschaft, 1966.

– *Homilies of Ælfric: A Supplemental Collection*. Ed. John C. Pope. EETS os. 259. 2 vols. London: Oxford University Press, 1967.

Bede. *Bede: A Biblical Miscellany*. Trans. W. Trent Foley and Arthur G. Holder. Liverpool: Liverpool Univeristy Press, 1999.

– *Ecclesiastical History of the English People*. Ed. B. Colgrave and R. Mynors. Oxford: Clarendon, 1969.

– *The Old English Version of Bede's Ecclesiastical History of the English People*. Ed. T. Miller. 4 vols. EETS os. 95, 96, 110, 111. (London) [repr. 1959–63].

Bowman, Bob. *If I Tell You a Hen Dips Snuff…* Lufkin: Best of East Texas Publishers, 1986.

Byrhtferth of Ramsey. *Byrhtferth's Enchiridion*. Ed. Peter S. Baker and Michael Lapidge. EETS ss. 15. London: Oxford University Press, 1996.

– *The Lives of St. Oswald and St. Ecgwine*. Ed. Michael Lapidge. Oxford: Oxford University Press, 2009.

Chaucer, Geoffrey. *The Canterbury Tales*. In *The Riverside Chaucer*. Ed. Larry D. Benson et al., 3–328. Boston: Houghton Mifflin, 1987.

de Glanvill, Ranulf. *The Treatise on the Laws and Customs of the Realm of England Commonly Called Glanvill*. Ed. G.D.G. Hall. Oxford: Clarendon Press, 1993.

Firmicus Maternus, Julius. *Mathesis*. Ed. Pierre Monat. Paris: Les Belles Lettres, 1992. 3 vols.

Geoffrey of Monmouth. *Vita Merlini*. Ed. Basil Clarke. Cardiff: University of Wales Press, 1973.

Gower, John. *Confessio Amantis, Volume 1*. Ed. Russell A. Peck, with Latin trans. by Andrew Galloway. Kalamazoo: Medieval Institutes Publications, 2000.

Higden, Ranulf. *Polychronicon Ranulphi Higden maonachi Cestrensis: Together with the English Translations of John Trevisa and of an Unknown Writer of the Fifteenth Century*. Vol. 6. Ed. Joseph Rawson Lumby. London: Longman, 1876.

Hoccleve, Thomas. *Regiment of Princes*. Ed. Charles R. Blyth. Kalamazoo: Medieval Institute Publications, 1999.

Laȝamon. *Brut*. Ed. G.L. Brook and R.F. Leslie. EETS os. 250, 277. 2 vols. London: Oxford University Press, 1978.

– *Brut (MS Cotton Caligula)*. Electronic Text Center, University of Virginia Library. http://etext.lib.virginia.edu/toc/modeng/public/LayBruC.html.

Langland, William. *Piers Plowman: The A Version; Will's Visions of Piers Plowman, Do-Well, Do-Better and Do-Best*. Ed. E. Talbot Donaldson and George Kane. London: Athlone, 1960.

– *Piers Plowman: The B Version; Will's Visions of Piers Plowman, Do-Well, Do-Better and Do-Best*. Ed. E. Talbot Donaldson and George Kane. London: Athlone, 1975.

– *Piers Plowman: A Facsimile of the Z-Text in Bodleian Library, Oxford, Ms Bodley 851*. Ed. George Rigg and Charlotte Brewer. Cambridge: D.S. Brewer, 1994.

– *Piers Plowman: A Parallel-Text Edition of the A, B, C and Z Versions*. Ed. A.V.C. Schmidt. London: Longman, 1995.

– *The Vision of Piers Plowman*. Ed. A.V.C. Schmidt. London: Everyman, 2002.

– *The Vision of William Concerning Piers the Plowman in Three Parallel Texts; Together with Richard the Redeless*. Ed. Walter W. Skeat. Oxford: Clarendon, 1886.

Macrobius. *Commentary on the Dream of Scipio*. Ed. and trans. W.H. Stahl. New York: Columbia University Press, 1952.

Pucci, Antonio. *I cantari della Reina d' Oriente*, Ed. Will Robins and Attillo Motta. Bologna: Commissione per i Testi di Lingua, 2007.

Stephen of Ripon. *The Life of Bishop Wilfrid*. Ed. Bertram Colgrave. Cambridge: Cambridge University Press, 1927.

Thomas of Marlborough. *History of the Abbey of Evesham*. Ed. and trans. Jane E. Sayers and Leslie Watkiss. Oxford: Clarendon, 2003.

Wace. *Wace's Roman De Brut: A History of the English: Text and Translation*. Ed. Judith Weiss. Exeter: University of Exeter Press, 1999.

William of Malmesbury. *Gesta regum Anglorum*. Ed. R.A.B. Mynors, Rodney M. Thomson, and Michael Winterbottom. Oxford: Clarendon, 1998.

– *Gesta pontificum Anglorum*. Ed. and trans. Rodney M. Thomson. Oxford: Clarendon, 2007.

Wulfstan, Archbishop II of York / I of Worcester. *Die "Institutes of Polity, Civil and Ecclesiastical," ein Werk Erzbischof Wulfstans von York*. Ed. Karl Jost. Bern: Francke, 1959.

– *Sammlung der ihm zugeschriebenen Homilien nebst Untersuchungen über ihre Echtheit*. Ed. Arthur Napier. Berlin: Weidmann, 1883.

– *Wulfstan's Canons of Edgar*. Ed. Roger Fowler. EETS os. 266. London: Oxford University Press, 1972.

Secondary Sources

Aers, David. *Sanctifying Signs: Making Christian Tradition in Late Medieval England*. South Bend, IN: University of Notre Dame Press, 2004.

Alford, John. "Design of the Poem." In *A Companion to Piers Plowman*. Ed. John Alford, 29–65. Berkeley: University of California Press, 1988.

– "Langland's Learning." *YLS* 9 (1995): 1–17.

– "Literature and Law in Medieval England." *PMLA* 92 (1977): 941–51.

– *Piers Plowman: A Glossary of Legal Diction*. Cambridge: D.S. Brewer, 1988.

– *Piers Plowman: A Guide to the Quotations*. Binghamton, NY: Medieval and Renaissance Texts and Studies, 1992.

– "The Role of the Quotations in *Piers Plowman*." *Speculum* 52, no. 1 (1977): 80–99.

Allen, Rosamund. "'Nv Seið mid Loft-Songe': A Re-Appraisal of Lawman's Verse Form." In *Laȝamon: Contexts, Language, and Interpretation*. Ed. Rosamund Allen, Lucy Perry, and Jane Roberts, 251–82. London: King's College London Centre for Late Antique and Medieval Studies, 2002.

Alvares, Alicia Rodriguez. "Oral Features in Late Middle English Legal Texts." *Neuphilologische Mitteilungen* 107, no. 2 (2006): 187–97.

Amodio, Mark. *Writing the Oral Tradition: Oral Poetics and Literate Culture in Medieval England*. South Bend, IN: University of Notre Dame Press, 2004.

Astell, Ann W. *Political Allegory in Late Medieval England*. Ithaca, NY: Cornell University Press, 1999.

Aston, Margaret. *Faith and Fire: Popular and Unpopular Religion, 1350–1600*. London: Hambledon Press, 1993.

Baer, Patricia. "Cato's Trace: Literacy, Readership, and the Process of Revision in *Piers Plowman*." *Studies in Medieval and Renaissance History* 3, no. 1 (2001): 123–47.

Baker, John Hamilton. *The Common Law Tradition: Lawyers, Books, and the Law*. London: Hambledon, 2000.

– *The Order of Serjeants at Law: A Chronicle of Creations*. London: Selden Society, 1984.

Baker, Nigel, and Richard Holt. *Urban Growth and the Medieval Church: Gloucester and Worcester*. Aldershot, UK: Ashgate, 2004.

Baldwin, Anna P. "The Historical Context." In *A Companion to Piers Plowman*. Ed. John Alford, 67–86. Berkeley: University of California Press, 1988.

– *The Theme of Government in Piers Plowman*. Cambridge: D.S. Brewer, 1981.

Barney, Stephen. "Langland's Prosody: The State of Study." In *The Endless Knot: Essays on Old and Middle English in Honor of Marie Borroff*. Ed. M. Teresa Tavormina and R.F. Yeager, 65–85. Cambridge: D.S. Brewer, 1995.
– "The Plowshare of the Tongue: The Progress of a Symbol from the Bible to *Piers Plowman*." *Mediæval Studies* 35 (1973): 261–93.
Barr, Helen. "The Dates of *Richard the Redeless* and *Mum and the Sothsegger*." *Notes and Queries* 37, no. 3 (1990): 270–5.
– *Signes and Sothe: Language in the Piers Plowman Tradition*. Piers Plowman Studies 10. Cambridge: D.S. Brewer, 1994.
– *Socioliterary Practice in Late Medieval England*. Oxford: Oxford University Press, 2001.
– "The Treatment of Natural Law in *Richard the Redeless* and *Mum and the Sothsegger*." *Leeds Studies in English* 23 (1992): 49–80.
Barron, W.R.J. "The Idiom and the Audience of Laȝamon's *Brut*." In *Laȝamon: Contexts, Language, and Interpretation*. Ed. Rosamund Allen, Lucy Perry, and Jane Roberts, 157–84. London: King's College London Centre for Late Antique and Medieval Studies, 2002.
Barrow, G.W.S. "Wales and Scotland in the Middle Ages." *Welsh History Review* 10, no. 81 (1981): 302–19.
Barrow, Julia. "Athelstan to Aigueblanche: 1056–1268." In *Hereford Cathedral: A History*. Ed. Gerald Aylmer and John Tiller, 21–47. London: Hambledon Press, 2000.
– "The Chronology of Forgery Production at Worcester from C. 1000 to the Early Twelfth Century." In *St. Wulfstan and His World*. Ed. Julia Barrow and N.P. Brooks, 105–22. Aldershot, UK: Ashgate, 2005.
– "The Community of Worcester, 961–c.1100." In *St. Oswald of Worcester*. Ed. Nicholas Brooks and Catherine Cubitt, 84–99. London: Leicester University Press, 1996.
– "William of Malmesbury's Use of Charters." In *Narrative and History in the Early Medieval West*. Ed. Elizabeth M. Tyler and Ross Balzaretti, 67–89. Turnhout: Brepols, 2006.
– "The Ideology of the Tenth-century English Benedictine 'Reform'." In *Texts, Histories, Historiographies: the Medieval Worlds of Timothy Reuter*. Ed. P. Skinner, 141–54. Turnhout: Brepols, 2010.
Barthes, Roland. "The Death of the Author." In *Image – Music – Text*. Trans. Stephen Heath. New York: Hill and Wang, 1977.
Bautier, Robert-Henri, ed. *Folia Caesaraugustana Vol. 1: Diplomatica et Sigillographica. Travaux Preliminaires de la Commission Internationale de Diplomatique et de la Commission Internationale de Sigillographie pour une Normalisation Internationale des Éditions de Documents et un Vocabulaire*

International de la Diplomatique et de la Sigillographie. Zaragoza, Spain: Institución "Fernando el Católico," 1984.

Baxter, Stephen. "Archbishop Wulfstan and the Administration of God's Property." In *Wulfstan, Archbishop of York: The Proceedings of the Second Alcuin Conference*. Ed. Matthew Townend, 161–205. Turnhout, Belgium: Brepols, 2004.

Bedingfield, M. Bradford. *The Dramatic Liturgy of ASE*. Anglo-Saxon Studies 1. Woodbridge, UK: Boydell & Brewer, 2002.

Bennett, J.A.W. "The Date of the B-Text of Piers Plowman." *MAe* 12 (1943): 55–64.

Benson, C. David. *Public Piers Plowman: Modern Scholarship and Late Medieval English Culture*. University Park: Pennsylvania State University Press, 2004.

Benson, C. David, and Lynne S. Blanchfield. *The Manuscripts of Piers Plowman: The B-Version*. Cambridge: D.S. Brewer, 1997.

Bethurum Loomis, Dorothy. "Regnum and Sacerdotium in the Early Eleventh Century." In *England before the Conquest: Studies in Primary Sources Presented to Dorothy Whitelock*. Ed. Peter Clemoes and Kathleen Hughes, 129–45. Cambridge: Cambridge University Press, 1971.

– "Stylistic Features of the Old English Laws." *MLR* 27 (1932): 263–79.

Biggs, Frederick M. *The Sources of Christ III: A Revision of Cook's Notes*. Old English Newsletter Subsidia 12. Binghamton, NY: CEMERS SUNY Binghamton, 1986.

Birkholz, Daniel. "Harley Lyrics and Hereford Clerics: The Implications of Mobility, c.1300–1351." *Studies in the Age of Chaucer* 31 (2009): 175–230.

Birnes, William J. "Christ as Advocate: The Legal Metaphor in Piers Plowman." *Annuale Mediaevale* 16 (1975): 71–93.

Bisson, Thomas N. *The Crisis of the Twelfth Century: Power, Lordship, and the Origins of European Government*. Princeton, NJ: Princeton University Press, 2009.

Bjork, Robert E. "Oppressed Hebrews and the Song of Azarias in the Old English *Daniel*." *Studies in Philology* 77, no. 3 (1980): 213–26.

Blair, John. "A Saint for Every Minster? Local Cults in Anglo-Saxon England." In *Local Saints and Local Churches in the Early Medieval West*. Ed. Alan Thacker and Richard Sharpe, 455–94. Oxford: Oxford University Press, 2002.

Blair, Peter H. *The World of Bede*. London: Secker and Warburg, 1970.

Blake, Norman. "Rhythmical Alliteration." *Modern Philology* 67, no. 2 (1969): 118–24.

Blamires, Alcuin. *The Case for Women in Medieval Culture*. Oxford: Oxford University Press, 1997.

– "*Mum and the Sothsegger* and the Langlandian Idiom." *Neuphilologische Mitteilungen* 76 (1975): 583–604.

Blanton, Virginia. "Counting Noses and Assessing the Numbers: Native Saints in the *South English Legendaries*." In *Rethinking the South English Legendaries*. Ed. Heather Blurton and Jocelyn Wogan-Browne, 251–70. Manchester: Manchester University Press, 2011.

Bliss, A.J. "The Spelling of *Sir Launfal*." *Anglia* 75 (1957): 276–87.

Bloomfield, Morton. *Piers Plowman as a Fourteenth-Century Apocalypse*. New Brunswick, NJ: Rutgers University Press,

Boffey, Julia. "Forms of Standardization in Terms for Middle English Lyrics in the Fourteenth Century." In *The Beginnings of Standardization: Language and Culture in Fourteenth-Century England*. Ed. Ursula Schaefer, 61–70. Frankfurt am Main: Peter Lang 2006.

Boone, Elizabeth Hill. "Introduction: Writing and Recording Knowledge." In *Writing Without Words: Alternative Literacies in Mesoamerica and the Andes*. Ed. Elizabeth Hill Boone and Walter Mignolo, 3–26. Durham, NC: Duke University Press, 1994.

Boureau, Alain. "How Law Came to the Monks: The Use of Law in English Society at the Beginning of the Thirteenth Century." *Past and Present* 167 (2000): 29–74.

Bowers, John. "*Piers Plowman*'s William Langland: Editing the Text, Writing the Author's Life." *YLS* 9 (1995): 87–124.

Boyle, Leonard E. "Diplomatics." In *Medieval Studies: An Introduction*. Ed. James M. Powell, 82–113. Syracuse, NY: Syracuse University Press, 1992.

Bradley, Henry. "The Misplaced Leaf of 'Piers the Plowman'." *Athenaeum* 21 April (1906): 481.

Brand, Paul. "Henry II and the Creation of the English Common Law." In *Henry II: New Interpretations*. Ed. Christopher Harper–Bill and Nicholas Vincent, 215–41. Woodbridge, UK: Boydell & Brewer, 2007.

– *Kings, Barons and Justices: The Making and Enforcement of Legislation in Thirteenth–Century England*. Cambridge: Cambridge University Press, 2003.

– "The Languages of the Law in Later Medieval England." In *Multilingualism in Later Medieval Britain*. Ed. D.A. Trotter, 63–76. Cambridge: D.S. Brewer, 2000.

Brasington, Bruce C. "Canon Law in the *Leges Henrici Primi*." *Zeitschrift der Savigny–Stiftung für Rechtsgeschichte. Kanonistische Abteilung* 123 (2006): 288–305.

Bredehoft, Thomas A. *Authors, Audiences, and Old English Verse*. Toronto: University of Toronto Press, 2009.

– *Early English Metre*. Toronto: University of Toronto Press, 2005.

Brehe, S.K. "Reassembling *the First Worcester Fragment*." *Speculum* 65 (1990): 521–36.

– "'Rhythmical Alliteration': Ælfric's Prose and the Origins of Layamon's Meter." In *The Text and Tradition of Layamon's Brut*. Ed. Françoise Le Saux, 65–89. Woodbridge, UK: Boydell & Brewer, 1994.

Bremmer, Rolf, Jr. "Dealing Dooms: Alliteration in the Old Frisian Laws." In *Alliteration in Culture*. Ed. Jonathan Roper, 74–92. New York: Palgrave MacMillan, 2011.

Bresslau, Harry. *Handbuch der Urkundenlehre für Deutschland und Italien*. 2nd ed. Leipzig: Veit, 1915.

Brooke, C.N.L. "The Teaching of Diplomatic." *Journal of the Society of Archivists* 4 (1970): 1–9.

Brundage, James A. *Medieval Canon Law*. London: Longman, 1995.

– "The Monk as Lawyer." In *The Profession and Practice of Medieval Canon Law*, 423–36. Aldershot, UK: Ashgate, 2004.

– "The Rise of Professional Canonists and Development of the *Ius Commune*." In *The Profession and Practice of Medieval Canon Law*, 26–63. Aldershot, UK: Ashgate, 2004.

Brunner, Ingrid A. "On Some of the Vernacular Translations of Cato's *Distichs*." In *Helen Adolf Festschrift*. Ed. Sheema Z. Buehne, James L. Hodge, and Lucille B. Pinto, 99–125. New York: Ungar, 1968.

Bryan, Elizabeth J. –*Collaborative Meaning in Medieval Scribal Culture: The Otho Laȝamon*. Ann Arbor: University of Michigan Press, 1999.

– "Truth and the Round Table in Lawman's Brut." *Quondam et Futurus* 2, no. 4 (1992): 27–35.

Bryer, Ronald. *Not the Least: The Story of Little Malvern*. Hanley, Worcester: Self-Publishing Association, 1993.

Burrow, J.A. "Audience of Piers Plowman." *Anglia* 73 (1957): 373–84.

– "Words, Works and Will: Theme and Structure in Piers Plowman." In *Piers Plowman: Critical Approaches*. Ed. S.S. Hussey. London: Methuen, 1969.

Cable, Thomas. "Early English Metre [Book Review]." *JEGP* 107, no. 3 (2008): 394–7.

– *The English Alliterative Tradition*. Philadelphia: University of Pennsylvania Press, 1991.

Campbell, James. "The Late Anglo-Saxon State: A Maximum View." In *The Anglo-Saxon State*, 1–20. Cambridge: Cambridge University Press, 2000.

– "The Sale of Land and the Economics of Power in Early England: Problems and Possibilities." In *The Anglo-Saxon State*, 227–47. Cambridge: Cambridge University Press, 2000.

– "Some Twelfth-Century Views of the Anglo-Saxon Past." In *Essays in Anglo-Saxon History*. Ed. James Campbell, 209–28. London: Hambledon, 1986.

Cannon, Christopher. "Langland's *Ars Grammatica*." *YLS* 22 (2008): 1–25.

– *The Grounds of English Literature*. Oxford: Oxford University Press, 2004.

– "The Style and Authorship of the Otho Revision of Layamon's *Brut*." *MAe* 62, no. 2 (1993): 187–209.

Carruthers, Mary. *The Search for St. Truth: A Study of Meaning in Piers Plowman*. Chicago: Northwestern University Press, 1973.

Catto, Jeremy. "Andrew Horn: Law and History in Fourteenth-Century England." In *Writing of History in the Middle Ages: Essays Presented to Richard William Southern*. Ed. R.H.C. Davis and J.M. Wallace–Hadrill, 367–91. Oxford: Clarendon, 1981.

– "The King's Servants." In *Henry V: The Practice of Kingship*. Ed. G.L. Harriss, 75–95. Oxford: Oxford University Press, 1985.

Cavill, Paul. *Maxims in Old English Poetry*. Cambridge: D.S. Brewer, 1999.

Chamberlin, J. Edward. "A New History of Reading: Hunting, Tracking, and Reading." In *For the Geography of a Soul: Emerging Perspectives on Kamau Brathwaite*. Ed. Timothy J. Reiss, 145–64. Trenton, NJ: Africa World Press, 2001.

Chambers, R.W. *On the Continuity of English Prose from Alfred to More and His School*. EETS os. 186. London: Oxford University Press, 1966.

– "The Original Form of the A Text of Piers Plowman." *MLR* 6 (1911): 302–23.

– "Robert or William Longland?" *London Medieval Studies* 1 (1948 for 1939): 430–62.

Chaplais, Pierre. "The Anglo-Saxon Chancery: From Diploma to Writ." In *Prisca Munimenta: Studies in Archival and Administrative History Presented to A.E.J. Hollaender*. Ed. F. Ranger, 43–62. London: University of London Press, 1973.

– "The Origin and Authenticity of the Royal Anglo-Saxon Diploma." In *Prisca Munimenta: Studies in Archival and Administrative History Presented to A.E.J. Hollaender*. Ed. F. Ranger, 28–42. London: University of London Press, 1973.

– "Who Introduced Charter into England? The Case for Augustine." In *Prisca Munimenta: Studies in Archival and Administrative History Presented to A.E.J. Hollaender*. Ed. F. Ranger, 88–107. London: University of London Press, 1973.

Chapman, Don William. "Germanic Tradition and Latin Learning in Wulfstan's Echoic Compounds." *JEGP* 101, no. 1 (2002): 1–18.

– "Motivations for Producing and Analyzing Compounds in Wulfstan's Sermons." In *Advances in English Historical Linguistics*. Ed. Jacek Fisiak and Marcin Krygier, 15–21. Berlin: Mouton de Gruyter, 1998.

– "Stylistic Use of Nominal Compounds in Wulfstan's Sermons." PhD diss., University of Toronto, 1996.

– "*Uterque Lingua / Ægðer Gereord*: Ælfric's Grammatical Vocabulary and the Winchester Tradition." *JEGP* 109, no. 4 (2010). 421–55.

Cheney, Mary. "The Litigation Between John Marshal and Archbishop Thomas Becket in 1164: A Pointer to the Origin of Novel Disseisin." In *Law and Social Change in British History*. Ed. J.A. Guy and H.G. Beale, 9–26. London: Royal Historical Society, 1984.

Chinca, Mark, and Christopher Young. "Introduction." In *Orality and Literacy in the Middle Ages: Essays on a Conjunction and Its Consequences in Honour of D.H. Green*. Turnhout, Belgium: Brepols, 2005.

Chism, Christine. *Alliterative Revivals*. Philadelphia: University of Pennsylvania Press, 2002.

Clanchy, M.T. *From Memory to Written Record: England 1066–1307*. 3rd ed. Cambridge: Blackwell, 2013.

– "Remembering the Past." *History* 55 (1970): 165–76.

Cole, Andrew. "Trifunctionality and the Tree of Charity: Literary and Social Practice in Piers Plowman." *English Literary History* 62 (1995): 1–27.

Coleman, Joyce. *Public Reading and the Reading Public in Late Medieval England and France*. Cambridge: Cambridge University Press, 1996.

Collier, Wendy E.J. "'Englishness' and the Worcester Tremulous Hand." *Leeds Studies in English* 26 (1995): 35–47.

– "The Tremulous Worcester Hand and Gregory's *Pastoral Care*." In *Rewriting Old English in the Twelfth Century*. Ed. Mary Swan and Elaine M. Treharne, 195–208. Cambridge: Cambridge University Press, 2000.

Constable, Giles. "The Orders of Society." In *Three Studies in Medieval Religious and Social Thought: The Interpretation of Mary and Martha, the Ideal of the Imitation of Christ, the Orders of Society*, 249–342. Cambridge: Cambridge University Press, 1998.

Conti, Aidan. "The Circulation of the Old English Homily in the Twelfth Century: New Evidence from Oxford, Bodleian Library, MS Bodley 343." In *Precedence, Practice and Appropriation: The Old English Homily*. Ed. Aaron Kleist, 365–402. Turnhout, Belgium: Brepols, 2007.

– "Preaching Scripture and Apocrypha: A Previously Unidentified Homiliary in an Old English Manuscript, Oxford, Bodleian Library, Ms Bodley 343." PhD diss., University of Toronto, 2004.

Cook, Albert S. "Cynewulf's Principal Source for the Third Part of 'Christ'." *Modern Language Notes* 4, no. 6 (1889): 171–6.

– "A Putative Charter to Aldhelm." In *Studies in English Philology: A Miscellany in Honor of Frederick Klaeber*. Ed. Kemp Malone and Martin Ruud, 254–7. Minneapolis: University of Minnesota Press, 1929.

Cornelius, Ian. "The Rhetoric of Advancement: Ars Dictaminis, Cursus, and Clerical Careerism in Late Medieval England. "*New Medieval Literatures* 12 (2010): 287–328.

Cox, R.S. "The Old English Dicts of Cato." *Anglia* 90 (1972): 1–42.

Cowan, Alice, "*Byrstas and bysmeres*: The Wounds of Sin in the Sermo Lupi ad Anglos." In *Wulfstan, Archbishop of York*. Ed. Matthew Townend, 397–411. Turnhout, Belgium: Brepols, 2004.

Crane, Susan. "The Writing Lesson of 1381." In *Chaucer's England: Literature in Historical Context*. Ed. Barbara Hanawalt, 201–21. Minneapolis: University of Minnesota Press, 1992.

Crépin, André. "Mentalités anglaises au temps d'Henry II Plantagenet d'après les *Proverbs of Alfred*." *Cahiers de Civilisation Médiévale* 37 (1994): 49–60.

Crick, Julia C. *Charters of St Albans*. Oxford: Oxford University Press, 2007.

 "Liberty and Fraternity: Creating and Defending the Liberty of St Albans." In *Expectations of the Law in the Middle Ages*. Ed. Anthony Musson, 91–103. Woodbridge, UK: Boydell, 2001.

– "*Pristina libertas*: Liberty and the Anglo-Saxons Revisited." *Transactions of the Royal Historical Society* 6, no. 14 (2004): 47–71.

– "St. Albans, Westminster, and Some Twelfth-Century Views of the Anglo-Saxon Past." *Anglo-Norman Studies* 25 (2003 for 2002): 65–83.

Cross, James E. "Missing Folios in Cotton MS Nero A.I." *British Library Journal* 16, no. 1 (1990): 99–100.

– "Wulfstan's *De Anticristo* in a Twelfth-Century Worcester Manuscript." *ASE* 20 (1991): 203–20.

Cross, James E, and Andrew Hamer. "Source-Identification and Manuscript Recovery: The British Library Wulfstan MS Cotton Nero A.I, 131v–132r." *Scriptorium* 50, no. 1 (1996): 132–7.

Cummings, Michael. "Paired Opposites in Wulfstan's *Sermo Lupi ad Anglos*." *Revue de l'Universitee d'Ottawa* 50, no. 2 (1980): 233–43.

Curzan, Anne, and Kimberly Emmons, eds. *Studies in the History of the English Language II: Unfolding Conversations*. Berlin: de Gruyter, 2004.

Damon, John. "Advisors for Peace in the Reign of Æthelred Unræd." In *Peace, Negotiation, and Reciprocity: Strategies of Co-existence in the Middle Ages and Renaissance*. Ed. Diane Wolfthal, 57–78. Turnhout, Belgium: Brepols, 2000.

Dance, Richard. "Interpreting Laȝamon: Linguistic Diversity and Some Cruces in Cotton Caligula A. IX, with Particular Regard to Norse-Derived Words." In *Laȝamon: Contexts, Language, and Interpretation*. Ed. Rosamund Allen, Lucy Perry, and Jane Roberts, 187–202. London: King's College London Centre for Late Antique and Medieval Studies, 2002.

– "Sound, Fury, and Signifiers; or Wulfstan's Language." In *Wulfstan, Archbishop of York: The Proceedings of the Second Alcuin Conference*. Ed. Matthew Townend, 29–61. Studies in the Early Middle Ages 10. Turnhout, Belgium: Brepols, 2004.

Danet, Brenda, and Bryna Bogoch. "Orality, Literacy, and Performativity in Anglo-Saxon Wills." In *Language and the Law*. Ed. John Gibbons, 100–35. London: Longman, 1994.

Das, S.K. *Cynewulf and the Cynewulf Canon*. Calcutta: University of Calcutta, 1942.

Dempsey, G.T. "Aldhelm of Malmesbury and High Ecclesiasticism in a Barbarian Kingdom." *Traditio* 63 (2008): 47–88.

Deskis, Susan. *"Beowulf" and the Medieval Proverb Tradition*. Tempe, AZ: Medieval & Renaissance Texts & Studies, 1996.

– "Echoes of Old English Alliterative Collocations in Middle English Alliterative Proverbs." In *Source of Wisdom: Old English and Early Medieval Latin Studies in Honour of Thomas D. Hill*. Ed. Charles D. Wright, Thomas N. Hall, and Frederick Biggs, 311–25. Toronto: University of Toronto Press, 2007.

Doane, A.N. "The Ethnography of Scribal Writing and Anglo-Saxon Poetry: Scribe as Performer." *Oral Tradition* 9 (1994): 420–39.

Donaldson, E.T. *Piers Plowman: The C-Text and Its Poet*. New Haven, CT: Yale University Press, 1949.

Donoghue, Daniel. "Laȝamon's Ambivalence." *Speculum* 65, no. 3 (1990): 537–63.

Doyle, A.I. "Remarks on Surviving Manuscripts of Piers Plowman." In *Medieval English Religious and Ethical Literature: Essays in Honour of G.H. Russell*. Ed. G. Hugh Russell, G.C. Kratzmann, and James Simpson. Cambridge: D.S. Brewer, 1986.

Duby, Georges. *The Chivalrous Society*. Trans. Cynthia Postan. Berkeley: University of California Press, 1981.

– *The Three Orders: Feudal Society Imagined*. Chicago: University of Chicago Press, 1980.

Dumville, D.N. *Liturgy and the Ecclesiastical History of Late ASE: Four Studies*. Studies in Anglo-Saxon History 5. Woodbridge, UK: Boydell & Brewer, 1992.

Duncan, Edwin. "The Middle English Bestiary: Missing Link in the Evolution of the Alliterative Long Line?" *Studia Neophilologica* 64 (1992): 25–33.

Dunning, T.P. "The Structure of the B-Text of *Piers Plowman*." *Review of English Studies* (1956): 225–37.

Dyer, Christopher. "Bishop Wulfstan and His Estates." *St Wulfstan and His World*. Ed. Julia S. Barrow and N.P. Brooks, 137–50. Aldershot, UK: Ashgate, 2005.

Earl, James W. "The Forbidden Beowulf: Haunted by Incest." *PMLA* 125 (2010): 289–305.

Edwards, Heather. *The Charters of the Early West Saxon Kingdom*. B.A.R. British Series 198. Oxford: B.A.R, 1988.

Embree, Dan. "*Richard the Redeless* and *Mum and the Sothsegger* – a Case of Mistaken Identity." *Notes and Queries* 22, no. 1 (1975): 4–12.

– "'The King's Ignorance': A Topos for Evil Times." *MAe* 56 (1985): 121–7.

England, Charlotte Patricia. "Layamon's *Brut*: Reading Between the Two Manuscripts." PhD diss., University of Toronto, 2006.

Faith, Rosamund. "The 'Great Rumour' of 1377 and Peasant Ideology." In *The English Rising of 1381*. Ed. T.H. Aston and R.H. Hilton, 43–73. Cambridge: Cambridge University Press, 1984.

Faletra, Michael A. "The Conquest of the Past in The History of the Kings of Britain." *Literature Compass* 4, no. 1 (2007): 121–33.

Farmer, Sharon. "Persuasive Voices: Clerical Images of Medieval Wives." *Speculum* 61, no. 3 (1986). 517–43.

Fell, Christine. "*Unfrið*: An Approach to a Definition." *Saga-Book* 21 (1982): 85–100.

Ferster, Judith. *Fictions of Advice: The Literature and Politics of Counsel in Late Medieval England*. Philadelphia: University of Pennsylvania Press, 1996.

Fields, P.J.C. "*Laȝamon's Brut*: Review Article." *Review of English Studies* 168 (1991): 560–1.

Finberg, H.P.R. *Early Charters of the West Midlands*. Leicester: Leicester University Press, 1961.

Finnegan, Ruth H. *Literacy and Orality: Studies in the Technology of Communication*. Oxford: Blackwell, 1988.

Fischer, Andreas. "Lexical Change in Late Old English: from *æ* to *lagu*." *The History and the Dialects of English: Festschrift for Eduard Kolb*. Ed. Andreas Fischer, 103–14. Heidelberg: Carl Winter, 1989.

Fletcher, Alan J. "The Essential (Ephemeral) William Langland: Textual Revision as Ethical Process in *Piers Plowman*." *YLS* 15 (2001): 61–98.

– *Preaching, Politics and Poetry in Late-Medieval England*. Dublin: Four Courts, 1998.

Foley, John Miles. "How Genres Leak in Traditional Verse." In *Unlocking the Word-Hord: Anglo-Saxon Studies in Memory of Edward B. Irving*. Ed. Mark Amodio and Katherine O'Brien O'Keeffe, 76–108. Toronto: University of Toronto Press, 2003.

– "Orality, Textuality, and Interpretation." In *Vox Intertexta: Orality and Textuality in the Middle Ages*, 35–45. Madison: University of Wisconsin Press, 1991.

Foot, Sarah. *Æthelstan: The First King of England*. New Haven, CT: Yale University Press, 2012.

– "The Historiography of the Anglo-Saxon 'Nation-State'." *Power and Nation in European History*. Ed. Len Scales and Oliver Zimmer, 125–42. Cambridge: Cambridge University Press, 2005.

– "Reading Anglo-Saxon Charters: Memory, Record, or Story?" *Narrative and History in the Early Medieval West*. Ed. Elizabeth M. Tyler and Ross Balzaretti, 39–65. Turnhout, Belgium: Brepols, 2006.

Forde, Simon, et al. *Concepts of National Identity in the Middle Ages*. Leeds: University of Leeds, 1995.

Foucault, Michel. "What Is an Author?" In *The Foucault Reader*. Ed. Paul Rabinow, 101–20. New York: Pantheon Books, 1984.

Fowler, David C. *The Life and Times of John Trevisa, Medieval Scholar*. Seattle: University of Washington Press, 1995.

Fowler, E. "A Crisis of Truth: Literature and Law in Ricardian England [Book Review]." *Speculum* 78, no. 1 (2003): 179–82.

Frank, Grace. "Proverbs in Medieval Literature." *Modern Language Notes* 58, no. 7 (1943): 508–15.

Frankis, John. "The Social Context of Vernacular Writing in Thirteenth Century England: The Evidence of the Manuscripts." *Thirteenth-Century England* 1 (1986): 175–84.

– "Towards a Regional Context for Lawman's *Brut*: Literary Activity in the Dioceses of Worcester and Hereford in the Twelfth Century." In *Laȝamon: Contexts, Language, and Interpretation*. Ed. Rosamund Allen, Lucy Perry, and Jane Roberts, 53–78. London: King's College London Centre for Late Antique and Medieval Studies, 2002.

Franzen, Christine. *The Tremulous Hand of Worcester: A Study of Old English in the Thirteenth Century*. Oxford: Clarendon, 1991.

Frederick, Jill. "*The South English Legendary*: Anglo-Saxon Saints and National Identity." In *Literary Appropriations of the Anglo–Saxons from the Thirteenth to the Twentieth Century*. Ed. Carole Weinberg and Donald Scragg, 57–73. Cambridge: Cambridge University Press, 2000.

Galloway, Andrew "Laȝamon's Gift." *PMLA* 121 (2006): 717–34.

– "Making History Legal: *Piers Plowman* and the Rebels of Fourteenth-Century England." In *William Langland's Piers Plowman*. Ed. Kathleen M. Hewett-Smith, 7–39. New York: Routledge, 2001.

– "Piers Plowman and the Schools." *YLS* 6 (1992): 89–107.

– "Private Selves and the Intellectual Marketplace in Late Fourteenth-Century England: The Case of the Two Usks." *New Literary History* 28, no. 2 (1997): 291–318.

Gameson, Richard. "St Wulfstan, the Library of Worcester and the Spirituality of the Medieval Book." In *St. Wulfstan and His World*. Ed. Julia Barrow and Nicholas Brooks, 59–91. Aldershot, UK: Ashgate, 2005.

Gauvard, Claude. "Justification and Theory of the Death Penalty at the Parlement of Paris in the Late Middle Ages." In *War, Government and Power in Late Medieval France*. Ed. C.T. Allmand, 190–208. Liverpool: Liverpool University Press, 2000.

Gayk, Shannon. "As Ploȝmen have Preued': The Alliterative Work of a Set of Lollard Sermons." *YLS* 20 (2006), 43–65.

Geary, Patrick J. "Land, Language, Memory." *Transactions of the Royal Historical Society (Sixth Series)* 9 (1999): 169–84.

– *Phantoms of Remembrance: Memory and Oblivion at the End of the First Millennium*. Princeton: Princeton University Press, 1994.

Gellrich, Jesse M. *Discourse and Dominion in the Fourteenth Century: Oral Contexts of Writing in Philosophy, Politics, and Poetry*. Princeton, NJ: Princeton University Press, 1995.

– *The Idea of the Book in the Middle Ages: Language Theory, Mythology, and Fiction*. Ithaca, NY: Cornell University Press, 1985.

Giancarlo, Matthew. *Parliament and Literature in Late Medieval England*. Cambridge Studies in Medieval Literature. Cambridge: Cambridge University Press, 2007.

Giandrea, Mary F. *Episcopal Culture in Late ASE*. Woodbridge, UK: Boydell, 2007.

– "Recent Approaches to Late Anglo-Saxon Episcopal Culture: Review Article." *Early Medieval Europe* 16, no. 1 (2008): 89–106.

Gilbert, B.B. "'Civil' and the Notaries in *Piers Plowman*." *MAe* 50, no. 1 (1981): 49–63.

Gillingham, John. *The English in the Twelfth Century*. Woodbridge, UK: Boydell & Brewer, 2000.

Giry, Arthur. *Manuel de Diplomatique*. Hildesheim: G. Olms, 1972.

Godden, Malcolm. "Ælfric's Changing Vocabulary." *English Studies* 61 (1980): 206–23.

– "Apocalypse and Invasion in Late Anglo-Saxon England." In *From Anglo-Saxon to Early Middle English: Studies Presented to E.G. Stanley*. Ed. Malcolm Godden, D. Gray and T. Hoad. Oxford: Clarendon, 1994.

– "Did King Alfred Write Anything?" *MAe* 76, no. 1 (2007): 1–23.

– *The Making of Piers Plowman*. London: Longman, 1990.

– "Plowmen and Hermits in Langland's Piers Plowman." *Review of English Studies* 35 (1984): 129–63.

– "The Relations of Wulfstan and Ælfric: A Reassessment." In *Wulfstan, Archbishop of York: The Proceedings of the Second Alcuin Conference*. Ed. Matthew Townend, 353–74. Studies in the Early Middle Ages 10. Turnhout, Belgium: Brepols, 2004.

Goody, Jack. *The Domestication of the Savage Mind*. Cambridge: Cambridge University Press, 1977.

Görlach, Manfred. *The Textual Tradition of the South English Legendary*. Leeds: University of Leeds, 1974.

Grady, Frank. "Contextualizing Alexander and Dindimus." *YLS* 18 (2004): 81–106.

– "The Generation of 1399." In *The Letter of the Law: Legal Practice and Literary Production in Medieval England*. Ed. Emily Steiner and Candace Barrington, 202–30. Ithaca, NY: Cornell University Press, 2002.

Gransden, Antonia. *Historical Writing In England, C.550 To C.1307*. London: Routledge and Kegan Paul, 1974.

– *Legends, Tradition and History in Medieval England*. London: Hambledon Press, 1992.

– "Prologues in the Historiography of Twelfth-Century England." In *England in the Twelfth Century*. Ed. D Williams, 55–81. Woodbridge, UK: Proceedings of the 1984 Harlaxton Symposium, 1990.

Green, Dennis Howard. *The Beginnings of Medieval Romance: Fact and Fiction, 1150–1220*. Cambridge: Cambridge University Press, 2002.

– "Fictive Orality: A Restriction on the Use of the Concept." In *Blütezeit: Festschrift für L. Peter Johnson zum 70*. Ed. Joachim Heinzle, Christopher Young, and Mark Chinca, 161–74. Tübingen: Niemeyer, 2000.

– *Language and History in the Early Germanic World*. Cambridge: Cambridge University Press, 1998.

– *Medieval Listening and Reading: The Primary Reception of German Literature 800–1300*. Cambridge: Cambridge University Press, 1994.

Green, Richard Firth. *A Crisis of Truth: Literature and Law in Ricardian England*. Philadelphia: University of Pennsylvania Press, 1999.

Greenaway, Diana E. "List 9: Archdeacons: York." In *Fasti Ecclesiae Anglicanae 1066–1300, vol 6: York* (1999). 31–6. http://www.british-history.ac.uk/report.as px?compid=6444&strquery=archdeacons york.

– "Worcester: Bishops." In *Fasti ecclesiae Anglicanae 1066–1300, vol. 2: Monastic Cathedrals* (1971). 99–102. http://www.british-history.ac.uk/report.aspx ?compid=33851.

Griffiths, Lavinia. *Personification in Piers Plowman*. Cambridge: D.S. Brewer, 1985.

Hadley, D.M. *The Northern Danelaw: Its Social Structure, c. 800–1100*. London: Leicester University Press, 2000.

Hagger M. "The *Gesta abbatum monasterii Sancti Albani*: Litigation and History at St. Albans." *Historical Research* 81, no. 213 (2008): 373–98.

Hahn, Thomas. "Early Middle English." In *The Cambridge History of Medieval English Literature*. Ed. David Wallace. Cambridge: Cambridge University Press, 1999. 61–91.

Hailey, R. Carter. "Robert Crowley and the Editing of Piers Plowman." *YLS* 21 (2007): 143–70.

Haines, Roy Martin. *The Administration of the Diocese of Worcester in the First Half of the Fourteenth Century*. London: S.P.C.K, 1965.

Hall, Hubert. *A Formula Book of English Official Historical Documents*. 2 vols. New York: B. Franklin, 1969.

Hall, Thomas N. "The Early Medieval Sermon." In *The Sermon*. Ed. Beverly Mayne Kienzle, 203–69. Turnhout, Belgium: Brepols, 2000.

Hanna, Ralph. "Alliterative Poetry." In *The Cambridge History of Medieval English Literature*. Ed. David Wallace, 488–512. Cambridge: Cambridge University Press, 1999.

– "Langland's Ymaginatif: Images and the Limits of Poetry." In *Images, Idolatry, and Iconoclasm*. Ed. Jeremy Dimmick, James Simpson, and Nicolette Zeeman, 81–94. Oxford: Oxford University Press, 2002.

– *London Literature, 1300–1380*. New York: Cambridge University Press, 2005.

– "Producing Manuscripts and Editions." In *Crux and Controversy in Middle English Textual Criticism*. Ed. Alistair Minnis and Charlotte Brewer. Cambridge: D.S. Brewer, 1992.

– *Pursuing History: Middle English Manuscripts and Their Texts*. Stanford, CA: Stanford University Press, 1996.

– "The Scribe of Huntingdon HM 114." *Studies in Bibliography* 42 (1989): 120–33.

– "Will's Work." In *Written Work: Langland, Labor, and Authorship*. Ed. Steven Justice and Kathryn Kerby-Fulton, 23–66. Philadelphia: University of Pennsylvania Press, 1997.

Hansen, Elaine Tuttle. *The Solomon Complex: Reading Wisdom in Old English Poetry*. Toronto: University of Toronto Press, 1988.

Hardman, Phillipa. "Windows into the Text: Unfilled Spaces in some Fifteenth-Century English Manuscripts." In *Texts and Their Contexts: Papers from the Early Book Society*. Ed. John Scattergood and Julia Boffey, 44–70. Dublin: Four Courts, 1996.

Harmer, Florence Elizabeth. *Anglo-Saxon Writs*. 2nd ed. Stamford, CT: Paul Watkins, 1989.

Harris, Stephen J. "An Overview of Race and Ethnicity in Pre-Norman England." *Literature Compass* 5 / 4 (2008): 740–54.

Hart, C.R. *The Danelaw*. London: Hambledon, 1992.

– *The Early Charters of Northern England and the North Midlands*. Leicester: Leicester University Press, 1975.

Havens, Jill C. "'As Englishe Is Comoun Langage to Oure Puple': The Lollards and Their Imagined 'English' Community." In *Imagining a Medieval English Nation*. Ed. Kathy Lavezzo, 96–128. Minneapolis: University of Minnesota Press, 2004.

Healey, Antonette diPaolo, et al., eds. "Dictionary of Old English: A to G online." Toronto: DOE Project, 2007. http://www.doe.utoronto.ca/.

Heningham, Eleanor K. "Old English Precursors of the Worcester Fragments." *PMLA* 55, no. 2 (1940): 291–307.

Herold, Jonathan R. "Memoranda and Memoria: Assessing the Preservation of Acta at Eleventh–Century Worcester Cathedral." PhD diss., University of Toronto, 2008.

Heslop, T.A. "Art and the Man: Archbishop Wulfstan and the York Gospelbook." In *Wulfstan, Archbishop of York: The Proceedings of the Second Alcuin Conference*. Ed. Matthew Townend, 279–308. Turnhout, Belgium: Brepols, 2004.

Hiatt, Alfred. *The Making of Medieval Forgeries: False Documents in Fifteenth–Century England*. Toronto: University of Toronto Press, 2004.

Hickes, G. *Antiquae literaturae septentrionalis liber alter*. Oxford: 1705.

Hill, Joyce. "Ælfric, Authorial Identity and the Changing Text." In *The Editing of Old English*. Ed. Donald Scragg and Paul Szarmach, 177–89. Woodbridge, UK: D.S. Brewer, 1994.

– "Ælfric's Grammatical Tradition." *Form and Content of Instruction in ASE in the Light of Contemporary Manuscript Evidence*. Ed. Patrizia Lendinara, Loredana Lazzari, and M.A. D'Aronoco, 285–307. Turnhout, Belgium: Brepols, 2007.

– "Archbishop Wulfstan: Reformer?" In *Wulfstan, Archbishop of York: The Proceedings of the Second Alcuin Conference*. Ed. Matthew Townend, 309–24. Turnhout: Brepols, 2004.

– "Authorial Adaptation: Ælfric, Wulfstan and the Pastoral Letters." *Text and Language in Medieval English Prose: A Festschrift for Tadao Kubouchi*. Ed. Akio Oizumi et al., 63–75. Frankfurt am Main: Peter Lang, 2005.

Hill, Thomas. "Wise Words: Old English Sapiential Poetry." In *Readings in Medieval Texts: Interpreting Old and Middle English Literature*. Ed. David F. Johnson and Elaine Treharne, 166–82. Oxford: Oxford University Press, 2005.

Hilmo, Maidie. *Medieval Images, Icons, and Illustrated English Literary Texts*. London: Ashgate, 2004.

Hohler, C.E. "Some Service-Books of the Later Saxon Church." *Tenth-Century Studies: Essays in Commemoration of the Millennium of the Council of Winchester and Regularis Concordia*. Ed. David Parsons, 60–83. London: Phillimore, 1975.

Hollis, Stephanie. "The Thematic Structure of the *Sermo Lupi*." *ASE* 6 (1977): 175–95. Repr. in *Old English Literature: Critical Essays*. Ed. R.M. Liuzza, 182–203. New Haven, CT: Yale University Press, 2002.

Hollister, C. Warren. "Anglo-Norman Political Culture and the Twelfth-Century Renaissance." *Anglo-Norman Political Culture and the Twelfth-Century Renaissance*. Ed. C. Warren Hollister, 1–17. Woodbridge: Boydell & Brewer, 1997.

Hollister, C. Warren, and John W. Baldwin. "The Rise of Administrative Kingship: Henry I and Philip Augustus." *American Historical Review* 83 (1978): 867–905.

Holt, J.C. "The Origins of the Constitutional Tradition in England." In *Magna Carta and Medieval Government*. Ed. J.C. Holt, 1–22. London: Hambledon, 1985.

Horobin, Simon. "Adam Pinkhurst and the Copying of British Library, MS Additional 35287 of the B Version of *Piers Plowman*." YLS 23 (2009): 61–83.

– "The Dialect and Authorship of *Richard the Redeless* and *Mum and the Sothsegger*." YLS 18 (2004): 133–52.

– "The Scribe of Bodleian Library, MS Digby 102 and the Circulation of the C Text of *Piers Plowman*." YLS 24 (2010): 89–112.

Horrall, S.M. "An Unknown Middle–English Translation of the 'Distichs' of Cato." *Anglia* 99 (1981): 1–2.

Horstmann, Carl. *Altenglische Legenden. Neue Folge. Mit Einleitung Und Anmerkungen Herausgegeben*. Heilbronn: Gebr. Henninger, 1881.

Howlett, D.R. *Sealed from Within: Self-Authenticating Insular Charters*. Dublin: Four Courts, 1999.

Hudson, Anne "Lollardy: The English Heresy?" *Studies in Church History* 18 (1982): 261–83.

– "A Lollard Sect Vocabulary?" In *So Meny People, Longages and Tonges: Philological Essays in Scots and Mediæval English Presented to Angus Mcintosh*. Ed. Michael Benskin and M.L. Samuels, 15–30. Edinburgh: Published by M. Benskin and M.L. Samuels, 1981.

Hudson, John. "Abbey of Abingdon, Its *Chronicle* and the Norman Conquest." *Anglo-Norman Studies* 19 (1996): 181–202.

– "Administration, Family and Perceptions of the Past in Late Twelfth–Century England: Richard Fitznigel and the Dialogue of the Exchequer." In *The Perception of the Past in Twelfth–Century Europe*. Ed. Paul Magdalino. London: Hambledon, 1992.

Huneycutt, Lois L. "Intercession and the High-Medieval Queen: The Esther Topos." In *Power of the Weak: Studies on Medieval Women*. Ed. Sally-Beth MacLean, Pauline Stafford, and Suzanne Wemple. Champagne: University of Illinois Press, 1995.

– *Matilda of Scotland: A Study in Medieval Queenship*. Woodbridge, UK: Boydell, 2003.

Hussey, S.S. "Langland, Hilton, and the Three Lives." *Review of English Studies* 7 (1956): 132–50.

Ingledew, Francis. "The Book of Troy and the Genealogical Construction of History: The Case of Geoffrey of Monmouth's *Historia regum Britanniae*." *Speculum* 69, no. 3 (1994): 665–704.

Irvine, Susan. "The Compilation and Use of Manuscripts Containing Old English in the Twelfth Century." In *Rewriting Old English in the Twelfth Century*. Ed. Mary Swan and Elaine M. Treharne, 41–61. Cambridge: Cambridge University Press, 2000.

Irving, Edward B., Jr. "Latin Prose Sources for Old English Verse." *JEGP* 56 (1957): 588–95.

Jackson, Elizabeth. "'Not Simply Lists': An Eddic Perspective on Short-Item Lists in Old English Poems." *Speculum* 73 (1998): 338–71.

Janin, Hunt. *Medieval Justice: Cases and Laws in France, England, and Germany, 500–1500*. Jefferson, NC: McFarland, 2004.

Jankofsky, Klaus P. "Entertainment, Edification, and Popular Education in the *South English Legendary*." *Journal of Popular Culture* 11, no. 3 (1977): 706–17.

– "National Characteristics in the Portrayal of English Saints in the South English Legendary." In *Images of Sainthood in Medieval Europe*. Ed. Renate Blumenfeld–Kosinski and Timea Szell, 81–93. Ithaca, NY: Cornell University Press, 1991.

Jayakumar, Sashi. "The 'Foreign Policies' of Edgar 'the Peaceable'." *Haskins Society Journal* 10 (2002): 17–37.

Jost, Karl. *Wulfstanstudien*. Bern: A. Francke, 1950.

Jurasinski, Stefan. "Andrew Horn, Alfredian Apocrypha, and the Anglo-Saxon Names of 'A Mirror of Justices'." *JEGP* 105, no. 4 (2006): 540–63.

– "The Continental Origins of Æthelberht's Code." *Philological Quarterly* 80 (2001): 1–15.

Jurkowski, Maureen. "Lawyers and Lollardy in the Early Fifteenth Century." In *Lollardy and the Gentry in the Later Middle Ages*. Ed. Margaret Aston and Colin Richmond. New York: St Martin's, 1997.

Jurovics, Raachel. "*Sermo Lupi* and the Moral Purpose of Rhetoric." In *The Old English Homily and Its Backgrounds*. Ed. Paul E. Szarmach and Bernard F. Huppe, 203–20. Albany: State University of New York Press, 1978.

Justice, Steven. "Introduction." *Written Work: Langland, Labor, and Authorship*. Ed. Steven Justice and Kathryn Kerby-Fulton, 1–12. Philadelphia: University of Pennsylvania Press, 1997.

– *Writing and Rebellion: England in 1381*. Berkeley: University of California Press, 1994.

Kane, George. *Piers Plowman: The Evidence for Authorship*. London: Athlone, 1965.

– "The 'Z Version' of *Piers Plowman*." *Speculum* 60, no. 4 (1985): 910–30.

Karn, Nicholas. "Rethinking the *Leges Henrici Primi*." In *English Law Before Magna Carta: Felix Liebermann and Die Gesetze der Angelsachsen*. Ed. Stefan Jurasinski, Lisi Oliver, and Andrew Rabin, 199–220. Leiden: Brill, 2010.

Kaske, R.E. "Piers Plowman and Local Iconography." *Journal of the Warburg and Courtauld Institutes* 31 (1968): 159–69.

Keith, W.J. "Laȝamon's *Brut*: The Literary Differences between the Two Texts." *MAe* 29 (1960): 161–72.

Kelly, Susan. "Anglo-Saxon Lay Society and the Written Word." In *The Uses of Literacy in Early Medieval Europe*. Ed. Rosamond McKitterick, 36–65. Cambridge: Cambridge University Press, 1990.

Kemble, John Mitchell. *Codex Diplomaticus Aevi Saxonici*. London, 1848.

Kennedy, A.G. "Cnut's Law Code of 1018." *Anglo Saxon England* 11 (1983): 57–82.

Kennedy, Ruth. "A Bird in Bishopwood: Some Newly-Discovered Lines of Alliterative Verse from the Late Fourteenth Century." In *Medieval Literature and Antiquities*. Ed. M. Stokes and T.L. Burton, 71–87. Cambridge: Cambridge University Press, 1987.

Ker, N.R. *Catalogue of Manuscripts Containing Anglo–Saxon*. Oxford: Clarendon, 1990.

– *English Manuscripts in the Century after the Norman Conquest*. Lyell Lectures, 1952–3. Oxford: Clarendon, 1960.

– "The Handwriting of Archbishop Wulfstan." In *England before the Conquest:Studies in Primary Sources Presented to Dorothy Whitelock*. Ed. Peter Clemoes and Kathleen Hughes, 315–31. Cambridge: Cambridge University Press, 1971.

– "Hemming's Cartulary: A Description of the Two Worcester Cartularies in Cotton Tiberius A. XIII." In *Studies in Medieval History Presented to Frederick Maurice Powicke*. Ed. R.W. Hunt, W.A. Pantin, and R.W. Southern, 49–75. Oxford: Clarendon, 1948.

– ed. *The Owl and the Nightingale. Reproduced in Facsimile from the Surviving Manuscripts, Jesus College, Oxford 29 and British Museum Cotton Caligula A. 9.* EETS os. 251. London: Oxford University Press, 1963.

Kerby-Fulton, Kathryn. *Books under Suspicion: Censorship and Tolerance of Revelatory Writing in Late Medieval England*. South Bend: University of Notre Dame Press, 2006.

– "Langland and the Bibliographic Ego." In *Written Work: Langland, Labor, and Authorship*. Ed. Steven Justice and Kathryn Kerby-Fulton, 67–113. Philadelphia: University of Pennsylvania, 1997.

– "*Piers Plowman." The Cambridge History of Medieval English Literature*. Ed. David Wallace, 513–38. Cambridge: Cambridge University Press, 1999.

– *Reformist Apocalypticism and Piers Plowman*. Cambridge: Cambridge University Press, 1990.

Kerby-Fulton, Kathryn, and Denise Louise Despres. *Iconography and the Professional Reader: The Politics of Book Production in the Douce Piers Plowman*. Minneapolis: University of Minnesota Press, 1999.

Kerby-Fulton, Kathryn, and Steven Justice. "Langlandian Reading Circles, and the Civil Service in London and Dublin, 1380–1427." *New Medieval Literatures* 1 (1997): 59–84.

Kern, Fritz, and S. B. Chrimes. *Kingship and Law in the Middle Ages*. 2 vols. New York: Harper Torchbooks, 1970.

Keynes, Simon. "An Abbot, an Archbishop, and the Viking Raids of 1006-7." *ASE* 36 (2007): 151–220.

– "The Additions in Old English." *The York Gospels*. Ed. N. Barker, 83–91. London: Roxburghe Club, 1986.

– "Cnut's Earls." *The Reign of Cnut: King of England, Denmark and Norway*. Ed. Alexander Rumble, 43–88. London: Leicester University Press, 1994.

– "The Declining Reputation of King Æthelred the Unready." In *Ethelred the Unready: Papers from the Millenary Conference*. Ed. David Hill. British Archaeological Reports 59 (1978): 227–53.

– *The Diplomas of King Æthelred "the Unready" (978–1016): A Study in Their Use as Historical Evidence*. Cambridge: Cambridge University Press, 1980.

– "Edgar, *rex admirabilis*." In *Edgar, King of the English, 959–975: New Interpretations*, 3–59. Woodbridge, UK: Boydell, 2008.

– *Facsimiles of Anglo-Saxon Charters*. Oxford: Oxford University Press, 1991.

– "King Athelstan's Books." In *Learning and Literature in ASE*. Ed. Michael Lapidge and Helmut Gneuss, 143–201. Cambridge: Cambridge University Press, 1985.

– "Re-Reading King Æthelred the Unready." In Writing Medieval Biography 750–1250: Essays in Honour of Professor Frank Barlow. Eds. D. Bates, J. Crick and S. Hamilton, 77–97. Woodbridge: Boydell & Brewer, 2006.

– "Royal Government and the Written Word in Late Anglo-Saxon England." In *The Uses of Literacy in Mediæval Europe*. Ed. Rosamond McKitterick, 226–57. Cambridge: Cambridge University Press, 1990.

Keynes, Simon, and Michael Lapidge. *Alfred the Great: Asser's Life of King Alfred and Other Contemporary Sources*. London: Penguin Classics, 1983.

Kienzle, Beverly Mayne. "The Typology of the Medieval Sermon and Its Development in the Middle Ages: Report on Work in Progress." In *De l'Homélie au Sermon: Histoire de la Prédication Médiévale: Actes du Colloque International de Louvain-la-Neuve (9–11 Juillet 1992)*. Ed. Xavier Hermand and Jacqueline Harnesse. Louvain-la-Neuve, Belgium: Institut d'Études Médiévales de l'Université Catholique de Louvain, 1993.

King, Henry Hall and Max Lainster. *Hand-list of Bede Manuscripts*. Ithaca: Cornell University Press, 1943.

Kirk, Elizabeth. "Langland's Plowman and the Recreation of Fourteenth-Century Religious Metaphor." *YLS* 2 (1988): 1–21.

Klaeber, F. "Textual Notes on *Beowulf*." *Modern Language Notes* 34 (1919): 129–34.

Klein, Stacy. *Ruling Women: Queenship and Gender in Anglo-Saxon Literature*. South Bend, IN: University of Notre Dame Press, 2006.

Kleinman, Scott. "Frið and Fredom: Royal Forests and the English Jurisprudence of Laȝmon's Brut and Its Readers." *Modern Philology* 109 (2011): 17–45.

Knapp, Ethan. *The Bureaucratic Muse: Thomas Hoccleve and the Literature of Late Medieval England*. University Park: Pennsylvania State University Press, 2001.

Kramer, Joanna. "The Study of Proverbs in Anglo-Saxon Literature: Recent Scholarship, Resources for Research, and the Future of the Field." *Literature Compass* 6, no. 1 (2009): 71–96.

Krikmann, Arvo. "On the Denotative Indefiniteness of Proverbs." *Proverbium* 1 (1984): 47–92.

Kruger, Steven F. *Dreaming in the Middle Ages*. Cambridge: Cambridge University Press, 1992.

Kubouchi, T. "A Note on Prose Rhythm in Wulfstan's *De Falsis Deis*." *Poetica* 15 / 16 (1983): 57–106.

Lahey, Stephen E. *Philosophy and Politics in the Thought of John Wyclif*. Cambridge: Cambridge University Press, 2003.

Lapidge, Michael. *Anglo–Latin Literature, 600–899*. London: Hambledon, 1996.

– *Anglo–Latin Literature, 900–1066*. London: Hambledon, 1993.

– "The Career of Aldhelm." *ASE* 36 (2007): 15–70.

– "The Hermeneutic Style in Tenth-Century Anglo-Latin Literature." *ASE* 4 (1975): 67–112.

– "The Medieval Hagiography of St. Ecgwine." *Vale of Evesham Historical Society Research Papers* 6 (1977): 77–93.

Lapidge, Michael, et al. *The Cult of St Swithun*. Oxford: Clarendon, 2003.

Lapidge, Michael, and Michael Winterbottom. *Wulfstan of Winchester: Life of St. Athelwold*. Oxford: Clarendon, 1991.

Larsen, Andrew. "Are Lollards Lollards?" In *Lollards and Their Influence in Late Medieval England*. Ed. Fiona Somerset, Jill Havens, and Derek Pitard, 59–72. Woodbridge, UK: Boydell & Brewer, 2003.

Law, Vivien. *Grammars and Grammarians in the Early Middle Ages*. London: Longman, 1997.

Lawler, Traugott. "The *Secular Clergy* in Piers Plowman." *Yearbook of Langland Studies* 16 (2002): 85–117.

Lawson, M.K. *Cnut: The Danes in England in the Early Eleventh Century.* London: Longman, 1993.

– "Wulfstan and the Homiletic Element in the Laws of Aethelred–II and Cnut." *EHR* 107, no. 424 (1992): 565–86.

Lawton, D.A. "Alliterative Style." In *A Companion to Piers Plowman.* Ed. John Alford, 223–50. Berkeley: University of California Press, 1988.

– "Gaytryge's Sermon, 'Dictamen,' and Middle English Alliterative Verse." *Modern Philology* 76, no. 4 (1979): 329–43.

– "The Idea of Alliterative Poetry: Alliterative Meter and *Piers Plowman.*" In *Suche Werkis to Werche: Essays on Piers Plowman in Honor of David C. Fowler.* Ed. Míceál F. Vaughan, 147–68. East Lansing, MI: Colleagues Press, 1993.

– "Lollardy and the *Piers Plowman* Tradition." *MLR* 76, no. 4 (1981): 780–93.

– "Middle English Unrhymed Alliterative Poetry and the *South English Legendary.*" *English Studies* 61, no. 5 (1980): 390–6.

– "The Unity of Middle English Alliterative Poetry." *Speculum* 58, no. 1 (1983): 72–94.

Le Saux, Françoise. *Layamon's Brut: The Poem and Its Sources.* Cambridge: D.S. Brewer, 1989.

– "Listening to the Manuscript: Editing Laȝamon's *Brut.*" In *Orality and Literacy in Early Middle English.* Ed. Herbert Pilch, 11–20. Tübingen: Gunter Narr Verlag, 1996.

Lendinara, Patrizia. "The Kentish Laws." In *Anglo-Saxons from the Migration Period to the Eighth Century: An Ethnographic Perspective.* Ed. John Hines, 211–44. Woodbridge, UK: Boydell, 1997.

-- "The Versus *De Die Iudicii.* Its Circulation and Use as a School Text in Late Anglo-Saxon England." In *Foundations of Learning: the Transfer of Encyclopaedic Knowledge in the Early Middle Ages.* Ed. Rolf Bremmer and K. Dekker, 175–212. Peeters: Leuven, 2007.

Lerer, Seth. *Inventing English: The Portable History of the English Language.* New York: Columbia University Press, 2007.

Levett, Ada Elizabeth. *Studies in Manorial History.* Eds. H.M. Cam, M. Coate, L.S. Sutherland. Oxford: Oxford University Press, 1938.

Lewis, Katherine J. "Anglo-Saxon Saints' Lives, History and National Identity in Late Medieval England." In *History, Nationhood and the Question of Britain.* Ed. Helen Brocklehurst and Phillips Robert, 160–70. New York: Palgrave Macmillan, 2003.

– "History, Historiography and Rewriting the Past." In *A Companion to Middle English Hagiography*. Ed. Sarah Salih, 70–86. Cambridge: D.S. Brewer, 2006.

Liebermann, Felix. "On the Instituta Cnuti aliorumque regnum anglorum." *Transactions of the Royal Historical Society*, ns. 7 (1893): 77–107.

– *Quadripartitus: ein Englische Rechtsbuch von 1114*. Halle: Niemeyer, 1896.

– *Über das Englische Rechtsbuch Leges Henrici*. Halle: Niemeyer, 1901.

Lionarons, Joyce Tally.–*The Homiletic Writings of Archbishop Wulfstan: A Critical Study*. Woodbridge, UK: Boydell & Brewer, 2010.

– "Napier Homily L: Wulfstan's Eschatology at the Close of His Career." In *Wulfstan, Archbishop of York: The Proceedings of the Second Alcuin Conference*. Ed. Matthew Townend, 413–28. Studies in the Early Middle Ages 10. Turnhout, Belgium: Brepols, 2004.

Little, Lester K. *Benedictine Maledictions*. Ithaca, NY: Cornell University Press, 1996.

Loomis, Roger Sherman. "The Oral Diffusion of the Arthurian Legend." In *Arthurian Literature in the Middle Ages: A Collaborative History*. Ed. Roger Sherman Loomis, 52–63. Oxford: Clarendon, 1959.

Lowe, Kathryn. "Bury St Edmunds and Its Liberty: A Charter-text and Its Afterlife." In *English Manuscripts Before 1400*. Eds. A.S.G. Edwards and Orietta da Rold, 155–72. London: The British Library, 2012.

Loyn, Henry R. "*De iure domini regis*: A Comment on Royal Authority in Eleventh-Century England." In *England in the Eleventh Century: Proceedings of the 1990 Harlaxton Symposium*. Ed. Carola Hicks, 17–24. Stamford, CT: Paul Watkins, 1992.

Lynch, Kathryn L. *The High Medieval Dream Vision: Poetry, Philosophy, and Literary Form*. Stanford, CA: Stanford University Press, 1988.

Mabillon, Jean. *De re diplomatica libri VI: in quibus quidquid ad veterum instrumentorum antiquitatem, materiam, scripturam, et stilum; quidquid ad sigilla, monogrammata, subscriptiones, ac notas chronologicas; quidquid inde ad antiquariam, historicam, forensemque disciplinam pertinet, explicatur et illustratur*. Paris: Sumtibus Louis Billaine, 1681.

Machan, Tim William. *Medieval Literature: Texts and Interpretation*. Medieval & Renaissance Texts & Studies 79. Binghamton, NY: Medieval & Renaissance Texts & Studies, 1991.

MacNeil, Heather. *Trusting Records: Legal, Historical and Diplomatic Perspectives*. Archivist's Library. Dordrecht: Kluwer Academic Publishers, 2000.

Magennis, Hugh. *Images of Community in Old English Poetry*. Cambridge: Cambridge University Press, 1996.

Makaryk, Irena R, ed. *Encyclopedia of Contemporary Literary Theory: Approaches, Scholars, Terms*. Toronto: University of Toronto Press, 1993.

Mann, Jill. "'He Knew Nat Catoun': Medieval School-Texts and Middle English Literature." In *Text in the Community: Essays on Medieval Works, Manuscripts, Authors, Readers*. Ed. Jill Mann and Maura Nolan, 41–74. South Bend, IN: University of Notre Dame Press, 2006.

Marafioti, Nicole. "Punishing Bodies and Saving Souls: Capital and Corporal Punishment in Late Anglo-Saxon England." *Haskins Society Journal* 20 (2008): 39–57.

Marsden, Richard. *The Text of the Old Testament in ASE*. Cambridge: Cambridge University Press, 1995.

Mason, Emma. *St. Wulfstan of Worcester*. Oxford: Blackwell, 1990.

Matonis, A.T.E. "Middle English Alliterative Poetry." In *So Meny People Longages and Tonges: Philological Essays in Scots and Mediæval English Presented to Angus McIntosh*. Ed. Michael Benskin and M.L. Samuels, 341–54. Edinburgh: Benskin and Samuels, 1981.

McDonald, Donald. "Proverbs, Sententiae, and Exempla in Chaucer's Comic Tales: The Function of Comic Misapplication." *Speculum* 41 (1966): 453–65.

McEntire, Sandra. "The Doctrine of Compunction form Bede to Margery Kempe." In *The Medieval Mystical Tradition in England: Exeter Symposium IV*. Ed. Marion Glasscoe, 77–90. Cambridge: D.S. Brewer, 1987.

McIntosh, Angus. "Early Middle English Alliterative Verse." In *Middle English Alliterative Poetry and its Literary Background: Seven Essays*. Ed. David A. Lawton, 20–33. Cambridge: D.S. Brewer, 1982.

– "Following the Scribal Trail: The BL Cotton Caligula A.IX Copy of Layamon's *Brut*." In *Rethinking Middle English: Linguistic and Literary Approaches*. Ed. Nikolaus Ritt and Herbert Schendl, 42–66. Frankfurt am Main: Peter Lang, 2005.

– "Wulfstan's Prose." *Proceedings of the British Academy* 35 (1949): 109–42.

Meaney, Audrey L. "*And we forbeodað eornostlice ælcne hæðenscipe*: Wulfstan and Late Anglo-Saxon and Norse 'Heathenism'." In *Wulfstan, Archbishop of York: The Proceedings of the Second Alcuin Conference*. Ed. Matthew Townend, 461–500. Turnhout, Belgium: Brepols, 2004.

– "Old English Legal and Penitential Penalties for 'Heathenism'." *Anglo-Saxons: Studies Presented to Cyril Roy Hart*. Ed. Simon Keynes and Alfred Smyth, 127–58. Dublin: Four Courts, 2006.

Meroney, Howard. "The Life and Death of Longe Wille." *ELH* 17 (1950): 1–35.

Middleton, Anne. "Acts of Vagrancy: The C–Version 'Autobiography' and the Statute of 1388." In *Written Work: Langland, Labor and Authorship*. Ed. Steven Justice and Kathryn Kerby-Fulton, 208–317. Philadelphia: University of Pennsylvania Press, 1997.

– "The Audience and Public of *Piers Plowman*." *Middle English Alliterative Poetry and Its Literary Background: Seven Essays*. Ed. David A. Lawton, 101–23. Cambridge: D.S. Brewer, 1982.

– "The Critical Heritage." *A Companion to Piers Plowman*. Ed. John Alford, 1–28. Berkeley: University of California Press, 1988.

 "The Idea of Public Poetry in the Reign of Richard II." *Speculum* 53, no. 1 (1978): 94–114.

– "Making a Good End: John But as a Reader of *Piers Plowman*." In *Medieval English Studies Presented to George Kane*. Ed. Ronald Waldron et al., 243–66. Wolfeboro, NH: D.S. Brewer, 1988.

– "Two Infinites: Grammatical Metaphor in *Piers Plowman*." *ELH* 39 (1972): 169–88.

– "William Langland's 'Kynde Name': Authorial Signature and Social Identity in Late Fourteenth-Century England." In *Literary Practice and Social Change in Britain, 1380–1530*. Ed. Lee Patterson, 206–45. Berkeley: University of California Press, 1990.

Miller, Sean, ed. "The New *Regesta Regum Anglorum*." http://www.trin.cam.ac .uk/chartwww/NewRegReg.html.

Minkova, Donka. "The Credibility of Pseudo-Alfred: Prosodic Insights in Post-Conquest Mongrel Meter." *Modern Philology* 94, no. 4 (1997): 427–54.

– "Early English Metre [Book Review]." *Speculum* 83, no. 3 (2008): 673–75.

Minnis, A.J. *Medieval Theory of Authorship: Scholastic Literary Attitudes in the Later Middle Ages*. 2nd rev. ed. Aldershot, UK: Ashgate, 1988.

– "Piers' Protean Pardon: The Letter and Spirit of Langland's Theology of Indulgences." In *English Court Culture in the Later Middle Ages*. Ed. Anne D'Arcy, 218–40. Dublin: Four Courts, 2005.

Mitchell, Bruce. "The Dangers of Disguise: Old English Texts in Modern Punctuation." *Review of English Studies* 31 (1980): 385–413.

Moffat, Douglas. "The Intonational Basis of Layamon's Verse." In *Prosody and Poetics in the Early Middle Ages: Essays in Honour of C.B. Hieatt*. Ed. M.J. Toswell, 133–46. Toronto: University of Toronto Press, 1995.

– *The Soul's Address to the Body: The Worcester Fragments*. East Lansing, MI: Colleagues Press, 1987.

Moreland, John. "Ethnicity, Power, and the English." In *Social Identity in Early Medieval Britain and Ireland*. Ed. B. Frazer and A. Tyrell, 23–51. Leicester: Leicester University Press, 2000. Repr. in *The Postmodern Beowulf*. Ed. Eileen Joy and Mary K. Ramsey, 163–98. Morgantown: West Virginia University Press, 1986.

Morey, James. "Plows, Laws and Sanctuary in Medieval England and in the Wakefield 'Mactacio Abel'." *Studies in Philology* 45 (1998): 41–55.

Morgan, Margery. "A Talking of the Love of God and the Continuity of Stylistic Tradition in Middle English Prose Meditations." *Review of English Studies* ns3 (1952): 97–116.

– "A treataise in Cadence." *Modern Language Review* 47 (1952): 156–64.

Morse, R. "Chaucer's Man of Law in Sequence." *Poetica* 28 (1988): 29–31.

Morrison, Stephen. "A Reminiscence of Wulfstan in the 12th-Century *Ormulum*, a Versified Gospel Harmony." *Neuphilologische Mitteilungen* 96, no. 3 (1995): 229–34.

Musson, Anthony. "Appealing to the Past: Perceptions of Law in Late-Medieval England." *Expectations of the Law in the Middle Ages*. Ed. Anthony Musson, 165–80. Woodbridge, UK: Boydell & Brewer, 2001.

– *Medieval Law in Context: The Growth of Legal Consciousness from Magna Carta to the Peasants' Revolt*. Manchester: Manchester University Press, 2001.

Musson, Anthony, and W.M. Ormrod. *The Evolution of English Justice: Law, Politics, and Society in the Fourteenth Century*. New York: St Martin's, 1999.

Nelson, Janet. "Rulers and Government." In *The Nùew Cambridge Medieval History c. 900 to c. 1024*. Ed. Timothy Reuter, 95–129. Cambridge: Cambridge University Press, 1999.

Newman, Barbara. "Redeeming the Time: Langland, Julian, and the Art of Life-long Revision." *YLS* 23 (2009): 1–32.

Noble, James. "Layamon's 'Ambivalence' Reconsidered." In *The Text and Tradition of Layamon's Brut*. Ed. Françoise Le Saux, 171–82. Woodbridge, UK: D.S. Brewer, 1994.

Nolan, Maura. "The Fortunes of Piers Plowman and Its Readers." *YLS* 20 (2006): 1–41.

O'Brien, Bruce. "The Becket Conflict and the Invention of the Myth of *Lex Non Scripta*." In *Learning the Law: Teaching and the Transmission of Law in England, 1150–1900*. Ed. Jonathan A. Bush and Alain Wijffels, 1–17. London: Hambledon, 1999.

– "Forgery and the Literacy of the Early Common Law." *Albion* 27, no. 1 (1995): 1–18.

– *God's Peace and King's Peace: The Laws of Edward the Confessor*. Philadelphia: University of Pennsylvania Press, 1999.

– "The *Instituta Cnuti* and the Translation of English Law." *Anglo Norman Studies* 25 (2002): 177–97.

O'Donovan, Mary Anne. "Episcopal Dates for the Province of Canterbury, 850–950." *ASE* 2 (1973): 91–113.

O'Keeffe, Katherine O'Brien. "Body and Law in Late Anglo-Saxon England."
  ASE 27 (1998): 209–32.
– "Death and Transformations: Thinking through the 'End' of Old English
  Verse." In *New Directions in Oral Theory*. Ed. Mark Amodio, 149–78. Tempe:
  Arizona Center for Medieval and Renaissance Studies, 2005.
– *Visible Song: Transitional Literacy in Old English Verse*. Cambridge:
  Cambridge University Press, 1990.
Oakden, J.P. *Alliterative Poetry in Middle English*. Hamden: Archon Books,
  1968.
Ogawa, H. "Revised Syntax in Wulfstan's Rewriting of Ælfric's Prose." In
  *Eigogaku no shiten: Aspects of Old English Linguistics: Essays Presented in
  Memory of Professor Saburo Ohye*, 3–17. Fukuoka: Kyushu University Press,
  1989.
Oliver, Lisi. *The Beginnings of English Law*. Toronto: University of Toronto
  Press, 2002.
Ong, Walter J. *Orality and Literacy: The Technologizing of the Word*. London:
  Methuen, 1982.
Orchard, Andy. *A Critical Companion to Beowulf*. Woodbridge, UK: D.S.
  Brewer, 2003.
– "Crying Wolf: Oral Style and the *Sermones Lupi*." *ASE* 21 (1992): 239–62.
– "On Editing Wulfstan." *Early Medieval English Texts and Interpretations*. Ed.
  Elaine Treharne and Susan Rosser, 311–40. Tempe: Arizona Center for Medieval
  and Renaissance Studies, 2002.
– "Parallel Lives: Wulfstan, William, Coleman and Christ." In *St. Wulfstan and
  His World*. Ed. Julia Barrow and Nicholas Brooks, 39–59. Aldershot, UK:
  Ashgate, 2005.
– *The Poetic Art of Aldhelm*. Cambridge: Cambridge University Press, 1994.
– "Re-Editing Wulfstan: Where's the Point?" *Wulfstan, Archbishop of York: The
  Proceedings of the Second Alcuin Conference*. Ed. Matthew Townend, 63–91.
  Turnhout, Belgium: Brepols, 2004.
– "Wulfstan as Reader, Writer, and Rewriter." In *The Old English Homily:
  Precedent, Practice, and Appropriation*. Ed. Aaron J. Kleist, 311–41. Turnhout,
  Belgium: Brepols, 2007.
Osberg, Richard H. "Alliterative Technique in the Lyrics of MS Harley 2253."
  Modern Philology 82, no. 2 (1984): 125–55.
Owst, G.R. *Literature and Pulpit in Medieval England*. Cambridge: Cambridge
  University Press, 1933.
– *Preaching in Medieval England*. Cambridge: Cambridge University Press, 1926.
Palmer, James. "*Compunctio* and the Heart of the Old English Wanderer,"
  Neophilologus 88, no. 3 (2004): 447–60.

Parkes, M.B. "*Rædan, areccan, smeagan*: How the Anglo–Saxons Read." *ASE* 26 (1997): 1–22.

Partner, Nancy. "Making Up Lost Time: Writing on the Writing of History." *Speculum* 61 (1986): 90–117.

– "The New Cornificius: Medieval History and the Artifice of Words." In *Classical Rhetoric and Medieval Historiography.* Ed. Ernst Breisach, 5–59. Kalamazoo: Medieval Institute Publications, 1985.

– Pasternack, Carol Braun. *The Textuality of Old English Poetry.* Cambridge Studies in Anglo-Saxon England 13. Cambridge: Cambridge University Press, 1995.

Patterson, Lee. "The Logic of Textual Criticism and the Way of Genius: The Kane-Donaldson *Piers Plowman* in Historical Perspective." In *Textual Criticism and Literary Interpretation.* Ed. Jerome McGann, 55–91. Chicago: University of Chicago Press, 1985.

– *Negotiating the Past: The Historical Understanding of Medieval Literature.* Madison: University of Wisconsin Press, 1987.

Pearsall, Derek. "The Origins of the Alliterative Revival." In *Middle English Alliterative Poetry and Its Literary Background: Seven Essays.* Ed. David A. Lawton, 34–53. Cambridge: D.S. Brewer, 1982.

Penn, Stephen. "Wyclif and the Sacraments." In *A Companion to John Wyclif.* Ed. Ian Levy, 241–92. Leiden: Brill, 2006.

Perry, Lucy. "Origins and Originality: Reading Lawman's *Brut* and the Rejection of British Library Ms Cotton Otho C. XIII." *Arthuriana* 10, no. 2 (2000): 66–90.

Phillips, Susan E. *Transforming Talk: The Problem with Gossip in Late Medieval England.* University Park: Pennsylvania State University Press, 2007.

Plucknett, T.F.T. *Legislation of Edward I.* Oxford: Clarendon Press, 1949.

Pollock, Frederick, and Frederic William Maitland. *The History of English Law before the Time of Edward I.* 2nd ed. Cambridge: Cambridge University Press, 1968.

Pons-Sanz, Sara M. *Norse-Derived Vocabulary in Late Old English Texts. Wulfstan's Works: A Case Study.* Odense: University Press of Southern Denmark, 2007.

Powell, Sue. "The Transmission and Circulation of The Lay Folks' Catechism." In *Late-Medieval Religious Texts and Their Transmission.* Ed. A.J. Minnis, 67–84. Cambridge: Boydell & Brewer, 1994.

Prestwich, Michael. "England and Scotland During the Wars of Independence." In *England and her Neighbors, 1066–1453.* Ed. M. Jones and M. Vale. London: Hambledon, 1989.

Putter, Ad, Judith Anne Jefferson, and Myra Stokes, eds. *Studies in the Metre of Alliterative Verse.* Oxford: Society for the Study of Medieval Languages and Literature, 2007.

Rabin, Andrew. "Old English *forespeca* and the Role of the Advocate in Old English Law." *Mediæval Studies* 69 (2007): 223–54.

– "The Wolf's Testimony to the English: Law and the Witness in the 'Sermo Lupi Ad Anglos' (Archbishop Wulfstan of York)." *JEGP* 105, no. 3 (2006): 388–414.

Ramsay, J.H. *The Angevin Empire.* Oxford: Oxford University Press, 1903.

Raw, Barbara. "Piers and the Image of God in Man." In *Piers Plowman: Critical Approaches.* Ed. S.S. Hussey, 143–79. London: Methuen, 1969.

Rex, Richard. *The Lollards.* Houndmills, UK: Palgrave, 2002.

Reynolds, Susan. "The Forged Charters of Barnstaple." *EHR* 84 (1969): 699–720.

– *Kingdoms and Communities in Western Europe, 900–1300.* 2nd ed. Oxford: Clarendon, 1997.

Richards, Mary P. "Anglo-Saxonism in the Old English Laws." In *Anglo-Saxonism and the Construction of Social Identity.* Ed. Allen J. Frantzen and John D. Niles, 40–59. Gainesville: University of Florida Press, 1997.

– "The Body as Text in Early Anglo-Saxon Law." In *Naked before God: Uncovering the Body in ASE.* Ed. Benjamin C. Withers and Jonathan Wilcox, 97–115. Morgantown: West Virginia University Press, 2003.

– "I–II Cnut: Wulfstan's *Summa*?" In *English Law Before Magna Carta: Felix Liebermann and Die Gesetze der Angelsachsen.* Ed. Stefan Jurasinski, Lisi Oliver, and Andrew Rabin, 137–56. Leiden: Brill, 2010.

– "The Manuscript Contexts of the Old English Laws: Tradition and Innovation." In *Studies in Earlier Old English Prose.* Ed. Paul E. Szarmach, 171–93. Albany: State University of New York Press, 1985.

– "Old Wine in a New Bottle: Recycled Instructional Materials in Seasons of Fasting." In *Precedence, Practice and Appropriation: The Old English Homily.* Ed. Aaron Kleist, 345–64. Turnhout, Belgium: Brepols, 2007.

– "Texts and Their Traditions in the Medieval Library of Rochester Cathedral Priory." *Transactions of the American Philosophical Society* 78, no. 3 (1988): 1–129.

Rickert, Edith. "John But, Messenger and Maker." *Modern Philology* 11, no. 1 (1913): 107–16.

Rider, Jeff. "The Fictional Margin: the Merlin of the Brut." *Modern Philology* 87, no. 1 (1989): 1–12.

Roberts, Jane. "A Preliminary Note on British Library, Cotton MS Caligula A. IX." In *The Text and Tradition of Layamon's Brut.* Ed. Françoise Le Saux, 1–14. Woodbridge, UK: D.S. Brewer, 1994.

Robertson, D.W., and Bernard Huppé. *Piers Plowman and the Scriptural Tradition.* New York: Octagon Books, 1969.

Robins, Will. "Towards a Disjunctive Philology." In *The Book Unbound.* Ed. Siân Echard and Stephen Partridge, 144–77. Toronto: University of Toronto Press, 2004.

Robinson, Fred. "Afterlife of Old English: A Brief History of Composition in Old English after the Close of the Anglo-Saxon Period." In *The Tomb of Beowulf and Other Essays on Old English*, 275–303. Oxford: Blackwell, 1993.

– "Old English Literature in its Most Immediate Context." In *Old English Literature in Context*. Ed. John Niles, 11–29. Woodbridge: Boydell & Brewer, 1980.

Rollason, D.W. *Saints and Relics in Anglo-Saxon England*. Oxford: Blackwell, 1989.

Rouse, Robert Allen. *The Idea of ASE in Middle English Romance*. Woodbridge, UK: Boydell and Brewer, 2005.

Rumble, Alexander R. "Purposes of the Codex Wintoniensis." *Anglo-Norman Studies* 4 (1981): 153–66.

Rydzeski, Justine. *Radical Nostalgia in the Age of Piers Plowman: Economics, Apocalypticism, and Discontent*. New York: Peter Lang, 1999.

Salter, Elizabeth. "'Alliterative Modes and Affiliations in the Fourteenth Century." *Neuphilologische Mitteilungen* 79 (1978): 25–35.

– "The Alliterative Revival." In *English and International: Studies in the Literature, Art and Patronage of Medieval England*. Ed. Elizabeth Salter, Derek Albert Pearsall, and Nicolette Zeeman, 101–10. Cambridge: Cambridge University Press, 1988.

– "*Piers Plowman* and *The Simonie*." *Archiv* 205 (1967): 241–54.

– *Piers Plowman: An Introduction*. Cambridge: Harvard University Press, 1962.

Samuels, M.L. "Dialect and Grammar." In *A Companion to Piers Plowman*. Ed. John Alford, 201–22. Berkeley: University of California Press, 1988.

Sayers, Jane E. "'Original,' Cartulary and Chronicle: The Case of the Abbey of Evesham." In *Fälschungen im Mittelalter. Internationaler Kongreß Der Monumenta Germaniae Historica, München, 16–19 September 1986*, 371–95. Monumenta Germaniae Historica 33. Hanover: Hansche Buchhandlung, 1988.

Scanlon, Larry. "King, Commons, and Kind Wit: Langland's National Vision." In *Imagining a Medieval English Nation*. Ed. Kathy Lavezzo, 191–231. Minneapolis: University of Minnesota Press, 2004.

Scase, Wendy. "Dauy Dicars Dreame and Robert Crowley's Prints of Piers Plowman." *YLS* 21 (2007): 171–98.

– "'First to reckon Richard': John But's *Piers Plowman* and the Politics of Allegiance." *YLS* 11 (1997): 49–66.

– *Literature and Complaint in England, 1272–1553*. Oxford: Oxford University Press, 2007.

– *Piers Plowman and the New Anticlericalism*. Cambridge: Cambridge University Press, 1989.

John Scattergood. "'Pierce the Ploughman's Crede': Lollardy and Texts." In *The Lost Tradition: Essays on Middle English Alliterative Poetry*, 160–78. Dublin: Four Courts, 2000.

– *Politics and Poetry in the Fifteenth Century*. London: Blandford Press, 1971.

Schaar, Claes. *Critical Studies in the Cynewulf Group*. Lund, Sweden: C.W.K. Gleerup, 1949.

Schiefele, Eleanor. "Richard and the Visual Arts." In *Richard II: The Art of Kingship*. Ed. Anthony Goodman and James Gillespie, 255–72. Oxford: Oxford UP, 2003.

Schmidt, A.V.C. *Clerkly Maker: Langland's Poetic Art*. Woodbridge, UK: D.S. Brewer, 1987.

– "Langland and Scholastic Philosophy." *MAe* 38 (1969): 134–56.

– "Visions and Revisions." *YLS* 14 (2000): 5–27.

Schwyter, J.R. *Old English Legal Language: The Lexical Field of Theft*. Odense, Denmark: Odense University Press, 1996.

Scott, Anne M. *Piers Plowman and the Poor*. Dublin: Four Courts, 2004.

Seipp, D. "Mirror of Justices." In *Learning the Law: Teaching and the Transmission of Law in England, 1150–1900*. Ed. Jonathan A. Bush and Alain Wijffels. London: Hambledon, 1999.

Sharpe, Richard. "Charters, Deeds, and Diplomatics." *Medieval Latin: An Introduction and Bibliographic Guide*. Ed. F.A.C. Mantello and A.G. Rigg, 230–40. Washington, D.C.: Catholic University Press of America, 1996.

– "The Prefaces of *Quadripartitus*." In *Law and Government in Medieval England and Normandy: Essays in Honour of Sir James Holt*. Ed. George Garnett and John Hudson, 148–73. Cambridge: Cambridge University Press, 1994.

– *Titulus: Identifying Medieval Latin Texts: An Evidence–Based Approach*. Turnhout, Belgium: Brepols, 2003.

Sheppard, Alice. "Noble Counsel, No Counsel: Advising Ethelred the Unready." In *Via Crucis: Essay on Early Medieval Sources and Ideas in Memory of J. E. Cross*. Ed. Thomas N. Hall and Thomas D. Hill, 393–422. Morgantown: West Virginia University Press, 2002.

Shichtman, Martin B. "Gawain in Wace and Layamon, a Case of Metahistorical Evolution." In *Medieval Texts and Contemporary Readers*. Ed. Laurie Finke and Martin Shichtman, 103–19. Ithaca, NY: Cornell University Press, 1987.

Shippey, Thomas. "Maxims in Old English Narrative: Literary Art or Traditional Wisdom?". In *Oral Tradition / Literary Tradition: A Symposium*. Ed. Hans Bekker-Hielsen, 28–46. Odense, Denmark: Odense University Press, 1977.

Shirley, Kevin J. *Secular Jurisdiction of Monasteries in Anglo–Norman and Angevin England*. Woodbridge, UK: Boydell, 2004.

Shogimen, Takashi. "Wyclif's Ecclesiology and Political Thought." In *A Companion to John Wyclif*. Ed. Ian Levy, 199–240. Leiden: Brill, 2006.

Shrader, Richard. "The Inharmonious Choristers and Blacksmiths of MS Arundel 292." *Studies in Philology* 104 (2007): 1–14.

Simpson, James. "The Constraints of Satire in *Piers Plowman* and *Mum and the Sothsegger*." In *Langland, the Mystics, and the Medieval English Religious Tradition: Essays in Honour of S.S. Hussey*. Ed. Helen Phillips, 11–30. Rochester, NY: Boydell & Brewer, 1990.

– "Saving Satire after Arundel's Constitutions: John Audelay's 'Marcol and Solomon'." In *Text and Controversy from Wyclif to Bale: Essays in Honour of Anne Hudson*. Ed. Helen Barr and Ann M. Hutchison, 387–404. Turnhout, Belgium: Brepols, 2005.

Sims-Williams, Patrick. "Thought, Word and Deed: An Irish Triad." *Eriú* 29 (1978): 78–111.

Smith, D. Vance. "Negative Langland." YLS 23 (2009): 33–59.

Smith, Macklin. "Langland's Alliterative Line(s)." *YLS* 23 (2009): 163–216.

Smith, Scott T. *Land and Book: Literature and Land Tenure in Anglo-Saxon England*. Toronto: University of Toronto Press, 2012.

Smyth, Alfred. *King Alfred the Great*. Oxford: Oxford University Press, 1995.

Somerset, Fiona. *Clerical Discourse and Lay Audience in Late Medieval England*. Cambridge: Cambridge University Press, 1998.

– "Expanding the Langlandian Canon: Radical Latin and the Stylistics of Reform." *YLS* 17 (2003): 73–92.

Southern, R.W. "The Classical Tradition." In *History and Historians: Selected Papers of R.W. Southern*. Ed. Robert Bartlett, 11–29. Oxford: Blackwell, 2004.

Spearing, A.C. *Medieval Dream-Poetry*. Cambridge: Cambridge University Press, 1976.

– "Verbal Repetition in Piers Plowman B and C." *JEGP* 62, no. 4 (1963): 722–37.

Speed, Diane. "The Construction of the Nation in Medieval English Romance." In *Readings in Medieval English Romance*. Ed. Carol M. Meale, 135–57. Cambridge: D.S. Brewer, 1994.

Stafford, Pauline. "The Laws of Cnut and the History of Anglo-Saxon Royal Promises." *Anglo Saxon England* 10 (1981): 173–90.

Stanley, Eric. "Layamon's Antiquarian Sentiments." *MAe* 38 (1969): 23–37.

– "Laȝamon: Priest and Historiographer." In *Laȝamon: Contexts, Language, and Interpretation*. Ed. Rosamund Allen, Lucy Perry, and Jane Roberts, 3–24. London: King's College London Centre for Late Antique and Medieval Studies, 2002.

– "On the Laws of King Alfred: The End of the Preface and the Beginning of the Laws." In *Alfred the Wise: Studies in Honour of Janet Bately on the Occasion of Her Sixty–Fifth Birthday*. Ed. Jane Roberts, Janet Nelson, and Malcolm Godden, 211–21. Oxford: D.S. Brewer, 1997.

Stanton, Robert. *The Culture of Translation in ASE*. Cambridge: D.S. Brewer, 2002.

Steadman, John. "Chaucer's Eagle, A Contemplative Symbol." *PMLA* 75 (1960): 153–91.

Stein, Robert. "Making History English: Cultural Identity and Historical Explanation in William of Malmesbury and Laȝamon's *Brut*." In *Text and Territory*. Ed. Sealy A. Gilles and Sylvia Tomasch, 97–115. Philadelphia: University of Pennsylvania Press, 1998.

Steiner, Emily. *Documentary Culture and the Making of Medieval English Literature*. Cambridge: Cambridge University Press, 2003.

Stenton, Doris Mary Parsons, and American Philosophical Society. *English Justice between the Norman Conquest and the Great Charter, 1066–1215*. London: G. Allen & Unwin, 1965.

Stenton, F.M. *The Latin Charters of the Anglo-Saxon Period*. Oxford: Clarendon, 1955.

– "The Supremacy of the Mercian Kings." *EHR* 33 (1918): 433–52.

Stock, Brian. *The Implications of Literacy: Written Language and Models of Interpretation in the Eleventh and Twelfth Centuries*. Princeton, NJ: Princeton University Press, 1983.

Stokes, Myra. *Justice and Mercy in Piers Plowman: A Reading of the B-Text Visio*. London: Croom Helm, 1983.

Strohm, Paul. "Counterfeiters, Lollards, and Lancastrian Unease." *New Medieval Literatures* 1 (1997): 31–58.

– "Introduction: False Fables and Historical Truth." In *Hochon's Arrow: The Social Imagination in Fourteenth-Century Texts*, 3–10. Princeton, NJ: Princeton University Press, 1992.

– "Queens as Intercessors." In *Hochon's Arrow: The Social Imagination in Fourteenth-Century Texts*. Princeton, NJ: Princeton University Press, 1992. 95–119.

Swan, Mary. "Authorship and Anonymity." In *A Companion to Anglo-Saxon Literature*. Ed. Philip Pulsiano and Elaine Treharne, 71–83. Oxford: Blackwell, 2001.

Szarmach, Paul. "Ælfric Revises: the Lives of Martin and the Idea of the Author." In *Unlocking the Wordhord: Anglo-Saxon Studies in Memory of Edward B. Iving, Jr.* Ed. Mark Amodio and Katherine O'Brien O'Keeffe, 38–61. Toronto: University of Toronto Press, 2003.

Szittya, Penn R. *The Antifraternal Tradition in Medieval Literature*. Princeton, NJ: Princeton University Press, 1986.

– "Domesday Bokes: The Apocalypse in Medieval English Literary Culture." In *The Apocalypse in the Middle Ages*. Ed. Richard K. Emmerson and Bernard McGinn, 374–97. Ithaca, NY: Cornell University Press, 1992.

Tatlock, John S.P. *The Legendary History of Britain: Geoffrey of Monmouth's Historia Regum Britanniae and Its Early Vernacular Versions.* Berkeley: University of California Press, 1950.

Thompson, Anne B. *Everyday Saints and the Art of Narrative in the South English Legendary.* Aldershot, UK: Ashgate, 2003.

Thompson, Susan D. *Anglo-Saxon Royal Diplomas: A Palaeography.* Woodbridge, UK: Boydell & Brewer, 2006.

Tiller, Kenneth Jack. *Laȝamon's Brut and the Anglo–Norman Vision of History.* Cardiff: University of Wales Press, 2007.

– "The Truth 'bi Arðure Pan kinge': Arthur's Role in Shaping Lawman's Vision of History." *Arthuriana* 10, no. 2 (2000): 27–49.

Tinti, Francesca. "From Episcopal Conception to Monastic Compilation: Hemming's Cartulary in Context." *Early Medieval Europe* 11, no. 3 (2002): 233–61.

Tolkien, J.R.R. "Ancrene Wisse and Hali Meiðhad." *Essays and Studies by Members of the English Association* 14 (1929): 104–26.

Treharne, Elaine. "Bishops and Their Texts in the Later Eleventh Century: Worcester and Exeter." In *Essays in Manuscript Geography: Vernacular Manuscripts of the English West Midlands from the Conquest to the Sixteenth Century.* Ed. Wendy Scase, Turnhout, 13–28. Belgium: Brepols, 2007.

– "Categorization, Periodization: The Silence of (the) English in the Twelfth Century." *New Medieval Literatures* 8 (2006): 247–69.

– "The Form and Function of the Twelfth-Century Old English Dicts of Cato." *JEGP* 102 (2003): 465–85.

– "The Life of English in the Mid-Twelfth Century: Ralph D'Escures' Homily on the Virgin Mary." In *Writers of the Reign of Henry II: Twelve Essays.* Ed. Ruth Kennedy and Simon Meecham-Jones, 169–86. New York: Palgrave MacMillan, 2006.

– *Living Through Conquest: The Politics of Early English, 1020–1220.* Oxford: Oxford University Press, 2012.

– "The Production and Script of Manuscripts Containing English Religious Texts in the First Half of the Twelfth Century." In *Rewriting Old English in the Twelfth Century.* Ed. Mary Swan and Elaine M. Treharne, 11–40. Cambridge: Cambridge University Press, 2000.

– "York, Minster Library, Additional 1." In *The Production and Use of English Manuscripts 1060 to 1220*, edited by Orietta Da Rold, Takako et al. University of Leicester 2010. Available at http://www.le.ac.uk/english/em1060to1220/mss/EM.YM.1.htm, accessed 13 September 2013.

Trilling, Renée R. "Sovereignty and Social Order: Archbishop Wulfstan and the *Institutes of Polity.*" In *The Bishop Reformed: Studies of Episcopal Power and*

Culture in the Central Middle Ages. Ed. John S. Ott and Anna Trumbore Jones, 58–85. Aldershot, UK, and Burlington, VT: Ashgate, 2007.

Troyon, H.W. "Who is Piers Plowman?" *PMLA* 49 (1932): 368–84.

Tsurishima, H. "The Fraternity of Rochester Cathedral Priory about 1100." *Anglo–Norman Studies* 14 (1992): 313–37.

Tunberg, Jennifer Morrish. "Introduction." In *The Copenhagen Wulfstan Collection.* Ed. J.E. Cross and Jennifer Morrish Tunberg. Copenhagen: EEMF 25, 1993.

Turville-Petre, Thorlac. *The Alliterative Revival.* Cambridge: D.S. Brewer, 1977.

– *England the Nation: Language, Literature, and National Identity, 1290–1340.* Oxford: Clarendon, 1996.

– "The Lament for Sir John Beverley." *Speculum* 57, no. 2 (1982): 332–9.

Tyler, E.M. *Old English Poetics: The Aesthetics of the Familiar in ASE.* Woodbridge: York Medieval Press, 2006.

Ullmann, W. "On the Influence of Geoffrey of Monmouth in English History." In *Speculum Historiale.* Ed. C. Bauer, L. Böhm, and M. Müller, 257–74. Munich and Freiburg: K. Alber, 1965.

Walker, Simon. "A Context for *Brunanburh*?" In *Warriors and Churchmen in the High Middle Ages: Essays Presented to Karl Leiser.* Ed. Timothy Reuter, 21–40. London: Hambledon, 1992.

Walling, Amanda. "Friar Flatterer: Glossing and the Hermeneutics of Flattery in *Piers Plowman.*" *YLS* 21 (2007). 57–76.

Warner, Lawrence. "John But and the Other Works that Will Wrought (*Piers Plowman* A XII 101–2)." *Notes and Queries* 52 (2005): 13–18.

– "An Overlooked Piers Plowman Excerpt and the Oral Circulation of Non-Reformist Prophecy c. 1520–55." *YLS* 21 (2007): 119––42.

Warren, W.L. *Henry II.* London: Eyre Methuen, 1973.

Waters, Claire. "Power and Authority." *A Companion to Middle English Hagiography.* Ed. Sarah Salih, 70–86. Cambridge: D.S. Brewer, 2006.

Watson, Nicholas. "Middle English Mystics." In *Cambridge History of Medieval English Literature.* Ed. David Wallace, 539–65. Cambridge: Cambridge Univesity Press, 2005.

– "*Piers Plowman*, Pastoral Theology, and Spiritual Perfectionism: Hawkyn's Cloak and Patience's *Pater Noster.*" *Yearbook of Langland Studies* 21 (2007): 83–118.

Watts, James W. "Ritual Legitimacy and Scriptural Authority." *Journal of Biblical Literature* 124, no. 3 (2005): 401–17.

Weinberg, Carole. "Marginal Illustration: A Clue to the Provenance of the Cotton Caligula Manuscript of Laȝamon's *Brut*?" In *Laȝamon: Contexts, Language, and Interpretation.* Ed. Rosamund Allen, Lucy Perry, and Jane

Roberts, 39–52. London: King's College London Centre for Late Antique and Medieval Studies, 2002.

Wells, Henry B. "The Construction of Piers Plowman." *PMLA* 44 (1929): 123–40.

Wenzel, Siegfried. "Medieval Sermons." In *A Companion to Piers Plowman*. Ed. John Alford, 155–72. Berkeley: University of California Press, 1988.

– *The Sin of Sloth: Acedia in Medieval Thought and Literature*. Chapel Hill: University of North Carolina Press, 1967.

– *Summa Virtutum de Remediis Anime*. Athens: University of Georgia Press, 1984.

White, Graeme J. *Restoration and Reform 1153–1165*. Cambridge: Cambridge University Press, 2000.

White, Hayden. "The Fictions of Factual Representation." In *The Literature of Fact: Selected Papers from the English Institute*. Ed. Angus Fletcher, 21–44. New York: Columbia University Press, 1976.

– "Rhetoric and History." In *Theories of History: Papers Read at a Clark Library Seminar, March 6, 1976*. Ed. Hayden White and Frank Emanuel. Los Angeles: William Andrews Clark Memorial Library, 1978.

Whitelock, Dorothy. "Archbishop Wulfstan, Homilist and Statesman." *Transactions of the Royal Historical Society* 24 (1942): 25–45.

– *English Historical Documents Volume 1, C. 500–1042*. London: Routledge, 1996.

– "*Institutes of Polity* [Book Review]." *Review of English Studies* n.s. 12 (1961): 61–6.

– "Some Charters in the Name of King Alfred." *Saints, Scholars and Heroes: Studies in Medieval Culture in Honour of Charles W. Jones*. Ed. M.H. King and W.M. Stevens, 77–98. Collegeville, MN: Hill Monastic Manuscript Library, Saint John's Abbey and University, 1979.

– "Wulfstan Cantor and Anglo-Saxon Law." In *Nordica Et Anglica: Studies in Honor of Stefan Einarsson*. Ed. Allan H. Orrick, 83–92. The Hague: Mouton, 1968.

– "Wulfstan and the Laws of Cnut." *The EHR* 63, no. 249 (1948): 433–52.

– "Wulfstan and the So-Called Laws of Edward and Guthrum." *The EHR* 56, no. 221 (1941): 1–21.

– "Wulfstan at York." In *Franciplegius: Medieval and Linguistic Studies in Honor of Francis Peabody Magoun*. Ed. J.B. Bessinger and R.P. Creed, 214–31. New York: G. Allen and Unwin, 1965.

– "Wulfstan's Authorship of Cnut's Laws." *The EHR* 70, no. 274 (1955): 72–85.

Whitman, Jon. *Allegory: The Dynamics of an Ancient and Medieval Technique*. Cambridge: Cambridge University Press, 1987.

Wickham-Crowley, Kelley M. *Writing the Future: Laʒamon's Prophetic History*. Cardiff: University of Wales Press, 2002.

Wilcox, Jonathan. "The Dissemination of Wulfstan's Homilies: The Wulfstan Tradition in Eleventh-Century Vernacular Preaching." In *England in the Eleventh Century*. Ed. Carola Hicks, 199–217. Stamford, CT: Paul Watkins, 1992.

– "Napier's Wulfstan Homilies XL and XLII: Two Anonymous Works from Winchester?" *JEGP* 90 (1991): 1–19.

– "The St. Brice's Day Massacre and Archbishop Wulfstan." In *Peace and Negotiation: Strategies for Coexistence in the Middle Ages and the Renaissance*. Ed. Diane Wolfthal, 79–91. Turnhout, Belgium: Brepols, 2000.

– "The Wolf on Shepherds: Wulfstan, Bishops, and the Context of the *Sermo Lupi Ad Anglos*." In *Old English Prose: Basic Readings*. Ed. Paul E. Szarmach, 395–418. New York: Garland, 2000.

– "Wulfstan and the Twelfth Century." In *Rewriting Old English in the Twelfth Century*. Ed. Mary Swan and Elaine M. Treharne, 83–97. Cambridge: Cambridge University Press, 2000.

– "Wulfstan's *Sermo Lupi Ad Anglos* as Political Performance: 16 February 1014 and Beyond." In *Wulfstan, Archbishop of York: The Proceedings of the Second Alcuin Conference*. Ed. Matthew Townend, 375–96. Turnhout, Belgium: Brepols, 2004.

Willard, Rudolph. "Vercelli Homily VIII and the Christ." *PMLA* 42, no. 2 (1927): 314–30.

Williams, Anne. "The Spoliation of Worcester." *Anglo-Norman Studies* 19 (1997): 383–408.

Williams, F. Carson. "Alliteration in English Versions of Current Widespread European Idioms and Proverbs." In *Alliteration in Culture*. Ed. Jonathan Roper, 34–44. New York: Palgrave MacMillan, 2011.

Winterbottom, Michael. "The Language of William of Malmesbury." In *Rhetoric and Renewal in the Latin West 1100–1540*. Ed. Constance J. Mews, Cary J. Nederman, and Rodney M. Thomson, 129–47. Turnhout, Belgium: Brepols, 2003.

Wittig, Joseph. *Piers Plowman: Concordance*. London: Athlone, 2001.

Wogan-Browne, Jocelyn, Nicholas Watson, Andrew Taylor, and Ruth Evans. *The Idea of the Vernacular: An Anthology of Middle English Literary Theory, 1280–1520*. Exeter: University of Exeter Press, 1999.

– "Locating Saints' Lives and Their Communities." In *Rethinking the South English Legendaries*. Ed. Heather Blurton and Jocelyn Wogan-Browne, 251–70. Manchester: Manchester University Press, 2011.

Woodman, D.A. "The Forging of the Anglo-Saxon Past in Fourteenth-Century Beverley." In *English Manuscripts Before 1400*. Eds. A.S.G. Edwards and Orietta da Rold, 26–42. London: The British Library, 2012.

Worley, Meg. "Using the *Ormulum* to Redefine Vernacularity." In *The Vulgar Tongue: Medieval and Postmedieval Vernacularity*. Ed. Fiona Somerset and Nicholas Watson. University Park, PA: Penn State Press, 2003.

Wormald, Patrick "Archbishop Wulfstan and the Holiness of Society." *Anglo-Saxon History: Basic Readings*. Ed. David A.E. Pelteret. New York: Routledge, 2000.

– "*Lex Scripta* and *Verbum Regis*: Legislation and Germanic Kingship from Euric to Cnut." In *Early Medieval Kingship*. Ed. P.H. Sawyer and I.N. Wood. Leeds: University of Leeds, 1977.

– "Lordship and Justice in the Early English Kingdom: Oswaldlaw Revisited." In *Legal Culture in the Early Medieval West: Law as Text, Image and Experience*, 313–32. London: Hambledon, 1999.

– "*Quadripartitus*." In *Law and Government in Medieval England and Normandy: Essays in Honour of Sir James Holt*. Ed. George Garnett and John Hudson, 111–47. Cambridge: Cambridge University Press, 1994.

Yeager, Stephen M. "Documents, Poetry, and Editorial Practice: The Case of 'St. Egwine'." In *Rethinking the South English Legendaries*. Ed. Heather Blurton and Jocelyn Wogan-Browne, 168–86. Manchester: Manchester University Press, 2001.

– "Lollardy in Mum and the Sothsegger: A Reconsideration." *Yearbook of Langland Studies* 25 (2011): 161–88.

– "The *South English Legendary* 'Life of St. Egwine': An Edition." *Traditio* 66 (2011): 171–87.

Yasuda, Jun. "On the Words of Scandinavian Origin." *Journal of Ryutsu Keisai University* 37, no. 4 (2003): 1–21.

Zacher, Samantha. "The Rewards of Poetry: 'Homiletic' Verse in Cambridge, Corpus Christi College, 201." *SELIM* 12 (2003–4): 83–108.

Zumthor, Paul. *Towards a Medieval Poetics*. Minneapolis: University of Minnesota Press, 1992.

Toronto Anglo-Saxon Series

General Editor
ANDY ORCHARD

Editorial Board
ROBERTA FRANK
THOMAS N. HALL
ANTONETTE DIPAOLO HEALEY
MICHAEL LAPIDGE
KATHERINE O'BRIEN O'KEEFFE